Preaching Power

Preaching Power

Gender, Politics, and Official Catholic Church
Discourses in Mexico City, 1720–1875

Charles A. Witschorik

◦PICKWICK *Publications* • Eugene, Oregon

PREACHING POWER
Gender, Politics, and Official Catholic Church Discourses in Mexico City, 1720–1875

Copyright © 2013 Charles A. Witschorik. All rights reserved. Except for brief quotations in critical publications or reviews, no part of this book may be reproduced in any manner without prior written permission from the publisher. Write: Permissions, Wipf and Stock Publishers, 199 W. 8th Ave., Suite 3, Eugene, OR 97401.

Pickwick Publications
An Imprint of Wipf and Stock Publishers
199 W. 8th Ave., Suite 3
Eugene, OR 97401

www.wipfandstock.com

ISBN 13: 978-1-62032-717-3

Cataloguing-in-Publication data:

Witschorik, Charles A.
    Preaching power : gender, politics, and official Catholic Church discourses in Mexico City, 1720–1875 / Charles A. Witschorik.

    x + 270 pp. ; 23 cm.

    Includes bibliographical references.

    ISBN 13: 978-1-62032-717-3

    1. Catholic Church—History—18th century. 2. Catholic Church—History—19th century. 3. Mexico—History. I. Title.

BR610 W55 2013

Manufactured in the U.S.A.

Contents

Acknowledgments | vii

List of Abbreviations | x

Introduction: Gender and Official Church Discourses in New Spain and Mexico | 1

1. Decorating Power: Sermons and the Baroque in Spain and Colonial Mexico | 19

2. Manly Virgins and Tender Fathers: Gender and Baroque Sermons in New Spain | 44

3. Reforming Discourses: Sermons and the Enlightenment in New Spain | 81

4. The French Connection: Sermons, Gender and Revolution in Late Eighteenth- and Early Nineteenth-Century New Spain | 110

5. Delicate Damsels and Perfidious Rebels: Preaching and Gender during the Insurgency | 140

6. Pious Women and New Foundations: Post-Independence Church Discourses | 164

7. Gendering Reform: Mid-Nineteenth Century Church Discourses | 186

Conclusion: Gendered Church Discourses Come Full Circle | 216

Bibliography | 221

Acknowledgments

I WISH TO THANK first the editors and staff at Wipf and Stock Publishers. Their dedication to the mission of advancing both classic and original works of scholarship makes an invaluable contribution to the fields of church history, theology, and biblical studies. I am also grateful to the University of California, Berkeley and its Department of History and Graduate Division for their support over the years of preparation of this project.

I owe a debt of gratitude to the many scholars and researchers who assisted me in my work in archives and libraries in Mexico, Spain, and the United States. At the Universidad Autónoma Metropolitana in Mexico City, Brian Connaughton was especially generous in sharing his time and helpful suggestions for my project. At El Colegio de Michoacán, Carlos Herrejón Peredo provided helpful suggestions for research on sermons. Manuel Ramos Medina at the Centro de Estudios de Historia de México CARSO was gracious in inviting me to study the CARSO collection. At the Universidad Nacional Autónoma de México, Francisco Iván Escamilla González and Jorge Traslosheros Hernández shared their wisdom and suggestions for directions in my research. Alfredo Ávila and Maru Vázquez extended a generous invitation for me to participate in their seminar course at UNAM during my time in Mexico City. At the Archivo Histórico del Arzobispado de México, Berenise Bravo Rubio and Marco A. Pérez Iturbe offered kind help and suggestions. At the Universidad Iberoamericana, Perla Chinchilla Pawling shared helpful insights for my research. At the Fondo Reservado of the Biblioteca Nacional de México, Sofía Brito Ocampo was generous with her time and advice. At the California State Library's Sutro Collection, Martha Whittaker offered valuable support in navigating the collection. At Stanford University, Paul Thomas introduced me to the university library's collection on Latin America. I am also grateful to Brian Larkin and Matthew O'Hara for their generosity in sharing research ideas and suggestions.

I extend a sincere thank you as well to my colleagues in the History Department at Berkeley for their support and encouragement. Stephanie

Acknowledgments

Ballenger, Sean McEnroe, and Brian Madigan gave helpful advice on living in Mexico City and working in various archives. Sarah Selvidge, Sarah Hines, and Pablo Palomino offered enduring support and encouragement for my project. Luis Peláez kindly assisted me with my work in Spain. I am thankful to the members of the Latin American History working group for their helpful comments and questions about one of this project's chapters.

I am particularly grateful to Hilja New, Ellen Thompson, Barbara Hayashida, and especially Mabel Lee for their friendly support and generous help at each stage of my time at Berkeley. Mia Mochizuki and Todd Olson shared generously of their time and wisdom in helping me to consider art and images as sources for historical thinking. Ivonne del Valle lent gracious support and ongoing encouragement to my project as I developed some of its connections with Spanish-language literature. Thomas Dandelet and John Efron offered valuable help in integrating my project with the history of Early Modern Europe. Mark Healey offered helpful suggestions and ideas for my project from its earliest beginnings. William Taylor shared especially generously of his time and wisdom from the beginning of my studies at Berkeley. I am particularly grateful for his insights and suggestions on connections between sermons and the culture of the Baroque. I wish to thank Margaret Chowning in a special way for her tireless support and invaluable advice through every stage of my project. Her appreciation for gender as a way of thinking about history inspired and encouraged me to tell the story of gendered public discourses that I encountered over the course of my research.

I also wish to thank my faculty and staff colleagues, as well as the students, at San Francisco University High School. It is a joy to work among such a talented and dedicated group of professionals and enthusiastically engaged students. I am grateful for the opportunity to share and grow in my knowledge of history as part of a community of such purpose and spirit.

Without the kindness and encouragement of friends and family this project would never have been possible. I am grateful to Jeffrey Cooper for his valuable insights and suggestions of connections between my project and larger church history. Jeffrey, along with Randy Rentner, Bruce Cecil, Brent Kruger, George Piggford, and many other members of the Congregation of Holy Cross, have been abiding sources of friendship and support. Francis McAloon, SJ, shared generously of his time and wisdom as an invaluable spiritual guide. The communities of Christ the Good Shepherd Lutheran Church in San Jose and St. Mark's Lutheran Church in San Francisco extended warm welcome and gracious championing of my work. Margaret Tillman, John Reardon, Bill Steigelmann, and Douglas Mack have offered enthusiastic and faithful friendship. Albert Wu and Michelle Kuo have been

Acknowledgments

wonderfully supportive, caring and loving friends. Melisa Galván is a treasured friend who has shared attentively of her support and care. Susan Carlson and her family believed in me and encouraged my interest in academics. I am particularly grateful to Susan for the generous time and wisdom she shared in helping me to develop my writing skills. Jeffrey and Gilda Mattison and their family have offered lifelong friendship and genuine kindness. Sarah Crary Gregory has been a steadfast source of wisdom and support and has generously shared of her time in helping me to revise and improve my writing. I am grateful for her sincere kindness as family and friend.

My heartfelt thanks to many other family members who have supported and believed in me from the beginning, especially my grandparents, my brother Mark and sister-in-law Molly, my uncles and aunts (especially Kathy, Mary, and Ellie), and my cousins. My husband, Adolfo Ramírez, has been an unfailing source of encouragement and support throughout my project. His patience, lively sense of humor, and sincere care have helped me more than I can say. Last but not least, I am deeply thankful to my parents, Charles and Cynthia, who inspired in me a love for learning and who have never wavered in their heartfelt support and love.

With sincere gratitude,
Chuck Witschorik
December, 2012

Abbreviations

AGN   Archivo General de la Nación, Mexico City
AHAM   Archivo Histórico del Arzobispado de México, Mexico City

Introduction

Gender and Official Church Discourses in New Spain and Mexico

"Disgraceful women! You conspire to your own ruin, to the dishonor of your husbands, to the desolation of your homes: you and all those who foment your lust and caprices conspire to expel our holy religion from this realm."[1]

ARCHBISHOP FRANCISCO XAVIER DE LIZANA Y BEAUMONT, MEXICO CITY, 1807, COMMENTING ON THE ADVENT OF NEW FASHION CURRENTS AMONG WOMEN.

"Once more we have seen with impotence, pain, and consternation how the legislative assembly has approved an immoral law . . . this pretension is nothing other than sinful pride and will inevitably lead society to ruin, which worries us deeply."[2]

CARDINAL NORBERTO RIVERA CARRERA, MEXICO CITY, 2009, REGARDING A LEGISLATIVE INITIATIVE TO LEGALIZE SAME-SEX MARRIAGE AND BROADEN ADOPTION RIGHTS.

THAT MEXICO CITY'S ARCHBISHOPS should condemn perceived moral crises in contemporary society, as Lizana and Rivera do in the epigraphs above, is not surprising. Moral crisis is, historically, a familiar theme in sermons. Many readers and listeners, however, may not be aware of how often churchmen use and have always used gender (e.g., citing some women and men as models of

1. Lizana y Beaumont, *Carta pastoral* (1807), 21.
2. León Zaragoza, "Inmorales y aberrantes."

virtue and other women and "effeminate" men as exemplars of immorality) to drive home their messages. This book shows that what I am calling gendered references—that is, language that either explicitly invoked patriarchal social norms or creatively reinforced them through adaptations of tropes of masculinity and femininity—were a pervasive aspect of church discourses in colonial and early-independent Mexico, occurring frequently in sermons, pastoral letters, and other official documents. Lizana, for example, in 1807 cited women's behavior as a root cause of social problems. He expressed dismay at recent novelties in fashion among female believers (e.g., uncovered necklines, jewelry, etc.), lamenting that the adoption of such trends—associated with France and therefore, by extension, with the anti-religious excesses of its revolution—would lead inexorably to social breakdown in New Spain as well. Two centuries later, Rivera also invoked gender, articulating a vision for the right ordering of society that centrally included traditional marriage and the "proper" relationship between men and women.[3]

In invoking imperiled gendered norms to which he demanded resolute fidelity on the part of the faithful, therefore, Rivera was not only responding to a contemporary social issue in the way he felt most suitable but also perpetuating a longstanding trend in Mexican church history.[4] Rivera's discourses shared with those of Lizana and other predecessors both a strong emphasis on conventions of gender that it was deemed essential to preserve and a location within a larger context of social upheaval and uncertainty—in the case of the early nineteenth century, the aftermath of the French Revolution and the Wars of Independence and, for the early twenty-first century, the waves of economic insecurity, drug violence and crime plaguing the country.[5] Addressing these worrisome circumstances, church leaders from both eras saw the violation of gender norms as part of the problem, and, perhaps not surprisingly, used gendered language to articulate their concerns and to propose a way forward—a path that would lead the nation back to a secure foundation in the faith.

3. See also Rodríguez, "Rivera defiende"; Cárdenas, "La cruz y la espada." Rivera instructed that his statement be read by the archdiocese's spokesman during a Sunday sermon in the Metropolitan Cathedral.

4. Parallels emerge on a broader level with other recent official Roman Catholic statements and policies, such as the United States bishops' 2012 "Fortnight for Freedom" campaign against insurance coverage of contraceptives. In a similar vein, in recent public comments the newly installed archbishop of San Francisco, Salvatore Cordileone, has suggested that attempts to legalize same-gender marriage constitute "the ultimate attack of the Evil One." See Goodstein, "Bishops Defend"; Garofoli, "Salvatore Cordileone's Key Prop. 8 Role."

5. For an account of some of the effects of drug violence on individual clergy and the institutional church in Mexico, see "12 Priests Slain in Mexico Over Last 4 Years."

Gender and Official Church Discourses in New Spain and Mexico

Gender and Church History

As recent scholarship has demonstrated, frequent gendered references were not exclusive to Mexico in this era. From the beginning of Christianity theologians appropriated misogynist elements of Judaism and Greek philosophy in their writings, fashioning gendered expectations of men's and women's behavior which they often buttressed through language designed to creatively affirm and reinforce those norms.[6] For example, as Grace M. Janzten has demonstrated, the case of the third-century martyrs Perpetua and Felicity—who had shown exceptional courage and steadfastness when, as public entertainment, they were forced into an arena with wild animals—and of other women like them proved problematic for a system founded on the presumptive strength of men and the imperfection of women.[7] To address the tension, a solution emerged through an idea expressed by Perpetua herself. In her personal diary, the saint had written of a dream in which she was "changed into a man" as a means of preparing for battle in the arena.[8] This "sex-change" supplied the necessary explanation for her courage and therefore "was expanded to fit many other cases. Women whose spirituality was beyond question were described as honorary males."[9] Women, in other words, although they could perform heroic deeds in service to the faith, could safely be made to fit within the broader reigning patriarchal system of the early Christian church through the creative adaptability of its discourses.[10]

---

6. Jantzen, *Power*, 43. Jantzen offers the following citation from the early Christian philosopher Philo as an example: "Philo, for instance, who did much to bring together Jewish and Hellenistic thought, and who was formative for the development of Christian theology, wrote, 'The male is more complete, more dominant than the female, closer akin to causal activity, for the female is incomplete and in subjection and belongs to the category of the passive rather than the active. So too with the two ingredients which constitute our life-principle, the rational and the irrational; the rational which belongs to mind and reason and is of the masculine gender, the irrational, the province of sense, is of the feminine. Mind belongs to a genus wholly superior to sense as man is to woman.'"

7. Jantzen, *Power*, 50. See also MacHaffie, *Readings in Her Story*, 27; Ruether, ed., *Religion and Sexism*.

8. Jantzen, *Power*, 50.

9. Ibid., 50–51.

10. See ibid., 2: "From the early days of the Christian church, struggles for authority were prominent; and throughout the medieval period, the struggles increased. It was crucial to the ecclesiastical establishment that those who claimed knowledge of the mysteries of God should be contained within the structures of the church, since the power of the church would be severely threatened if it should be acknowledged that access to divine authority was possible outside its confines."

Working from the established normative presumption of women's weakness, clerics were thus free to employ creative language like that used to describe Perpetua and Felicity (e.g., as "manly" or "virile" virgins) as a means of reinforcing underlying gendered norms while keeping the articulation of those norms supple and flexible enough to adjust to varying ambient and historical circumstances. Such adjustments would continue in the medieval and early modern periods of Church history, including, for example, in feminized monastic religious language, in discourses related to female mystics and the ambiguous, layered dimensions of power they shared with male spiritual authorities, as well as in evolving missionary discourses on women's culpability for sin and vice.[11] In other words, from the beginning of church history ecclesiastical authorities found in the creative fashioning of gendered language an important means by which to reaffirm the patriarchal norms that underlay the institution's power and authority. As I argue, during periods of time when these underlying norms were relatively secure, there was less need to remind believers of them and therefore the gendered language used to frame them could be employed more flexibly, allowing for the development of creative approaches like that used for Perpetua and Felicity. Conversely, during moments of crisis—both for the security of gendered social norms and for society in general—it would become more important for clerics to refer directly to the gendered transgressions of actual believers, leaving less openness for creativity of gendered language. Above all, it is my argument that, for the Church, gendered social norms were an essential, if often unconscious, aspect of its institutional authority and power. Whether explicitly rearticulating those norms, creatively reimagining them, or instinctively redirecting them, the Church used normative ideas of gender and creative adaptations of gendered language as an important means by which to fortify and secure its institutional authority, integrity and power.[12]

---

11. See Walker Bynum, *Jesus as Mother*, chapter 4; Coakley, *Women, Men, and Spiritual Power*, Introduction and chapter 1; Selwyn, *A Paradise*, 66–81.

12. In speaking of the Church I am referring to the hierarchical institution and its authority as exercised discursively in the documents under consideration. While individual preachers, in order to secure permission for the publication for their sermons, would have had to conform their writings to the guidance and norms of the hierarchy, some room for individual modes of expression and approach did remain—as will be evident in the examinations of particular sermons featured in each chapter. Preachers enjoyed even more latitude in their unpublished (manuscript) sermons, a study of which is beyond the scope of this book but is nevertheless important to acknowledge.

Gender and Official Church Discourses in New Spain and Mexico

Discourses of Gender and Power

In this book I will be examining both gendered language and direct references to women and men in sermons from eighteenth- and nineteenth-century Mexico City. I am interested, ultimately, in understanding how the Church attempted to preserve power and negotiate a way forward in difficult times. To this end, I have been guided by the theoretical literature on discourses, power and gender, especially the work of Michel Foucault on the history of discourses and sexuality and that of Joan Scott on connections between gender and discourses of power.[13] In his efforts at constructing what he called an "archaeology" and a "genealogy" of knowledge, Foucault sought to explain how discourses are fashioned to support structures of power and how changes within those discourses often serve to strengthen and promote these structures. As the work of Joan Scott has demonstrated, an important aspect of the connection between power and discourses is located in notions of gender. As institutions such as the Church define and regulate norms of masculinity and femininity over time, the institutions create the impression that these notions of what it means to be a man or a woman are fixed and immutable.[14] Moreover, these definitions eventually become so closely enmeshed with the power and authority wielded by the institution that potential threats to the normative status of the definitions imperil the institution's own security as well. In the case of the patriarchal system that developed over many centuries in the Church, normative definitions of masculinity and femininity thus took on added significance as guarantors of institutional stability, which, when secure, ensured the ongoing functioning of the institution, but, when contested or undermined, threatened the entire sacred enterprise.

Accordingly, studying the Church's discourses through the lens of gender has the potential to reveal not simply how the institution perceived and responded to contemporary events but also something of the internal, ingrained logic it used to adapt itself in ways it sensed most likely to safeguard and perpetuate its authority. In order to illustrate the functioning of this dynamic, I have chosen a span of time during colonial and early independent Mexico in which there was both confidence and stability in gendered norms as well insecurity and a resulting volatility. However, although my analysis will show how the Church's approach to gendered social norms changed over time, I am not proposing that the institution's understanding of the norms

---

13. See Foucault, *The History of Sexuality*. See also Weeks, *Making Sexual History*; Halperin, "Is There a History of Sexuality?"; Scott, "Gender"; French and Bliss, *Gender, Sexuality, and Power*, 12.

14. Scott, "Gender," 1067–70.

themselves changed significantly. Instead, preachers and other church officials used the flexibility and adaptability of their discourses as a means of adjusting to contemporary developments. Unlike conventions of rhetoric or even advocacy for varying models of government and sovereignty—which also changed over time in sermons and other church discourses—gender constituted a less conscious, more deeply enduring repertoire of assumptions and values that changed less in its essence than in the ways in which it was articulated depending on the needs of the time. In other words, as circumstances changed around it, the Church turned frequently to gender throughout the periods studied in this project not so much as a conscious strategy for renewal but as a deeper-seated response to ongoing societal developments—a response which, because of the close connections between notions of gender and power, provides important indications of how the institution measured the security of its place in society and how its mission would need to adjust accordingly. For that reason, study of the evolution of gender—that is, references to gendered social norms and the language used to articulate them—as a significant element of official church discourses is important for its potential to reveal how the Church perceived its mission in light of an essential element of its historical and institutional authority and makeup, and how it adapted its practices and discursive strategies as a result.

Sermons and the Public Sphere

This book focuses on sermons as a key public space in which the Church attempted to advance its institutional interests. Relevant, therefore, is Jürgen Habermas's study of the public sphere, especially his 1962 *The Structural Transformation of the Public Sphere*.[15] Habermas posited that early movements toward capitalism in the seventeenth and eighteenth centuries contributed to the development of a public realm or "sphere" distinct from yet also interrelated with the state.[16] Originating as a means by which the bourgeoisie could articulate and defend publicly its economic and political interests, the modern public sphere gradually developed as a discursive space—often embodied in newspapers and other periodicals—in which

---

15. Habermas, *Structural Transformation*. For studies that examine aspects of Habermas' thought on the public sphere see the following: Goode, *Jürgen Habermas*; Eriksen and Weigård, *Understanding Habermas*; Hahn, ed., *Perspectives on Habermas*; Outhwaite, ed., *Habermas Reader*; Calhoun, ed., *Habermas*; Thompson and Held, eds., *Habermas: Critical Debates*.

16. Calhoun, ed., *Habermas*, 6–7; Eriksen and Weigård, *Understanding Habermas*, 8; Kellner, "Habermas," 263.

citizens could speak with increasingly equal voice. Whereas in the medieval period—when the concept of a public was associated closely, and sometimes coterminously, with the king or ruler and his presence "before" the public—now the public itself was coming to have a distinct voice by which it could both speak its mind and express its will.[17]

As other scholars have pointed out, one weakness of Habermas' analysis is his lack of consideration for the ongoing presence and significance of religion in society both in the early modern world and even into the twentieth century and beyond.[18] Even more crucially, as David Zaret observes in a recent study of religion and the public sphere in seventeenth-century England, what Habermas fails to account for is the development of religion itself as an additional, unique, and even original iteration of the public sphere. As Zaret explains, in the seventeenth and eighteenth-century contexts in which Habermas discerns the emergence of the secular public sphere, religion remained a key social idiom with which virtually all contemporaries would have been familiar and in which many were heavily, personally invested.[19] Therefore, just as Habermas' identification and characterization of the secular public sphere has advanced understanding of the history and workings of the state, so too it is now important that similar analysis be applied to the historical development of religion.

For the specific case of Mexico, other scholars of this period have also noted the importance of the development of a nascent public sphere in the eighteenth and nineteenth centuries, including François-Xavier Guerra, Victor Uribe-Uran, and Peter Guardino.[20] Unlike Guerra and others, who have argued that a significant public sphere did not emerge in Mexico until the advent of political competition and the free circulation of newspapers following independence, Uribe-Uran and Guardino posit that such spheres did exist, at least in isolated contexts—for instance, the operations of political culture which Guardino observes among Indians in Oaxaca in the

---

17. Goode, *Jürgen Habermas*, 4–6; Thompson and Held, eds., *Habermas: Critical Debates*, 4.

18. For example, see Zaret, "Religion," 213: "Aside from a few scattered references and a long footnote, Habermas's account glosses over the relevance of religion for the emergence of a public sphere in politics at a time when religious discourse was a, if not the, predominant means by which individuals defined and debated issues in this sphere."

19. Ibid., 221. Moreover, Zaret argues that the religious public sphere he describes was in fact an important precursor of some of the later public spheres studied by Habermas.

20. See the following studies by François-Xavier Guerra: "La desintegración"; "Revolución Francesa." See also Uribe-Uran, "Birth of a Public Sphere"; Guardino, *Time of Liberty*.

late colonial period and the actions of lawyers and intellectuals (*letrados*) studied by Uribe-Uran. In a similar way, it is my argument in this book that the official printed discourses of the Church in the late colonial period likewise constituted a limited public sphere that developed prior to those secular versions that emerged around the time of independence. Functioning as a semi-public, religious discursive space, published sermons and other church documents provided a means for clerics and a limited portion of the lay public to communicate amongst one another—or, in the case of the laity, at least to observe and follow the communications of the clerical elite—affirming common values and convictions while also supporting those reigning social and cultural norms most advantageous to the Church.

However, the relatively unchallenged nature of this early ecclesiastical public sphere in the Baroque period did not last. One of the significant ways in which the Church changed later in the eighteenth century was in response to the growing secular sphere in Mexico (e.g., newspapers, cafés, fashions, etc.), including what the Church perceived as the instability and insecurity of gendered norms within it. Therefore, with the advent of public spaces increasingly beyond its control, the institutional church would need to adjust its discursive strategies if it wished to secure and reinforce its institutional prominence and authority—that is, it would have to find a way to expand beyond the limits of its earlier internal public sphere in order to enter into and compete within the larger emerging public sphere of independent Mexico.

To this task, as my research shows, the Mexican church responded both swiftly and adroitly. Unlike in Habermas' analysis, which discounts the importance of the Church after the advent of the public spheres he describes, my research does not reveal an institution grown hardened or increasingly irrelevant in the face of challenges to its spiritual authority. On the contrary, the official church pushed back vigorously against these threats precisely through the same increasingly open public sphere in which its opponents had begun to operate.[21] Marshalling and reimagining earlier strains within its official discourses (e.g., those embodied in gendered language associated with female piety), the Church adapted to the new challenges and emerged with a resurgent public presence and voice in independent Mexico—a phenomenon observable in the frequency and intensity of the various church-state skirmishes that populate Mexico's nineteenth-century history. As my

---

21. As will be discussed in later chapters, the work of Brian Connaughton and other scholars also confirms that the Church responded decisively and often compellingly through its discourses to the various challenges that it faced following independence. See Connaughton, *Clerical Ideology*; Ávila, "Interpretaciones"; Pani, "Para difundir"; Staples, "La participación."

project shows, by returning to gender as a perennially constitutive aspect of its public discourses and authority, the Church successfully negotiated the transition from its earlier, more limited internal public sphere to a hard-won place for itself within the nascent modern public sphere of early independent Mexico, thereby ensuring its ability to continue promoting its particular discursive and political goals for many decades to follow.

Medieval and Peninsular Precedents

Although use of the sermon as a historical source constitutes a relatively novel direction in scholarship on New Spain and early independent Mexico, it also follows a longer tradition of study in other contexts, especially theology.[22] For the earliest Christians—influenced both by Jewish and Greco-Roman rhetorical conventions—preaching happened regularly at worship ceremonies and normally featured running exegesis of biblical passages, which were then related to everyday life and often interpreted allegorically.[23] Following further developments in the middle ages, a significant new type of preaching emerged toward the end of the medieval period that would influence Baroque sermons in Spain and Colonial Mexico. Referred to as epideictic preaching, this new, more demonstrative style grew out of late medieval rediscoveries of elements of classical rhetoric and emphasized elaborate praise and adulation for the sermons' subjects—for example, saints or religious figures.[24] As John W. O'Malley has shown, this new type of preaching worked especially well in the context of the Renaissance papal court.[25] At the court, preachers sought less to convey doctrine and more to foster a mood or experience of awe and wonder at the glories, both heavenly and earthly, of the papacy. This new aesthetic emphasis also found resonance in the mid sixteenth century among the early members of the Society of Jesus, or Jesuits, whose training featured special regimens in preaching and who often gave sermons and sacred lectures even outside the context of the mass.[26] Though the mid-sixteenth-century Council of Trent—treated more extensively in chapter 1—further codified expectations for preaching

22. For the long trajectory of the history of Christian preaching, two scholarly surveys constitute the principal sources in English for a synoptic sense of the development of the genre and its relationship to surrounding events over the course of many centuries. See Dargan, *History;* Edwards, *History.*

23. Dargan, *History,* 51.

24. Edwards, *History,* 272.

25. O'Malley, *Praise and Blame.*

26. Edwards, *History,* 332–45.

in the Catholic world and called for the renewal of priestly training, the legacy of earlier Christian preaching left contemporary preachers in the early modern period with an extensive repertoire of methods and approaches for preparing their sermons, which they could utilize in crafting the words and images they felt appropriate to the particular circumstances of their parishioners and congregations.

In the context of Early Modern Spain a wide stylistic and topical variety found favor among preachers.[27] Many authors published their sermons, sometimes in order to document and represent their careers or to serve as models for seminary study.[28] Most of these sermons were delivered originally from notes and later revised for publication based on the preacher's own redactions or from notations sometimes made by someone in the congregation. Stylistically, many of the sermons focused on a single theme and featured vivid figures of speech such as comparisons, similes, and paradoxes.[29] In their content, the sermons were highly moral, often seeking to reproach their congregations for perceived sins, though also recognizing the need for the life of the preacher himself to be beyond reproach. To more effectively convey their messages, many preachers tended toward the epideictic, employing gestures and dramatic effects such as holding a crucifix as they preached and seeking to create a kind of virtual reality in which the words they used helped simulate the original experiences being described in the sermons.[30]

In recent studies, historians Hilary Dansey Smith and Félix Herrero Salgado further elaborate on the specific characteristics of early modern Spanish preaching.[31] Although secular clergy also preached, Smith notes they were outnumbered in this period by regulars, likely as a result of the latter's greater access to advanced theological training and erudition.[32] The average preaching career for clergy spanned some approximately thirty years, or, as Smith notes from a contemporary source, "until they lost their teeth."[33] Among qualities expected in preachers, significant academic and

---

27. Herrero García, *Sermonario clásico*, xix. As Herrero García puts it, "[L]os Sermones españoles son de una variedad orgánica desconcertante. No hay un patrón, no hay un *marcador de cañamazo* para bordar, a lo más, con distintos hilos y colores, pero sujetos a la immutable cuadrícula. Campea la genialidad, el talento, la bizarría de cada predicador, que va a su fin por diversísimos caminos."

28. Edwards, *History*, 340.

29. Ibid.

30. Ibid., 340–341.

31. Smith, *Preaching*, 1; Herrero Salgado, *La oratoria*.

32. Smith, *Preaching*, 22.

33. Ibid., 28. For elaboration of desired qualities in preachers, see also Herrero

intellectual preparation was required, along with mastery of biblical and patristic authors as well as contemporary developments in the humanities and sciences, a deep life of prayer, and exceptional personal sanctity.[34]

Regarding the financial details surrounding the preaching and publication of sermons, Smith explains that preachers were normally paid for a daily ration of food (*lo común*) and an additional *limosna* or stipend whose amount depended on the occasion for which the sermon had been commissioned.[35] If preachers wished to have their sermons published normally they would need to serve as their own agents unless they were able to secure the support of a patron, publisher or their religious order.[36] In terms of the publication itself, printed sermons were normally prepared by their authors from their original notes and often augmented with additional quotations and citations, especially in Latin.[37] Manuscript sermons also circulated both as texts from which preachers delivered sermons and also as models for other preachers, though this practice was officially outlawed by the Inquisition in the mid-sixteenth century, likely because the doctrinal content of manuscript versions was difficult to supervise.[38] As a result, the last decades of the sixteenth century saw a significant rise in the publication of *sermonarios*, or collections often gathered and published by individual preachers to represent the output of their preaching careers, to provide models for aspiring preachers, and, increasingly by the 1630s, to serve an expanding lay, devotional readership of published sermons.[39] Sermons were also printed in loose (*suelto*) form, whose publication normally followed shortly after the pronouncement of the sermon and therefore usually constituted a more closely accurate record of what was said when the sermon was preached.[40]

With regard to the practicalities of sermon delivery, Smith explains that both the rote reading and complete memorization of sermons were

---

Salgado, *La oratoria*, 158: "Buena voz, sonora y agradable; buen entendimiento, claro y magistral, para que con estas dos cosas perciban y entiendan lo que dijere; buena memoria para aprender el sermón y decirlo sin confusión, sino por el orden que lo escribió, o propuso decirlo; buen gusto o, por otro nombre, buena elección, esto es lo más sustancial; y, sobre todo, buena gracia y donaire sabroso para dar vida a lo que dice; buena lengua, no tartamuda, ni zazo o borrosa; buenos dientes para pronunciar distinto y cortado lo que dice, y otros muchos dotes de la naturaleza."

34. Herrero Salgado, *La oratoria*, 159–62.
35. Smith, *Preaching*, 21.
36. Ibid., 34–35.
37. Ibid., 42.
38. Ibid., 35–36.
39. Ibid., 36, 30, 40.
40. Ibid., 29.

discouraged, while the delivery of sermons from notes with recourse to various memorization schemes and devices was normative.[41] The length of most sermons when delivered was approximately one hour and not usually more than ninety minutes, and was often shorter and less frequent in the summer months due to the various difficulties occasioned by warmer temperatures.[42] Smith also cites the recommendations of contemporary sermon manuals that preachers speak loudly enough to be heard at the back of the church but without shouting. Extreme motions or gestures were discouraged, including the following colorful list of forbidden actions cited by Herrero Salgado—the commonality of which is, of course, implied by their proscription: the imitation of gladiators' movements, immoderate clapping, the agitation of the body, the cracking of knuckles, the wiping of sweat or fanning of oneself with the clerical cape, spitting, especially into the congregation, playing with handkerchiefs, uncovering the arms up to the elbows, or the stomping of feet.[43] Some moderate use of audiovisual aids was permitted—such as the display of crucifixes and other images—while various rhetorical techniques such as enumeration, hyperbole, and comparison were also used to heighten the effectiveness of communication.[44]

Regarding sermon attendance, Herrero Salgado explains that there is contradictory evidence from sixteenth-century sources, with some witnesses testifying to abundant attendance and others to a scarcity.[45] However, what appears clear is that some preachers were successful enough to attract followings not necessarily related to the religious fervor or devotion of their hearers.[46] As Smith points out, whatever the nature of church attendance and readership of sermons in their printed form, the sermons that have survived offer an ample field of inquiry for historians as they provide a reflection of the shared cultural norms current at the time of their pronouncement and publication: "The sermon form itself, although it retains the constants of Biblical exposition and the division of texts, is intrinsically flexible, and

41. Ibid., 31–32.

42. Ibid., 42–43.

43. Herrero Salgado, *La oratoria*, 213–14.

44. Smith, *Preaching*, 63–67, 108. Smith also mentions hourglasses and even skeletons' heads as other common props used in the pulpit.

45. Herrero Salgado, *Oratoria*, 167.

46. Ibid., 171–72. As Herrero Salgado also puts it: "Ir al sermón era un acto social, como ir a las comedias. Cuando el predicador era de los de campanillas, horas antes de la función religiosa las calles que confluían en la iglesia se convertían en ríos de gentes que se encaminaban a ella para asegurarse un buen lugar, o, al menos, un sitio cualquiera dentro del templo. La expectación del exigente público tenía su correspondiente repercusión en el ánimo del orador." See Herrero Salgado, *La oratoria*, 212.

easily becomes a vehicle to mediate not only the Word of God but also a set of cultural assumptions from preacher to people[.]"⁴⁷

Preaching in Eighteenth and Nineteenth-Century Mexico

With the exception of the period of the Conquest and its immediate aftermath, there have been relatively few scholarly studies on the subject of preaching in New Spain and nineteenth-century Mexico until quite recently.⁴⁸ Perla Chinchilla Pawling's examination of seventeenth-century Jesuit sermons, one of the recent additions to the literature, illuminates some of the ways in which preaching in New Spain developed over the course of the second century of Spanish rule, and is particularly useful in considering the emergence of the ecclesiastical public sphere in sermons under consideration in this book.⁴⁹ According to Chinchilla Pawling, beginning in the seventeenth century the function of sermons in society took on a more artistic bent, gradually eschewing the traditional doctrinal purpose of preaching.⁵⁰ As a result, the longstanding challenge of communication between orator and audience slowly gave way to what the author terms a "republic of letters," in which preachers spoke and wrote more to and among themselves than to their congregations. While audiences increasingly came to mass more to admire the wonders of rhetoric and secure their social standing and increasingly less to be instructed in the essentials of the faith, preachers and a limited portion of the lay reading public meanwhile engaged in sustained public dialogue and interaction through the medium of printed sermons and the accompanying letters of approval and recommendation (*pareceres*) that were included with their publication.⁵¹ Chinchilla Pawling argues that

---

47. Smith, *Preaching*, 159.

48. For preaching following the Spanish Conquest, see: Clenndinen, *Ambivalent Conquests*; Burkhart, *Slippery Earth*; Klaus, *Uprooted Christianity*; Megged, *Exporting*; Pita Moreda, *Los predicadores*; Lockhart, *Nahuas*; Schwaller, *Church and Clergy*; Morales, ed., *Franciscan Presence*; Gibson, *Aztecs*; Borges Moran, *Los métodos*; Ricard, *Spiritual Conquest*. For studies of aspects of preaching and rhetoric in New Spain after the sixteenth century, see: Terán, *El artificio*; Osorio, *Conquistar el eco*; Ponce, *La elocuencia*; Pedraza, *La oratoria*.

49. Chincilla Pawling, *Compositio*.

50. Ibid., 16. Chinchilla Pawling explains that this transition is related to changes in norms for preaching promulgated by the Council of Trent, including an emphasis on "amplifying" or improvising on established doctrines and themes rather than opening up questions of biblical interpretation like those associated with the Protestant Reformation.

51. Ibid., 46. As Chinchilla Pawling points out, because of the increasing presence

sermons thus provide an instructive discursive space in which to observe in action what she calls the transition of a traditionally religious society to elements of modernity—again, in other words, the emergence of a nascent religious public sphere.

Carlos Herrejón Peredo's work on the history of sermons in colonial Mexico is also instructive for understanding the development of a culture of printed sermons.[52] Herrejón Peredo suggests a three-part periodization for colonial Mexican sermons. The first period, spanning the years from 1584–1665, represented the consolidation of the formal printing of sermons and the stylistic integration of them by preachers with traditions from Europe. In the second period, from 1666–1760, the sermon in New Spain reached the culmination of its splendor in the Baroque period. From there, in the years between 1760 and 1821, Herrejón Peredo argues that the sermon entered into a period of crisis in light of political, economic, and social developments both in the Iberian peninsula and in New Spain.[53] Later, following the Wars of Independence, Herrejón Peredo outlines some of the ways in which the conventions of sacred oratory carried over into secular speeches, though he acknowledges that the trajectory of preaching following independence remains an important topic for further study.

To this end, a number of recent studies have begun to raise important questions about the role of sermons in the formation of Catholic discourses and Mexican national identity in the periods immediately preceding and following independence.[54] For example, Brian Connaughton, a pioneer in the study of sermons around the period of independence, proposes the idea of a clerical public space in which prelates interacted with other political and social actors more creatively than has usually been acknowledged. Overall, this literature on sermons has been important in beginning to build a picture of a Church that is neither monolithic nor fully reactionary and is

---

and length of these perambulatory materials, sermons grew from an average of twenty pages in length in the mid-sixteenth century to forty pages on average by the start of the seventeenth century, and continued to lengthen throughout the Baroque period.

52. Herrejón Peredo, *Del sermón*. See also the extensive additional work of Herrejón Peredo on sermons, including the following studies: "La oratoria"; "La Revolución Francesa"; "El sermón"; "Catolicismo y violencia"; "Sermones y discursos"; "El sermón barroco"; "Los sermones novohispanos." For other recent studies on eighteenth- and nineteenth-century sermons in Mexico, see Connaughton, "El ajedrez"; Vázquez Parada, "Del barroco." Vázquez Parada's study is of particular note for its study of a collection of manuscript sermons.

53. Herrejón Peredo, *Del sermón*, 29.

54. For example, as noted above (footnote 21), some of the scholars who have pursued this direction include Brian Connaughton, Erika Pani, Alfredo Ávila, and Anne Staples.

Gender and Official Church Discourses in New Spain and Mexico

a part of scholarship on the Church to which this book, especially through the added dimension of gender, seeks to make a contribution.

Methodology and Organization

As mentioned above, methodologically I have chosen a period of time spanning late colonial and early independent Mexico in which there were times both of confidence and stability in gendered norms as well a lack of such security and resulting uncertainty. My purpose in studying this period—the approximately 150 years from 1720 to 1875—is to illustrate how the Church employed gendered language (especially tropes of masculinity and femininity) throughout this era but did so in varying ways and with changing degrees of emphasis on underlying gendered social norms (especially the normative places and roles of men and women in society) depending on the exigencies of surrounding circumstances. Beginning in the second decade of the eighteenth century, my study follows Herrejón's suggested periodization in order to narrow its focus to sermons that both exemplify the most important characteristics of Baroque preaching and also fall relatively close chronologically to subsequent decades in which the dominant style would shift. I then trace changes in references to men's and women's behavior and social customs and the frequently gendered language that framed them in sermons and other church discourses in the Enlightenment, pre- and post-Independence, and Reform periods, examining how the Church adapted its approach according to the needs of each successive age and, ultimately, how it used gendered language to secure a place for itself in the nascent public sphere of independent Mexico.

This book adopts a more or less chronological organizational scheme. In chapters 1 and 2, I examine some of the Spanish precedents of Baroque preaching in Mexico, as well as how New Spanish sermons developed in unique ways. Specifically, I study how, during the Baroque period—which, following Herrejón, I see as lasting well into the eighteenth century—preachers operated within a cultural and ecclesiastical context that encouraged a significant degree of freedom in choosing imagery, analogies, and metaphors to employ in their sermons. Like the elaborate *retablos*, architectural flourishes, and Baroque paintings and music that framed their sermons—all of which will be considered in these chapters—preachers would often construct intricate analogies and comparisons related to the events which their sermons celebrated or commemorated, such as the profession to a convent of a wealthy novice or the death of an important person. Preachers might invoke the image of *Santa Inés*, for example, as a model for an especially

15

pious nun, wondering aloud how the saint could have summoned the courage to face martyrdom rather than renounce her virginity. An archbishop in death might be compared to *San José*, who managed to serve both as Christ's mother and father.

As these examples suggest, for many of the Baroque preachers studied in this book, a way to drive home to listeners the exceptional nature of the person(s) being honored was to emphasize how they and the saints to whom the preacher compared them seemed to transcend the customary limits of their gender as part of their sacred mission. Displaying "manly courage" if they were women or sometimes serving as spiritual "mothers" if they were men, the implicit message of many sermons from this period was that the boundaries of gender roles and their expectations were flexible and that sometimes it was necessary to step beyond the limits of one's own gender in order to fulfill a higher calling. Nevertheless, this unusual flexibility did not normally indicate any significant openness on the part of preachers to substantially altering accepted *societal* gender roles. Rather, as part of a larger Baroque aesthetic in which opposites and excesses were celebrated, unusual gendered language and associations provided a way for prelates to engage their audiences, even while affirming, albeit paradoxically, received conventions. Through this imaginative, almost playful approach, preachers both captured their audiences' attention and contributed to the triumphal celebration of the Church's foundational role in society that was central to the Baroque in New Spain. Though not without limits, I argue that this relative degree of discursive flexibility with respect to gender in Baroque sermons provided an important means by which sermons in New Spain, as an artistic and discursive medium, participated in the larger Baroque aesthetic.

In chapter 3, I examine how, beginning around the middle decades of the eighteenth century, the earlier openness of the Baroque gave way to a less flexible understanding of gender in official Church discourses. As "enlightened" ideas began to penetrate New Spain, preachers' visions of gender evolved according to the prevailing reformist spirit. As with church architecture, paintings and other media, so also in sermons those stylistic elements which had formerly displayed the Baroque spirit were increasingly jettisoned in favor of new, more austere features, resulting, in the case of sermons, in less flexibility in how men and women were portrayed. Additionally, as regalist bishops and high clergy sought to implement the reform program of the Bourbon monarchy, scientific rationalism and calls for reform aimed at securing greater social order resulted in diminished discursive flexibility concerning gender. The earlier flights of imagination were dispensed with, in favor of more sober language and a stricter, more biologically inspired assignment of gender roles.

Gender and Official Church Discourses in New Spain and Mexico

Political and military struggles on the Iberian Peninsula likewise called for a decisive response on the part of the Church in New Spain, and official discourses such as sermons and pastoral letters were key tools by which the Church either supported or (later) criticized the Crown. In mid-eighteenth-century sermons, men were no longer applauded for their "motherly" qualities, but rather were urged to follow the example of the many brave Spanish soldiers who had given their lives for the Fatherland, exhibiting courage and virtue in all their dealings. With regard to women, the discourses preachers used were less changed in that they continued to recommend cultivation of "manly" virtue and other masculine attributes. In a context in which preachers perceived a need for "military" discipline on the part of all Christians in battling various threats, language referring to women's "manly" qualities became less figurative and theoretical than in the Baroque period. Now the nature of the times and of the challenges to the Church called for imitation of saints' virtues and not merely admiration of them.

Chapter 4 shows how, in the decades immediately preceding independence (1821), beginning in the 1790s, preaching once again changed course as the realities of contemporary events settled in. Where reformers had promoted various Bourbon projects, later prelates turned their attentions increasingly to the deeply alarming events of the French Revolution and the rational, sometimes even secular ideas and trends they associated with it, which seemed to be taking hold in New Spain with a tenacity beyond the Church's ability to control. As a result of some of these developments, prelates in the final years preceding the wars of independence sought to restore order, especially through emphasis on moral renewal and reinvigorated obedience to "legitimate" authority—that is, to God and to the institutional Church as well as to the Crown as the legitimate political authority. Since moral regeneration was considered by prelates as key to restoring proper order, and decadent social customs—especially those purportedly engaged in by women—were among the primary perceived offenses, official discourses focused significant energies on gendered social customs and behavior. Still called upon to be "manly" and strong, both men and women now were also reminded by many clergymen of the duties proper to their sexes. Men were to battle courageously for the cause of God against the tyranny of Spain's enemies, while women could best express their own bravery by remaining "subjects" of their husbands, mostly confined to the home, where they would avoid temptations to "pomp" and "display," thereby setting an edifying example for other members of society.

Chapters 5 and 6 study the periods of the insurgency and the aftermath of Mexico's proclamation of its independence in 1821, when the country entered into a long period of contention and contestation over how the polity would be governed and whose vision of Mexican nationhood would ultimately come to dominate. In this context, the Church intensified its efforts to make its own voice heard. As civic discourses (speeches) given by politicians and other members of the laity became important shapers of public opinion—that is, as public speaking expanded to include speakers other than preachers—sermons, pastoral letters, and decrees remained important means by which the Church articulated and promoted its own vision for Mexican society. As in prior decades, gender occupied an important place within these official Church discourses. Less caustic and more positive, post-independence gendered discourses often celebrated the contributions of women to society, especially through their piety, and encouraged men along the same lines. Unlike those who wished to turn Mexico in the direction of a secular state, women's piety and the example it could give had the potential to shore up the centrality of Catholicism as a foundation of national identity. Put another way, whereas in the late colonial period women were called upon to be more manly in their defense of the Church, after independence, as the Church tried to negotiate its role in the new nation, men were called to be more like women in their own piety.

As demonstrated in chapter 7, this tendency became even more pronounced with the struggles of the period of the *Reforma* in the 1850s and the increasingly venomous relationship between church and state. The Church again responded forcefully and decisively to what it perceived to be attacks on its legitimate rights, turning often to women and the piety they embodied—because their devoutness contradicted so clearly the "atheism" of the Church's opponents—as a means of both defending against perceived threats and outlining a vision for how members of the Church were to operate in the world. By the end of the period under consideration in this study, the Church had reached a point at which it was now a commonplace within its official discourses that the sort of piety and devotedness it had once strained to associate with women while men engaged in various "battles," constituted precisely the "manly" ideal by which all believers, men and women alike, could respond to the Church's new call to arms against the reigning "impiety of the age."

Chapter 1

Decorating Power

Sermons and the Baroque in Spain and Colonial Mexico

"Overcharged decoration . . . of ritual space . . . sought to impose itself massively . . . on the spectator and to capture in that way his or her will, operating more in the realm of emotional persuasion than of rational knowledge."[1]

REFERENCING THE VISCERAL POWER of Baroque art in the seventeenth- and eighteenth-century Hispanic world, this analysis by a contemporary scholar points to ways in which the Baroque aesthetic employed abundance and excess as a means of imposing meaning on its audiences. Drawing its beholders and listeners in through wonder and adornment, Baroque art sought to win over the will and secure loyalty to the underlying values and power structures that it served. Among the forms in which this Baroque aesthetic manifested itself—for example, architecture, painting, and music—an important but less frequently studied instance was the sermon. Likewise elaborate, mesmerizing and even spectacles in themselves, sermons in the Baroque period in Spain and New Spain served as a way for the Catholic Church, as an arbiter of reigning social norms and power structures, both to celebrate and reinforce its privileged social place.

In order to understand how sermons may contribute to our understanding of the Catholic Church in colonial and early-independent Mexico,

---

1. R. de la Flor, *Emblemas*, 26.

this chapter will first examine the context out of which they arose—namely, early modern Roman Catholic preaching in general and Baroque Spanish sermons in particular. Understanding this context will help to illuminate some of the ways in which Baroque sermons in New Spain differed from their peninsular counterparts—especially with regard to the gendered discourses employed within them—and what that may suggest about the state of the institutional Church in New Spain in the first part of the eighteenth century. Later chapters will explore the nature of this difference in greater depth and point to ways in which the Church's position changed over time in the wake of political and cultural developments later in the eighteenth and early nineteenth centuries.

Early-Modern Catholicism and the Baroque

Common to both Catholic and Protestant Early Modern societies, preaching was frequent and ubiquitous, found not just at mass and church services but also in the contexts of hospitals, outdoor events, religious processions, and *autos-de-fe*, among others.[2] In Catholic and Protestant settings alike, preaching included both a doctrinal component as well as a social dimension reflective of surrounding circumstances.[3] However, where Roman Catholic and Protestant preachers parted ways was in the style of preaching emphasized in each movement's normative statements of reform. While Protestants emphasized the bible and scriptural exegesis in their sermons, Catholic preaching tended to favor reaffirmations of doctrines challenged by reformers, including the authority of the papacy, the cult of the saints, and the centrality of the Eucharist—a trend codified at the Council of Trent (1545–1563) in its decrees on preaching. Nevertheless, while traditional narratives have tended to portray this Catholic response as reactionary—as observable in terms such as *Counter*-Reformation—more recent scholarship on Trent, beginning with the seminal mid-twentieth-century work of H. Outram Evennett, has shown that neither the council nor the various Roman Catholic reform movements that preceded and followed it were strictly reactionary or focused solely on the past.[4] For that reason, other scholars such as John W. O'Malley have suggested various alternate ways

---

2. Edwards, *History*, 339.
3. Mack Crew, *Calvinist Preaching*, Introduction.
4. Evennett, *Spirit*. For further discussion on the nature of the Counter or Catholic Reformation, see Cochrane, "Counter-Reformation"; Dickens, *Counter Reformation*.

of describing Catholic reform movements, including Catholic Reformation and Early Modern Catholicism, among others.[5]

Still, if the term Counter Reformation is appropriate in any sense for describing early modern Catholicism it is likely in the realm of preaching—an important discursive platform by which the Church sought to combat the gains of Protestantism.[6] Nevertheless, Catholic preaching post-Trent was not monolithic—though sharing in common a desire to defend the faith, Catholic sermons embodied a diverse assortment of older and more contemporary forms tailored to the needs of specific situations.[7] Officially, the approach mandated by Trent represented a break from earlier times in the sense that it now called for sermons to be given in the context of greater pastoral care on the part of bishops and parish priests—as opposed to the late medieval practice of leaving pastoral concerns largely to religious orders.[8] In the words of the Council, bishops and priests were instructed as follows:

> [To] feed the people committed to them with wholesome words in proportion to their own and their people's mental capacity, by teaching them those things that are necessary for all to know in order to be saved and by impressing upon them with briefness and plainness of speech the vices that they must avoid and the virtues that they must cultivate, in order that they may escape eternal punishment and obtain the glory of heaven.[9]

This emphasis on clear speaking indicated a desire on the part of the council at least implicitly to warn preachers against some of the excesses of medieval preaching, in which extended asides on subtle points of philosophy and theology had tended to obscure more essential moral and spiritual messages.[10]

Also crucial to the council was the issue of who was to preach.[11] Although parish priests and members of religious orders would continue to give sermons, Trent specifically called for bishops to preach whenever possible and to maintain oversight and control of preaching in their respective dioceses.[12] Since little mention was made of the types of sermons considered

5. O'Malley, *Trent*, 143.
6. Old, *Reading and Preaching*, 160.
7. Taylor, *Preachers and People*, xi.
8. Edwards, *History*, 334.
9. Worcester, "Catholic Sermons," 18–19.
10. Ibid., 19.
11. Wright, *Counter-Reformation*, 37.
12. Worcester, "Catholic Sermons," 19.

normative, following Trent responsibility for the type of preaching to be encouraged and/or disallowed in particular dioceses largely devolved upon the local bishop.[13] Though efforts on the part of some bishops—notably, the archbishop of Milan, Charles Borromeo—resulted in some systematization of Catholic preaching, one of the important legacies of Trent for Catholic preaching was the implicit flexibility it gave for a diversity of styles and genres of sermons to be preached in particular areas according to specific local needs and circumstances.[14] Overall, Catholic preaching in the Early Modern period consisted of a diverse, hybrid assortment of many earlier forms, all of which were available to and could be employed by preachers according to the specific needs of the communities in which they preached.[15]

For the purposes of this study, one important need manifested in the Catholicism of this period found expression in the culture of the Baroque that flowered after Trent.[16] Although the council had recommended clarity and economy of style, an even greater priority in many Catholic contexts was the need to guard against defections to Protestantism—a goal often pursued through new artistic and discursive strategies aimed at producing a visceral impact in their audiences, thereby underlining for them the power and majesty of the Church and clarifying what was at stake in either staying or leaving. Often highly theatrical, the lively culture and spirituality of what became known as the Baroque stemmed, in other words, from the perceived need to reconnect with believers' everyday lives—to help establish for them the continuity between the human and the divine. If salvation was to be considered a drama lived out in daily life, then the churches in which believers worshipped were its principal theaters.[17] In architectural terms, this meant creating the illusion of continuity between the sacred and the mundane and providing a foretaste of heaven on earth, while also facilitating the efficacious delivery of sermons that would complement and enhance the aesthetics of the surroundings.[18] For example, the architecturally elaborate Baroque church of *Il Gesù* in Rome—the spiritual headquarters of the iconic Counter-Reformation order, the Society of Jesus or Jesuits—was constructed with an expansive, open nave and a flat, wooden roof to improve acoustics

---

13. Ibid., 20.
14. Edwards, *History*, 338–39.
15. Worcester, "Catholic Sermons," 30.
16. For synoptic studies of the Baroque style, see the following: Wölfflin, *Renaissance and Baroque*; Friedrich, *Age of the Baroque*; Tapié, *Age of Grandeur*; Calloway, *Baroque*; Harbison, *Reflections*.
17. Hsia, *World*, 168.
18. Ibid. See also Early, *Colonial Architecture of Mexico*, 63–64.

and promote effective delivery of sermons to large crowds.[19] Like the art and architecture that framed them, many of these sermons, while promoting Trent's programmatic goals vis-à-vis Protestantism, harnessed the creative impulse of artists, preachers, and other exponents of the Church's overarching vision of the centrality of the divine in human life.

Accordingly, official norms of preaching notwithstanding, for the purposes of this study what is most important to understand about the Baroque and its place in early modern Catholicism is its aesthetic of creating and sustaining religious experiences in its beholders and hearers in a manner that furthered the discursive exigencies of particular times and places. Much like the experience of those who would have worshipped at the Gesù in Rome, those who listened to sermons there and in many other Baroque churches throughout the Early Modern Catholic world, including Spain and Colonial Mexico, would have encountered them as part of the overall religious experience being called forth and sustained in their presence, including within it sufficient discursive flexibility for the various messages churchmen desired to convey. It will be the task of the following two sections of this chapter to examine the functioning of this Baroque aesthetic in the particular contexts of Spanish and colonial Mexican sermons and of the next chapter to analyze particular examples of the latter.

Spanish Baroque Sermons

Like the Baroque in general, Spanish Baroque sermons evince a flair for the theatrical at the service of larger discursive purposes—though, for reasons discussed below, they exhibit less of the openness and flexibility of meaning evident in other manifestations of the Baroque. In many cases—as in the Italian Jesuit Robert Bellarmine's early-seventeenth century essay on preaching, *De ratione formandae concionis*—the message of sermons was best conveyed precisely by means of the style employed in their delivery.[20] For example, since he was especially concerned with the moral message to be conveyed through preaching, Bellarmine counseled sermonizers against overly harsh language and instead favored recourse to rhetorical tools such as examples, illustrations, and similes as means by which to capture and move audiences.[21] Over time, especially in Spain, this style proliferated as preachers sought to draw their hearers in with elaborate rhetorical displays—for example, extended improvisations on the spiritual implications

19. Hsia, *World*, 163–69.
20. Old, *Reading and Preaching*, 218.
21. Ibid., 220.

of a simile on divine love—putatively at the service of the moralizing agenda of the Church hierarchy but also fashioned so as to inundate and win over their audiences through the sheer wonder of the divine.

Theatricality in Spanish Baroque Sermons

One way that preachers sought to create theatrical experiences among their listeners was through the conveying and shaping of mental images. Theologian and historian José Ramos Domingo suggests the concept of "convoked presence" in sermons, by which he means that the truths and dogmas of faith would not simply be invoked but "palpably visualized and demonstrated" for listeners.[22] Like Baroque altarpieces, paintings, or architecture, sermons in this way, through the construction of elaborate mental images, could likewise inspire a sense of connection between the human and the divine, thereby eliciting both awe and imitation. For example, in a 1607 sermon, one author described as his goal "to make seen" the sorrowful moments of Christ's passion and death though painstaking descriptions of his suffering—thereby evoking the presence of this crucial moment in Christian history for his audience.[23] Perhaps yet more powerfully, in a 1725 nun's profession sermon the author constructed an indelible mental image in which the body of Christ on a crucifix (*corpus*) came suddenly to life, pursuing, knocking down, wounding and leaving "half-dead" a nun who had succumbed to the fateful desires of the flesh.[24] Reporting in vivid detail the image of the Christ figure coming alive and descending upon the unhappy nun, the author made a point of emphasizing that the right hand and arm of the same figure still remained detached from the cross—as if to remind his audience that an equally dreadful fate awaited any who might succumb to similar temptations.

Significantly, this emphasis on the construction of mental images in sermons also coincides with the rise of Baroque *retablos* or altarpieces, in which the rhetorical power of sermons and the images preached within them could be paired with the devotional and pious scenes and images contained in the *retablos*.[25] Also significant in this context were the influ-

---

22. Ramos Domingo, *Retórica*, 353.

23. Ibid., 355–56.

24. Ibid., 358.

25. Ibid., 360–361. This correspondence between sermons and images only continued to grow in importance as moments such as the purchase of new clothing or jewels for a devotional image became occasions that called for special sermons to solemnize and promote the event.

ential *Spiritual Exercises* of Ignatius of Loyola—founder of the Society of Jesus—which likewise called for the construction of and engagement with elaborate mental images as essential to proper religious devotion.[26] Whether mental or physical, the construction of and the proliferation of references to images in Spanish Baroque sermons thus constituted one of the principal characteristics of sermons in early modern Spain.[27]

Another characteristic trait of these sermons, studied by historian Miguel Ángel Núñez Beltrán, is the use of contradictions and paradoxes.[28] Among such devices, the trope of the juxtaposition of death and life was particularly significant—utilized in order to touch audiences' emotions in the most profound way possible.[29] Through paradox, for example, a preacher who emphasized the somber side of human reality was then charged with turning the message around and demonstrating how new life could arise from death and how moral, virtuous conduct could facilitate this transformation. In this juxtaposition of death and life, a larger characteristic of the Baroque sermon thus also emerged: the paradox of unity among seeming opposites.[30] In a dialectical way, and utilizing tropes such as that of life from death, Baroque Spanish sermonizers preached a generally pessimistic view of human beings and the world precisely as a means of strengthening their case for the primacy of the divine. This same attitude also expressed itself in sermons as a favoring of the soul over the body, laments over the effects of original sin, emphasis on the fleeting, illusory nature of life, and a view of the world as a vale of tears subject to the tyranny of death—all which would also find expression in varying ways in sermons from New Spain.[31]

Therefore, it was precisely with the profusion of rhetorical devices such as mental images, contradictions and paradoxes that early modern Catholic preaching, especially in Spain, came to take on its Baroque character—both

---

26. For Jesuit spirituality and the *Spiritual Exercises* as well as their connection to the construction of other types of images, see the following: Arrupe, "Art"; De Nicolas, *Powers of Imagining*; Alcalá et al., eds., *Fundaciones Jesuíticas*; Corder, "Spiritual Senses"; O'Malley and Bailey, *Jesuits*. O'Malley and Bailey emphasize the importance for Ignatius of engaging audiences in the world of images as part of their devotion. Likewise, in the case of sermons, Alcalá points out that Jesuit preachers in colonial Latin America favored a strong association between the images they constructed in their sermons and others available around them in churches.

27. For further examples of the Baroque style of preaching, see Callahan, *Church*, chapters 2 and 3.

28. Núñez Beltrán, *La oratoria*.

29. Ibid., 294.

30. Ibid.

31. Ibid., 294–323.

for better and for worse. Citing contemporary norms and criticism, José Ramos Domingo has shown how, despite their power to shore up points of doctrine and morals, the perceived excesses of some of these rhetorical devices highlighted tensions between economy of style and emotive displays in sermons.[32] For example, various actions and gestures grew common in sixteenth- and seventeenth-century Spanish preaching, including mimicry and the use of props, some of which were recommended in sermon manuals of the time but which also could easily devolve into excess.[33] In criticism of this tendency, the early-seventeenth century author Don Francisco Terrones del Caño's *Arte o Instrucción* lamented that the Baroque form of preaching had turned the voice of the preacher into "gallantry and flowers" for the ears of audiences.[34] Instead of a faithful reflection of doctrine, preaching was now a "vain foliage of words," with little regard for received conventions.[35] Later in the seventeenth century, don Gonzalo Pérez Ledesma's *Censura de la elocuencia* also offered a strong critique of the state of contemporary preaching. Pérez Ledesma outlined several problematic trends, among them the *hinchado* or "overblown" style, in which preachers indulged in vanity, composing sermons he termed a "lamentable rosary of incomprehensible, mysterious metaphors" and the "miscellaneous" sermon, in which, like a "salad of quite unequal herbs," preachers chose indiscriminately among various unrelated themes and examples, which they would then parse together inelegantly.[36] Even into the eighteenth-century, as William J. Callahan has shown, Baroque sermons continued to draw criticism, suggesting that, especially toward the end of the Baroque period, attempts at the reform of sermons may have reflected institutional divisions within the Church. For example, while mission preachers in peninsular Spain were often famed for their colorful, magnetic approach to preaching, by the middle of the eighteenth century tensions had developed between this emotive style and the vision of reform offered by the Church hierarchy and royal officials—a

---

32. Ramos Domingo, *Retórica*, 238.

33. Ibid., 266, 282. The author cites the following helpful examples of this phenomenon: "En efecto, <<si hablaban de la curación de un enfermo se tomaban el pulso como debían hacerlo los médicos; si tenían que hablar de un músico movían los dedos a modo del que toca las cuerdas de un instrumento. Si querían representar el sonido de un clarín llegaban las manos a la boca y moviendo los dedos les faltaba poco para silvar>>."

34. Ibid., 147–48.

35. Ibid., 148.

36. Ibid., 154–55.

development that would have consequences for internal ecclesiastical unity later in the century.[37]

Interpretations of the Spanish Baroque

Recent scholarship has offered several ways to interpret the theatricality and the embrace of contradiction and paradox of the early modern Spanish baroque, among them as a means of bolstering traditional institutions and networks of power and as a support for reigning societal misogyny. Regarding the ability of the Spanish Baroque to serve and reaffirm traditional networks of power and privilege, the seminal work of historian José Antonio Maravall is an appropriate place to begin.[38] For Maravall, the Spanish Baroque was a response to the concrete historical conditions of the seventeenth century and the rupture it represented from the time of creative and artistic expansion of the Renaissance.[39] With the economic and social crises of the time—among them the fiscal decline of Castile vis-à-vis peripheral regions such as Cataluña and País Vasco, the growth of foreign debts, political corruption, urbanization, population decline, and contemporary perceptions of moral decadence—a new aesthetic was needed: one in which the expansive energy of the Renaissance (for example, as manifested in what some would have seen as the social and religious anarchy of the Reformation) could be contained and the power of traditional authorities reasserted.[40] The rhetoric of persuasion and the aesthetic of adornment and exuberance characteristic of the Baroque in Spain therefore formed part of a common artistic strategy of celebrating authority, including that of the Church.[41] Baroque art was to be at the service of power, encouraging listeners, viewers, and passersby to revel in fiestas and adornment, not out of a sense of freedom from strictures but

---

37. Callahan, *Church*, 64. Callahan cites the following particularly memorable example: "The Capuchin Fray Diego de Cádiz, described by a contemporary as 'a prophet whose lips were purified with a burning coal,' preached with such emotion against comedies . . . that those present shouted spontaneously that they 'hated them and wished to destroy them,' which, indeed, they did at the close of the service by pulling the local theater to the ground."

38. Maravall, *Culture*.

39. Ibid., 28–30.

40. Ringrose, *Madrid*; Fernández Álvarez, *La sociedad*; Elliott, *Count*-Duke; Kamen, *Golden Age*.

41. See Maravall, *Culture*, 13: "[R]ather than a question of religion, the baroque was a question of the Church, and especially the Catholic Church because of its status as an absolute monarchical power."

rather as a means of celebrating and reaffirming their power from within.[42] At the same time, as other scholars have emphasized, Maravall's emphasis on culture as power need not exclude other interpretations—for instance, the capacity of the Baroque precisely to negotiate and harmonize tensions between arbiters of power and alternate voices in creative, original ways.[43]

Literary critics Nicholas Spadaccini and Luis Martín-Estudillo agree that an important dimension of the Spanish Baroque was its unique capacity to legitimize established networks of power.[44] For these authors, the Baroque constitutes a clear example of Michel Foucault's conception of power less as a force that imposes itself or says "no" than as a producer of knowledge, speech and pleasure.[45] In this sense, the Baroque represented a kind of dialogue between freedom and limits, where opportunities for self-discovery and encounters with the other existed in tension with tropes of deception and discourses at the service of power. José Luis Sánchez Lora takes up this same question in his study of Spanish Baroque religiosity, noting that a key to understanding the Baroque comes in perceiving its function at the service of social control.[46] In the Spanish context, this meant that the Baroque served the function of fixing or stabilizing each individual in his or her place in society and the family, thereby maintaining and assuring the perpetuation of social structures portrayed as immutable. In other words, precisely at the moment in which these structures were beginning to give way and be challenged, the genius of the Baroque emerged in its ability to appropriate the energy of contemporary crises and redirect it to the service of existing social norms.[47]

Writing about early modern Spanish sermons, Fernando Negredo del Cerro and Gwendolyn Barnes-Karol explain how this dynamic emerged in preaching, arguing that the coercive power that sermons came to acquire stemmed less from a fear of punishment by authorities and more from the sense of wonderment and awe they produced and the prospect of social marginalization they often played upon.[48] Preaching, according to this argument, had the power both to include and exclude members within the bounds of the community provided by the Church—a function which served

---

42. Maravall, *Culture*, 129.

43. Valverde, *El barroco*; Chiampi, *Barroco*; Mujica Pinilla, *El barroco*; Achim, "Mysteries."

44. Spadaccini and Martín-Estudillo, *Libertad y límites*.

45. Ibid., 22–23.

46. Sánchez Lora, *Mujeres*.

47. Ibid., 41.

48. Negredo del Cerro, "Levantar la doctrina"; Barnes-Karol, "Religious Oratory."

the crucial role of promoting guidelines of behavior in a cultural context in which values were communicated largely orally.[49] The study of sermons in the early modern period, then, has the potential to illuminate the values the Church was trying to promote at the time and the social conflicts and tensions whose energies it cooperated in repressing and/or redirecting by means of the creativity and adaptability of its official discourses.[50] In Spain and other Catholic countries, in other words, sermons had the potential to advance the Church's efforts at setting boundaries, reconsolidating its authority and securing a place for itself within established power structures.

Gender in Spanish Baroque Sermons

Among those social norms and structures most frequently reinforced and defended in sermons were those related to women and their place in society and the Church. Constrained largely to the two principal paths of marriage or the convent, early modern Spanish women's appearances in official Church discourses largely conformed to these two categories, often serving as reflections of how the Church considered it necessary for women to behave in order to consolidate the vision of society it sought to promote.[51] Moreover, these reflections on women's behavior, as a number of scholars have pointed out, tended frequently toward the misogynistic. For example, Núñez Beltrán refers to a tendency within sermons to presume the inherent weakness of women in comparison to men.[52] From this starting point, it followed that women were inferior to men, possessed of what one contemporary preacher termed a "weak nature," which contrasted with the "strong, intrepid spirit that commits great and heroic deeds" present in men.[53] The success of any woman who overcame the weakness of her sex and performed heroic deeds was therefore solely attributable to and a reflection of God's transforming grace.[54]

Based on the biblical story of Eve's temptation of her husband Adam—a sin interpreted by many Baroque preachers as a concession to impudent

---

49. Negredo del Cerro, "Levantar la doctrina," 56.

50. Ibid., 63. As the author puts it, "[Los sermones eran] la pieza clave que hac[ía]n adoptar a multitud de personas unos comportamientos y unas actitudes mentales que hubiesen sido incapaces de tomar sin la intervención de un ecclesiástico."

51. For recent studies on women and religion in early modern Spain, see the following: Sánchez Ortega, "La mujer"; Aguado et al., eds., *Textos para la historia*.

52. Núñez Beltrán, *La oratoria*, 360.

53. Ibid.

54. Ibid., 361.

ambition—women were also seen as given to vanity and worldly ambition, occasions for men's downfall, and even agents of the devil.[55] Hilary Dansey Smith, for example, cites multiple accounts of women as fickle and easily deceived by demonic forces in her study of Golden Age preaching.[56] One preacher cited the contemporary practice of wealthy women who consumed clay in order to lighten their complexions as a confirmation of his own critique of women's vain character, while another had stern words of warning to incoming university students about the moral dangers posed to them by women.[57] As Sánchez Lora explains, the reason for the harsh character of much of this language relates to the key role that discourses about women played in upholding the surrounding patriarchal social structures from which the Church benefited and of which it was a part.[58] As these structures—among them legitimacy and honor, for example—grew more rigid in response to the various challenges aimed at them, the role of women as the ideological underpinning of the system grew all the more crucial.[59] For many preachers in this period, it was to women that the responsibility for preserving the chastity and virtue of men fell. Virtuous women, empowered by God's grace, could uphold the honor and good name of a family or community; however, women who gave in to their baser nature could expect to bear the wrath of those charged with upholding social mores, primary among them the Church.[60]

55. Ibid., 362–63. See the following citation that Núñez Beltrán offers from another sermon: "Muger, puerta del Diablo eres, primera despreciadora del precepto de Dios, y tal que te atreviste al hombre, a quien el demonio cobarde no llegava, y diste con la imagen de Dios en el lodo. Imitadora de las que he referido, y no desigual en nada de malicia a las passadas, llena de falsas revelaciones, fue occasion de cayda a quien crédulo escuchó sus mentiras y celebró sus errores."

56. Dansey Smith, *Preaching,* 124.

57. Smith, *Preaching,* 124–25.

58. To this end, the declarations of the Council of Trent were influential. According to one recent study, the Council's mandates limited women's options in choosing husbands and tied more explicitly their role as wives to their salvation. As the authors explain, these efforts to control and restrict women's marriage choices, along with other analogous attempts through sermons, were part of a larger context in Spain in which the repression or channeling of sexuality was used as a means of perpetuating patriarchal social structures. See Barnes-Karol and Spadaccini, "Sexuality, Marriage, and Power."

59. For a helpful account of the gendered significance of honor in the Spanish context see Vieira Powers, *Women in the Crucible,* 123. See also Clark, *Desire,* chapter 6; Sánchez Lora, *Mujeres,* 456. See also chapter 2 for a discussion of recent scholarship on the topic of honor as it relates to circumstances in New Spain.

60. Núñez Beltrán, *La oratoria,* 364.

Another way in which sermons could manifest contemporary gendered conventions was through the language they employed related to men and norms of masculinity. According to Smith, in addition to women's mode of dress, attention was also drawn in sermons "to over-dressed fops and 'carpet knights', who [had] succeeded the hardy, hirsute warriors of old. [One author] describe[d] them as ['excessively delicate, flowery, presumptuous, and weak'] and comment[ed] that ['in the past they smelled of gun powder but now many reek of amber, and all of starch']."[61] Likewise, even preachers themselves were not immune to criticism and questions about their own masculinity, as several scholars make mention of purportedly "effeminate" preachers.[62]

One key to understanding the favor and preference given to masculinity during this period lies in notions of the location of social decadence in alleged aspects of femininity—ideas deeply rooted in Iberian conceptions of sexuality.[63] According to this understanding, women, through their tendency to moral weakness and vanity, could easily bring about the downfall of society while men, as long as they did not give in to "effeminacy"—and the "adultery" of self-preoccupation, "luxury" and "opulence" that went along with it—could fortify social cohesion. Given contemporary understandings which also characterized women as having originated from a man's rib, it is therefore not surprising that women would be seen as defective and even "monstrous" within Baroque culture.[64] Thus, an important aspect of Baroque culture in Spain included underlying currents of misogyny directed toward women and "effeminate" behavior in men as the putative origins of contemporary social ills.

Tapping into these currents of misogyny, Baroque preachers in Spain employed language about women and men as part of a larger effort on the part of the Church—as in Maravall's interpretation—to transmit those cultural values and norms that it perceived would best safeguard its position of power in Spanish society.[65] Key to this moral and cultural voice of the Church was its understanding of the proper roles men and women should play in the family and society—roles whose affirmation occupied many

61. Smith, *Preaching*, 125. Translations are my own from Smith's text.

62. Herrero Salgado, *La oratoria sagrada*, 279; Smith, *Preaching*, 102–3.

63. One important manifestation of these notions appeared in legends surrounding the medieval Iberian saint and martyr Pelagius (*Pelayo*)—a figure referred to frequently in sermons. According to these stories, the saint's renown stemmed from his heroic resistance to same-gender sexual advances and his preference for mystical union with Christ. See Jordan, *Invention*, 17; Díaz y Díaz, "La pasión."

64. Sánchez Lora, *Mujeres*, 48.

65. Núñez Beltrán, *La oratoria*, 423–24.

preachers' energies and whose forceful articulation in sermons exercised significant influence over the lives and destinies of their hearers.

The Development of Mexican Sermons

Trained in and familiar with the conventions of preaching in Early Modern Spain, the first preachers in colonial Mexico brought with them their experiences of hearing and giving sermons in their own country and sought to adapt them to the variety of circumstances that awaited them in New Spain. The first part of this section will review briefly the history of preaching in New Spain in the sixteenth and seventeenth centuries as preachers adapted the styles and conventions they were familiar with from Spain to the particular needs of their communities in Mexico. The second part will take up the flowering of the Baroque sermon in the early eighteenth century and the importance of questions of gender for understanding this development—leading to the beginning of the historical period under primary consideration in this book.

Early Colonial Preaching

Some of the earliest preachers in colonial Mexico, among them the first Franciscans who arrived in 1524 and successive waves of members of other religious orders who came soon thereafter, rapidly commenced study of indigenous languages such as Nahuatl, Mayan, Zapotec and others and sought to develop a level of proficiency that would allow them to preach to Indians in their own tongues.[66] A printing press was soon set up in Mexico City, which published catechisms, manuals on doctrine and the sacraments, and some early homilies in various native languages, including the Dominican text, published in 1548, *Doctrina christiana en lengua española y mexicana*.[67] The purpose of much of this early preaching was primarily catechetical (that is, with an emphasis on teaching) and doctrinal, aimed at inculcating doctrine and piety and less concerned with creating some of the more visceral experiences of faith seen in later sermons.[68]

---

66. Old, *Reading and Preaching*, 178–79. See also the introduction for additional treatments of preaching in the aftermath of the Conquest.

67. Ibid., 179–81.

68. Ibid., 182; Sánchez Herrero, *Historia de la Iglesia*, 223–24. According to Sánchez Herrero the methodology of the early evangelizers alternated between emphasis on external ceremonial gestures such as crucifixes, blessings, and body movements and the more abstract ideas and concepts of normative Christian doctrine.

Decorating Power

Historian María Teresa Pita Moreda points out that many of the early mendicant evangelizers of New Spain strained for analogies capable of helping them grasp the magnitude of the task before them.[69] In the centuries before their arrival in Mexico, the Dominicans and other mendicant orders had labored in the evangelization of heretical groups starting in the thirteenth century and, in the particular case of the Iberian peninsula, had extensive experience working with and evangelizing the *morisco* population following the conquest of Granada. Nevertheless, the circumstances these groups encountered in the New World were quite different. Here, preachers and evangelizers faced the reality of a large indigenous population totally unaware of the existence of Christianity and completely unfamiliar with its essential tenets. For that reason, the Dominicans looked back to the early history of the Christian Church for an appropriate analogy. In that history they found a match in the image of the first apostles, who faced the task of evangelizing a vast number of people unfamiliar with the teachings of Christ, and so it seemed natural for these first missionaries to employ methods similar to those of the apostles in early Christian church.[70] Viewing themselves as latter-day heirs to the apostles, the early mendicant evangelizers of New Spain created a legacy of hope that the new Church they had founded would transcend the problems and failings of the old Church in Europe and offer a fresh start for Christianity in the New World.

Nevertheless, by the seventeenth century, with the consolidation of the Church's privileged role in Mexican colonial society, many of the sermons that survive appear to have settled into patterns that both correspond with those studied for Spain and also prove significantly distinctive.[71] As historian Perla Chincilla Pawling points out in a recent study of Jesuit sermons in New Spain, by the seventeenth century a transition had occurred from a catechetical to an artistic emphasis in preaching.[72] Avoiding controversial doctrinal points, sermons, like other contemporaneous artistic media, came to "amplify" and elaborate on sacred texts and traditions in artful ways while, in light of the specter of Protestants' speculations on central dogmas in their preaching, steering clear of the unchangeable realm of divine truth.[73]

---

69. Pita Moreda, *Los predicadores*, 85.

70. Ibid.

71. This development likely stemmed from the influence of the Council of Trent and New Spain's three sixteenth-century provincial church councils (1555, 1565, and 1585) and their decrees on preaching. See Connaughton, "El ajedrez," 197–200.

72. Chinchilla Pawling, *Compositio*.

73. Ibid., 20–32.

Preaching Power

Before turning to specific studies related to sermons, however, it will be helpful first to elucidate recent directions in scholarship on the Mexican Baroque in general, especially art and architecture, in order better to situate the place of sermons within the larger Baroque aesthetic in New Spain as it differed from its Spanish counterpart. Encompassing a variety of different art forms and spanning several centuries, the phenomenon of Baroque art in colonial Mexico was complex and multi-dimensional.[74] Necessarily, any account of such a wide-ranging topic necessarily must narrow its focus and concentrate on certain select aspects of the question at hand. Here, the primary objective will be to review scholarship on the New Spanish Baroque, paying special attention to those conceptions of the Baroque most relevant to sermons.

Abundance and Excess

Within scholarship on the Baroque in New Spain, as in some of the studies of the European and Spanish Baroque cited above, one important theme is that of theatricality, or sumptuous abundance and excess—found notably in examples of colonial religious architecture and sculpture, especially following a phase of renewed creative energy and building in the first half of the eighteenth century.[75] However, despite its similarities, what distinguished the Mexican Baroque from European precedents was the remarkable degree of its sumptuousness and artistic excess—both in the plastic arts as well in preaching. One explanation for this phenomenon offered by many scholars of the plastic arts emphasizes the role of Indian artisans in shaping the Mexican Baroque. For instance, in her study of Mexican Baroque sculpture, Elizabeth Wilder Weismann attributes the unique character of the Mexican Baroque to the fact that by the seventeenth and eighteenth centuries artisans were left more or less to themselves with less direct supervision than had been exercised by the Spanish in the sixteenth century.[76] As a result, sculptors were free to draw from received European styles while also introducing

---

74. For an introduction to the various art forms of the Baroque in New Spain, see Bailey, *Art of Colonial Latin America*. Among the different media in which the Baroque aesthetic in New Spain manifested itself, Bailey highlights triumphal arches constructed for the arrival of new viceroys, *biombos* or painted screens, architecture, painting, murals, *retablos*, and sculpture.

75. Brading, "Tridentine Catholicism." See also Kubler and Soria, *Art and Architecture*.

76. Weismann, *Mexico*, 115–29.

Decorating Power

their own innovations, reflective of a preference for richness, splendor, light, movement, and a desire to leaving no surface undecorated.[77]

Such peculiarly Mexican artistic ideals are embodied admirably in Spanish architect Jerónimo de Balbás' *Altar de los reyes*, placed prominently in the rear center of the Mexico City cathedral. Referring to Balbás as a kind of artistic apostle to Mexican artisans, Weismann explains that he provided the inspiration artists in New Spain were seeking for their unique style, which came to be known as the Churrigueresque.[78] As Weismann puts it in her comments on the *Altar*: "Everything is in flight . . . The very walls disintegrate, and heaven opens up . . . to receive the worshipper . . . [The *Altar*] is one of the great religious arts, theatrical, perhaps, but a just setting for ecstatic devotion. To contemplate it is like reading a chapter in the Apocalypse, all color and rich words and mysticism."[79]

Thus, notwithstanding the derision of some critics, all was not chaos and disorder but in fact the art in question encompassed a conscious set of guiding principles.[80] To illustrate these principles, the *estípite*, or pilaster in the shape of an inverted obelisk—featured prominently in the *Altar de los reyes* and other colonial art—provides an ideal example. Instead of fulfilling its usual function of support, the *estípite*-type column created the illusion that the column itself was floating in a way that defied gravity and everything earthbound.[81] This effect was meant to create a kind of alternate reality meant not just to be seen but experienced with all the senses.[82] This engendering of a parallel reality was intimately related to the theological purpose of the art, which sought to "absorb the worshipper into the mystery" and provide respite from the difficult realities of daily life.[83] As in other Mexican Baroque churches such as Santa Prisca, in Taxco, Guerrero, the ensemble or *conjunto* of various art forms all worked together in lending to each church what Weismann describes as a "personality" and another scholar has characterized as an overall "verve" to the space.[84]

Other recent scholarship highlights the religious and theological underpinnings of the unique sumptuousness of the Baroque in New Spain.[85] For

77. See also Weismann's more recent study, Weismann, *Art and Time*, 50.
78. Weismann, *Mexico*, 130.
79. Ibid.
80. Ibid., 132.
81. Ibid.
82. Ibid., 134.
83. Ibid.
84. Weismann, *Art and Time*, 61; Armstrong Baird Jr., *The Churches of Mexico*, 114.
85. Mazín, "El altar."

example, according to Oscar Mazín, the orientation of colonial society toward the sacred had an important effect on the nature of the art produced at the time.[86] In the case of one church, the design of two of its principal altars was meant to evoke an enormous processional monstrance, serving as a reminder of the importance of devotion to the Eucharistic sacrament, and drawing viewers into a sense of the sacred that was larger than life.[87] Similar to sculpture, other scholars characterize Mexican Baroque architecture as an attempt to distract from the miseries of life and provide the faithful with a foretaste of heaven, and note its contradictory tendencies toward both a conservative repetition of older formulas and an openness to and imitation of new trends from Europe.[88] Overall, Mexican Baroque sculpture and architecture did not represent so much an imitation as an attempt to out-do or surpass European models, serving as evidence of New Spain's unmatched religiosity and eliciting a profound religious experience in those who beheld it.[89]

In addition to architecture, sculpture, and other art forms, in their studies of preaching in New Spain, historians Carlos Herrejón Peredo and Edelmira Ramírez suggest ways in which sermons also served as a medium for the expression of the New Spanish Baroque's characteristic aesthetic of excess or abundance.[90] According to Herrejón Peredo, the distinguishing characteristic of this aesthetic as manifested in sermons was what he describes as the playful discovery of endless similarities and antitheses.[91] In this play of similitudes and contradictions, preachers utilized techniques such as chiaroscuro, counterpoint, sound and echo, mirror and reflection, symbol and symbolized, and paradox to achieve the desired effects of wonder and awe in their audiences—a point Ramírez also highlights in emphasizing that an important goal of preachers was to use the various rhetorical techniques at their disposal to inspire profound religious experiences in their audiences.[92] To this end, for Baroque preachers in New Spain, it was

86. Ibid., 207.

87. Ibid., 222–24.

88. Early, *Colonial Architecture*; Gómez Martínez, *Historicismos*.

89. Gómez Martínez, *Historicismos*, 17–19, 30–33.

90. Herrejón Peredo, *Del sermón*; Ramírez, *Persuasión*. For studies that treat the Baroque aesthetic in the additional literary genre of lives of saints, see the following: Rubial García, *La santidad controvertida*; Morgan, *Spanish American Saints*.

91. See Herrejón Peredo, *Del sermón*, 32.

92. See Ramírez, *Persuasión*, 15. Like other scholars, the author also emphasizes the importance of sermons as a means for the Church to defend and secure its spiritual power and authority. For another study of a specific preacher—in this case an influential peninsular Franciscan active in Mexico in the 1720s and 30s—see Mercedes Alonso de Diego, "Retórica."

the figurative sense of scripture that often found favor. As in the case of early Christian theologians many centuries before, these preachers favored allegory in their interpretations of sacred texts and sought connections everywhere they could between the sacred and the world around them.[93]

Regarding the mechanics of how preachers composed their sermons in this way, Herrejón Peredo explains that sermonizers in New Spain opened up the discursive possibilities of their art form through the use of symbols.[94] The search for symbolism was something already codified in manuals for preachers, which offered instruction on how to prepare sermons in this style. For example, one important text was *Mundus Symbolicus* by the seventeenth century Italian friar Filippo Picinelli.[95] Picinelli's work was particularly influential in its emphasis on the rhetorical device of emblems, in which a preacher could call to mind for his audience an image of particular relevance for the topic at hand. Normally there were four essential elements common to the emblems priests used in sermons: first, the principal theme or value the preacher sought to promote; second, an epigraph or motto in Latin associated with the main theme; third, the image or representation; fourth, its application to a saint or theme.[96] Among different examples of such emblems, preachers used clocks, eagles, columns of fire, and various others, along with a variety of other symbols—for example, the human heart—all of which would have served to elicit a variety of meanings and heighten the visceral impact of their sermons on congregations.[97] Sometimes the images or objects in question were actually present in the church and could be used as props for sermons, but even if they were not physically present preachers used them to enhance the rhetorical effectiveness of their sermons.[98]

93. Herrejón Peredo, *Del sermón*, 32.

94. Ibid., 50–58. For a study of the rhetorical mechanics of one particular sermon, see Ramírez, *Persuasión*.

95. Herrejón Peredo, *Del sermón*, 50.

96. Ibid., 50–51.

97. See Achim, "Mysteries of the Heart." Recounting the story of the bequest of the late seventeenth-century bishop Manuel Fernández de Santa Cruz—the same prelate who had corresponded with Sor Juana as "Sor Filotea"—of his heart to a Puebla convent, Achim interprets the act as a means of bridging spaces—a way to hold in creative tension the opposing and competing forces and movements of the age, such as those witnessed in the bishop's earlier interactions with Sor Juana.

98. Herrejón Peredo, *Del sermón*, 57. In his study of the emblem in Spanish literature, R. de la Flor, following Maravall, argues that the device played an important role in strengthening discourses of power, both secular and ecclesiastical—especially through its ability to elicit visceral reactions among audiences. See R. de la Flor, *Emblemas*, 26.

Preaching Power

Like architects, sculptors and other artists, therefore, New Spanish Baroque preachers were servants of a greater aesthetic—one in which practitioners of each art form participated in and contributed to a larger ensemble or *conjunto*, consisting of a strikingly visceral multi-medium, multi-dimensional sensory experience meant to draw audiences in and enfold them within the divine.[99] As in a contemporary pulpits, often built alongside and integrated into the elaborate Baroque sculpture surrounding it, sermons were part of a dynamic artistic and religious aesthetic in which worshippers would have found themselves immersed in colonial Mexican Baroque churches.[100]

Epistemological Openness

In addition to questions of abundance and excess, another significant theme in the scholarly literature on the Mexican Baroque is that of openness to a multiplicity of meanings in various art forms—a theme also found in the European and Spanish Baroque but, as in the case of abundance and excess, which took on a life of its own in New Spain.[101] For example, in an essay on creole identity, Solange Alberro highlights the multivalence of meaning made possible by the Baroque, citing the example of an arch of triumph constructed for the arrival of a mid seventeenth-century viceroy, which held

---

99. Weismann, *Art and Time*, 60; Early, *Colonial Architecture*, 77; Valverde, *El barroco*, 10–11; Taylor, *Magistrates*, 266; Larkin, *Very Nature*, 4–6, 80. Taylor describes vividly what it might have been like to behold and participate in the *conjunto* experience of the New Spanish Baroque: "The elaborate altars, the paintings and sculpted figures, the play of light on polished silver and three-dimensional forms coated with gold leaf created precious surfaces pulsating with life . . . to be inside a well-furnished colonial church or chapel was to approach the heavenly realm, to be transported toward the divine in an atmosphere that engaged all the senses" (Taylor, *Magistrates*, 266). Similarly, Larkin characterizes the sacred as inherently immanent for New Spanish Baroque Catholicism. As he puts it, "In essence, richly adorned sacred space induced a corporeal experience of the sacred's awesome presence in Catholics and fomented a deeply felt, affective adoration for God and the saints. Splendor and drama were integral components of baroque Catholicism that manifested the divine kingdom, demonstrated devotion, and inspired religious fervor all at the same time" (Larkin, *Very Nature*, 4–6, 80).

100. Larkin, *Very Nature*, 4–5, 91. Larkin emphasizes that worshippers in Baroque New Spain served as active participants in the *conjunto* described above, often through the wills they left behind.

101. Bailey, *Art of Colonial Latin America*, 238. In terms of the plastic arts, Bailey describes this tendency as a freer interpretation of classical models in colonial Latin America.

in tension Spanish and Indian artistic sensibilities.[102] Comparing the logic of the Baroque in New Spain to an allegory or metaphor, Alberro argues that it was the unique capacity of the Baroque to bring together disparate or seemingly opposing truths that ensured its success in Mexico.[103] In other words, the Baroque aesthetic in New Spain facilitated the coexistence of diverse ways of viewing the world by holding multiple traditions together in creative tension through various artistic media.[104]

In his recent study on the origins of Protestantism in Mexico, Joel Morales Cruz likewise points to the polyvalence of Baroque epistemology in New Spain.[105] According to Morales Cruz, "Baroque spirituality and epistemology served as a unifying umbrella by which many religious forms could be deemed legitimate."[106] In other words, part of the success of the Baroque in New Spain can be attributed to its ability to hold together creatively and fruitfully various indigenous and European traditions and spiritualities and, "[a]s a consequence of this (and of the actual potential of perceiving the divine in so many areas) religion in the Baroque leaned towards pluralism and enculturation."[107] While these scholars, who have identified and studied the characteristic openness of Baroque epistemology in New Spain, deploy the concept primarily as a lens through which to consider the coexistence of indigenous and European traditions, another avenue of inquiry consists in evaluating how this defining characteristic of the Baroque in New Spain may have functioned discursively. In other words, in addition to providing artistic space in the plastic arts for the coexistence of diverse forms, in its written and spoken forms the Baroque aesthetic in New Spain also opened up new opportunities for creole self-expression and identification.[108]

One example of how the Baroque aesthetic in New Spain manifested itself in the written word was in the literary output of the celebrated creole Jeronymite nun, Sor Juana Inés de la Cruz (1651–1695).[109] According to

102. Alberro, "Barroquismo."

103. Ibid., 460.

104. Literary scholar Leo Cabranes-Grant reaches a similar conclusion in his study of the Mexican Baroque aesthetic. In contrast to the European Baroque—which some scholars understand to have allowed for little cultural change or shifting—Cabranes-Grant argues, citing the output of Sor Juana, that the Mexican Baroque "show[s] that cultures, once translocalized, are indeed changeable." See Cabranes-Grant, "Fold of Difference," 477.

105. Morales Cruz, "Origins."

106. Ibid., chapters 2, 4.

107. Ibid., chapter 2.

108. Rubial García, *La santidad controvertida*, 53.

109. For recent studies on aspects of Sor Juana's writings, see Buxó, "Sor Juana";

recent scholarship, the writings of Sor Juana share much in common with other forms of Baroque art in that they too speak in terms of doubles and deceptions in order to express deeper truths—both in spite of yet also by means of the tensions engendered by the constraints of the time.[110] For example, in her 1691 *Letter to Sor Filotea*, Sor Juana used the medium of the written letter, in this case under the pretext that her addressee was a fellow nun rather than in fact the then-bishop of Puebla, Manuel Fernández de Santa Cruz (1676–1699), in order to defend her desire to pursue learning.[111] Sor Juana explained the tension between her thirst for knowledge and her awareness that study was an activity largely prohibited to women—a tension she used to her advantage in playing along with the ruse of the bishop's letter while also employing a degree of satire of her own. Though confined to a fixed, gendered identity, with its attendant social expectations, by exploiting the polyvalence of that identity from within Sor Juana seized on the potential of the Baroque to convey multiple meanings in order to defend her own position and challenge that of her interlocutor—though ultimately her transgressions of gendered norms would prove far less acceptable to ecclesiastical authorities than those frequently expressed by contemporary purveyors of the Church's own officially-endorsed discourses.

In the case of the spoken and printed sermons under consideration in this study, preachers likewise found themselves freed by the Baroque aesthetic of excess and epistemological openness to employ language that otherwise may not have proved socially acceptable at the time. For preachers, as for Sor Juana, this transgression often took the form of language centered around gendered norms and social expectations. However, unlike Sor Juana, these churchmen usually did not openly challenge the Church's authority or its normative conceptions of gender. Rather, as literary scholars have pointed out, the type of challenge to gendered norms that they preached more likely constituted a strategic transgression rather than, necessarily, an attempted subversion of the established patriarchal system.[112] In other words, what

---

Bosse et al., eds., *La creatividad femenina*; Ruiz Barrionuevo, "El barroco"; López-Portillo, *Sor Juana*; Paz, *Sor Juana*.

110. Ruiz Barrionuevo, "El barroco," 235.

111. Mills et al., eds., *Colonial Latin America*, 207–14. For a study of this letter see Schüller, "Disputa."

112. See Albers and Felten, eds., *Escenas de transgresión*, 22–23. Referring to the Baroque novels of the Spanish Golden Age writer María de Zayas, the authors describe this type of transgression (rather than subversion) as "un gesto que toca lo prohibido sin suprimirlo y tiene por objetivo experimentar con el límite mismo[.]" See also Schwartz, "Discursos." In her study Schwartz points to some ways in which de Zayas inverted the typically anti-feminine language of reigning masculine discourses by

was distinctive about this particular kind of epistemological openness—in contrast to that of Sor Juana, whose own challenges to established gender norms were perceived as threats by elements of the Church hierarchy—was the way in which its flexibility does not appear to have proved threatening to ecclesiastical or civil authorities at the time, given its prevalence in officially sanctioned texts.[113] Rather, church authorities seem to have at least tolerated if not enthusiastically approved of this style—a fact which indicates that the transgressions of gender contained within them were, at least at the time, perceived by ecclesiastical officials to be supportive rather than subversive of the reigning patriarchal system.[114]

---

appropriating elements of the discourses for her own ends, even while not necessarily subverting the larger patriarchal system.

113. One way to understand this phenomenon may relate to the manner in which church figures understood their own discourses on women—that is, as elements of their own creation rather than of women themselves. For example, as recent scholarship has demonstrated for the case of colonial women's autobiographies later redacted by male authorities, with a change of narrative voice came significant alterations in the tone, style, and meaning of the texts. This trend is noticeable by its contrast with the example of Sor Juana, whose insistence on maintaining authorial integrity for her own autobiography resulted in the lack of publication of a volume on her life comparable to others produced about other nuns in the same period. In contrast, despite their lack of originality, the redacted autobiographies—not unlike the sermons studied in chapter 2—garnered church support and popular interest through their characteristic dramatic and mystical elements. See Peña, "Manipulación," 600–603; Lavrin, "La religiosa."

114. One instructive indication of how the Church's sensibilities on what constituted acceptable transgression versus problematic subversion changed over time can be found in a mid eighteenth-century church document that occasioned significant controversy prior to its publication. Finally printed in 1748, the massive, two-volume, 1400-page document—*Espejo de luz*, by the peninsular Dominican Fray Matías Diéguez—had spent most of the previous decade languishing in review as church figures debated its merits. Extremely virulent in its critiques of women and their social customs and habits, the document was criticized by some churchmen as excessively harsh and was only given final approval for publication after more than twelve *pareceres* arguing for its orthodoxy were collected and appended to the printing. Thus, for the purposes of this study, what is significant about the document is the suggestion it makes of the difficulty one particularly scrupulous priest faced in publishing his views on women during the height of the Baroque era, with its more open and flexible discursive application of gendered norms. In contrast, a half-century later, in the context of a series of crises which ushered in the end of the colonial era, the very attitudes and opinions expressed by Diéguez and which proved controversial within the church at the time were now issued openly, frequently, and largely without question by contemporary preachers. In other words, the changes in surrounding political, economic, and social circumstances likewise occasioned evolution in the Church's institutional understanding and prioritization of normative gendered roles and expectations. See Diéguez, *Espejo de luz*.

However, as study of sermons in later chapters will show, this situation of relative openness and flexibility in the use of gendered norms was not to last. In the wake of new intellectual and cultural developments, and as church authorities began to discern an accumulation of threats to the reigning system of power in which they participated—and of which gendered norms were an important foundational support—the former openness of the Baroque was exchanged for increasingly stricter, more rigid understandings of gender in sermons later in the eighteenth century.

Conclusion

Thus, as the work of the scholars studied in this chapter has shown and as further analysis of specific examples in chapter 2 will also demonstrate, the sermon—with its tendency toward rhetorical excess and its ability to hold together creatively a multiplicity of meanings—represents a particularly rich source from which to draw in studying the culture of the New Spanish Baroque. However, one aspect of these sermons and thus of the operation of the Baroque in New Spain not yet analyzed in depth by scholars is the recurring presence within them of gender-themed messages and tropes—related to perceptions about and recommendations and assertions concerning women and men on the part of preachers. Unlike in Spain, in colonial Mexico the appearance of themes and questions about the nature and character of men and women was not limited largely to criticism of purported feminine and "effeminate" vices. Although these tropes also carried over into New Spanish sermons, what distinguishes these sermons is the simultaneous presence of discourses that at least to some degree appear to defy or transcend normative gender expectations. I argue that these common themes, in which women often take on normatively masculine characteristics and vice versa, while not unprecedented in other contexts, appear to have assumed a unique discursive power in New Spain because of the extraordinary greatness of the religiosity implied as having inspired them. Therefore, seizing on surrounding motifs of sumptuousness and epistemological openness, Baroque preaching in New Spain employed wonder-inducing transgressions of gender as part of its participation in the larger colonial Baroque aesthetic even while also affirming the more enduring patriarchal societal norms on which the Church's own authority and prominence in society rested.

In other words, it is my argument that it was especially through the devices of unconventional gendered language and imagery featured within them that preachers displayed in their sermons the characteristic artistic excess and epistemological openness of the New Spanish Baroque. The Baroque sermon in New Spain, understood in gendered terms, therefore constituted a privileged art form—a means by which, through rhetorical excess as well as symbolic openness to a variety of possible meanings, the Church could contribute to the surrounding Baroque aesthetic even while also reaffirming, celebrating, and securing, albeit temporarily, its own institutional interests.

Chapter 2

Manly Virgins and Tender Fathers
Gender and Baroque Sermons in New Spain

"To call a woman strong means she is a manly woman, intrepid and militaristic, who orders and commands troops, squadrons, and armies."[1]

OFFERED BY ONE OF New Spain's most accomplished, prolific and celebrated preachers, the creole priest Juan José de Eguiara y Eguren, these words spoken in praise of the late queen María Bárbara of Portugal in 1759 embody an important aspect of preaching in Colonial Mexico: frequent, often unusual gendered references—both to historical saints and contemporary male and female believers. As established in the previous chapter, an important key to understanding how the Baroque aesthetic in New Spain operated in official church discourses such as sermons lies with what is both a frequent topic in sermons and yet also an often unacknowledged presumption underlying them: namely, gender—considered here as contemporary understandings of the nature of women and men and the respective social roles assigned to them. Whether regarding a nun's profession, the "manly" virtue of a female saint, or the admirable virginity of male saints, Baroque preachers in New Spain employed gendered language and concepts as a means of conveying their messages and in doing so both responded to and participated in the surrounding context of gendered social norms. In fact, if sermons from this period can be considered Baroque in the sense associated with the various other art forms discussed in the previous chapter, one important way in which this occurred was through rhetorical flourishes frequently employed

---

1. Eguiara y Eguren, *La muger fuerte*, 5–6.

Manly Virgins and Tender Fathers

at the service of commentary on the nature of men and women and their respective roles in society.

In other words, like a column transformed into an *estípite* or a church façade intensified through adornment, one of the ways sermons in New Spain became Baroque was through the rhetorical devices—often featuring gendered language—which preachers employed as they delivered their sermons and readied them for printing. The elaborateness of language and unusual nature of many of the gendered references in these sermons were not simply for show, however. Careful study of these discourses demonstrates that, like other art forms, they were part of a context in which the sumptuousness of the Baroque helped to underline what made New Spain unique and exceptional. Specifically, the message was that if men and women in the pews followed the extraordinary, gender-transcending examples of the saints, they too could honor God and secure blessing for the land. It would be this remarkable devotion, as the thinking went, that could make Mexico unique and perhaps even central to the divine plan of salvation. Thus, the principal aim of this chapter will be to examine particular examples of these discourses in order better to understand how New Spain's characteristic Baroque aesthtic of excess and paradox came alive through them.

Sermons and the Baroque Conjunto in New Spain

As established in chapter 1, Baroque sermons emerged out of a context in which they functioned as one among a number of art forms united in a multi-medium, poly-dimensional aesthetic and religious experience, or *conjunto*. Aimed at overwhelming audiences and beholders with florid displays while also celebrating and affirming reigning social norms and hierarchies, the Baroque *conjunto* in New Spain functioned by combining individual artistic forms—among them sermons—and transfiguring and subsuming them into a larger whole.[2] To elucidate this phenomenon, it will be helpful to turn to some examples of sermons for which ample information is preserved regarding their place amid the accompanying circumstances in which they were given. For example, as noted above, in May of 1759 on the occasion of the funeral of Queen María Magdalena Bárbara of Portugal, the celebrated creole preacher and scholar Juan José de Eguiara y Eguren offered a sermon amid elaborate accompanying rites, providing an opening glance into what it might have been like to experience a Baroque sermon within its surrounding context.[3]

2. Weismann, *Art and Time*, 168.
3. *Tristes ayes.*

Beginning with an extensive introduction, the opening section preceding the sermon described the construction of an elaborate funeral pyre for the late queen, on which were inscribed more than fifty poems of tribute. Among some of the poems were several significant references to men and women that featured gendered language comparable to that found in many of the sermons studied in this chapter. For example, one poem lauded the late queen's "manly" strength in the face of harsh bouts with illness.[4] With masculine fortitude and effort, María Bárbara endured heroic battles with her torments and emerged victorious. Though disadvantaged by the characteristic "weakness" of her sex, the queen overcame such disadvantages through her heroic virtue. In the author's words, because "strength does not have just heroes but also heroines," it followed that "an invincible constancy is not tied to men alone, as a characteristic quality of the manly sex, but can also shine in the weak, and beautiful sex, with equal, and even superior rays."[5] As the author implied, though women were normally to be considered part of the "weak" and "beautiful" sex, on rare occasions they could surpass even men in the "superior rays" of their virtue.

The author noted that these and other inscriptions on the pyre were finished three days before the funeral, which afforded time for "the most numerous Mexican People [to] satiate their curiosity and renew their sentiment [for the queen]," by passing by and examining the pyre and its inscriptions.[6] Then, on May 18th – the first day of the funeral rites – the solemnities began with hourly artillery fire and the ringing of church bells throughout the city. In the afternoon an elaborate procession made up of the leading members of the viceregal government, cavalry, infantry, and members of the high clergy and various religious orders wound its way through the streets to the cathedral. Entering a church structure whose construction had commenced only a few years after the conquest of Mexico and which was as yet still not complete at the time, worshippers entered the cathedral, passing the *coro* (separate choir area) through the *vía de crujía* (processional walkway), both of which had only been finished in recent decades.[7] There, in the main part of the church, alongside sixteen side chapels and before the imposing *Altar de los reyes*, solemn vespers and the first sermon, in Latin, were offered before the rites paused for the night.[8] The following morning,

4. *Tristes ayes*, Introduction.
5. See ibid.
6. Ibid.
7. Armstrong Baird, *Churches of Mexico*, 95–96.
8. Baird, *Churches of Mexico*, 96. See chapter 1 for a discussion of the artistic character and religious significance of the *Altar de los reyes*.

May 19th, the same dignitaries gathered again in the cathedral for the solemn pontifical Mass, presided over by the archbishop Dr. Don Manuel José Rubio y Salinas, in which Juan José de Eguiara y Eguren offered the *sermón de honras* in Spanish.[9]

Entitling his sermon "The Strong Woman," Eguiara used his reflections to elaborate some of the ways in which María Bárbara had exemplified virtues normally associated with men. In his words, as noted above, Eguiara y Eguren argued that María Bárbara was a strong woman—that is, "a manly woman" who was "intrepid" and "militaristic."[10] Though the queen never literally commanded armies, Eguiara y Eguren pointed out that she did serve as a "warrior heroine" through her efforts to recruit and bring to Spain various religious orders such as the Visitation and Salesian Sisters.[11] The late queen was also heroic in her piety and especially her devotion to the Sacred Heart—qualities which, as will be noted later in this chapter in the context of other sermons, confirmed her status as a "virile" woman well on the way to overcoming the "weakness" of her sex.[12]

Though Eguiara's sermon provides a fitting introduction to the larger *conjunto* of which Baroque sermons formed a part, it was by no means the first sermon to function in this way. As recent scholarship demonstrates, ceremonies like those surrounding the funeral of the late queen had been occurring in New Spain since at least the mid-sixteenth century.[13] Connected to ongoing evangelization efforts, "[t]he interconnection of visual, auditory, and other sensory experience in these events was similar to the way that native people had been taught Christian tenets through visual representations."[14] Also significant and unique to the Spanish and colonial Mexican contexts was the emphasis placed in these funeral rites not simply on liturgical music for the Requiem mass itself but for the procession which preceded it. Passing through the streets of the capital and drawing in large numbers of participant-observers, these processions functioned as another element, along with preached sermons and their later printed versions, within the larger Baroque *conjunto* experience—which could also

---

9. For studies of Eguiara y Eguren, including his contributions to creole erudition through his famed project, *Biblioteca mexicana*, see Alejos-Grau, "La contribución"; *Teología*, ed. Saranyana and Alejos Grau, 220–29; Brading, *First America*, 388–90.

10. Eguiara y Eguren, *La muger fuerte*, 5–6.

11. Ibid., 6–7, 15.

12. Ibid., 20–21.

13. García Ayluardo, "World of Images"; Wagstaff, "Processions"; Larkin, *Very Nature*.

14. Wagstaff, "Processions," 169.

feature numerous additional displays, including theater troupes, dancers, fireworks, games, and bullfights.[15] Likewise, funerary monuments were an important part of the Baroque experience of funerals, often, as in the case of the pyre constructed for María Bárbara, featuring elaborate epithets and engravings related to the deceased person's life and virtues.[16]

However, the *conjunto* experience was not limited just to funerals. As two additional examples demonstrate, the New Spanish Baroque was a phenomenon that pervaded multiple aspects of daily life. For instance, the first of these examples—a bound volume of eight printed sermons along with *pareceres* and introductions given on the occasion of the inauguration of the Dominican Rosary Chapel in Puebla in 1690—illustrates vividly how sermons functioned in tandem with other art forms in New Spain.[17] Given once per day over the course of the eight days of celebration of the chapel's dedication, the sermons formed part of a much larger celebration which, outside the chapel, included torches kept lit all night to create the effect of an endless day, tapestries draped from rooftops and balconies, roses adorning windows and doors, gun salutes, sound effects, fireworks, and an elaborate procession with a statue of the Virgin of the Rosary into the Chapel.[18]

Inside the chapel, over the course of the week-long celebration, the eight preachers praised the magnificence of the space surrounding them, calling their listeners' attention to the ways in which the wonders of the chapel ought to call forth devotion and faith within them.[19] Describing these marvels, one study notes that the chapel "seems to be alive with an ecstasy of heavenly joy in the midst of a fantastic ornamental jungle[.]"[20] Featuring gold strapwork, carved stucco, and a variety of statuary, including saints, angels and insignia, the surface of the chapel's walls and ceiligs were designed to seem to disappear amid the adornment, creating the dizzying effect of constant, ongoing motion.[21] And, as evaluators of the sermons noted,

---

15. Ibid., 169, 178. Wagstaff argues that processions also served a pedagogical function in New Spain as a means of introducing new Christians both to the Church and its teachings as well as Spanish society. See also Larkin, *Very Nature*, 37. For numerous descriptions of religious processions in early eighteenth-century Mexico City, along with the frequent presence of sermons as part of the context of larger celebrations, see *Gacetas de México*.

16. de la Maza, *Las piras*.

17. *Octava Maravilla*.

18. Ibid., XII.

19. Ibid., XII–XIII; Gorospe, *Sermón*.

20. Baird, *Churches of Mexico*, 106.

21. Ibid.; Early, *Colonial Architecture*, 85–87; Artigas, "Juegos." For a complete description of the iconography of the Rosary Chapel, see de la Maza, "La decoración."

the preachers did not hesitate to harmonize this ambient sumptuousness with the rhetorical elaborateness of their sermons. As one *parecer* writer put it, the wonders of the religious art with which the chapel was full found echo and complement in the sermons that were preached there. Making reference to the compositional technique of counterpoint often utilized in Baroque music, the author noted that "in order to sing the glories of the Rosary in its Chapel," preachers "gave the counterpoint" from the pulpit, all of which proved a "sweet attraction" to "devout souls."[22] Likewise, another cleric in his *aprobación* described the sermons as "rare, solid, well-founded, conceptual, and sharp," pointing out that either hearing them in person or reading them in print provided so "faithful [a] copy" of the Chapel that even "for those who have not seen it, it will become visible."[23]

Among the creative representations and interpretations of the Chapel expounded in the sermons, one preacher made an especially memorable comparison of the Dominican preachers who would utilize the space to the "fishers of men" mentioned by Christ in the Gospel of John.[24] According to this author, preachers who "catch" many "fish" (i.e., souls) through their sermons could not simply abandon their catches on the beach or throw them back into the water, as they would be lost. Rather, a "sacred swimming pool" (*piscina sagrada*) would be necessary in order to provide the "fish" with a safe place to swim.[25] This "pond of crystalline waters of grace" was of course nothing other than the Rosary Chapel—a place where the faithful could come to encounter the solace of sacred doctrine and the renewal of heartfelt devotion. Similarly, in other sermons one preacher compared the abundant gold of the Chapel's walls and ceiling to the purity of the Virgin Mary's virtue and charity, while another likened the Chapel's splendor to ornate music and still another labeled the place a living Temple, adorned with the saving mysteries of the faith.[26] Awash in comparisons, analogies, and praise, these sermons provided to worshippers a fitting reflection of the splendors and wonders they viewed, heard, sensed, smelled, felt, and touched as beholders of and active participants in the Baroque *conjunto* by which they were surrounded there in the chapel.

22. Amphoso, *Parecer*.

23. Gómez de la Parra, *Aprobación*. There is no internal pagination within this document.

24. See John 21; Victoria Salazar, *Sermón*.

25. Victoria Salazar, *Sermón*, 63.

26. Bailey, *Art of Colonial Latin America*, 289–90; del Valle, *Sermón*, 119; Espinosa, *Triumpho festivo*, 151; Pérez Carballo, *Sermón*, 196.

A few decades later, in Mexico City, another event of significance called for festivities and religious celebrations like those surrounding the earlier dedication of the Rosary Chapel in Puebla. Commemorating the recent canonization of the sixteenth-century Spanish Carmelite mystic John of the Cross in 1726, the Carmelite Order in New Spain organized another eight days of celebration.[27] As Karen Melvin explains in a recent study of these events, the festivities in celebration of the new saint included fireworks, plays, processions—one even featuring an enormous, fire-breathing dragon—and also, as in Puebla, sermons.[28] Altering the Carmelites' local church itself, the building was remodeled in preparation for the celebrations, including the construction of a new high altar that was "painted a brilliant vermillion, so that it would stand out as the 'most exquisite' and 'most extraordinary' altar in the church" and which included a statue of John himself at the center."[29] Situated among other saints with local associations, the figure of John in the center of the *retablo* helped situate the importance of his canonization locally, as did the inclusion of items collected from lay persons, including multiple mirrors, some covering the ceiling and "some located directly across from one another 'so that what was represented in one was multiplied in the other' and all that one could see were mirrors of crystal and their gold frames."[30]

Sermons, as they had been in Puebla, were also an important aspect of the celebrations. Highlighting the importance of John of the Cross for Mexico City, preachers cited the multiple mirrors, comparing John to a mirror of Carmelite virtues and a reflection or magnification of God's light—as also evident in the rays of light descending upon John in an image included with the commemorative edition of the printed sermons—and even proclaiming that John was canonized during his own lifetime by Christ himself.[31] Evincing familiarity with contemporary gendered discursive conventions as well, one preacher did not hesitate to liken John, in the midst of a spiritual ecstasy, to a bride who, "like a dove flies in ecstasy to the throne of [her husband's] delights."[32] Hearing the voice of his "Divine Spouse" as that of a turtledove, the preacher noted that John "united it with flowers, transforming pains . . . into delights of glory."[33]

27. Melvin, "Rearranging Spaces."
28. Ibid., 1–2.
29. Ibid., 3.
30. Ibid., 5.
31. Ibid., 6. See also Ita y Parra, *Canonizacion*, 294–95.
32. Díaz, *Sermon* (1729), 364.
33. See ibid., 365.

Manly Virgins and Tender Fathers

Also of special significance, preachers highlighted the date of John's feast day, January 15th—the anniversary of violent uprisings in Mexico City just over one hundred years earlier, in 1624, but now a date redefined and associated with the joyful occasion of John's canonization and its local celebration in Mexico City.[34] Finally, just outside the church on its main patio, the Carmelites included a number of displays and, according to the descriptions' author, "curiosities to amuse the common people."[35] One such curiosity was a small stage featuring a model of the hill of Tepeyac, where tradition held that the Virgin of Guadalupe appeared near Mexico City not long after the Spanish conquest of Mexico. In addition to the Guadalupan shrine, the display included a replica of the *Calzada de Guadalupe*, a well-known local road on which pilgrims traveled to the shrine. Significantly, making their way along the *calzada* were the figures of two pilgrims—St. John of the Cross and St. Teresa of Avila, another important Carmelite saint and sixteenth-century religious reformer. As the author of the descriptions put it, the figures appeared so real, "that it seemed they were walking while going on pilgrimage to visit the Sanctuary."[36]

Thus, displays such as those featuring saints in local contexts, along with decorations, paintings and other elements of accompanying celebrations, all worked together as part of a larger, multi-dimensional *conjunto* experience of the sacred within the New Spanish Baroque aesthetic—an important dimension of which sermons also provided. In the words of a contemporary evaluator regarding the merits of one preacher: "In the pulpits, there is no first, or second in his sermons; because each one seems to be the only one . . . the discourses are so well put together and understood: the intonations with which he says them . . . are soft chains, made from the most pure gold of his knowledge, with which, like another Hercules, he beguiles his hearers, and sweetly imprisons them."[37] Likewise, describing the "most deserved applause" received by Eguiara y Eguren—in 1729, near the beginning of his long preaching career—for a sermon he had given as part of a theological exam in the Mexico City cathedral, the evaluator spoke of the "profound authority" of his arguments and the "beautiful variety of his tropes."[38] Similarly, characterizing the importance of sermons as an integral

34. Melvin, "Rearranging Spaces," 6–7.
35. Ibid., 7.
36. Ibid., 7–8.
37. See Alvarado, *Parecer*.
38. For a study of Eguiara y Eguren's preaching career see de la Torre Villar, "Eguiara y Eguren." According to de la Torre Villar, Eguiara y Eguren started preaching at a very young age (twenty-two years), remaining prolific for decades and leaving behind at least twenty-eight tomes of sermons, some of which are preserved in manuscript

part of the sumptuousness of a *retablo* dedication ceremony in 1732 and of a church dedication celebration in 1736, contemporary reports described the sermons as both equal in importance to the music and fireworks featured in the first celebration and, "giving complement to such a solemn and important occasion," in the second—echoing with spoken words the solemn beauty and "exquistite" splendor of the celebrations.[39]

As part of the larger Baroque aesthetic in New Spain, therefore, sermons served as way to "sweetly imprison" audiences rhetorically through the force of preachers' words and ideas, drawing them that much more fully into the "exquisite" world of religious devotion which surrounded them. Although such celebratory events and artistic and architectural expressions continued to frame sermons throughout the Baroque period in New Spain, the remainder of this chapter will turn to a more detailed analysis of sermons themselves and the rhetorical devices preachers deployed within them which, like the *retablos*, columns, paintings, music, and other art forms that accompanied them, formed an integral part of the *conjunto* of the Baroque in New Spain.

Gender and Rhetorical Devices in Baroque Sermons

Though the sheer length of many Baroque sermons from New Spain, along with the abundance of biblical and classical allusions and quotations included within them alone merit their consideration as Baroque, this chapter argues that a specific topic and emphasis in many of the sermons—namely, gendered language and tropes—provides a key to understanding how the Baroque aesthetic came alive in preaching during this period. In contrast to later decades in the eighteenth and early nineteenth centuries—in which gendered church discourses appear to have grown more rigid in response to (mostly peninsular) Church leaders' attempts to appease secular authorities through demonstrations of political allegiance—New Spanish Baroque sermons featured a relatively flexible, open understanding of gender that allowed preachers to decorate and embellish them much as contemporary creole artists might execute an *estípite* column or compose a sacred motet.[40] In fact, as some scholars

---

form. See also Aroche, *Aprobacion.*

39. *Gacetas de México*, 34.

40. See Seed, *To Love;* Myers, *Neither Saints Nor Sinners*, 62; Taylor, *Magistrates of the Sacred*, chapter 1. As Seed points out, even before the Bourbons, the Council of the Indies under the Hapsburgs was already starting to promte the authority of the state over the Church, a movement that would be consolidated under the Bourbons by the end of the eighteenth century.

have argued, the persistence of elements of this earlier style well into the late eighteenth century may also point to a relationship between the elaborate, extraordinary nature of the New Spanish Baroque—including its manifestations in Church discourses—and the gradual emergence of creole self-awareness and identity in the same period.[41]

Whatever its genesis, the convergence of gender and power in the Church's evolving official discourses which appears later in the eighteenth century was less fully realized and explicit in the Baroque period.[42] Rather, preachers in this period—especially creoles but some peninsulars as well—were freer to experiment with some of the conventions that would later be tightened by church authorities. Although they continued to celebrate and affirm reigning gendered norms and hierarchies in their sermons, members of the high clergy could do so in flexible, playful ways that highlighted New Spain's unique religious greatness.[43] In other words, although as one scholar has forcefully put it, "[t]he 'natural' weakness of women was the ideological pin that rotated the axis of [church] power," the seeming stability of the system during the Baroque period allowed for a more pliable approach to gender—one in which it was not necessary to strictly enforce or frequently rearticulate this foundational axiom, as would happen later.[44] Instead, the apparent security of prevailing hierarchies allowed for a degree of flexibility of gendered conventions in sermons on saints as well as male and female believers—a discursive strategy that provided an ideal means by which preachers could engage larger Baroque motifs of excess and paradox while also reaffirming traditional gendered power structures, thereby exhibiting New Spain's unique collective greatness.

Opening Examples

Preached in 1720, the first year of the period under consideration for this study, a sermon by the creole Franciscan friar Miguel Díaz Romero on the

41. See Alejos-Grau, "La contribución"; Higgins, "(Post-) Colonial"; Taylor, "Mexico's Virgin of Guadalupe"; Brading, *Mexican Phoenix*, chapter 7; Brading, "La ideología"; Cañizares Esguerra, "Racial, Religious, and Civic"; Herrejón Peredo, *Del sermón*, 32–33; Escamilla González, *José Patricio*, 259–60.

42. For a study in which this convergence figures prominently, see Jantzen, *Power, Gender and Christian Mysticism*. For an insightful recent articulation of how this worked in the context of New Spain, see Franco, *Plotting Women*, xiii.

43. For ways in which church and secular authorities maintained vigilance over actual gender-transgressive practices in the colonial period, see Tortorici, "Contra Natura," chapters 2–3; De Los Reyes-Heredia, "Sodomy and Society," chapters 3–4.

44. Franco, *Plotting Women*, xiii–xiv.

marriage rites of St. Joseph and Mary offers a fitting place to begin consideration of how Baroque sermons functioned discursively.[45] Focusing on the image of the "giving of hands" inherent in the marriage rite, Díaz Romero utilized this trope as a means by which to deliver his doctrinal message. The author began by comparing Mary and Joseph to the unity between the sun and moon. Referring to the biblical account of creation and its report of God's celebration of the creation of the sun and moon on the fourth day, Díaz Romero noted the special nature of the union.[46] At this celestial marriage of Mary and Joseph, as in God the Father's presence at the union of sun and moon in creation, the author reported that Christ himself, along with angels and representatives of all the tribes of the Earth, were present.

In addition to their celestial marriage, Mary and Joseph's union had important earthly implications that likewise called for praise. For example, Díaz Romero cited Thomas Aquinas and other church authorities in support of his contention that Joseph's act of giving Mary his hand constituted an act of preserving the integrity of her virginity. According to Díaz Romero, Joseph was "the cloth for the protection of her decency . . . the cape of her virginal purity."[47] The author then went on to provide a list of a number of possible allegorical interpretations for this "cape," among them "original purity," "virginal perfection," "legitimate motherhood," the Assumption, and the chaste love of the Virgin's spouse.[48] From among these interpretations, Díaz Romero favored the latter, explaining that Joseph, as a "good man," protected the virginity of Mary, thereby giving "shadow" (*sombra*) to her purity and assuring her "immunity" from worldly corruption.[49]

Joseph's dignity and greatness were even further cemented by a heavenly vision in which his chosen status was symbolized by the appearance of a dove over his head and the flowering of his staff.[50] In this way, Díaz Romero explained that the Holy Spirit was able to "redraw" both Joseph's and Mary's purity and ensure their special role as the parents of Christ, offering an extended artistic analogy by way of explanation.[51] As the "substitute of the Holy

---

45. Díaz Romero. *Ornamento*. For the status as creole or peninsular of this preacher and the others examined in this book, I have consulted Carlos Herrejón Peredo's seminal study on the subject of colonial preaching, *Del sermón*.

46. Díaz Romero, *Ornamento*. This sermon contains no internal pagination.

47. See ibid.

48. Ibid.

49. Ibid.

50. For the iconography of images of St. Joseph and Mary in this period, including implicit gendered interpretations, see Villaseñor Black, "Love and Marriage."

51. Díaz Romero, *Ornamento*.

Spirit," Joseph was both Mary's spouse and also the guarantor of her virginity and purity. He was her protector and her husband and, in the dynamic of God's creation, he provided the means by which Mary was to be preserved for her role as the mother of Christ. For that reason, Díaz Romero concluded that the marriage of Joseph and Mary was "the new emblem of virginity" – the unexpected yet unmistakably efficacious symbol of the purity necessary in the lives of all Christians.[52] In other words, turning the reigning association of the holding of hands with concupiscence and sin on its head, Díaz Romero made the claim that, in the case of the chaste marriage of Joseph and Mary, the outcome of their union was instead even greater moral purity and the integrity of a virginity offered for the glory of God.

Díaz Romero's text is an instructive place to begin as it provides a clear example of a preacher employing the tools of oratory—in this case, the emblem—at the service of a doctrinal message—here, moral purity—while also employing gendered language.[53] Díaz Romero himself referred to the image he had constructed of Joseph and Mary holding hands at their wedding ceremony as "the new emblem of virginity." Beginning with this image, Díaz Romero developed its implications over the course of his sermon, citing Church Fathers in support and drawing out the moral for his audience. Specifically, the author employed the ironic image of a kind of hand-holding that was, paradoxically, utterly chaste, in order to reinforce the superiority of virginity and therefore too the appropriateness of contemporary gendered norms, even while also avoiding doctrinal error.[54] In other words, by engaging a familiar image in a compelling and memorable way, Díaz Romero exemplified the capacity of Baroque sermons in general and those from New Spain in particular to creatively and compellingly reimagine and reinterpret some of the tradition's most important and resonant gendered symbols, even while shoring up traditional doctrine in the process.

Further examples of this capacity of the Baroque sermon to creatively reinforce gendered doctrinal and social norms abound in printed sermons. For example, in a sermon given the same year in the Mexico City convent of *capuchinas*, the creole Franciscan friar Lorenzo Fraguas took up the topic of the Eucharistic sacrament, offering a sustained comparison between it and what he called the *"hermanada idea"* of some of the ways in which the

52. Ibid.

53. See chapter 1 for more information on the rhetorical device of the emblem, in which a preacher called to mind for his audience an image of particular relevance for the topic at hand. For more information on emblems, see Herrejón Peredo, *Del sermón*, 50–58; R. de la Flor, *Emblemas*.

54. Denunciation to the Inquisition was an ever-present risk for preachers in this period, as one study notes: González Casanova, *La literatura perseguida*, 27.

holiness and devotions of nuns and priests complemented one another.[55] In the introduction to his sermon, Fraguas opened with what he saw as the harmony and complementarity between nuns and priests, comparing nuns to "virgin butterflies" and describing the vocation of priests as that of a "consecrated phoenix."[56] United in their devotion to the "divine sacramented sun" of the Eucharist, priests and nuns together could form the vanguard of proper devotion and thus serve as an example for other believers.

In order to illustrate how this phenomenon worked, Fraguas employed an extended emblematic comparison involving eagles, roosters, and the sun—another apt example of a rhetorical device at the service of a preacher's desired message. In the first section of his sermon, Fraguas outlined the comparison he wished to make between eagles and the sun.[57] For Fraguas, those who had assembled for the celebration had come as "eagles"—that is, those who admired and venerated the sacrifice of both consecrated virgins and priests at the altar and who therefore ressembled eagles that never lost sight of the sun or, in this case, God. As Fraguas went on to say, extending the analogy, priests and nuns were like "roosters" and "sunflowers of light," whose vows and respective sacrifices gave honor and glory to God and received the praises of the whole world. Here again Fraguas highlighted the indispensable connection between the sacrifices of nuns and priests. Like roosters that began calling and waking the world at the first rays of the sun, so nuns who prayed the first office of the early morning called other Christians to awaken to the rising light of Christ.[58] However, to do this Christ needed to be sacramentally present, in order to shine this light, and this necessary step could be possible solely through the instrumentality of priests.[59] In other words, priests' sacrifice at the altar produced the Eucharist, thereby creating the light to which nuns, as spiritual "roosters," responded.

Also of particular significance in this section is the language about men and women that was used. Here men, in the form of priests who performed the Eucharistic sacrifice, were "sunflowers of light" who awakened their fellow believers to the celestial light of Christ. However, also crucial was the agency of women—here the nuns in question—who arose at dawn to serve as "roosters" who called others to the rising of the Eucharistic "sun." In this comparison, it is especially significant to note how a traditionally masculine image (i.e., the rooster) came to take on an association not just

55. Fraguas, *Hermanada*.
56. Ibid., Introduction.
57. Ibid., 3.
58. Ibid., 4.
59. Ibid.

with men but also the women whose virtue was being praised, while an often feminine image (i.e., flowers) was associated unproblematically with exceptionally holy men. In other words, here and in other Baroque sermons, language and images normally associated with either men or women often were transformed and reimagined in order to underline the seriousness and importance of whatever point the preacher wished to make. As in this example, the use of traditionally male imagery for women and female imagery for men almost certainly did not signify any desire on the part of the preacher to upend traditional gender roles or social norms—on the contrary these sermons tended to reinforce those norms. Instead, the images constituted a means by which the fluidity of language could serve creatively to reinforce accepted social norms—in this case the place and roles of women and men in the Church—even while also underlining the exceptional nature of the individuals in question and, by implication, the larger communities to which they belonged.

Something of a creative, transcendent reinforcement of received gender norms does, therefore, appear to emerge in sermons like Fraguas' as we read them more closely. For example, after offering the above images of the rooster, eagle, and sun, Fraguas proceeded to outline the perfections of each state—how men most perfectly embodied the dignity of the priesthood and how women most ideally glorified God as nuns. Beginning with priests, Fraguas returned to the theme of the dignity of the priesthood, noting that although priests were men they were in fact more like the Cherubic angels—completely spiritual and no longer embodied.[60] Consisting of "all spirit," priests left behind their bodies and assumed an other-worldly nature at the altar.[61] Likewise, women who professed vows and lived the consecrated life were like spiritual "roosters" who awakened others to the rising sun of Christ through their purity and chastity.[62]

Again, what is instructive is the language of gender directed toward priests, nuns, and the faithful. They were to to be spiritual "roosters," "eagles," and "sunflowers"—all images with varying degrees of gendered associations—and yet they were also to transcend their respective genders and even their own bodies in order to arrive at the ideal of entirely spiritual service to God. Fraguas thus outlined what would emerge as a common theme in many sermons from the Baroque period in New Spain—namely, the transcendence of normative gender expectations at the service of higher ideals. As Fraguas' sermon affirmed, in suggesting the possibility of reimagining

60. Ibid.
61. Ibid.
62. Ibid., 5.

gendered norms for the good of spiritual service, Baroque sermons opened up a discursive space in which traditional gender roles could be rearranged and yet also reaffirmed. It was this relatively open, flexible discursive space and its attendant collection of ambiguously orthodox images and rhetorical devices that would come to characterize Baroque preaching in New Spain.

Still another example of how Baroque preachers employed rhetorical devices as a means of commenting on questions of gender is found in the Franciscan fray Francisco Moreno's 1723 convent sermon on St. Gertrude.[63] Working from the assumption that the heart was the foundational principle of life, Moreno described how Christ saw in Gertrude the need for a heart and gave to her his own, thereby essentially making her coequal with him and therefore also with God.[64] In Moreno's words, Gertrude, no longer having any heart or principle of life than that of her celestial Spouse, therefore had essentially *become* (the normatively-gendered-as-male) God.[65] As Moreno went on to say, the hearts of Gertrude and Christ were so intimately united that not even Mary Magdalene enjoyed the privileges that Gertrude did in possessing the heart of Christ."[66] Again, for Moreno the union of Christ and Gertrude through the heart that they shared rendered them all but one and therefore made Gertrude next to God—and, by extension, male—at the essence of her being. Employing another analogy, Moreno called Gertrude a "dipthong"—a letter composed of two other letters which is neither the former nor the latter but a combination of both. In the case of Gertrude, Moreno described her as the æ in the Latin word *Hæc* since in her heart she bridged the gap between the human and the divine.[67] Not only did Gertrude unite the divine and human in her person, by doing so Moreno proclaimed that she actually *became* another (male) Christ.[68]

Thus, because of her virtue and piety, which had brought her as close to Christ as the combined sounds of a dipthong in speech, Gertrude transcended the boundaries both of her humanity and of her gender as a woman to actually become Christ—and, therefore, male—in a profound way. This idea appears to be at play in one final section of Moreno's sermon in which

---

63. Moreno, *Gertrudis*. It is not clear whether Moreno was peninsular or creole.

64. See chapter 1's discussion of the heart as symbol of the intellect and soul in the Baroque period. See also Moreno, *Gertrudis*, 9–10; Gutiérrez Haces, "Sacred Heart of Jesus."

65. Moreno, *Gertrudis*, 10.

66. Ibid., 12–13.

67. Ibid., 11.

68. Ibid., 15.

he compared Gertrude to the Eucharist.[69] Like the sacrament, in which what was once a common and ordinary thing is definitively transformed into something completely different, so Gertrude, having received Christ's heart, now "dispense[d] splendors" as she was subsumed completely into God—a point that corresponds to a recent study on the discursive significance of the Eucharist in the Baroque period.[70] Also notable, therefore, in Moreno's comparison is the fact that Gertrude was associated intimately with the Eucharist—normally a domain reserved exclusively to the sacred power of (male) priests. Here too, then, because of her extreme holiness, Gertrude overcame the limits of her gender and assumed a power, normally reserved exclusively to men, to turn a given entity into something completely different, thereby assuring her status as the effective coequal of Christ and, by extension, a male.

The Blessed Virgin Mary

Although preachers of Baroque sermons in New Spain employed emblems and other rhetorical devices in describing and praising a variety of male and female saints and addressing various theological topics, one of the most important subjects of their discursive flourishes was the singular, frequently gender-transcending nature and virtues of the Blessed Virgin Mary. For example, in his December 12, 1723 sermon on the Immaculate Conception of Mary, given at the Mexico City Convent of la Limpia Concepción, the creole Franciscan friar Diego Antonio de Escobar offered an extended meditation on the opening words of the Gospel of John, in which the figure of John the Baptist identified himself as a voice crying out in the wilderness, proclaim the coming of Christ.[71] According to Escobar, this passage not only referred to the special calling of John the Baptist as a herald of Christ but also on a deeper level to the unparalled holiness of the Virgin. For instance, referring to the question posed in this passage of whether anyone holier had ever been lifted up among those born of a woman, Escobar explained that Mary in fact superseded John, a male, in dignity.[72] Christ himself, according to Escobar, proclaimed the exalted character of his mother, which stemmed from the belief that, in order likewise to prepare the way for him, she was

69. Ibid., 18.

70. Brading, *Nueve sermones*, 50. According to Brading, one important characteristic of Baroque sermons was their tendency to employ sacramental language related to a greater emphasis in the Baroque period on the worship of the eucharistic sacrament.

71. Escobar, *Ultimo*.

72. Ibid., 12.

conceived without the stain of the original sin of the first man and woman, Adam and Eve.

The theological question of the sinless or immaculate conception of Mary was very much on the minds of many churchmen and other believers in the early modern Catholic world and especially in New Spain, even as late as the eighteenth century.[73] Since the medieval period theologians, church authorities, and members of various religious orders had discussed and debated the merits of the theological claim that, by necessity, the Virgin Mary, as the mother of Christ and therefore of God, must have been conceived without original sin. While there was some degree of theological dispute and disagreement in Europe over the need for official ecclesiastical recognition and proclamation of this doctrine, in New Spain the doctrine of the Immaculate Conception quickly took on association with devotion to the Virgin of Guadalupe and therefore also a character closely related to a growing sense of consciousness among creoles, which had first begun in the seventeenth century.[74] Additionally, as many of the priests who offered the sermons under consideration in this chapter were formed at Mexico City's colonial *Universidad de México*, it is significant to note that, as with the University of Salamanca, all students took a special oath of loyalty to the Immaculate Conception, without which the titles of *doctor*, *licenciado*, and *bachiller* were not conferred.[75]

Though there was some diversity of opinion among Dominican friars as to the orthodoxy of the Immaculate Conception, members of the other major orders, especially the Franciscans, Jesuits, Mercedarians, and Carmelites all agreed on the central importance of the doctrine.[76] In his sermon, Escobar—a Franciscan—wondered out loud if the long-awaited official papal proclamation of the Immaculate Conception, whenever it might come,

73. For a discussion of this question as well as some of the ways in which it manifested itself artistically, see Stratton, *Immaculate Conception*.

74. See Taylor, "Mexico's Virgin of Guadalupe," 293. See also Taylor, "The Virgin of Guadalupe"; Brading, *Mexican Phoenix*, chapter 6. As Taylor and Brading demonstrate, the period of the 1730s–50s, not long after Escobar's sermon was published, witnessed significant advances in the development of *guadalupanismo* near Mexico City—for example, through the elevation by the viceroy of the *pueblo* where the Virgin's shrine was located to the more elevated status of *villa*, a papal declaration of the Virgin's status as official patroness of the viceroyalty, and the publication of official church endorsements in sermons and episcopal pastoral letters.

75. Saranyana et al., eds., *Teología*, 491–92.

76. While some Dominicans supported the doctrine of the Immaculate Conception, others, citing St. Thomas Aquinas, argued against it. As Carlos Herrejón Peredo points out, the position of Aquinas on this question remains disputed even in contemporary theology. See Herrejón Peredo, *Del sermón*, 186; Saranyana et al., eds., *Teología*, 492.

could signify the final step necessary before the culmination of time and the end of the world.[77] Just as John the Baptist learned from Christ that his questions would only fully be answered at the time of the Last Judgment, so Escobar implied that the final definitive pronouncement of the Immaculate Conception by the pope would signal the coming of the end of the world.

Although the apocalypse might well arrive at the time of a papal proclamation of Mary's Immaculate Conception, Escobar went on to explain that this process could be hastened if Christians learned to follow more closely Mary's example of moral purity.[78] Recommending a return to "good customs" and ardent devotion, Escobar suggested to his audience that they might hasten along the final consummation of the world if they reformed their ways and lived with sincere piety. Or, in other words, Escobar here drew an important connection between individuals' purity of life and that of the Virgin Mary. Indeed, it was the moral integrity and exalted virginity of a woman, albeit a most exceptional one, combined with a call for moral reform on an individual and collective level, that emerged as a key to understanding and preparing for an apocalyptic future. By extension then, it is not surprising that moral purity, especially that of women, would come to receive special attention and emphasis in sermons from this period and in subsequent ones. Specifically, women's potential for unusual, "heroic," and "manly" courage constituted a singular component of the message many New Spanish preachers sought to convey both in the Baroque period and beyond.

Offering another example of praise for the Virgin Mary, in his 1728 sermon for the Assumption of the Virgin Mary, given before the assembled dignitaries of New Spain in the metropolitan cathedral, the peninsular Mercedarian friar Joseph Cubero Ramírez de Arellano opened his reflections by proclaiming Mary's exaltedness as a "Deity"—that is, as fundamentally similar to (the normatively male) God—to be revered with solemn silence.[79] There, among the gathered dignitaries and important members of society, the Virgin Mary's status as a near-God could rightly be recognized.[80] Erupting with applause, yet with "silent music," Cubero Ramírez de Arellano called those gathered in the cathedral to a particular reverence for the Virgin Mary—one born of the special nature of her virtue and moral purity as the mother of Christ and of God. For Cubero Ramírez de Arellano, he could

---

77. Escobar, *Ultimo*, 25. For another sermon, given in Querétero, in which the theme of apocalyptic expectations associated with devotion to the Virgin was also underlined, see Brading, *Mexican Phoenix*, chapter 7.

78. Escobar, *Ultimo*, 15.

79. Cubero Ramírez de Arellano, *Musica*, 2.

80. Ibid.

think of no more appropriate way to offer devotion and praise to the Virgin than through the image of music that accompanies a wedding.[81] Evoking the ornate sacred music which would have been heard in the context of his and other sermons, the preacher pointed out that for this celestial marriage, in which the Virgin was to be espoused to the Holy Trinity, various sacred figures would play musical instruments to accompany the festivities and only "royal" musicians would do.[82]

One privileged way for preachers to render even more explicit the connection between Mary's purity and virtue and the need for moral greatness among their listeners was through reference to the Virgin of Guadalupe.[83] Following the consolidation of the Guadalupan tradition in the middle decades of the seventeenth century, creole preachers enthusiastically embraced the Virgin of Guadalupe as an advocation of Mary well suited to their rhetorical purposes, doing so with even greater alacrity in the eighteenth century in light of developments such as the 1746 papal proclamation of Guadalupe as the official patroness of New Spain.[84] As noted above, an apocalyptic reference in one sermon from the 1720s referred to the possibility that an official papal proclamation of the Immaculate Conception might coincide with the end of the world. By the 1730s, if not before, this association had also taken on resonance with devotion to Guadalupe, as is evident in a 1738 sermon by the peninsular Mercedarian friar Miguel Picazo in which he drew a strong association between *la Purísima* and Guadalupe.[85] In other words, even the indisputable superiority of Mary's purity was, in a sense, not sufficient in itself. Although the moral purity and immaculate character of Mary's life were beyond question and were professed with notable zeal throughout peninsular Spain, for preachers in New Spain the unique gift of Mary's apparition as *la Guadalupana* rendered Mexico that much more exalted in the tribute it could render to Mary.[86] Highlighting the perceived similarities between the Virgin of Guadalupe and the bib-

---

81. Ibid., 6.

82. For studies of sacred music in New Spain, see Bowers, "Golden Age"; Long, "Music"; Lemmon, "Los jesuitas." See also Cubero Ramírez de Arellano, *Musica*, 6–7.

83. For a study of the long-term development of the Guadalupan devotion see Brading, *Mexican Phoenix*. For studies of Guadalupan themes in sermons, including the role of preaching in promoting the devotion, see Brading, *Nueve sermones*; Mayer, *Flor de primavera*; Traslosheros Hernández, "Santa María de Guadalupe."

84. Brading, *Mexican Phoenix*, Introduction, chapters 3 and 7; Taylor, "Mexico's Virgin of Guadalupe"; Taylor, "The Virgin of Guadalupe"; Saranyana, ed., *Teología*, 500.

85. Picazo, *Imagen humana*, 8.

86. See Brading, *Nueve sermones*.

Manly Virgins and Tender Fathers

lical Woman of the Apocalypse, preachers offered what some scholars view as the beginnings of a language of Mexican nationalism.[87] As Picazo noted later in his sermon: "I want to state that although in itself the Conception of Mary is a praiseworthy mystery which, against the corruption of sin, carries the victorious palm, with the florid painting of Guadalupe it becomes outstanding and multiplies palms in its triumph."[88]

If Picazo was correct and even the wonder of Mary's immaculate conception itself paled in comparison to its florid, triumphal manifestation in the Guadalupan image, it followed that those entrusted with devotion to the image—namely, the populace of New Spain—would be required, out of necessity, to display extraordinary moral character and virtue in order to live up to the dignity of their collective calling. This quasi-messianic quality is also reflected in a sermon preached by the creole Jesuit Nicolás de Segura in 1742.[89] According to Segura, the unique gift of the image of Guadalupe, belonging to all the inhabitants of America "without any exception," implied an aspiration to moral greatness that could empower those who came to the Virgin with their needs and wants. This sacred, healing and empowering character of Guadalupe therefore could function as a means of strengthening the moral virtue and character of those who heard these sermons, thereby giving honor to the Virgin and perhaps even serving to hasten the coming proclamation of the Immaculate Conception, with its attendant apocalyptic effects.

Echoes of the aspiration of preachers to inculcate moral purity continued to resonate in the sermons from the 1740s and 1750s. Here again it is evident that, through the elaborate rhetorical devices they employed to describe the exalted character of Mary's purity, these preachers were also attempting to persuade their congregations of the need for virtue in their own lives.[90] For example, in a sermon from the 1740s, the creole Dominican friar Manuel Romualdo Dallo y Zavala drew a connection between Mary's

---

87. See Brading, *Mexican Phoenix*, Introduction, chatpers 3 and 7; Mayer, *Flor de primavera*, 143–83; Taylor, "Mexico's Virgin of Guadalupe"; Taylor, "The Virgin of Guadalupe"; Saranyana, ed., *Teología*, 500.

88. See Picazo, *Imagen*, 12. For ways in which preachers likened the Virgin of Guadalupe to the advocation of the Immaculate Conception, see Mayer, *Flor de primavera*, 102–11.

89. Segura, *Platica*, 6.

90. It should be noted, of course, that a desire to promote morality and virtue was not unique to preachers in the decades of the 1740s and 50s. However, as will emerge in the next chapter on sermons from the Enlightenment period, priests placed different emphases on the topic of virtue in different time periods, depending on their discursive goals.

purity and its implications for sinners.[91] For this author, his listeners needed to consider themselves warned: Mary herself did not wish to judge them, but her heavenly son would soon return and would impose divine justice according to the extraordinarily high standards set by Mary's example. If those who heard the sermon were living in ways less-than-reflective of the integral purity of Mary's virtue, they were placing in jeopardy not only their own salvation but also, by their lack of witness, the prospect of bringing about the official proclamation of the Immaculate Conception and therefore, at least potentially, the consummation of the world. In other words, since, as Dallo y Zavala put it later in the sermon, "her most pure Conception was for the most holy Mary the root of her greatness," it followed that those not living up to these standards were thereby imperiling their own greatness, both individual and collective.[92]

A sense of this connection between an emerging creole identity and the purity of Mary's conception as reflected in Guadalupe emerges in a sermon by another creole Jesuit, Antonio de Paredes.[93] According to Paredes, like the Ark of the Covenant for the Hebrew people, the sacred image of Guadalupe was for preachers a visible sign of the chosen status of America before the world and before God. For Paredes and others, the unique nature of the Guadalupe image had clear implications for what it might mean for his hearers not just to be Spaniards but also to now form part of a new collectivity—Mexico.[94] According to Paredes, Mexico itself was a most perfect image of Mary, its model and protector. The image of Guadalupe was both a sign and a confirmation of this fact. However, for this reality to hold true, the mostly creole audiences who would have listened to and read this and other sermons like it would need to live up to the extraordinarily high standards—often articulated in gender-transcending terms—set for them by the Virgin Mary in her exalted virtue.

For this reason, to reflect the greatness of virtue to which they aspired for their congregants, Baroque preachers found an ideal rhetorical aesthetic in the ornate and elaborate language of the Baroque. Demonstrating memorably the rhetorical extremes to which these preachers often resorted in trying to instruct their listeners, a sermon from 1747 on the triple purity of Mary, once again by the famed creole preacher and scholar Juan José de Eguiara y Eguren, is instructive.[95] Not just in a singular man-

91. Dallo y Zavala, *El Trono*, 15.
92. Ibid., 21–22.
93. Paredes, *La autentica*, 8.
94. Ibid., 10–11.
95. Eguiara y Eguren, *Purificacion*, 3.

ner, for Eguiara y Eguren the purity of the Virgin Mary was "triplicated" in nature and therefore worthy of the highest, most elaborate praise.[96] Citing the traditional Jewish purification ritual that she, like other Jewish women, would have undergone after giving birth, Eguiara y Eguren proclaimed that the Virgin not only transcended the need for such a ritual but even, in her person, constituted the means of purification not just for herself but also Joseph, all other human beings, and even Christ himself. In other words, extraordinarily, not only did the Virgin not have any need for a purification ritual devised, imposed and administered by men toward putatively "impure" women, in fact she herself could be said to have purified males—both her husband, Joseph, and even Jesus himself. In other words, according to Eguiara y Eguren, Mary "gave birth before having given birth," precisely by giving birth, through her extraordinary purity, to herself. She then gave birth to Christ as she gave birth in this fashion and then gave birth once again, after giving birth the first time, by doing so for all people. Through this extraordinarily complex series of "births," the Virgin remained innately pure and thus could be considered three times purified and therefore unassailably pure. Thus, through these elaborate improvisations on the word *parir* ("to give birth"), Eguiara y Eguren's sermon provides another instructive example of how preachers in Baroque New Spain employed the tools of rhetoric at their disposal in intricate and complex ways in order to demonstrate the Virgin's purity and reflect on some of the implications of that truth for their listeners.

As reflected in sermons on the Virgin, it is evident that Baroque preachers in New Spain employed extraordinary, unusual gendered language and imagery in characterizing saints and figures like the Virgin not so much to question normative understandings of gender as to reinforce them in order to inspire societal transformation. In other words, if women and men would only conform their lives to the example of the Virgin—that is, acting in extraordinary, gender-transcending ways in service of the faith—they too held the potential to reform society from within, perhaps even hastening the second coming of Christ. As another preacher commented about the Virgin of Guadalupe, "In order to transform ourselves into the Sacramented Christ . . . it is not sufficient merely to receive Him; each must prove first his strength, each must examine his purity[.]"[97] Here, as in other examples, the message was that gendered understandings of piety held the key to societal transformation. In a time in which pious adherence to devotions like the cult of the Virgin of Guadalupe held the key for many preachers to an

---

96. Ibid., 3–4.
97. Folgar, Varela, y Amunarriz, *Las circunstancias*, 112.

emerging sense of what made Mexico unique and distinctive, the hope was that if only male and female believers honored sufficiently the sacraments and worshipped God in these ways, they too could attain not just individual salvation but spiritual transformation of their society into the collective Body of Christ.

Explicit Gendered References in Sermons

So far this chapter has examined some of the rhetorical devices and thematic emphases—among them elaborate praise for the Virgin—employed by Baroque preachers in New Spain at the service of what was often a message affirmative of established gendered social norms, albeit in ways that often seemed to challenge those norms as a means of highlighting New Spain's unique greatness. However, there remains the task of providing an account of what explicitly preachers said about women and men and the ways in which they thought they should live and act in society. Though important indications of these attitudes have emerged in the sermons already examined above, it will be helpful to turn to specific sermons in which preachers offered more explicit commentary on what they viewed as appropriate social roles for men and women, especially sermons preached in convents, others given on particular male or female saints, and additional examples from occasions like religious professions and funerals. Though a complete account of the social contexts of convent life, laywomen and men, and masculinity in eighteenth-century Mexico is beyond the scope of this study, attention will be paid in this section to understanding those aspects of these contexts most relevant to the study of sermons.

Convents

Among sermons on or about women, many come from the context of convents. Often focused on the lives and virtues of female saints, these sermons, as with those on the Virgin Mary, tended to emphasize the extraordinary virtue of the women in question—virtue which rendered them near equals of (a male-gendered) God—and also focused often on the implications of the saints' lives for the nuns and other women in the audience. Regarding the context of convent life, Rosalva Loreto López points out in a recent study that convents played an especially important social role in New

Manly Virgins and Tender Fathers

Spanish society, both culturally and morally.[98] Convents in eighteenth-century Mexico were important symbolic centers for the promotion of social and cultural values, serving as spiritual and cultural bulwarks and calling believers to emulate the religious observance they were expected, ideally, to embody, even while also reflecting an awareness of happenings in both local and broader contexts.[99]

As Margaret Chowning points out in a recent study of eighteenth-century convent life in New Spain, "the convent was thought to have a positive influence on laypeople's religious habits and even their characters . . . it acted as a 'fortress standing against moral lapses and worldly perversity,' a place where character traits that were treasured not only in the church, but also in the secular world – humility, modesty, austerity, chastity, self-abnegation, obedience, and respect for authority – were modeled by nuns."[100] Asunción Lavrin makes a similar point, noting the understanding held by many contemporaries of the spiritual importance of convents: "[Nuns'] prayers had a special value . . . and people understood their relation to nunneries as one of exchange of material support for the spiritual benefits derived from the salvific mediation of the brides of Christ."[101] Thus, for members of the high clergy hoping to promote obedience and respect for ecclesiastical authority among lay people, the idealized example of nuns provided a fitting point of reference both for promoting their discursive goals, and serving in juxtaposition to movements and elements contrary to the vision of social order promoted by the Church.[102] By extension, since the relative degree of spiritual freedom and autonomy enjoyed by nuns in convents could at times—as

---

98. Loreto López, *Los conventos*, 21.

99. Ramos Medina, *Místicas y descalzas*, 113–14; Chowning, *Rebellious Nuns*; Cañizares-Esguerra, *Puritan Conquistadors*.

100. Chowning, *Rebellious Nuns*, 64.

101. Lavrin, *Brides of Christ*, 5.

102. López, *Los conventos*, 89; Chowning, "Convent Reform"; Gunnarsdóttir, *Mexican Karismata*, 3; Salazar de Garza, *La vida común*, 12–13. Significant differences prevailed in the rigor and style of observance in convents, ranging from the austere Carmelite and Capuchin *descalzas* to the more relaxed *calzadas*. Given the symbolic moral importance of convents for society, when questions arose over the course of the eighteenth century concerning the faithful observance of vows in some *calzada* convents, these doubts proved relevant not just for the small number of nuns in question but for Catholic society in general. By the middle of the eighteenth century, many church authorities agreed that observance of religious vows in some convents had grown lax. The dispute over convent reform that would soon come to a head related to the question of how nuns' lives should be structured in community. Reforming bishops and some prioresses initiated certain reforms of convent life in the mid eighteenth century, requiring a more traditionally observant lifestyle known as the *vida común*.

in the case of Sor Juana and other nuns—be perceived by members of the ecclesiastical hierarchy as dangerous or subversive, ensuring that nuns were offering the right kind of example was also crucial.[103]

As in the case of sermons on the Virgin Mary and other saints studied above, convent life and, in particular, the spiritual lives of nuns also proved an ideal vehicle for the expression of Baroque preachers' at times seemingly unorthodox views of gender. As Lavrin states regarding an example she cites,

> The metaphor of triumph and conquest over self and evil conferred on nuns as women the valor and strength of soldiers sustained by the love of Christ. In fact, one preacher exceeded his imagination by envisioning the professing nun having conquered Christ himself and holding him forever in her arms as her captive, a defeated lover embraced by his new bride. Mixing this allusion to a lover's embrace with the imagery of war, the preacher fused feminine and masculine values to define the merits of profession and the merits of divine love. But, by capturing Christ the bride was performing an act of possession that was uncommon in a period in which the female was always yielding rather than exerting her authority.[104]

As this chapter attempts to show, such seemingly unorthodox displays, metaphors and analogies—with their frequent transcendence of normative gender roles and expectations—were, at least within the realm of Baroque religiosity and preaching, perhaps in fact more common than might be expected.[105]

Among sermons in which the phenomenon of nuns' mystical unions emerges, at a celebration of the 1734 beatification of the sixteenth-century Italian saint Catarina de Ricci, the Dominican friar José de Sosa y Peña gave a sermon in the Mexico City Convent of Santo Domingo in which he related an anecdote from Catarina's life. As he put it, like St. Gertrude in another sermon studied above, Catarina in this story appeared essentially to have *become* (the male) Christ. According to Sosa y Peña, another nun in Catarina's convent once questioned the saint's "sovereign ecstasies" and "celestial visions" but was relieved of her doubts upon encountering Catarina in the chapel in a state "out of her senses": "Then the Saint turned her face and said to her: Who am I, Catarina or Jesus? 'Jesus,' responded the Religious

---

103. Franco, *Plotting*, xv.

104. Lavrin, *Brides of Christ*, 91–92.

105. For analysis of some of the gendered language applied to Hispanic nuns in this period, see Arenal and Schlau, *Untold Sisters*, 11–12; Lavrin, *Brides of Christ*, 321; Kirk, *Convent Life*.

Manly Virgins and Tender Fathers

(because her semblance appeared that way). 'Well, I *am* Jesus,' said the Saint. Then, prostrate and undone in tears, the Religious was left free of doubts and assured of such sovereign glories."[106]

As this story demonstrates, Catarina's personal holiness and piety were sufficient not only to place her above the level of most of her fellow nuns but in fact brought her so close to her celestial (male) spouse that the two were no longer distinguishable. Having received the gift not only of displaying the wounds of Christ's passion in her hands but also of spiritual visions and visitations in which the crucified Christ came to rest in her arms, Sosa y Peña declared that Catarina had transcended the realms of finite reality, taking on the infinite (and, again, normatively male) nature of God.[107] Catarina's mystical flights and heroic virtue had taken her so far from the bounds of human existence that she had in essence become omnipotent. Catarina now was all but coequal with the male figures of Christ and the Father and enjoyed along with them the exercise of omnipotence in heaven.[108] With all the powers of omnipotence literally "in her hands," Catarina, as described by Sosa y Peña, appeared more as a divine (male) being than human.

In a similar way, another preacher—the creole Franciscan friar Felipe Montalvo—in a 1748 sermon on Santa Clara mentioned how Clara's extraordinary virtues rendered her nothing short of a captain in a celestial army.[109] As Montalvo pointed out, Clara's status as a kind of general of heavenly troops rested on the extraordinary purity and moral virtue she attained during her earthly life.[110] As a "mystic cup," Clara learned to receive heavenly graces, guard them closely and use them at the service of her own sanctification and honor, thereby assuring herself a privileged role in the celestial army of heaven. Comparing Clara to the (all-male) high priests of biblical times, whose exercise of heroic virtue assured them their place at the helm of leadership, Montalvo confessed that something like this same honor was due to Clara as well.[111] For Montalvo, the "prodigious splendors" and "extraordinary lights" of Clara's heroic virtues qualified her not just for leadership status in the heavenly armies but for the dignity and responsibility associated with the (male) high priesthood.

---

106. Sosa y Peña, *Complemento*, 4; emphasis added. It is not clear whether this preacher was a peninsular or creole.

107. Ibid., 18.

108. Ibid., 28.

109. Montalvo, *Mistico vaso*, 1.

110. Ibid., 2–3.

111. Ibid., 6–7.

Preaching Power

As is evident from the above examples, for Baroque preachers in New Spain the extraordinary virtues of women saints did not just assure them a place in heaven; rather, they represented a step on the part of these women toward transcending their gender and assuming roles and characteristics often associated with men—e.g., becoming army captains and high priests and exercising omnipotence, though doing so in ways that conformed to expectations of the official Church and not, as discussed in chapter 1, in a manner improperly defiant of authority—for example, as in the case of Sor Juana Inés de la Cruz. In characterizing certain female saints in this way—that is, as, in a sense, "becoming" men—the preachers studied here were carving out a unique, open discursive space in which gendered language could transcend normative expectations, thereby emphasizing the extraordinary nature of the saints being honored.[112]

This same dynamic is evident in other sermons, such as one offered by the secular priest Antonio Manuel de Folgar in which he praised the heroic virtues and purity of the early Christian martyr Santa Inés, who accepted martyrdom in place of compromising her virginity.[113] For Folgar, Inés' heroic defense of her purity was of such great value that it overshadowed even the sacrifice she made of her life in martyrdom.[114] In fact, Inés' virtue and courage were so remarkable that for Folgar they surpassed even those of the heroic patriarch Alexander the Great.[115] More valiant even than Alexander, according to Folgar Inés ought to be honored for the exemplary virtue that enabled her to resist temptation and which therefore rendered her, like Christ, a sacrificial lamb of God.[116] Likewise, essentially equal to (the male) Christ as the Lamb of God and heroic enough to merit "eternal triumph" in the celestial "castles of glory," Inés in Folgar's sermon, as in the case of other sermons on female saints studied above, appeared to transcend the limitations of her gender, essentially becoming male.

Similar sentiments are evident in a variety of sermons for other occasions related to convent life. For example, in a sermon given near the end of the first period under consideration in this study, the Franciscan friar Diego Ossorio elaborated a long list of explanations for the greatness of the life lived by women in convents.[117] According to Ossorio, female religious

---

112. See the introduction for ways in which this type of discourse dated back much earlier in church history.

113. Folgar, Varela, y Amunarriz, *La mayor*. Folgar's birthplace is unknown.

114. Ibid., 74.

115. Ibid., 74–75.

116. Ibid., 88–89.

117. Ossorio, *Exaltacion*. It is not certain whether Ossorio was peninsular or creole.

life was a "heroic" and "divine" calling which closed the nun off from the world and left her entirely in the care of her divine spouse.[118] For a nun to profess her vows meant to wed herself entirely and exclusively to Christ and thus to overcome the limits of her gender.[119] Serving Christ and committing herself to become perfect by walking in the path of virtue, each nun had the capacity to transcend her status as "just a woman" and become a queen, an angel or even a "God"—equal to the (male) Christ and Father and therefore worthy of the highest praise and admiration.

Laywomen

Turning to sermons on laywomen, as in the case of convent life it is also important to understand the context in which women lived in this period in order to appreciate more fully the significance of their place in sermons. In their work on gender and families in colonial Mexico, Susan Migden Socolow and Pilar Gonzalbo Aizpuru have shown how, by the end of the sixteenth century, peninsular and creole women had come to assume the place they would occupy in normative Church discourses throughout the colonial period—namely, as practitioners of virtue subject to the authority of their husbands.[120] Gonzalbo also points out that, following the Council of Trent's emphasis on what she terms a contractual model of marriage, prevailing understandings of marriage evolved—at least at the elite level—to defend families' economic interests.[121] As another recent study has shown, an important dimension of laywomen's lives in the wake of these changes centered on definitions of honor within the family, often related to idealized notions of sexual and racial purity.[122] One author explains that these gendered understandings of honor were tied to contemporary assumptions about the intrinsic nature of men and women.[123] Nevertheless, as the work of scholars such as Ann Twinam and Steve Stern has also demonstrated,

---

118. Ibid., 3–4.

119. Ibid., 5.

120. Migden Socolow, *Women of Colonial Latin America*, 15; Gonzalbo, "Tradición." For some of the ways in which women negotiated power and exercised some degree of agency in the context of the patriarchal society of New Spain, see also Gonzalbo Aizpuru, "Las mujeres novohispanas."

121. Gonzalbo, "Nuevo mundo."

122. Johnson and Lipsett-Rivera, eds., *Faces of Honor*, 4–5; Lavrin, ed., *Sexuality and Marriage*, 10.

123. Spurling, "Honor."

even within the rigidity of the honor system there existed degrees of flexibility and contestation.[124]

Regarding women's social circumstances, another study on women and families for this period notes that despite the existence of special schools for elite young women and a few for poorer children the education of women in New Spain was significantly deficient at least through the end of the eighteenth century.[125] Even more than education or social status, however, the generalized patriarchal character of society was frequently determinative of women's place within it.[126] As Richard Boyer notes in a recent study of marriage and family for this period, "Girls . . . had a more protected and more closely supervised childhood. It centered on hearth and home and so offered far fewer chances for enrichment . . . than . . . their brothers. Marriage ended their childhood but not their legal minority[.]"[127] Submitted first to the absolute authority of their fathers and then to their husbands, women faced few opportunities for the exercise at least of public authority, though their confinement to the home and the traditional roles of wife and mother was never complete.[128] Moreover, in a study of a nun's autobiography, Kathleen Ann Myers shows how limits placed on women's agency and choices were not always exclusively imposed by men but also could be determined by female family members, while Pilar Gonzalbo also points to ways in which some women acted to limit their own choices.[129]

Studies by Patricia Seed illuminate how the Church likewise played a role in shaping women's marriage choices, both through canonical rules of consanguinity among marriage partners and by means of the ostensible limits imposed by its expectation that marriage be contracted freely by both

---

124. Twinam, "Negotiation of Honor"; Twinam, *Public Lives*; Stern, *Secret History*, 16.

125. Giraud, "Mujeres," 65. Giraud notes in support of this conclusion the high rates of illiteracy among many women.

126. Ibid., 67–68. Also of significance, it appears that the average age of women at the time of their marriages (eighteen years) rose with higher social class, a trend that appears to point to some degree of flexibility of the timing of their marriages for women of higher social standing. Also influential in this regard was the apparent advantage enjoyed by women of mostly Spanish origin; their later average age of marriage and greater likelihood to remarry if widowed indicates that they were both more likely to marry and possessed more options for potential suitors than their Indian or black counterparts in colonial society.

127. Boyer, *Lives of the Bigamists*, 59.

128. Arrom, *Women of Mexico City*, 62. See also Lavrin and Couturier, "Dowries and Wills."

129. See Myers, "Glimpse of Family Life"; Gonzalbo, "Autoridad masculina."

parties.[130] Adherence to this latter stricture gradually waned over the course of the colonial period, however, as rivalries between peninsular and creole families heightened the influence of parents over their children's marriage choices, sometimes even disposing some parents to resort to violence in order to influence their children's decisions.[131] As Seed notes, the increasing degree of authority exercised by parents over their children's marriage choices by the eighteenth century points to what she calls a new normative patriarchy which emerged in this period. As this happened, the Church and state—as normative arbiters of social authority—responded in kind and adjusted their policies in order to support these social changes.[132] As a result, in order to assure their best chances for propitious matches, young women's lives fell increasingly under their parents and others' vigilance over the course of the eighteenth century.[133] Among the popular classes this was less true as there was less financial risk at stake on the part of parents and as a result young people enjoyed a greater degree of freedom in choosing marriage partners.[134]

Within the Church's public discourses in sermons, laywomen were featured less frequently than nuns and female saints, although when they were referenced it was often in terms similar to those already seen in convent sermons. Though few sermons dedicated exclusively to the topic of laywomen's devotion are preserved, one telling exception, in addition to Eguiara y Eguren's sermon cited at the beginning of this chapter, is a 1738 funeral sermon for the deceased creole noblewoman Doña Gertrudis de la Peña. In his sermon, the creole Jesuit priest Juan Antonio de Oviedo referred to his subject in both the title and throughout the text of his oration as "the strong woman."[135] For Oviedo this very title was a contradiction in terms since women were by nature weak and imperfect: "Because, 'woman and strong,' how can that be, when the very word woman denotes weakness, softness, and debilitation?"[136] In contrast to the abject weakness of women, men were naturally strong and in fact supplied the linguistic origins of the

---

130. Giraud, "Mujeres," 68. See also Seed, *To Love*.

131. Seed, "Marriage Promises."

132. Seed, *To Love*, 5.

133. Giraud, "Mujeres," 69. For example, young women were often not allowed to leave home without the accompaniment of a guardian ("*dueña*").

134. Ibid.

135. Oviedo, *La muger fuerte*. Oviedo was born in Nueva Granada, in northern South America.

136. Ibid., 1.

words courage and virtue.[137] For that reason, Oviedo pointed out that it was an exceptional thing to encounter a truly strong woman, though he insisted that he had found just such an example in Doña Gertrudis.[138]

Oviedo went on to elaborate some of the ways in which this strong, "military" woman had overcome the "armies" at war with the weakness of her sex. First, she did battle with the temptation to laziness.[139] To this example of virtue Oviedo called upon the women of Mexico in his congregation to pay particularly close attention, as Doña Gertrudis too was a Mexican woman who, "to no other woman ceded anything in nobility of blood, abundance of riches, and the other trappings and endowments which adorn the female sex."[140] According to Oviedo, the ideal to which the women of Mexico, imitating Doña Gertrudis, ought to aspire was to serve as stable "edifices" or "houses" for their husbands—solid structures of virtue which, by definition, did not move about but instead remained firmly and steadfastly in place.[141] If women succeeded in following this counsel and emulating the example of Doña Gertrudis and other heroic female witnesses, they too could become "manly" women who displayed courage and virtue and served as examples for other women both in their families and in the larger society.[142] Thus, as in the case of convent sermons, laywomen too were called by preachers to overcome the innate "weakness" of their sex not only to assure their own personal salvation but to shore up the strength, stability, and holiness of surrounding society.

Men and Masculinity

Turning now to sermons preached on various male saints and in which norms of masculininty were invoked, it seems the opposite of the trend toward the masculinizing of women saints was true for their male counterparts. For example, among all the male saints who served as the topic for various Baroque sermons in New Spain, one of the most crucial was Saint Joseph, the adoptive father of Jesus. For many preachers, Joseph was not only a crucial father figure for Christ, and therefore strong, courageous and masculine; instead, he also embodied a number of significant traditionally female characteristics

137. Ibid.
138. Ibid., 2.
139. Ibid., 4.
140. Ibid., 4–5.
141. Ibid., 7.

142. Ibid., 18. For an additional account of the phenomenon of "virile" women in ecclesiastical discourses in this period, see Myers, *Neither Saints Nor Sinners*, 13.

as a result of the extraordinary moral purity he was held to have exercised in serving as Mary's husband but never engaging in a sexual relationship with her. This characterization of Joseph as motherly and nurturing in his care for Christ accords with a trend noted by Charlene Villaseñor Black in a recent study of the cult of Saint Joseph in the Spanish empire. As Villaseñor Black notes, Colonial Mexico differed from Spain in its devotion to Joseph in matriarchal terms.[143] Among other possibilities, Villaseñor Black suggests that, "[t]he preference for the extended matriarchal family in Mexican Holy Family images may . . . be traceable to the influence of indigenous family structures, which were more matriarchal in nature and frequently composed of extended kin networks."[144] Moreover, in another study, Villaseñor Black suggests that depictions of Joseph in both paintings and sermons in this period may point to connections between these discourses and changing notions of masculinity in the early modern period.[145]

Pointing to another possible explanation, this trend is also noteworthy in light of the work of Grace M. Jantzen, outlined in the introduction, with regard to female mystics. According to Jantzen, for many early Christian writers the ideal path for women to achieve holiness would involve the transcendence of their gender, leading them to become "manly and perfect."[146] However, the same was not usually true for men: "[Holy men] do not thereby become unmasculine, let alone female. For a man to develop in spirituality, he must become even more manly, with the manliness of Christ, transcending the demands of the flesh and living by the spirit."[147] Intriguingly, then, as will be demonstrated below, this same trend does not appear to have held consistently for Baroque sermons in New Spain; instead, a more expansive discursive flexibility and openness seems to have admitted the possibility that holy men could appropriate positive feminine attributes.[148] As in the case of laywomen, such discursive openness may reflect a degree of flexibility within expectations of men in colonial society—especially in the eighteenth century, as studied by scholars such as Pete Sigal and Zeb Tortorici—even though norms of masculinity were an important aspect of relations of power throughout the colonial period.[149]

143. Villaseñor Black, *Creating*, 81.

144. Ibid., 84.

145. Villaseñor Black, "Love and Marriage," 667.

146. Jantzen, *Power*, 53.

147. Ibid.

148. For a study of another period in which male and female spiritual authority appear to have coexisted creatively, see Coakley, *Women, Men, and Spiritual Power*.

149. For example, for accounts of how notions of sodomy developed during the

Turning to a specific sermon on Saint Joseph, another work by Antonio Folgar praised Joseph's virtues and compared them to those of the biblical matriarchs Rachel and Sarah, who had endured difficult births in order to bring forth their children. In the case of Rachel, Folgar addressed Joseph and pointed to how the saint's love for his son made Jesus "your Benjamin."[150] As the son of "the Eternal Father's delights" and of the pain, silence and sorrows of Joseph, the spiritual birth of Jesus from Joseph paralleled that of Benjamin, whose mother Rachel, referring to his difficult birth, gave him the name "son of her pain." Accordingly, Folgar seemed to be suggesting that Jesus was likewise the son of Joseph's own pain and therefore that, in a sense, Joseph had birthed Jesus much as a mother would. Turning to a comparison with Sarah, Folgar highlighted the story of a biblical figure who, like Joseph, loved a child born originally to someone else.[151] Here, like Sarah, Joseph was an adoptive parent—caring for Jesus with an exceptionally great, even motherly love. Folgar saw no difficulty in comparing Joseph's love to a biblical matriarch's nor, presumably, with the logical implications of that comparison—namely, that part of the perfection of masculinity included the taking on of positive feminine, even motherly attributes at the service of a divine calling or mission.

Similar openness and flexibility around masculine conventions of gender in emerge in a sermon from 1735 in which a celebrated anecdote from the life of San Bernardo was recounted and highlighted.[152] In the sermon, the peninsular Carmelite preacher, fray Nicolás de Jesús María, showed no hesitation in elaborating on how both St. Joseph and Bernardo competed for nourishment from Mary's breasts, with Bernardo emerging a clear winner because, "to Joseph from the chaste breasts of Mary were only dispensed blessings . . . but to Bernardo was given food."[153]

As already seen earlier in this chapter in language that depicted St. John of the Cross as a loving "bride" of Christ, additional discourses of

---

colonial period, how accusations could be negotiated, and how the severity of punishments against the accused actually decreased in Mexico during the eighteenth and early nineteenth centuries, see Spurling, "Honor," 47; Tortorici, "Contra Natura," chapters 1–4; De Los Reyes-Heredia, "Sodomy and Society," chapters 1–3; Gruzinski, "Ashes of Desire"; Sigal, ed., *Infamous Desire*. Likewise, for treatments of theological discourses of sodomy and their transformation into secular categories during the enlightenment period, see Garza Carvajal, *Butterflies Will Burn*; Allaín Bracamonte, "Los nefandos placeres."

150 Folgar, *Competencias* 8–9.
151. Ibid., 11.
152. Jesús María, *El codicioso*.
153. Ibid., 22.

Manly Virgins and Tender Fathers

unexpected masculinity abounded in other sermons in this period. For example, in a 1743 sermon on St. Peter of Verona in the Mexico City Convent of Santo Domingo, the creole Dominican friar Manuel Romualdo Dallo y Zabala highlighted among the saint's many virtues his special affinity for assisting women at childbirth.[154] As a kind of spiritual midwife, Dallo y Zabala proclaimed that St. Peter's miracles on behalf of women seeking to become pregnant or in the pangs of childbirth would require "entire books" to elaborate. Likewise, in another sermon from the same period given in the Mexico City cathedral by the Franciscan friar Anastasio Antonio Pérez, the preacher extoled the virtues of the seventh-century French saint Eloi. Renowned as the patron saint of metal workers, according to Pérez Eloi was even more notable for the work of purification he accomplished within his own soul—a feat which transformed him into a "Vice God."[155] In this case, Eloi's labors at self-mastery resulted not just in his moral sanctification but in fact his becoming, "with God's help, God." Crucially, Pérez went on to elaborate that one of the keys to Eloi's transformation was the way in which he emulated the virtues of female virgins, following their example of moral purity and thereby attaining perfection.[156] Thus, having molded his life according to the pattern of holy women, Eloi achieved the perfection of transformation not simply into a saint but into God himself.

Thus, as the above examples have demonstrated, a marked tendency emerges in Baroque New Spanish sermons toward portraying female saints with positive attributes of masculintity and male saints with affirming feminine charcteristics. However, while the advocacy given by these preachers to various moral virtues on the part of saints has been apparent, what has proved less readily obvious are some of the assumptions about gender that undergird many of these assertions. To elucidate some of these more hidden presuppositions, another sermon on saints, this time on both a male and a female saint, will be instructive. Written in 1754, near the end of the first time period under consideration in this study, the creole priest José Mariano Gregorio de Elizalde Itta y Parra's sermon on Sts. Joachim and Anne—the parents of the Virgin Mary—was quite frank in its transparency concerning normative conventions of gender.[157]

Turning first to Anne, Itta y Parra offered an opening query as to why the saint should be worthy of veneration. According to Itta y Parra, "a bad son is better than a good daughter, because her sex is so naturally imperfect

154. Dallo y Zabala, *San Pedro*, 19.
155. Pérez, *El Vice-Dios*, 5–6. Pérez's status as either peninsular or creole is uncertain.
156. Ibid., 9.
157. Itta y Parra, *El desempeño*.

77

that even the desire to have daughters is contrary to the impetus of nature, which always tends toward that which is most perfect."[158] If daughters, as females, were "naturally imperfect" and therefore the desire to have them itself constituted an impetus "against nature," Itta y Parra wondered what possible merit could devolve upon Anne if all that she did was merely give birth to a child who was "just a daughter." The author addressed this question, suggesting that this lack of appreciation for the birth of a mere daughter would indeed be appropriate for every female birth that had ever been, "[in the] universe," save in the extraordinarily exceptional cases of those of Anne and her daughter Mary.[159] Why were Anne's and Mary's births unique among all the other innumerable and unremarkable female births in history? Itta y Parra explained that the dignity of Anne's birth stemmed from that of her daughter, Mary, and the latter's unparalleled ability to "defeat the impossible things of nature" in "singularly grand" fecundity. By this Itta y Parra explained that he meant that Mary, as the mother of Christ, miraculously superseded both the male and female sexes, essentially transcending the limits of gender itself as a means of proving worthy to bear the Christ child.[160] Despite the "imperfection of her sex," Mary "supersede[d] both sexes put together," thereby overcoming the problem of her birth as "just a daughter" and assuring the consummation of the divine plan both for herself and her son.[161]

In other words, as Itta y Parra also put it, Mary, because of her superlative purity and perfection, was not in fact really so much Anne's daughter as, remarkably, her "son."[162] In truth, Mary was the "equivalent" of a son for Anne since, perhaps pushing the bounds of orthodox belief, Itta y Parra proclaimed that Jesus too in fact had become incarnate in Anne's womb through Mary.[163] In this process Anne's husband, Joachim also had a role. According to Itta y Parra, Joachim and Anne were destined by God to bring about the re-edification of the ancient Jewish temple—they were to be the source of the restoration of the promises made by God to their ancestors.[164] Here Joachim's role was to be "heaven" and Anne's to be "earth," which, in

---

158. Ibid., 10.

159. Ibid., 11.

160. Ibid..

161. For a recent study of the iconography of the Holy Family and especially of St. Anne, see Villaseñor Black, "St. Anne."

162. Itta y Parra, *El desempeño*, 12–13.

163. Ibid., 17.

164. Ibid., 1–2.

coming together, would form the "pure and clean" material (i.e., Mary), through which the world would be saved.

In other words, in this sermon as in the others examined above which speak in praise of various male and female saints and address the nature of men and women and their roles in society in the context of religious professions and funerals, the working assumptions about gender betrayed within them appear clear. First, women were "naturally imperfect" and weak and therefore customarily not to be looked to for inspiration to moral excellence and virtue. However, very exceptional women had, with God's help, overcome the weakness of their sex and excelled in purity, thereby displaying "manly" virtue and all but becoming both male and even coequals with God. Second, men, while members of the more perfect sex, also needed to practice virtue and purity. To do so, they were advised to look to the purity of heroic female virgins and become spiritual, mystical lovers and even "brides" of Christ and, as with women, near equals to God. If both women and men, in these ways, overcame their tendencies to sin and thus exercised virtue heroically, they too would be like the saints who now lived in heaven and had become "vice-Gods." Finally, perhaps most importantly of all, if the people of Mexico City to whom the priests made their appeals would only follow the example of these "manly" women and "maternal" men, they too would assure not only their own individual salvation but also reconfirm and perpetuate the collective greatness of the emerging polity of which they were a part—that is, Mexico.

Conclusion

As this chapter has thus demonstrated, gendered language in sermons was used in the Baroque period both to affirm normative gender expectations and to transcend them, often as a means of promoting New Spain's collective greatness. For example, according to these narratives, women were by nature weaker than men and yet, paradoxically, female saints who acted like men redeemed their sex, while men who acted like women in embodying virginity and birthing spiritual children though their pain and sorrows were considered the most admirable of all males. In the case of both women and men, these heroic and remarkable virtues, when also embodied by the faithful, could secure divine blessing. As suggested earlier, these tropes of flexible masculinity and femininity and the discursive practices used to convey them were not coincidental occurances; rather, they point at once both to a nexus of patriarchal authority and gender and to a degree of flexibility at play in the Church's public discourses in this period. Unlike examples from subsequent decades, in which underlying gendered norms would be made much more explicit in sermons and other official Church discourses, in the Baroque period they were more latent and less frequently specified, thereby allowing preachers more flexibility in using conventions of gender to promote their larger discursive goals.

Therefore, as this chapter has sought to demonstrate, the language that Baroque preachers in New Spain employed to characterize and praise various saints and contemporary figures created a distinctive discursive space in which gendered norms could both be reaffirmed and transcended at the service of larger goals. For these preachers, this essential element of the Baroque aesthetic as it operated in Mexican Baroque sermons—the officially sanctioned transgression of normative gender boundaries by means of rhetorical devices—supplied a key both to understanding the workings of heavenly forces and to demonstrating the uniquely extraordinary and singular ways in which they were operative in the context of New Spain.

Chapter 3

Reforming Discourses

Sermons and the Enlightenment in New Spain

> *"Adjusting himself to the circumstances . . . the orator skillfully combined poetic inspiration with doctrine . . . the useful with the pleasant, in order to delight while convincing and persuade while edifying his great and numerous audience."*[1]

EVEN AS PREACHERS WELL into the middle and later decades of the eighteenth century in New Spain continued to offer sermons steeped in the Baroque aesthetic described in the previous chapter, by the middle of the century movements for change were in the air. As reflected in the above excerpt from an introductory review (*parecer*) of a sermon in this period, starting with reforms imposed by the new Bourbon rulers of Spain but soon taking root among church leaders as well, the cluster of ideas and reforms that came to be known collectively as the Enlightenment proved significantly influential in colonial Mexico. Not only in the realms of politics and governmental reforms but also in the arts and, specifically, in the style of preaching that came to be embraced by ecclesiastical authorities, the Enlightenment brought changes to styles of preaching—specifically, often in the gendered language and imagery employed in them—that would have important consequences in subsequent decades. After first introducing the surrounding context of enlightened reforms, this chapter will examine some of the ways in which preachers and other purveyors of official church discourses in colonial Mexico City adapted as the new ideas and sensibilities of the Enlightenment took sway.

1. Omaña, *Parecer*.

The Enlightenment Context

Although the Bourbon dynasty had assumed control of the Spanish monarchy following the War of Spanish Succession near the beginning of the eighteenth century, it was not until the middle decades of the century that Bourbon administrative changes would begin to take effect in New Spain. Especially with the advent of Charles III's reign (1759–1788), Bourbon authorities started to promulgate new policies designed to bring order to urban environments, populations, and institutions—including the Church—and increase revenues for the crown.[2] As William Taylor and Stanley and Barbara Stein have noted, many aspects of the Bourbon Reforms were part of a "defensive modernization" engaged in as a way to strengthen Spanish imperial interests in response to contemporary political developments—for example, the Seven Years' War (1756–1763) and its aftermath with the cession of Florida as well as the temporary loss of Havana to the British in 1762.[3] As a result, the new defining values of Bourbon rule in New Spain were centralization under royal governors, standardization, efficiency, precision, and the rule of law through *reglas fijas*—laws not subject to extensive debate or interpretation.[4] Overall, the new ambient ethos was one of sobriety and austerity, especially in the public arena, along with subjection of colonial interests to those of the metropole.[5]

In the artistic world, the establishment of the Royal Academy of San Carlos in Mexico City in 1785 signified the codification of trends toward classicism in art and architecture that had begun earlier in the eighteenth century.[6] In painting, for example, in contrast to earlier portraits, which of-

---

2. O'Hara, *Flock Divided*, 56. See also Larkin, *Very Nature*, 119–23; Brading, *Miners*; Lynch, *Spanish American Revolutions*; Viqueira Albán, *Propriety*. Among the changes imposed by the Bourbons after 1750 these scholars emphasize the following: reorganization of the financial system, increased mining production, opening of free trade, the increased presence of the regular army, and the subordination of church interests to those of the state, among others.

3. Taylor, *Magistrates*, 13; Stein and Stein, *Colonial Heritage*, 88. Recent studies by Stanley and Barbara Stein have continued to examine economic aspects of Bourbon reformism. For example, see Stein and Stein: *Silver; Apogee of Empire; Edge of Crisis*. In *Apogee of Empire* the Steins explain how some of the economic aspects of the Bourbon reforms proved disadvantageous and therefore unpopular with significant elements of New Spanish monied interests, thereby affecting the manner in which some reforms were received in the colony.

4. Taylor, *Magistrates*, 13.

5. Florescano and Menegus, "La época," 369.

6. For the context surrounding the foundation of the Royal Academy, see Burke, *Treasures*, 83–85. See also Weismann, *Art and Time*, 66; Early, *Colonial Architecture*,

ten displayed signs of their sitters' rank and privilege, late eighteenth-century portraits were more intimate, emphasizing individuality and realism and featuring geometrical forms and simplicity of background.[7] In the field of architecture, the selection in 1786 of the creole architect José Damián Ortiz de Castro's design for the completion of the Mexico City cathedral marked another significant victory for the classicizing tastes of the Academy of San Carlos, evident in the evenness of line and simplicity of decoration of the church's twin bell towers.[8] The classicism of Ortiz de Castro's plan emerged in sharp relief to that of a competing plan—with its abundant curves, projections, and recesses—from Isidro Vicente de Balbás, son of Jerónimo de Balbás, the designer of the cathedral's great Baroque altarpiece, the *Altar de los reyes*.[9] Abandoning the purported excesses represented by Balbás' design, the new, classically-inspired design of Ortiz de Castro corresponded to the prevailing norms of the Academy of San Carlos and represented a victory for its exponents in their efforts to reimagine Mexico City visually and architecturally.

In addition to Bourbon reformism's strong "top-down" impetus, it is also true that prevailing social circumstances in the latter part of the eighteenth century influenced the formulation of some policy reforms. As populations expanded and crises of subsistence and disease ensued, traditional social relationships from the Hapsburg era began to break down and the Bourbon state viewed a new approach to governance as necessary. For example, as Brian Larkin has pointed out, with traditional patron-client relationships weakened in the second half of the eighteenth century, "an expanding state apparatus began to intervene systematically in the realm of charity. This ever more pervasive state also attempted to reform the plebian class by ordering the urban landscape and regulating the minutiae of daily life."[10] However, as greater space for social mobility emerged for some sectors of society, elites sought to reaffirm ethnic and racial differences—for example, in the genre of *casta* paintings—to preserve their traditional privileges.[11]

192; Mullen, *Architecture*, 204.

7. Burke, *Treasures*, 94–96.
8. Early, *Colonial Architecture*, 193–94.
9. Ibid.
10. Larkin, "Baroque," 32. See also Larkin, *Very Nature*, 121.
11. Viqueira Albán, *Propriety*, xxii. See also recent studies on *casta* paintings: Carrera, *Imagining Identity*; Katzew, *Casta Painting*.

Enlightened Reform and the Church

Parallel to the political, social, and artistic shifts promoted by Bourbon reformers in this period were changes in the Church's approach to spirituality and its own internal governance that likewise proved significant. As secular authorities implemented reformist programs, church officials sought increasingly to promote and enforce the formation of a more regalist church, in which the institution's interests would be tied closely to those of the state.[12] For prelates like Francisco Lorenzana y Butrón (1766–1771) and other like-minded church leaders, authority would now need to reside more clearly with bishops and less with the traditionally powerful religious orders, a tendency evinced in the secularization of rural parishes—a continuation of earlier sixteenth- and seventeenth-century efforts—and the expulsion of the Society of Jesus from New Spain.[13] The expulsion of the Jesuits was linked for reformers to what they saw as the order's excessive influence over the education and spiritual lives of New Spaniards, though it would elicit episodes of violent opposition among some creoles.[14]

In the midst of these changes, and to a greater degree than in earlier decades, questions of power and the loss of institutional prominence were also on the minds of New Spanish church leaders in the mid-to-late eighteenth century. For the Church, as Nancy Farriss and other scholars have demonstrated, the Bourbon reforms also meant increased supervision and sometimes usurpation by the state of traditional manifestations of its authority—a development which, as Oscar Mazín has shown, represented a significant break from previous models of church-state relations.[15] For example, reforms directed at the Church included limitations on the jurisdiction of ecclesiastical courts, restrictions on traditional *fueros*, the trying

---

12. See Farriss, *Crown and Clergy*, 8.

13. For the effects of Bourbon reformism on the Church, see Brading, *First America*, chapter 22; Brading, *Church and State*; Melvin, "Urban Religions," chapter 2; Taylor, *Magistrates*, 83–84; Larkin, *Very Nature*, 122; Florescano and Menegus, "La época," 369–70.

14. See Brading, *First America*, 467–68; Brading, *Church and State*, chapter 1; Brading, "Tridentine Catholicism." For studies on the expulsion and its aftermath, see Andrés-Gallego, ed., *Tres grandes cuestiones*; Vargas Alquicira, *La singularidad*; Mörner, *Expulsion*.

15. See Farriss, *Crown and Clergy*, 4–12, 91. See also: Taylor, *Magistrates*, 13–17; Larkin, *Very Nature*, 122–23; Mazín, *Entre dos majestades*, 13; Mazín, "El poder," 53. Mazín refers to a "crisis de convivencia" between church and state—though one that unfolded gradually and in complex ways—in the wake of these trends.

of priests who committed crimes in civil courts, increased taxation and the undermining of the work of some revenue-generating foundations.[16]

Whether in support or protest of greater secular reforms and trends, pastoral letters were another important aspect of the Church's institutional development in the period of the Bourbon Reforms. Published by Mexico City's prelates with increasing frequency in the periods corresponding to the reigns of Charles III and Charles IV and to the tenures of archbishops Lorenzana, Alonso Núñez de Haro y Peralta (1772–1800), and Francisco Xavier de Lizana y Beaumont (1803–1811), these discourses provided an important means by which church leaders could seek to implement desired reforms.[17] Although Lorenzana's immediate predecessor, Manuel José Rubio y Salinas (1748–1765), did publish a few significant letters and decrees—including a moralizing entreaty in response to the infamous Lima earthquake of 1755—it appears that the publication of archbishops' pastoral letters in Mexico City did not increase notably until Lorenzana's reign as archbishop.[18] As William Callahan and William Taylor have pointed out, part of the reason for this significant increase relates to Lorenzana's and other prelates' perceived need to cooperate in the Crown's reforming efforts.[19] For example, in contrast to Rubio y Salinas' six total letters and decrees, given over the course of a seventeen-year term as archbishop, Lorenzana, within the first four years of his arrival, had already published no fewer than thirty-three pastoral documents, a collection of which appeared in 1770, and which were further affirmed in the decrees of

---

16. See Farriss, *Crown and Clergy*, 6. See also Larkin, *Very Nature*, 121; Pérez Puente, "El obispo." Pérez Puente suggests the importance of viewing bishops as both political and religious figures in this period, defending and seeking to further the interests of the Church, though not always in uniform ways.

17. Larkin, *Very Nature*, 127. For the significance of the Church's more assured predominance under the earlier archbishop (and viceroy) Juan Antonio de Vizarrón y Eguiarreta (1730–1747), see Brading, "Tridentine," 2.

18. For the initial decades of the period under consideration in this study, I was able to identify only seven total published pastoral letters or decrees from Lorenzana's two immediate predecessors, Juan Antonio de Vizarrón y Eguiarreta (1730–1747) and Manuel José Rubio y Salinas (1748–1765). I found only one decree from Vizarrón y Eguiarreta, which dealt with regulation of religious celebrations. For Rubio y Salinas I found six letters and decrees dealing with matters such as *diezmos* and clerical discipline. Though Vizarrón's single decree dealt with a relatively minor internal church matter, Rubio's letters did exhibit some evidence of a growing sense of anxiety on the part of leadership of the archdiocese concerning contemporary events and practices—for example the Lima earthquake. See Rubio y Salinas, *Carta pastoral*.

19. Callahan, *Church*, 11; Taylor, *Magistrates*, 16–17.

the Fourth Provincial Council in the early 1770s—studied in greater detail below in the context of sermons.[20]

Succeeding Lorenzana after the latter's elevation to the primatial see of Toledo in 1772, Alonso Núñez de Haro y Peralta continued many of his predecessor's reforming initiatives and was similarly prolific in his published output.[21] One of Núñez de Haro's most lasting impacts on the Church in New Spain and Mexico came in the form of his response to the crisis surrounding a famous sermon given by the creole Dominican theologian Fray Servando Teresa y Mier (1763-1827)—a sermon that would provoke a definitive final condemnation from the church hierarchy of the style of discourse and approach to spirituality, studied in chapter 2, that had developed among creole preachers in the Baroque period.[22] Offered before both the viceroy and the archbishop on the occasion of the feast of the Virgin of Guadalupe in 1794, Mier's sermon quickly veered from established standards of orthodoxy when he suggested that the recent discovery of the Aztec calendar stone in central Mexico City indicated that the image of Guadalupe had been painted by the Virgin Mary herself on the cape of the apostle St. Thomas, who subsequently traveled to America, evangelized the Indians and then, following their apostasy, hid the image until its location was revealed to Juan Diego by the Virgin following the Spanish Conquest.[23]

This startling, highly speculative interpretation did not sit well with Núñez de Haro and other church authorities who denounced the purported excesses of such a non-rational "fable" in a decree issued the following year.[24] As Iván Escamilla González argues, this condemnation of what was essentially a continuation of earlier traditions from the Baroque period—which had included a degree of freedom for speculation and improvisation within sermons—represented an attempt finally to bring such interpreta-

20. Lorenzana, *Cartas*. For treatments of Lorenzana and the significance of his term as archbishop, see Taylor, *Magistrates*, 13-17; de la Hera, "El regalismo"; Zahino Peñafort, ed., *El Cardenal*; Sierra Nava-Lasa, *El Cardenal*.

21. As was the case with Lorenzana, Núñez de Haro's long term as archbishop—almost 30 years, from 1772 to 1800—was characterized by the publication of many letters, decrees, and instructions dealing with matters such as the sacraments, public order, nuns and convents, priests' conduct, the suppression of Jesuit theology, obedience to the Crown, and charitable initiatives. From among these many writings, I was able to identify and consult twenty-two examples. See also Larkin, *Very Nature*, for study of some of Núñez de Haro's writings, including his additional output of sermons.

22. For accounts of the Mier episode, see: Mayer, *Flor de primavera*, 202-20; Brading, *First America*, chapter 26; Escamilla González, *José Patricio*, chapter 7; Alejos Grau, "Génesis," 691-786.

23. Brading, *First America*, 583.

24. Núñez de Haro y Peralta, *Nos el doctor* (1795).

tions into line with new, enlightened religious sensibilities and priorities.[25] Describing this new spirituality, Matthew O'Hara points out that church authorities considered many "popular religious practices [to be] spiritually and materially damaging to the faithful . . . Spiritually, they distracted the mind . . . Economically, they wasted resources that could be directed toward more productive activities."[26] Like their secular counterparts, religious reformers in eighteenth-century New Spain sought to achieve a greater degree of control over the lives of those under their direction. For church leaders, this meant promoting a more strictly spiritual approach to the divine and a renewed emphasis on the power and authority of the hierarchy.

As Brian Larkin points out, the changes proposed in religious language by the Enlightenment touched on the very nature of God himself: "Catholic reformers of the second half of the eighteenth century advocated a new religious practice. They sought to interiorize and simplify piety. For them, God was eminently spiritual and thus largely incapable of being confined within the physical world."[27] Among new models or images of God proposed by reformers, William Taylor and Pamela Voekel point to ways in which God was now to be seen less as suffering or in agony and more closely associated with Christ's resurrection.[28] Likewise, St. Paul and the Ten Commandments grew in favor, while the Seven Deadly Sins, the devil, and more pessimistic views of the human condition were deemphasized.[29] Also problematic were some of the more emotive aspects of the earlier spirituality. As Voekel puts it, "[t]he passions were no longer a road to God . . . Rather, they represented a serious social threat that the Christian must overcome through the exercise of secular reason."[30] No longer could the perceived excesses of the Baroque be tolerated, in which the divine could be equated or at least intimately as-

---

25. Escamilla González, *José Patricio*, 259-61. Escamilla González argues that, since its codification in the mid-seventeenth century, the Guadalupan tradition had always been the product of the negotiation between popular piety and creole authors' creativity. With this freedom to interpret the image and its tradition stifled by reforming authorities, Escamilla González suggests that the creativity of the tradition might be seen as eventually finding new outlets—for example, in movements toward independence in the early nineteenth century. See also Pérez Memén, *El episcopado*, 51; Ampudia, *La Iglesia*, 236; Brading, *First America*, 494-97; Taylor, *Magistrates*, 16-19; Larkin, *Very Nature*, 121-23; Farriss, *Crown and Clergy*, 11-12.

26. O'Hara, *Flock Divided*, 65.

27. Larkin, *Very Nature*, 7.

28. Taylor, *Magistrates*, 19; Voekel, *Alone Before God*, 1-3. See also Connaughton, "Mudanzas."

29. Taylor, *Magistrates*, 19.

30. Voekel, *Alone Before God*, 2-3.

sociated with elements of the material world. Instead, the faithful were to meditate on spiritual matters and seek moral perfection, eschewing earlier, more material approaches to God.

In short, in Larkin's words, "reformers sought to redefine the balance in Catholic practice between ritual action and pious contemplation in favor of the latter," though, as Voekel insists, it is also important to emphasize that such reason-centered reforms did not preclude sincerity of religious feeling or belief.[31] Whatever they were communicating, as the remainder of this chapter will show, one of the most significant ways in which church authorities promoted their reform-minded goals was by means of spoken and printed sermons—both through their content as well as stylistic changes that called for cleaner, sparer language with which to communicate more efficiently the divine message.

Changing Styles and Themes in Enlightenment-Era Preaching

Carlos Herrejón Peredo traces the beginnings of the transition from Baroque sermons to a style of sacred oratory more attuned to enlightened sensibilities to approximately 1760, around the time of the death of Ferdinand VI and the accession of Charles III—when a number of changes became noticeable in the style and content of sermons.[32] For that reason, and because of the political context surrounding the policies of Charles III in which the sermons were preached, the examples studied below will correspond to the three decades of Charles' reign (1759-1788). In this period, as Church authorities increasingly sought to placate and win favor with their secular counterparts, royal figures came to take on greater prominence in sermons—for example, even individual viceroys could at times serve as the subject of sermons.[33] Along with this emphasis on authority figures came increased attention to questions of political theory, such as the definition and role of sovereignty within political bodies as well as the nature of despotism, just war, and appropriate national self-defense, especially in the wake of later events in the Iberian peninsula during the decades of the 1790s and 1800-1810.[34]

---

31. Larkin, "Baroque," 17-18; Larkin, *Very Nature*, 7-8; Voekel, *Alone Before God*, 3-4.

32. Herrejón Peredo, *Del sermón*, 61, 90-96.

33. Ibid., 66-67.

34. Ibid., 78-80.

Sermons and the Enlightenment

In general, the transitional period under consideration in this chapter was characterized by a marked increase in preaching on the cultivation of moral virtue in everyday life.[35] Trying to make the requirements of religion more accessible and thus potentially more easily subject to accountability, church reformers and preachers emphasized morality and the pursuit of virtue in their sermons as part of their larger efforts at promoting interior over exterior modes of piety and devotion.[36] To this end, preachers advocated interior devotion to the Eucharist and criticized and sometimes persecuted other more popular or local devotions associated with the older, Baroque style.[37] Likewise, certain saints received renewed emphasis and attention from preachers, including St. Thomas Aquinas, whose notable chastity served as a model against which to compare what some preachers saw as the decay of public morals over the course of the eighteenth century.[38] In preaching about saints, sermonizers in this period were also likely to speak less of the inimitable, super-human greatness of their subjects and were more disposed to offer examples from the lives of the saints as models to be followed by their congregations.[39]

Also significant for understanding the development of preaching in New Spain in the mid eighteenth century are the decrees of the Fourth Provincial Council, which met and deliberated in the early 1770s during the tenure of Archbishop Lorenzana.[40] Especially significant for the purposes of this study are the council's decrees on the reform of preaching in New Spain, featured second in order of importance only to a declaration on the creed.[41] Specifically, among the values the council promoted related to preaching, the first was that of consistency within the texts of sermons.[42] Preachers were to remain faithful to received interpretations of Scripture and were advised to avoid challenging them with novel, alien interpreta-

---

35. Ibid., 142.
36. Ibid., 225.
37. Ibid., 242–45; Taylor, *Magistrates*, 47–73.
38. Herrejón Peredo, *Del sermón*, 195.
39. Ibid., *Del sermón*, 115.
40. For treatments of the Fourth Provincial Council, see Luque Alcaide, "Los concilios"; Zahino Peñafort, *Iglesia*, 213–14. Zahino Peñafort characterizes the Council and a number of other church-related reforms (including reform of *diezmos*, convent reform, integration of Indian *doctrinas*, and the expulsion of the Jesuits) as notable failures due to their lack of sensitivity to creole traditions.
41. Herrejón Peredo, *Del sermón*, 89.
42. *El Cardenal Lorenzana*, 55.

tions wed to individual caprices.[43] Similarly, preaching was to be useful and not to indulge in vain tangents and asides.[44] Sermons should also be clear and easy to follow and understand, avoiding unnecessary complications and extravagant abstractions.[45] Other values mentioned included cirumspection, consideration of the witness value and knowledge of the preacher, the prohibition of challenging ecclesiastical superiors in publc, obedience, and counsels toward charitableness and prudence.[46]

Herrejón Peredo cites an instructive example of how considerations of style and language changed in this period in the form of an introductory *parecer* for a 1760 sermon. In his evaluation of the sermon, the author of the *parecer*, the creole Jesuit humanist Agustín Pablo de Castro, made a point of insisting that changes in the style of sermons were necessary in order to overcome the excesses of the Baroque period.[47] According to Castro, the Baroque had represented an era of oratorical backsliding as preachers reverted to a medieval style reminiscent of the times in which Spain had lived under Muslim rule. For Castro this "barbaric" period, characterized by values of "ingenuity" and "admiration" in sermons, had ended only with the advent of Catholic reformism, as witnessed in the Renaissance and finally codified at the Council of Trent. Therefore, according to the author's narrative, new, enlightened styles of preaching represented a renunciation of the excesses and regressions of the Baroque and a return to the values of the Renaissance and of Trent.[48] Although not necessarily representative of all preachers in New Spain, the values of rhetorical simplicity and directness presented in Castro's account would come to take hold in many sermons printed in Mexico City by the late eighteenth century.

Another example of how these new ideas came to be expressed emerges in a *parecer* offered by the peninsular priest don Juan Ignacio de la Rocha for a 1762 sermon by the creole Jesuit preacher Joseph Julián Parreño.[49] According to de la Rocha, Parreño's sermon on Guadalupe represented "a most manly image" of Christian eloquence, given by an orator de la Rocha did not hesitate to label a "deity of eloquence."[50] As mentioned by Castro above, here de la Rocha likewise highlighted the importance of

43. Ibid.
44. Ibid.
45 Ibid.
46. Herrejón Peredo, *Del sermón*, 89–90.
47. Ibid., 99–100.
48. Ibid., 100.
49. de la Rocha, *Parecer*. Records indicate that Parreño was born in Cuba.
50. Ibid. There is no internal pagination within the *parecer*.

Reforming Discourses

classical rhetoric for the composition of good sermons, citing, for example, a maxim of Cicero on the primacy of thought over the senses.[51] Similarly, in his *aprobación*, another Jesuit, the creole Salvador Dávila, also praised the virtues of ancient Greek rhetorical arts.[52] Mentioning Cicero, Athens, and various Roman orators, Dávila explained that the erudition of these ancient authors provided the standard to which contemporary preachers ought to aspire.[53] Making reference to the influence of European Enlightenment conventions in New Spain, according to Dávila, this "French" style of preaching should serve as a model for sermons in New Spain as well since it reflected "the golden age of eloquence."[54] Thus, by returning to the "golden age" of the "nervous simplicity" of Athens, preaching in New Spain could likewise aspire to greatness—a goal also reflected in the 1767 performance of another preacher, who, according to his creole evaluator, knew how to combine skillfully the necessary attributes of good preaching, including eloquence, solid doctrine, grace, delight and persuasion.[55]

The advantages of reforming sacred oratory according to the conventions of classical rhetoric were not just aesthetic in character. Concretely, referring again to Parreño's sermon, Dávila pointed out that one of the benefits of such an approach was the response it had the potential to elicit among audiences.[56] By "exciting affections" of piety and virtue, Dávila argued that the discipline of classical rhetoric could help preachers to assist their congregants in reforming their lives, even while also permitting the preachers to exercise greater authority over them in the process. The key was to know how to deploy the conventions of oratory prudently and artfully so that audiences would be won over. For that reason, it is important to emphasize that the purpose of the reforms in preaching implemented during the latter half of the eighteenth century in New Spain was not so much to drain preaching of its emotional or rhetorical impact. On the contrary, the aspiration of reformers was to heighten the persuasive force of sermons by making them clearer and more accessible to audiences, thereby increasing their effectiveness and, as a result, consolidating the Church's spiritual power in an age in which it was starting to be more frequently questioned and even undermined.

51. Ibid.
52. Dávila, *Aprobacion*. There is no internal pagination within this *aprobación*.
53. See ibid.
54. See ibid.
55. Omaña, *Parecer*.
56. Dávila, *Aprobación*.

Changing Notions of Masculinity and Femininity in Sermons

Even as preachers adjusted their approaches to preparing and delivering their sermons in light of reformist sensibilities, one element that remained consistent was the presence and importance of gendered language and imagery. As before, references to women—whether female saints, nuns, or laywomen—often invoked notions of masculinity in describing remarkable female virtue. However, whereas in the Baroque period especially virtuous men were often likened to spiritual mothers or tender virgins, sermons in the enlightenment period offered more masculinized portraits of ideal men—a convention that could be applied to some women as well. For instance, among sermons on women, in one example from 1760 the peninsular Dominican Miguel Rodríguez de Santo Thomás lauded the virtues of a deceased nun, Sor Antonia del Señor San Joaquín, and, as in earlier Baroque sermons, praised her for transcending the expectations of her sex.[57] With the fortitude of a brave and virtuous man, Rodríguez implied that Sor Antonia had transcended the normal boundaries of her gender and won recognition as a saintly figure to be admired and emulated both inside and outside the convent—a circumstance likely seen by church authorities as all the more crucial in light of their campaigns for convent reform during this period.[58]

Similar imagery emerged in another funeral sermon for a nun, in this case Sor María Ignacia de Azlor, given in 1768 by the creole priest Luis de Torres.[59] In the introduction to the sermon, offered by the prioress and other members of the convent, the nuns themselves demonstrated familiarity with the conventions of gendered official church language, lauding Sor María Ignacia's "manly" courage, which had rendered her a "truly strong woman."[60] References to these same conventions appear within the body of the sermon as well. At the beginning of his sermon, Torres declared that Sor María Ignacia had in fact been more like a man than a woman—so much so that she could be said to have acted like a "great man."[61] Comparing the late nun to the biblical patriarch Abraham, Torres cited the Book of Genesis and its declaration that Abraham's "seed" would be as numerous as the stars. For

---

57. Rodríguez de Santo Thomás, *Memorial*, 24–25.

58. See chapter 2 for the context of eighteenth-century convent reform campaigns. As examined in chapter 2, see also Lavrin, *Brides of Christ*; Kirk, *Convent Life*; Chowning, *Rebellious Nuns*; Chowning, "Convent Reform"; Gunnarsdóttir, *Mexican Karismata*; Loreto López, *Los conventos*; Ramos Medina, *Místicas*; Salazar de Garza, *La vida común*; Arenal and Schlau, *Untold Sisters*.

59. Torres, *Sermon funebre*. Records indicate that Torres was born in Panama.

60. Ibid., Introduction. There is no internal pagination within the introduction.

61. Ibid., 3.

Torres, it was Sor María Ignacia's fidelity to her vocation that had also made possible the multiplication of her own virile "seed."[62] Through faithfulness to God's calling, which led her from her native Mexico to profession in a convent in Spain, Sor María Ignacia had taken on resemblance to Abraham even as she became a mother for the many spiritual daughters who also professed vows in the convents she founded in New Spain.

Taking up the figure of the Virgin Mary, two other sermons—by the creole Oratorian José Gómez de Escontría and the peninsular Carmelite Francisco de San Cirilo—highlighted what would also represent an important change in Enlightenment-era sermons. In the cases of Gómez de Escontría and San Cirilo, as in earlier, Baroque sermons, both preachers spoke with notable enthusiasm in praise of the Virgin's extraordinary holiness. However, what was different now was that the sermonizers were extolling her less as the quasi-divine being of many earlier sermons than as a model of virtue for others to follow.[63] According to Gómez de Escontría, for example, the Virgin "had no other path to heaven than the very one signaled by providence to all mortals."[64] Emphasizing the cultivation of virtue as essential to salvation, the preacher insisted that "each person is the architect of his own eternal salvation or reprobation. The entire vast expanse of the world is nothing other than a universal office where all work incessantly, fashioning for themselves, by the choice of their free will, either rewards or punishments, through which they must arrive at last into the realm of eternity."[65] In his own sermon, San Cirilo argued that Mary's true greatness rested in the "interior" works she performed, "listening attentively to the words of God and assenting to the power of his truths."[66] This interior faith was therefore, according to San Cirilo, an "enlightened" one—that is, one illuminated by proximity to God and therefore empowering to the soul in the path of virtue.[67] Recommending the Virgin therefore as a model to be followed, Gómez de Escontría likewise concluded that all were called, "with steps proportionate to [their] weakness," to exercise virtue and thus play an

---

62. Ibid., 20–21.
63. See Gómez de Escontría, *Sermon* (1772); San Cirilo, *La mejor parte*.
64. Gómez de Escontría, *Sermon* (1772), 10.
65. Ibid., 10–11.
66. San Cirilo, *La mejor parte*, 7–8. For another sermon by San Cirilo in which he speaks in greater depth of the distinction between "interior" and "exterior" devotion, see San Cirilo, *Obligacion*.
67. San Cirilo, *La mejor parte*, 10.

active role in securing both their own salvation and, by implication, that of the surrounding society.[68]

Intriguingly, evidence of Gómez de Escontría's influence in New Spain at the time his sermon was preached emerges in other contemporary evidence. As Jaime Cuadriello points out in a study of a painting from the same era, Gómez de Escontría and other members of the Oratorian religious order, not long after the expulsion of the Jesuits from New Spain, successfully petitioned the Crown to assume control of the former Jesuit house of *La Profesa* in Mexico City.[69] Seeking to acknowledge the depth of creole devotion to Jesuit spiritual practices, the Crown granted the request, requiring the Oratorians to live under the Ignatian rule and assigning them, with royal approval and protection, to some of the ministries formerly undertaken by the Jesuits.[70] As Cuadriello points out, the figure of Gómez de Escontría appears in the lower right-hand corner of the painting, along with other Oratorians, holding a piece of paper with the words *Salvos fac servos tuos* (Let your servants be safe), "thus declaring themselves benefited by the intercession of the patriarch Joseph—transfigured into Charles III—under whose titles they then gathered for protection: Saint Joseph the Royal."[71] In other words, Gómez de Escontría, both in his sermons as well as in contemporaneous iconography, provides an example of how sermonizers could play influential roles in pursuing ecclesiastical and political interests they perceived to be advantageous both to themselves and their religious communities.

The cultivation of virtues in men was also an important topic covered in many sermons in this period. Among various male saints and exemplars, one of particular significance was St. Thomas Aquinas.[72] Though Aquinas was important to late eighteenth-century preachers in New Spain for a variety of reasons, especially significant among them was his famed moral virtue. One sermon, given by the Dominican creole Joseph Gallegos in 1771, demonstrates well this emphasis even in its title: *Paragon of Chastity*.[73] In his *parecer* for the sermon, the Oratorian priest Pedro Josef Rodríguez Arizpe praised Aquinas' virtues and singled out in particular the saint's renowned virginity and the "marvelous connection" between this virtue and his renowned wisdom.[74] For Rodríguez Arizpe, Aquinas' virtues and especially

---

68. Gómez de Escontría, *Sermon* (1772), 11.
69. Cuadriello, "Ministry."
70. Ibid., 261.
71. Ibid.
72. See Herrejón Peredo, *Del sermón*, 195–96.
73. Gallegos, *Dechado*.
74. See Rodríguez Arizpe, *Parecer*. It is not certain whether Rodríguez Arizpe was

Reforming Discourses

his virginity were of such a remarkable nature that in a sense they constituted the foundation on which all the truths that the Church taught rested.[75] In other words, as an "invincible column" of virtue, Thomas Aquinas' heroic character had the capacity to support and embolden the Church in its battles against sin and vice.

Like some of the references to male saints during the Baroque period studied in chapter 2, here too a male saint received praise for the extraordinary character of his virginity. Yet in this sermon a differing emphasis more characteristic of the Enlightenment period also emerged—namely the belief that saints could be imitated and not just supply material for wonderment and awe.[76] Specifically, within the main body of his sermon, Gallegos engaged his audience, asking them directly whether or not saints' examples were to be followed and imitated.[77] For Gallegos, the answer to this question was, of course, to be answered resolutely in the affirmative. Unlike previous conceptions of their extraordinary, superhuman virtues, Gallegos emphasized that saints were in fact fashioned from the same material as all other human beings—they too were flawed and broken and in need of redemption. However, what set them apart from the vast majority of other human beings was their "cooperation" with God—their openness to the light of grace, which redeemed them and rendered them worthy examples or "paragons" to be imitated by others.

Among all the ways that saints could cooperate with grace, Gallegos named as highly significant their battles against lust and lasciviousness, manifested "not just in profane and provocative dresses, but also in familial relations between men and women."[78] In the case of St. Thomas this campaign for chastity had taken on the specific character of a struggle with a "provocative" woman sent into a cell in which he was being held against his will in order to attempt to dissuade him from his divine calling.[79] Though Aquinas soundly defeated the temptress, "body to body," as in Gallegos' earlier comments, here too he emphasizeed for his audience the fact that the saint's circumstances would have been much like their own in facing similar temptations of lust. Like them, he too would have found himself put to the test at the precise moment in which he was least prepared or energized for the battle to fend off temptation. For that reason, as Gallegos argued, it was

---

a creole or *peninsular*.

75. Ibid.
76. Herrejón Peredo, *Del sermón*, 115.
77. Gallegos, *Dechado*, 2.
78. Ibid., 3.
79. Ibid., 5.

crucial both for Thomas Aquinas and for contemporary listeners to arm themselves well against temptation since it could arrive without warning, often at the most inopportune and unexpected of moments.

Battling the weaknesses of the flesh and remaining always on guard, the portrait of Aquinas that emerged in Gallegos' sermon was one in which the saints—both those already canonized along with potential aspirants to holiness among his hearers—were called to engage in spiritual combat for the good of the faith. No longer mere observers or beholders of the supernatural greatness of the saints as in earlier, Baroque sermons, Gallegos and other preachers in the second half of the eighteenth century called their listeners to a more active role of combat in the pursuit of virtue. For example, in praising Aquinas' virtues and his battle against the temptations of the woman who attempted to seduce him, Gallegos referred to the saint as a "valorous combatant" in the heroic fight for virtue.[80] Similarly, having "legitimately fought" in the necessary battle, once Aquinas had passed the test of virtue and emerged victorious he was gifted with the ability to leave behind altogether the temptations of the flesh.[81] This "perpetual virginity" which Gallegos espoused also applied to women. For Gallegos, women played a particularly important role in following the example of saints like Aquinas in that they could either contribute decisively to the edification of society or assure its decadence.[82] Either they would inspire their fellow citizens to virtue or seal their perdition by "flirting," giving "performances," and soliciting applause in "the most public of places."

For Gallegos, because women's witness either of virtue or vice had the power either to save or to condemn those around them, women in particular were called to the spiritual warfare Aquinas had exemplified.[83] As would emerge with even greater clarity in the final years of the eighteenth century and well into the nineteenth, when Church leaders in New Spain preached about women in this period they came to do so less to hold up individual, exceptional examples and more to call on all women to fulfill a quasi-salvific role in shoring up society's religious underpinnings. As for men, preachers increasingly called them to serve as "valorous combatants" in the battle to defend church and state from various threats, both internal and external. In short, within the context of a Church hierarchy increasingly focused on reforming society, preachers called upon individual men and women among their audiences not merely to behold the heroic witness of

80. Ibid., 7.
81. Ibid., 11–12.
82. Ibid., 17.
83. Ibid.

saintly predecessors but to actively cultivate lives of virtue that would secure blessing and prosperity for both church and state.

One additional example of a sermon on St. Thomas Aquinas is also instructive concerning attitudes on the part of the high clergy toward gender and the importance of virtue. Given on the occasion of the opening of the Fourth Provincial Council in 1771, the royalist bishop of Puebla Francisco Fabián y Fuero's sermon on St. Thomas Aquinas likewise focused on the saint's virginity and admirable virtue.[84] According to Fabián y Fuero, Aquinas' virtues were valuable to the Church and should be allowed to shine forth for the edification of all.[85] To this end, Fabián y Fuero described the role of the Fourth Provincial Council as one of promoting devotion to Aquinas for the good of all in "Septentrional America."[86] Working toward the "utility of all," the mission of the council was to promote Aquinas as an example of the sort of virtue that would benefit society—in this case, by implication, those virtues most in harmony with the principal tenets of the regalist position, including subordination of the interests and traditions of the Church in New Spain to those of the Crown.[87] To that end, Fabián y Fuero continued by characterizing what was at stake in promoting devotion to Aquinas as nothing less than the triumph of the Church in New Spain—that is, the successful integration of its own priorities with those of the Bourbon monarchy.[88] In an increasingly militarized surrounding political context—discussed below—awareness of Aquinas' doctrines and teachings, especially regarding the Eucharist, was crucial, according to Fabián y Fuero, to combat a "diabolical army" that had arisen in opposition to the forces of good.[89] Against these enemies, St. Thomas' teachings had the power to secure victory, since, through his doctrine, this "heroic champion" would defeat the "army of hell" and secure victory for Christ, "the God of armies."[90]

Again, as is apparent in the above excerpts as well as in the conclusion to his sermon in which he referred to the "militant Mexican church," it is evident that Fabián y Fuero perceived a connection between the promotion of St. Thomas Aquinas as an example of virtue and as a heroic inspiration for

84. Fabián y Fuero, *Oracion*.
85. Ibid., 22–23.
86. Ibid., 24–25.
87. See Zahino Peñafort, *Iglesia*, 214; Farriss, *Crown and Clergy*, 8.
88. Fabián y Fuero, *Oracion*, 44–45.
89. Ibid., 45–47.
90. Ibid., 45–49. In this section of Fabián y Fuero's sermon he invokes the biblical story of the Maccabees and the legendary prowess of Hernán Cortés as examples of the Church's militaristic calling.

the many "battles" in which regalist church leaders percieved themselves and society in general to be engaged at the time. The militaristic language, in this case employed as way to promote a particular vision of the Church, was, in general, often used in connection with renewed emphasis on the promotion of virtue and began to appear with increasing frequency in mid eighteenth-century New Spanish sermons. It is therefore worthy of further examination as a subset of the discourses under consideration in this chapter.

Militaristic Themes and the Promotion of Virtue in Sermons

During the second half of the eighteenth century in New Spain various political and social developments both inside and outside the Church contributed to a trend evident in Fabián y Fuero's sermon and others—namely, the militarization of language tied to political developments in both Spain and America.[91] For example, in the aftermath of 1766 riots in Madrid, royal officials on both sides of the Atlantic worried that clerics, especially the Jesuits, were responsible for these and other affronts to royal authority.[92] In New Spain, this took the form of concern on the part of Viceroy Carlos Francisco de Croix that clergymen had been responsible for uprisings that occurred following the expulsion of the Jesuits in 1767.[93] As a result of this development, members of the high clergy, among them Lorenzana and Fabián y Fuero, perceived a need to demonstrate more than ever the sincerity of their loyalty to the crown—that is, their regalism.[94] One important way in which this change manifested itself was through gendered language used in some sermons, which came to take on a more masculine character as the virtues of military prowess and victory found favor as a means of conveying ecclesiastical loyalty to the Crown. This trend appeared clearly by the mid-1760s in the form of sermons preached regularly in tribute to members of the Spanish military killed in various offensives such as the Seven Years' War (1756-1763), and also began to manifest itself in sermons focused on Spain's historical military victories—a trend that, as chapter 4 will show, would be taken up with even greater fervor in subsequent decades.[95]

91. See Farriss, *Crown and Clergy*, 129-31 for an account of some of these circumstances.

92. For an explanation of the context for this uprising, the *Motín de Esquilache*, see ibid., 125.

93. See Brading, *First America*, 499-500; Farriss, *Crown and Clergy*, 131.

94. See Seed, *To Love*, Introduction and chapter 10; Farriss, *Crown and Clergy*, 135.

95. Regarding the militarization of society in general in this period, see García Peña, "El encierro"; Kahle, *El ejército*; Archer, *Army*; Brading, "Bourbon Spain." For

Within a late eighteenth-century context of an increased presence and awareness of the operation of the army in everyday life, along with the high clergy's perceived need to demonstrate its loyalty to the Crown, preachers thus turned with increasing frequency in their sermons to themes related to military heroism and virtue, often expressing them in increasingly masculinized language. For example, preached in November of 1767 by the creole Franciscan Joseph Manuel Rodríguez, the first of four in a consecutive, yearly series of sermons in commemoration of Spain's fallen soldiers was offered in the Convento Grande de San Francisco under the explicit orders of Viceroy de Croix, a fact which received attention in an elaborate, fawning introductory letter by an official in the Franciscan order.[96] In another introductory *dictamen* on the sermon, the peninsular priest Juan Ignacio de la Rocha made explicit the connections between the glory of military service and that of heaven.[97] Not only were Catholic soldiers to recall that the glories of the present world were passing; they were also to pray for the expiation of their companions' sins, especially given the "defects" that tended to accompany military service. Within the text of his sermon, Rodríguez had even higher praise for the potential of soldiers to promote good order and prosperity for societies. According to Rodríguez, Charles III himself wished to speak words of thanks to these soldiers.[98] In the king's hypothetical words, the glory of the Spanish monarchy rested upon the "robust" bodies of those soliders who had given their lives for the honor of the Crown. These soldiers helped to preserve order and safeguard against social temptations such as insolence and licentiousness.[99] As a result—confirming in no uncertain terms the loyalty of the Church to the Crown—in Rodríguez's words, "it is the God of battles who will grant victory to the arms of Spain."[100]

Similar militaristic themes emerged in a sermon given one year after Rodríguez's, in which the creole secular priest don Gregorio de Omaña, also in the presence of Viceroy de Croix, offered reflections on the virtues and glories of Spain's fallen soldiers. Comparing the soliders to the brave heroes of the biblical Book of Maccabees, Omaña declared that they "died like men" at the service of Spain.[101] To their last breath, Omaña proclaimed that these

---

examples of these sermons, see Gallegos, *Glorias de España*; Morfi, *La nobleza*.

96. Rodríguez, *Oracion funebre*. Rodríguez was a creole born in Cuba.
97. de la Rocha, *Dictamen*. There is no internal pagination within this *dictamen*.
98. Rodríguez, *Oracion*, 3–4.
99. Ibid., 6.
100. Ibid., 15.
101. Omaña, *Oracion funebre* (1768).

soldiers not only defended their country bravely but also proved themselves heroic witnesses in the even more critical "war of the passions." As men adept thus at defeating enemies both material and spiritual, these soldiers for Omaña represented ideal paragons of masculine virtue—examples of men worthy of immortality as well as fitting vehicles for the message of loyalty that church leaders also wished to convey, through de Croix, to the Crown.

The following year, in 1769, a similar occasion was celebrated in the Mexico City cathedral in memory of Spain's fallen soldiers, again in the presence of Viceroy de Croix and once more featuring a funeral sermon given by Omaña.[102] In his sermon, Omaña once again took up the theme of how "famous men," in this case soldiers, assured social tranquility and order.[103] According to Omaña, those who lived only for themselves awaited an ignominious death, while those who died for others secured a place in heaven.[104] For Omaña, those who died with heroic virtue—like Judas Maccabeus and other biblical and historical exemplars—would in fact live on forever.[105] The virtues of these soldiers not only carried them forth bravely into battle, often costing them their lives, but also gave them the courage to engage in an even more crucial battle—the combat against sin and vice. Labeling men and women's innate sinful inclinations as "domestic enemies of the soul," Omaña warned his listeners of the dangers of vice.[106] As both "domestic enemies" and "rebels," "machines" and "mines," human beings' in-born vices—and, by implication, any rebelious elements of society—had to be rooted out through God's grace and the patient practice of virtue.[107] Only then would these same individuals, whether soldiers or civilians, emerge victorious and social harmony and peace ensue.

The final sermon of those published over four consecutive years in commemoration of Spain's fallen soldiers was given in November, 1770 by the creole Oratorian Joseph Gómez de Escontría—mentioned above—likewise in the Mexico City Cathedral and in the presence of Viceroy de Croix.[108] In line with many Enlightenment-period sermons, Gómez de Escontría placed a marked emphasis on the accessibility of personal holiness both to the soldiers about whom he spoke and the general body of believers

---

102. Gregorio de Omaña, *Oracion funebre* (1770).
103. Omaña, *Oracion* (1770), 3–4.
104. Ibid., 7–8.
105. Ibid., 10.
106. Ibid., 14–15.
107. Ibid., 15.
108. Gómez de Escontría, *Oracion funebre* (1770).

he was addressing.¹⁰⁹ Although the preacher agreed that there existed a "friendly alliance" between holiness and military service, he did not wish to imply that personal sanctity was not within the reach of all believers.¹¹⁰ Rather than the visions of superhuman holiness and other-wordly flights of Baroque sermons, Gómez de Escontría emphasized that sanctity was accessible to all.¹¹¹ Instead of the "inaccesible mountains" into which "self-love" had sometimes placed it, holiness was to be found in the ample opportunities provided in everyday life for the exercise of virtue and the combatting of vice—again, with social implications for the combatting of collective vice and rebellion as a clear subtext. In this struggle for virtue Catholic soldiers and the faithful in general were to find their strength in charity, humility, and chastity and to persevere in cultivating personal virtue.¹¹²

One additional New Spanish military funeral sermon from the period of Charles III's reign—given in the Mexico City cathedral in 1786, about fifteen years after the series of four sermons studied above—illustrates how the regalist and militaristic trends described for those sermons grew even more intensified in subsequent years as well as how some of the earlier enthusiasm preachers had expressed for "French" styles was now starting to wane.¹¹³ As the author of the sermon, the creole secular priest Francisco Xavier Conde y Oquendo, indicated, the virtue exhibited by Spanish soldiers in supporting and defending the king had only grown in importance as "soulless" philosophers—a clear reference to the growing threat posed to the Church by Enlightenment writers—had dared to challenge royal authority.¹¹⁴ In contrast to such effrontery, Conde y Oquendo insisted that the extraordinary heavenly power of no fewer than one billion angels was ready to fight for God's righteous cause—that is, that of the king.¹¹⁵ Likewise, God too was a man of war—indeed a *conquistador*—while the Church was portrayed as blessing and approving war at the service of such righteous causes. As Conde y Oquendo put it quite starkly: "To the victors it is permitted to sheath . . . their blood-gushing swords, and to hang the spoils of the defeated by the nails of the tabernacle and the cornices of the temples; not as trophies of vanity for some, nor as patterns of ignominy for others; rather as signs

109. Ibid., 19.
110. Ibid.
111. Ibid., 20.
112. Ibid., 25.
113. Conde y Oquendo, *Oración fúnebre*.
114. Ibid., 8. See chapter 4 for a more extended treatment of the Church's reaction to Enlightenement ideas and trends, especially those associated with France.
115. Ibid., 9.

of their mutual concord, given to the arbiter of peace, and as monuments of gratitude erected to the God and Lord of battles[.]"[116] For this preacher, Christians too were called to serve as soliders in the "blood-gushing" battle against sin and vice.[117] In fact, the good of society itself was at stake in the current conflicts being waged against God's will and therefore it was to be taken as an article of faith that God's avenging sword and that of the king were in fact one—conjoined through the righteous, divine mandate authorizing them to eradicate all opposing forces.[118]

As the analysis of sermons undertaken in this section has shown, the genre of military-themed sermons in the middle decades of the eighteenth century, arising as it did from a context in which Church officials encouraged greater fervor in displays of loyalty to the Crown, offered a number of ideas about gender and the proper roles men were to play in society and the Church. According to the preachers studied here, in order for social renewal to take place and for the Church to retain its proper glory, both soldiers and Catholics in general would need to engage in difficult spiritual combat, fighting enemies both internal and external. The temptations of vice were strong and therefore people who "fought like men" were needed in order properly to guide society toward the peace and tranquility that flowed from appropriate order and discipline. This would only be possible, however, if everyone practiced virtue—if they acted with bravery and fearlessness analogous to that of Spanish soldiers in the field of combat, especially as affronts to royal authority and the impudence of "philosophers" both progressed, signalling the need to defend virtue that much more urgently. Seemingly, both physical and spiritual warfare were called for in this age and as a result the sermons studied above evince progressively less of the discursive openness to alternative ways of envisioning femininity and especially masculinity found in Baroque sermons. Instead, at the service of an official Church concerned with demonstrating fealty to the Crown and also increasingly concerned with the implications of modern philsophical ideas, men were more and more called upon to be virtuous and heroic, while women, where they did have a role to play, were to emulate those same virtues at the service of their families and of the public order. In other words, all were to "fight like men" against the shared enemies of the ever-more closely tied Crown and Church.

116. Ibid., 12–15.
117. Ibid., 17.
118. Ibid., 24–28.

Political Themes in Sermons

Among the other thematic changes observed in sermons during the advent of the Enlightenement in New Spain in the middle decades of the eighteenth century, of additional significance was an increased emphasis on and connection to the surrounding political situation of Spain and America.[119] Preached in 1761 at the beginning of this period, the Jesuit Joseph del Castillo's sermon on the coronation of Charles III provides an appropriate place to begin consideration of this theme.[120] In the extended introduction to the sermon, the author provided an account of the ceremonies which took place in Mexico City in celebration of the accession of the new king.[121] Within the commentary provided, one excerpt is particularly illuminating of its author's regalist understanding of the close and mutually interdependent relationships that existed between religion and the Spanish Empire.[122] According to the author, religion and piety were integral components of the empire. Without proper devotion to God the "walls" of kingdoms would not hold. However, equally important was the role of kings; without the intervention of the royal majesty of the Crown, the fear of God and the love of others would be irreconcilable. In other words, both religion and royal authority were necessary for the right functioning of society and could not be separated without imperiling proper social cohesion and order. The author went on to describe the elaborate decorations with which the Iglesia del Hospital de Jesús Nazareno was adorned for the occasion and then described the cermony in detail, including its "costly adornments," "carpets," and other "rich" decorations.[123]

In his sermon, Castillo began by declaring the unquestioned loyalty of the present assembly to the king, wondering aloud what it was that distinguished the praises of New Spain for its new king.[124] According to Castillo, what made the devotion and praise of New Spain stand out was its particular wisdom and knowledge, founded upon reason, manifested especially in its keen appreciation of the king's greatness. In other words, the outstanding character of the gathering was its loyalty to the primacy of reason at the service of royal authority. Castillo confirmed this observation with a comment

---

119. For studies of political themes in sermons from this period, see the following by Herrejón Peredo: "La potestad"; *Del sermón*, 61–80.

120. del Castillo, *El Salomon*. del Castillo's birthplace is not known.

121. Ibid., 1.

122. Ibid., 3.

123. Ibid., 4–5.

124. Ibid., 25.

on Charles' own enlightened use of reason and the assurance it gave that his reign would be long and prosperous.[125]

Castillo proceeded to praise Charles III as himself characterized in a particular way by the gifts of wisdom and reason. Comparing him to the biblical king Solomon and attributing to the king the desire to be known as "the wise," Castillo explained that, in the king's hypothetical words, what he had intended to say was: "I do not want empty names, vain or apparent, that only serve for ostentation: nor that of *Wise*, as great and appropriate as it may be to my natural inclination, if not earned by merit."[126] Castillo proclaimed that Charles III embodied this wisdom in his style of governing, something of which those he was addressing should be aware.[127] Castillo counseled his listeners to leave passion behind in their own doings and, engaging the faculty of reason, see for themselves the goodness and wisdom of their king in his efforts to govern wisely—for example, in forgiving debts. In this way, Castillo demonstrated through language emphasizing the importance of reason the greatness of Spain's king and the importace of fidelity to the monarchy on the part of its subjects in Mexico City.

A similar political strain in preaching also emerged in a sermon by the creole Franciscan friar Pedro Francisco de Oronsoro, in which he associated devotion to the Immaculate Conception of Mary with the glories of New Spain.[128] According to Oronsoro, Mary in her advocation as the Immaculate Conception had received dominion over all kingdoms and principalities.[129] Oronsoro went on to explain how the Immaculate Conception had come to replace St. James (*Santiago*) as the principal patron of Spain and of New Spain.[130] As in the previous sermon, here too mention was made of Charles III's virtues, this time in special connection with the patronage of Mary as the Immaculate Conception. No other kingdom throughout the world had seen the great works of such a mighty patron nor of such an exalted king. For that reason, Oronsoro expressed confidence in the ability of Charles III to triumph, thereby perpetuating the glory of Spain through the graceful intercession and patronage of Mary in her Immaculate Conception.

In another sermon from the 1760s, the creole Franciscan friar Joseph Manuel Rodríguez offered extended reflections on the question of how

125. Ibid., 26.
126. Ibid., 29.
127. Ibid., 115.
128. Oronsoro, *Oracion*.
129. Ibid., 5.
130. Ibid., 27.

subjects should relate to kings.¹³¹ Near the beginning of his sermon, Rodríguez proclaimed it as the duty of "ministers of the Divine Word" like himself to teach forcefully the obligation of honor owed by subjects to their sovereigns.¹³² Fulfilling this "absolutely indispensable obligation," Rodríguez offered a harsh rebuke to any who would dare question the dominion of their sovereign.¹³³ As "abominable monster[s]," those who disobeyed God's rule and law by challenging the sovereignty of their legitimate rulers could expect punishment and righteous vengance.¹³⁴ Thankfully, however, according to Rodríguez kings such as Charles III afforded hope to their people as their wise and prudent rule brought tranquilty and good order to society.¹³⁵ Again, as with the regalist positions expressed in the above sermons, Rodríguez likewise believed that Charles III was uniquely gifted to bring peace and stability to both Spain and New Spain, provided he received the cooperation and support of willing and faithful subjects in both lands.

Another interpretation of how sacred and secular power could combine emerged in a 1770 sermon by the creole Dominican Joseph Vergara.¹³⁶ According to Vergara, virtue in general and right religious belief in particular were the essential foundations of kingdoms.¹³⁷ Without religion, kingdoms faltered and disorder reigned.¹³⁸ Piety, right belief, and "divine politics" were indispensable elements of any successful and sustainable government and therefore were to be respected and defended in the interest of the public good. To this end, Vergara, like the other preachers above, praised Charles III as an examplar of the virtues and wisdom necessary for leading and governing his kingdom in this way.¹³⁹

Praising the virtues of a closer, more immediately familiar sovereign—the viceroy Antonio María Bucareli y Ursua—the creole priest José Fernández de Uribe's 1779 sermon for Bucareli's funeral offers an instructive example of how members of the high clergy perceived the local political situation in New Spain.¹⁴⁰ As Iván Escamilla González points out in a recent

131. Rodríguez, *Como deben haverse*. Rodríguez was born in Cuba.
132. Ibid., 1.
133. Ibid., 4.
134. Ibid., 11–12.
135. Ibid., 24.
136. Vergara, *La virtud*.
137. Ibid., 11–12.
138. Ibid., 12.
139. Ibid., 14. For a similar perspective on the close relationship between God's sovereignty and that of the king, see the following sermon: Enebro, *Sermon*, 4–5.
140. Uribe, *Elogio funebre*.

study, Fernández de Uribe, as a confidant of Archbishop Lorenzana and a promotor of education as the rector of the *Real Universidad*, was well positioned to promote the Church hierarchy's vision of reform in his sermons.[141] However, as a member of the cathedral chapter (*cabildo*), Fernández de Uribe also participated in an institution dominated by creole interests. Therefore, providing an opportunity both to extol reformist virtues and praise a viceroy at least some of whose policies had corresponded to creole interests, Fernández de Uribe utilized his sermon at the viceroy's funeral to stake out his position.

Referring to an episode in which Bucareli had opposed efforts on the part of the Crown to reform the *repartimiento* system of sales of Spanish goods to Indians at the expense of creole commercial interests, Fernández de Uribe praised the late viceroy for "furthering the interests of the sovereign without prejudicing those of the vassal."[142] In other words, according to Fernández de Uribe one of Bucareli's virtues was his ability to smooth over potential sources of tension between the Crown and some of its most powerful creole subjects in New Spain, thereby preserving peace. Calling Bucareli therefore a "Christian hero," Fernández de Uribe opened his sermon with praise for the ways in which the deceased viceroy had brought tranquility to New Spain, noting how "voices of religious bitterness," accompanied by "laments and tears" resounded through Mexico City's streets and plazas upon the news of his death.[143] As a revered leader, Uribe praised Bucareli for his spirit of "religious politics," which facilitated and consolidated the peace that had characterized his rule. Moreover, by combining all the virtues of a "pleasant heroism," Bucareli was thus able to govern effectively and assure peace for the people of the viceroyalty.[144] Among Bucareli's most important virtues were also his lack of timidity in the face of military ventures and his proper respect for the Church and its prelates. To this end, Uribe characterized Bucareli as having been in possession of "a noble, strong, generous heart, no less disposed to crown its temples with martial laurels dyed in the blood of the enemies of the state and of religion than inclined to plant peaceful olive branches among those who belong to him."[145] Crucially, Bucareli demonstrated proper deference to the Church as well.[146] Never daring

---

141. Escamilla González, *José Patricio*, 15–16.

142. Uribe, *Elogio fúnebre*, 18–19. See also Florescano and Menegus, "La época," 374.

143. Uribe, *Elogio funebre*, 2–4.

144. Ibid., 6.

145. Ibid., 11.

146. Ibid., 19.

to "penetrate the sacred limits of the sanctuary," Bucareli exhibited proper respect for religious authority and its ministers and thus contributed that much more fully to the social harmony and concord which had characterized the years of his reign.

Approximately five years after the sermon on viceroy Bucareli, Fernández de Uribe again preached in tribute to another late viceroy: Don Matías de Gálvez.[147] According to Fernández de Uribe, one of Gálvez's most important virtues was his "sincerity of heart."[148] A man of enlightened sensibilities, Gálvez was characterized by "sobriety of inclinations," which lead him to seek "moderation in everything," a trait which had secured his status as a "simple man" in the positive sense Fernández de Uribe wished to convey.[149] Unfortunately Gálvez had only lived nine months after his entrance into New Spain as viceroy, a fact Fernández de Uribe lamented on behalf of all the people of Mexico.[150] According to Fernández de Uribe, Gálvez's heroism emerged not in prideful displays of "studied hyperboles" and multiple "noisy actions" but in the sincerity with which he lived, from his heart—including the work of education he sponsored and promoted in his brief tenure, especially his support for the Academy of San Carlos and its work in educating artists.[151] Like Gálvez—"*el virrey sincero*"—therefore, the people of New Spain could find outlets for the heroism to which they were called in defending Church and State through the cultivation of domestic and civic virtues, among them education and the arts.[152]

Finally, having begun with a sermon celebrating Charles III's accession, study of a sermon lamenting the monarch's death provides an instructive summation of the state of preaching in New Spain immediately preceding the events in Spain and Europe that would shape its development in the 1790s and beyond.[153] Taking place on May 26 and 27, 1789, less than two months before the advent of the French Revolution, the Mexico City funeral rites for the late king paid lavish tribute to his absolutist rule. According to the printed introductory comments which preceded the sermons for the two-day occasion, the author noted that the solemnity had begun at 4:00 in the afternoon on May 26th with the gathering of ecclesiastical and

---

147. Fernández de Uribe, *Solemnes exêquias*.
148. Ibid., 4–5.
149. Ibid., 9.
150. Ibid., 2.
151. Ibid., 4.
152. Ibid., 5.
153. Serruto y Nava, *Elogio funebre*. Serruto's birthplace is not known.

secular officials.[154] On display for the occasion was the elaborate funeral pyre, illuminated by hundreds of large candles all lit in prepraration for the first evening's solemn vespers.[155] Then, at 6:30 the following morning, with all the candles lit, masses were offered and vigils sung in different chapels throughout the cathedral, after which a procession departed through the streets. At 9:00 all entered the cathedral and mass was celebrated, presided over by the archbishop.[156] Finally, after mass was completed, the cleric José Serruto y Nava offered what the author described as a "pathetic and edifying" sermon in which the glorious actions and virtues of the deceased king were recounted.[157]

In the text of his sermon, Serruto y Nava outlined the late monarch's virtues, praising him as "a king valorous in the defense of his dominions [and] disposed to providing for the good of his subjects . . . edifying in his personal proceedings . . . [who] presents to all of you the foundations of the most solid hopes."[158] According to Serruto, the "solid hopes" that Charles' example afforded were relevant not merely for other sovereigns and monarchs but for his subjects as well, since all were considered vassals before the most high sovereign—God.[159] Reviewing the history of Charles' many military victories, Serruto y Nava praised the king for his bravery and, "the military prowesses, the right providences [and] the virtues" that accompanied his reign, and concluded that the king had been a "Christian hero," motivated above all by his faith in God.[160] Without doubt, Charles had ruled wisely and justly as the divinely appointed sovereign of New Spain—a ruler destined to bring victory to his armies and peace to his people through their obedience and loyalty to him and thus also to God.[161]

As had been the case in other sermons from this period, Serruto y Nava's comments demonstrate once more the increasing priority given by the mid eighteenth-century Church in New Spain to promoting the closeness of its ties to royal authority as well as its vision for the perpetuation of the established political system in which it too participated. Demonstrating both loyalty and high esteem for the monarchy and its functionaries and yet also returning frequently in its discourses to its own place within reigning

154. *Reales exequias*, 6.
155. Ibid., 7.
156. Ibid., 7–8.
157. Ibid., 8.
158. Serruto y Nava, *Elogio*, 4.
159. Ibid., *Elogio*, 5.
160. Ibid., 4–5.
161. Ibid., 28.

power structures, the Church, through the public voice of its high clergy, sought to navigate the political shifts occurring around it in the mid eighteenth century in ways that would preserve and strengthen its authority in New Spanish society.

Conclusion

This chapter has considered some of the ways in which sermons changed during the second half of the eighteenth century in Mexico City, roughly corresponding to the reign of Charles III (1759–88). Among the most significant changes, preachers employed greater economy of style and language, sought to inculcate virtue in their listeners, and extolled specific virtues associated with a vision of masculinity founded on militaristic values and virtues. Preachers also sought to give voice to a particular vision of how society should be structured and how the Church, in concert with royal authorities, ought to retain its traditionally prominent place in social and political life. Thus, by the final decades of the eighteenth century, the Church, through its public ministers, had developed an extensive repertoire of gendered conventions, discourses of virtue, and political visions which could be deployed, refined, adjusted, and reworked as it encountered and responded to the unique, often unprecedented challenges that would await it in the final decade of the eighteenth century and the opening years of the century to follow.

4

The French Connection

Sermons, Gender and Revolution in Late Eighteenth- and Early Nineteenth-Century New Spain

> "[The French are] the authors and inventors who have introduced and promoted in Mexico perverse customs and abominable, poisonous fashions, designed to destroy our faith, seize power over us, and divest us of everything we have."[1]

As reflected in these words of Mexico City's archbishop Francisco Xavier de Lizana y Beaumont (1803–1811), changing political and social realities in late eighteenth- and early nineteenth-century Europe and New Spain had begun to shape the form and content of sermons even more explicitly than in earlier decades. Though sermonizers in this period continued to favor a mode of preaching associated with Enlightenment-era reforms, including economy of style and calls to virtue on the part of audiences, their preaching on the subject of the nature of men and women and their respective roles in society and the church betrays noticeable shifts that reflect an increasingly militarized and traumatized polity and society—one in which politics was intimately tied to gendered language and conventions. This chapter will examine the sermons and pastoral letters of Mexico City's high clergy from this period and will suggest how these prelates' understandings of gender changed even as they also continued to serve as an important means by which both to make sense of surrounding events and respond to them in ways they believed would help restore proper order and balance to society.

---

1. Lizana y Beaumont, *Instrucccion* (1808).

The French Connection

The Late Colonial Context

By the turn of the nineteenth century, the regalism of the Spanish and New Spanish Church—its primary allegiance to the King, rather than the Pope—was beginning to be questioned. The ambitious and correct Charles III had commanded loyalty from his bishops, but his son Charles IV and many of his officials were embroiled in failings and scandals, including the anti-clerical machinations of the king's prime minister Manuel de Godoy along with the latter's romantic affair with the queen, María Luisa.[2] Meanwhile, amid wars and shifting alliances between Great Britain, France and Spain, both prior to and following the French Revolution, the Crown lost a great deal of its international prestige, along with significant territories in America, and suffered a blockade of the port of Cádiz and the subsequent inability to supply markets in America.[3] In this context of economic hardship for the Crown, Church wealth proved an increasingly attractive target for Godoy and other royal officials, resulting in the disentailment (*consolidación*) and auction of some church property in Spain in 1798 and similar measures in America in 1804—moves widely contested and resented by the Church.[4] As David Brading has pointed out, the Crown's assaults on traditional Church privileges and wealth would not prove inconsequential:

> The attack on the church signaled the imminent demise of the traditional authority of the crown. For priests throughout the empire had always preached obedience to monarchy as a divine commandment . . . But the Bourbon dynasty slowly dissipated the moral and political capital bequeathed by their Hapsburg predecessors. Although the Divine Right of Kings was still sedulously purveyed, the doctrine was increasingly

---

2. For treatments of the state of the Spanish monarchy under Charles IV and its relationship to New Spain, see Stein and Stein, *Edge of Crisis*; Brading, *Church and State*; Sánchez Bella, *Iglesia y estado*; Farriss, *Crown and Clergy*; Taylor, *Magistrates*, chapter 1; Elliott, *Empires*, chapters 11 and 12; Brading, *First America*, chapters 22 and 24; Torres Puga, "Beristáin"; Villoro, "La revolución."

3. Stein and Stein, *Edge of Crisis*, chapter 1; Brading, "Bourbon Spain," 136–37; Brading, "Tridentine"; Elliott, *Empires*, 373. For recent synoptic views of significant aspects of the historiography of the French Revolution, see Kates, ed., *French Revolution*; Doyle, *French Revolution*; Hunt, *French Revolution*; Chartier, *Cultural Origins*; Baker, *Inventing*.

4. For studies of Church wealth in New Spain and the *consolidación*, see Wobeser, *Dominación*; Stein and Stein, *Edge of Crisis*, chapter 11; Chowning, "Consolidación"; Marichal, *La bancarrota*; Herr, *Rural Change*; Flores Caballero, "La Consolidación"; Lavrin, "Execution"; Sugawara H., ed., *La deuda*; Sugawara H., "Los antecedentes."

detached from its natural background in scholastic theology and baroque sensibility.[5]

As a result, as Nancy Farriss and J.H. Elliott have also shown, Bourbon policies during the final decades of colonial rule served ultimately to undermine an essential aspect of the Crown's legitimacy: its "sacral aura."[6] In Elliott's words, "the church-state alliance, the central pillar of the elaborate edifice of Spain's empire of the Indies, was beginning to totter."[7]

The Aftermath of Revolution

Of even greater concern to both Church and Crown, however, were the unfolding events of the French Revolution, especially the notorious excesses of anti-religious sentiment and, ultimately, regicide, which it produced.[8] As Brading and William Taylor have pointed out, recent decades had witnessed a vogue of French-inspired political and cultural changes—e.g., the primacy of reason, loss of traditional church privileges, and the neo-classical style that came to predominate in New Spain both architecturally and in sermons—associated with the Bourbon Reforms, only now to be confronted with what appeared, at least to the Church, to be some of the pernicious consequences of those changes.[9] By 1808, the specter of such events drew even closer to home as the delicate reigning political order in Spain collapsed upon the abdication of both Charles IV and his son Ferdinand VII and the installation of Napoleon's brother, Joseph, on the Spanish throne within the space of only a few months.[10] Creating an unprecedented crisis of political legitimacy, these events left no clear, universally accepted forum for the solution of the questions raised in their wake. Different areas in America therefore adopted varying strategies and, in general, the question of the

---

5. Brading, "Bourbon Spain," 160. See also Brading, "Tridentine," 1–2.

6. Brading, "Bourbon Spain," 160. See also Brading, *Church and State*, 222–27; Farriss, *Crown and Clergy*, Introduction; Elliott, *Empires*, chapter 12.

7. Elliott, *Empires*, 373.

8. For some of the ways in which the French church was affected by anti-religious revolutionary campaigns, including violence against clergy, see McManners, *French Revolution*; Desan, *Reclaiming*; Vovelle, *Religion*; Vovelle, *La Révolution*; Dommanget, *La déchristianisation*.

9. See Brading, "Bourbon Spain," 160–161; Taylor, *Magistrates*, 14–26.

10. Elliott, *Empires*, 374. For a study of some of the different ways in which the symbolic importance of Ferdinand VII developed for various groups in New Spain following the events of 1808 see Landavazo, *La máscara*. For preaching and the contemporary actions of the Church in another Latin American setting, see di Stefano, *El púlpito*.

nature of legitimate sovereignty remained an open and contested one.[11] In New Spain, peninsular Spaniards and some creoles maintained loyalty to Spain for reasons related both to economic interests and to fear, especially following an attempted coup in 1808 and then the Bajío parish priest Miguel Hidalgo's rebellion in 1810—events which will be discussed in greater detail in chapter 5.[12]

Conscious of these political, economic, and social developments and often personally affected by many of the changes, preachers and other members of Mexico City's high clergy responded with increasing dismay and alarm in their published discourses during this period. Although concerned with recent affronts to the Church on the part of the Crown, as Carlos Herrejón Peredo has pointed out, without doubt the specter of the French Revolution and especially the anti-religious attacks associated with it loomed especially large for many preachers.[13] Frequently criticizing figures such as Napoleon, sermonizers lamented especially the horrors perpetrated against the Church and its leaders in France, including "drastic measures such as the closing of churches; the destruction or confiscation of sacred objects, bells, and statues; the resignation of priests; the renaming of towns and streets; and the performance of burlesques of Catholic practice."[14] In the minds of many church leaders, especially following the French seizure of the Spanish throne, the fear was that such events would soon befall New Spain as well, barring serious moral and spiritual reform.

For these leaders, as also appears to have occurred in the French church, a key aspect of the necessary reform involved the gendered behavioral and social customs of their parishioners, especially women.[15] Excoriating the vices of "the weak sex," clergymen scolded women amid their audiences—along with some men whom they accused of acting in "effeminate" ways by pursuing "luxuries"—for their purported moral laxity, which the priests perceived reflected in women's modes of dress, speech, gait, and social customs. According to the preachers, these customs had provoked divine wrath

---

11. Elliott, *Empires*, 375–77. For an explanation of the process leading to the calling of a general *Cortes* see Brading, *First America*, 540–541. For a collection of studies on various aspects of the events of 1808 in Iberian America see Ávila and Pérez Herrero, ed., *Las experiencias*.

12. See Brading, *Church and State*, 236–37; Farriss, *Crown and Clergy*, 197–98; Elliott, *Empires*, 381–82.

13. Herrejón Peredo, *Del sermón*, 275–82.

14. Desan, *Reclaiming*, 8–9.

15. For studies that include discussion of the place of women in the discourses of religious authorities in France, see Ford, *Divided Houses*, chapter 1; Desan, *Reclaiming*; Hufton, "Reconstruction."

in the form of events like those already witnessed in France and, barring serious moral reform, would soon do so in New Spain as well, leading in short order to catastrophic social breakdown. Nevertheless, all hope was not yet lost. In addition to their admonitions, preachers also upheld ways in which women could reform their habits by returning to the example of historical figures and saints, thereby aiding in the restoration of social order. Likewise, men who had strayed could return to the fold by acting with valor once more in defense of the *patria*. If both men and women, in deference to legitimate religious authority, reformed their behavior in these ways, proper social order would thus be restored and imminent crisis averted. Accordingly, as surrounding circumstances grew progressively more grave and desperate, Mexico City's high clergy turned with increasing frequency to conventions of gender both as a readily identifiable explanation for and a concrete solution to the manifold problems at hand.[16]

Gender and the Late Colonial Context

Regarding the gendered social context of late colonial Mexico City to which preachers often made reference in their sermons, while recent scholarship has demonstrated continuity in women's subjection to the authority of Church and State it has also pointed to ways in which women were beginning to transcend some of the restrictions traditionally placed on them. For instance, in her study of the women of Mexico City in this period, Silvia Arrom details various ways in which women began to enter the public sphere (albeit somewhat tentatively and more poor than elite women) and to claim rights in a modernizing world.[17] For example, as Pilar Gonzalbo Aizpuru and Marie Francois also note, by the late eighteenth century women were receiving more extensive education, becoming a part of the work force, cooperating in military campaigns, acting as heads of households upon the death of fathers or spouses and, after independence, organizing politically and civically.[18] Steve J. Stern and Juan Javier Pescador also address the question of women's evolving social roles in their studies of gender in late

16. For possible connections between the positions on social order and religious authority of these late eighteenth- and early nineteenth-century New Spanish prelates and those adopted by conservatives in independent Mexico, see Schmidt, "Contra."

17. Arrom, *Women*, chapters 1 and 2. For studies of the role of women in the public sphere amid political and economic changes in late eighteenth- and early nineteenth-century Europe and the United States, see: Landes, *Women*; Outram, *Body*; Davidoff and Hall, *Family Fortunes*; Smith, *Emerging Female*; Kerber, "Separate Spheres."

18. Gonzalbo Aizpuru, *Las mujeres*, chapter 2; Francois, "Cloth and Silver"; Arrom, *Women*, chapters 1 and 2.

colonial period. According to Stern and Pescador, conditions in Mexico City in this period proved especially conducive to the challenging of traditional gender roles, especially among plebeian women, who migrated to Mexico City with increasing frequency in this period and who often succeeded in exercising agency through opportunities for employment, including in factories and artisanal workshops, as wet nurses and street vendors, and even in the management of prostitution rings.[19]

Another aspect of this gendered social context, and one that seems especially to have influenced preachers, was women's embrace of French fashions and social customs. For instance, Anne Staples has demonstrated in a recent study how one manifestation of the influence of the Enlightenment in Mexico emerged in social customs reflective of a society, "more extroverted, enjoyable and pleasant than in earlier times."[20] Staples cites the influence of French customs and styles of fashion, which grew in popularity in New Spain under the increased openness of Bourbon rule, describing one late-colonial society gathering in which 180 "well-groomed ladies," along with 222 other women of slightly lower rank but still "highly decent," attended a dance in honor of the accession of Ferdinand VII.[21] Still, as Pilar Gonzalbo Aizpuru has noted in a study of notarial records from this period, although styles of dress were changing—including adoption of new fashions and habits of conspicuous consumption—some of the reasons for these changes may also relate to evolving notions of hygiene and aesthetics, which resulted in some of the lighter, more open dresses condemned by some church officials.[22] Nevertheless, by the late eighteenth century women in Mexico City had begun to adopt styles of dress and comportment often associated with French fashions and therefore also, in the minds of many church leaders, with the deleterious, anti-religious consequences such decadence had already engendered in Europe.[23] In light of this trend, therefore, the presence within many of the official Church discourses examined in this chapter of sharp criticism of women's perceived social infractions, along with those of some men as well, points not simply to increased sensitivity and vigilance on the part of clergy but also to the

19. Stern, *Secret History*, chapters 1, 2, and 11; Pescador, "Vanishing Woman."

20. Beside the sermons and other official Church discourses under consideration in this chapter, Anne Staples points to other evidence regarding women's activity outside the home in the final years of the colonial period. See Staples, "Sociabilidad."

21. Staples, "Sociabilidad," 102. See also López-Cordón Cortezo, "Women."

22. Gonzalbo Aizpuru, "Del decoro."

23. For other studies of fashion trends in Spain, France, and England in this period, including their relationship to developing notions of gender and morality, see Valverde, "Love of Finery"; Batchelor, "Fashion and Frugality"; Jones, "Repacking"; Jones, *Sexing*; Molina and Vega, *Vestir*.

close associations drawn by many of these officials between feminine—and, sometimes, "effeminate"—habits and customs and the nefarious effects they seemed already to have wrought in Europe, which were now in imminent danger of erupting in New Spain as well.

As the remainder of this chapter will demonstrate, members of the high clergy in New Spain, like their lay contemporaries, found themselves caught up during these years in the confusion and chaos of the events that would ultimately lead to the wars of independence. One response was to rearticulate and reaffirm gendered norms, the transgression of which church officials frequently associated with the pernicious influence of trends originating in revolutionary France. Through public discourses such as sermons and pastoral letters, therefore, prelates could air their concerns with troubling aspects of their flocks' behavior and with what such actions could portend for society, even while also expressing support for traditional power structures perceived to be under threat and exercising at least some degree of control and authority in an age that appeared to many of them to be leading precipitously toward moral chaos and social dissolution. The remaining sections will examine church discourses from this period and will demonstrate how, as political and social realities continually shifted around them, the high clergy once more turned to gendered language and concepts as a significant, albeit largely unconscious, dimension of their discursive strategies—this time as a means of restoring order amid the array of crises occasioned by unfolding contemporary events.

Gender and Politics in Archepiscopal Pastoral Letters and Sermons

As the eighteenth century drew to a close and in the opening decade of the nineteenth century, Mexico City's highest ecclesiastical authorities, archbishops Alonso Núñez de Haro y Peralta (1772–1800) and Francisco Xavier de Lizana y Beamont (1803–1811), noted with increasing alarm the inability of the Crown to defend against the dangers to Spain and America represented by revolutionary France. Setting the tone for other preachers, these leaders' visions of what was ailing society and how it could be ameliorated proved influential in shaping the development of official church discourses in this period and therefore merit extended consideration before turning to the output of other sermonizers.

The Archbishops' Concerns

Although troubled as well with affronts on the part of the Crown to traditional church privileges, what was of foremost concern to Núñez de Haro and Lizana was the seeming inability of royal officials to grasp the gravity of the current situation.[24] With religion and the Church under active attack in France, it was all the more crucial for the Spanish monarchy to reaffirm its own loyalty to the Church, lest in failing to do so it imperil the very foundations of its own legitimacy.[25] By the mid-1790s and into the first decade of the nineteenth century, however, both Núñez de Haro and Lizana concluded that the Crown was failing in this grave responsibility. Forfeiting its sacred duty by attacking Church privileges and generally failing to diminish the French menace, the monarchy, in the minds of the archbishops, was hastening the impending doom of the entire colonial system. For these prelates, it was not so much the case that the Crown now represented an oppressive power to be cast off—on the contrary, church leaders throughout this period continued to preach on the decisive importance of monarchy amid the chaos of the events surrounding the French Revolution. Instead, if anything Church leaders saw the Crown as insufficiently regal—as having imperiled its own legitimacy through ill-advised political decisions and policies, especially those perceived by ecclesiastics as representing attacks on traditional church privileges. For Núñez de Haro and Lizana, if the Crown was now acting in its own interests then the Church must likewise defend its privileged position—both for its own sake and ultimately that of the ordered society for which it alone constituted the authentic foundation.

Accordingly, in the final years of the eighteenth century and the opening of the nineteenth, New Spain's high clergy, led by Núñez de Haro and his successor, Lizana y Beaumont, began condemning the anti-religious excesses of the age, which they saw as in danger of penetrating New Spain as well through the increasingly free circulation of books, ideas and fashions.[26] In particular, signaling a shift in discursive emphasis and strategy, Núñez

24. Escamilla González, *José Patricio*, 199. In New Spain this reality became manifest in tensions between viceregal and ecclesiastical authorities. For example, as Escamilla González notes, the second viceroy Revillagigedo and Núñez de Haro clashed on issues such as the church's legal jurisdiction, innovations in governance, the remodeling of the cathedral plaza, and other perceived affronts to the archbishop's authority.

25. Ibid., 226.

26. Pérez Memén, *El episcopado*, 51; Ampudia, *La Iglesia*, 236. See also Ávila, "Interpretaciones," 37–39; Herrejón Peredo, *Del sermón*, chapter 8. As both Ávila and Herrejón Peredo point out, starting in the first years of the nineteenth century a noticeable transition occurred in sermons from a previous doctrinal emphasis to increasingly political content.

de Haro and especially Lizana looked to discourses of gender as a means of restoring proper order. While other scholars have pointed to increasingly direct references to turmoil through increased political content in sermons, my research shows that an important discursive element of this change—led by Núñez de Haro and Lizana—came through gendered language and conventions.[27] Among other reasons, as noted already for scholarship on the French Revolution itself, prelates seem to have turned to language of gender—especially regarding women and their behavior—precisely because women and some men appeared increasingly to be embodying the very values the Church associated with the French Revolution and which, therefore, it abhorred. For example, prelates singled out women's frequent immodesty of dress, frivolity of comportment, and generalized vanity, all of which had led, in their assessment, to the breakdown of social order and the extreme manifestations of anti-religious sentiment witnessed in France. These, among others, were some of the horrors that awaited New Spain, so the message went, if women in particular—though some men as well—did not mend their ways and eschew the pernicious trends and vogues of fashion to which they had succumbed.

In the case of Núñez de Haro, for example, one decree published by the archbishop in 1790 addressed issues related to women's dress and behavior. In his decree the archbishop expressed dismay concerning a growing custom among women to dress as *beatas*, donning habits that covered their faces, and sometimes their bodies, entirely. As noted by Edelmira Ramírez in a study of *beatas* in this period, the women in question formed an intermediary group in colonial society—between nuns and lay women—and, in the late eighteenth century, were the subjects both of clerical campaigns to document and encourage their religious devotion as well as efforts on the part of higher church authorities to suppress what some saw as the unorthodox, excessive nature of their piety.[28] For example, in his decree Núñez de Haro complained that the "tight and vulgar" articles of clothing worn by some *beatas* invited "delinquents" to take advantage of the women, committing various "crimes and excesses," all hidden from the view of judges and magistrates. For this reason, in order to bring the women back under the Church's jurisdiction, Núñez de Haro declared excommunicated anyone wearing the habits who had not been previously authorized to do so by the

---

27. Herrejón Peredo, *Del sermón*, chapter 8.

28. Ramírez L., *María Rita*, 10–39. See also Atienza López, "De beaterios." According to Atienza López, concern was longstanding on the part of church authorities with reigning in *beatas*' abilities to practice religious devotion outside the conventual context.

Church.²⁹ For Núñez de Haro and, later, Lizana as well, such episodes were outward manifestations of a larger trend of societal decadence and the need to bring women's behavior into line, which, if not reversed, would lead inevitably to the erosion and possible destruction of the only true foundation for civilized society: the Church.

The Arrival of Archbishop Lizana

Among church leaders and preachers, Archbishop Lizana's published output stands out as more particularly focused on women and concepts of gender as significant focal points for moral reform and renewal than any of his predecessors. Arriving in New Spain in late 1802 after a long, arduous journey to assume his post as archbishop of Mexico City, Francisco Xavier de Lizana y Beaumont entered the city on January 11, 1803 and lost little time in addressing his new flock.[30] Beginning first with the priests under his spiritual authority, Lizana directed a pastoral letter to them later that month in which he described the perils and "fatigues" of the journey he had undertaken, along with a call to reform of their own personal customs and observances as a means of inspiring similar virtue among their flocks.[31]

Publishing no fewer then nine additional letters and other declarations during the year of his arrival, Lizana proved to be by far the most prolific of Mexico City's recent archbishops.[32] As Ana Carolina Ibarra points out in a recent study of Lizana, the archbishop recognized from the beginning a climate of tensions at play in New Spain as the Church and Crown faced rising discontent with colonial rule along with external threats from the U.S. and Great Britain.[33] Additionally, as Lizana expressed in another letter from 1803, a further troubling situation had arisen in the form of recent affronts by the Crown on ecclesiastical privilege and authority, including attacks on clerical immunity, *cofradías*, and clerical privileges.[34] To Lizana, these abuses were attacks not only on individual clergy members but on the institution of the Church itself and therefore also on the only true "cornerstone" on which, in a most delicate and imperiled political moment, Spanish

29. See AGN GD 14 Bienes Nacionales. Año: 1790. Vol. 829, exp. 18.
30. Ibarra, "De tareas"; Schwaller, "Episcopal Succession."
31. Lizana y Beaumont, *Nos* (1803).
32. From his eight-year tenure as archbishop and, briefly, viceroy, I was able to identify and consult forty-five different printed documents, including at least two sermons, numerous pastoral letters and decrees, and other proclamations.
33. Ibarra, "De tareas," 339.
34. Ibid., 341.

authority in America rested. In Lizana's words, "if the influence and faculties of priests are not maintained within the terms in which they existed previously, these dominions could be lost."[35] With these and other issues such as the cooperation and obedience of creole clergy occupying him, Lizana pursued a policy which promoted moral reform and renewal of piety among clergy and laity—for example promoting retreats for clergy and spiritual renewal in parishes—while simultaneously negotiating the increasingly difficult challenges posed by the political situation facing New Spain in the first decade of the nineteenth century.[36]

Lizana and Gendered Discourses

To succeed in promoting his vision for the Church while confronting the unique challenges posed by deteriorating church-state relations, Lizana would need a strong discursive foundation upon which to base his efforts. Though Ibarra and other scholars have studied various aspects of the archbishop's discursive output, especially as they relate to the surrounding political climate, my research shows that a significant additional way in which Lizana, along with various other clerics, understood his pastoral task in this period was in strongly gendered terms.[37] More than either of his two immediate predecessors, Lizana spoke to his flock and admonished them to conform to a precise vision of the right ordering of masculinity and femininity in society and the Church—an understanding which Lizana associated with avoidance of the deadly pitfalls of the example of revolutionary France. For Lizana, if the Church—and therefore Spain's dominion in America, too—were to be preserved it would happen by reversing the trends that had led to moral dissolution in France—that is, largely through moral and ethical renewal embodied in right behavior among male and female believers. Absent conformity of this sort, Lizana proclaimed his belief that the cause of the Church in America would ineluctably be lost. As he stated quite frankly in the context of the aftermath of the Napoleonic invasion of the Iberian Peninsula in 1808:

---

35. Ibid. For further studies on church-state relations at the close of the colonial period, see Farriss, *Crown and Clergy*; Brading, *Church and State*.

36. Ibarra, "De tareas," 342–42, 347. As Ibarra points out, Lizana was well known for being particularly pious and devout. He engaged in various penitential practices and was know to live austerely in the archbishop's house.

37. See ibid., 345–49 for an analysis of some aspects of Lizana's sermons. See also Connaughton, "Mudanzas," 252.

The French Connection

> Who would have thought that—at the same time as the ministers of the Lord are clamoring in prayer between the vestibule and the altar, begging that God's inheritance be spared perdition, confusion, and opprobrium; in the same age in which our most kind King Ferdinand VII is imprisoned as a result of the most infamous treason, our Most Holy Father Pius VII is sacrilegiously oppressed by a perfidious ingrate, so much blood is being spilled in Spain, so many tears shed in America and in all the Christian world; in the very days and circumstances in which it would be most appropriate for the faithful inhabitants of this most devout and opulent city of Mexico—an object so desired by the greed of the usurper—to multiply supplications, frequent the sacraments and come to implore the mercy of God in the churches—who, indeed, would have thought that, since they have not dressed in mourning as they ought and have not moderated the cost of the galas they attend and the dresses they wear, at least the city's women might reform the shameful nudity with which they present themselves in public?[38]

As this strongly worded condemnation indicates, Lizana understood the various crises facing Spain and America as almost apocalyptic signs that were to be intimately associated with and interpreted in gendered terms—especially related to women's behavior—precisely because it was in gendered terms that society had gone astray. For Lizana and other preachers in this period, gendered conventions and expectations were not merely incidental means by which to frame discursive stories and examples or even to inculcate moral virtue and religious sentiment; rather, they formed the very essence of what was at stake in the fight to the death in which they believed the Church and its enemies were engaged in the present age.

Hinting at the emphasis on questions of gender that would come to mark his discursive output, just a few months after his arrival in Mexico City Lizana published another pastoral letter, this time addressed to all the faithful, in which he indicated that an important religious obligation of leaders was to berate and admonish their flocks, to reform "belief and practice."[39] According to the archbishop, women's behavior in particular stood in need of reform. Calling women's tendency to embrace luxury "diabolical," he condemned "that nakedness among common people that transforms each woman into . . . a phantasm of hell."[40] Many elite women in early nineteenth-century Mexico had begun to adopt French fashions, including

---

38. Lizana y Beaumont, *Instrucccion* (1808), 1–2.
39. Lizana y Beaumont, *Carta* (1803).
40. Ibid., 26–27.

dresses which featured cuts deemed provocative by religious authorities.[41] Addressing these scandalous women, Lizana queried,

> How do you defend yourself, impudent woman, when, either with provocative dress (if you have the riches with which to adorn yourself and are a woman of quality), or all but naked (if you are from the common class), you present yourself at the foot of the altar? You, who with excessive adornment of your criminal body, with elevated neck, breathing lust, are not satisfied with circulating and wandering through the streets, plazas, walkways and other places, releasing flames of impure love, but rather go to the temple to provoke your God, and return home full of pride for having commanded the attentions of all.[42]

According to Lizana, the solution to such effrontery to God himself could lie solely with a return by women to more modest modes of dress, "to manifest to all the purity of your heart if you are a damsel, conjugal chastity if you are married, and appropriate continence if you are a widow."[43]

Similar patterns emerged throughout Lizana's pastoral letters and other writings in the years following his accession as archbishop. For example, in another letter from the following year, Lizana lamented the practices of "secular women" (*mujeres del siglo*), dedicated as they seemed to be to "diversions and fashions."[44] Likewise, in an 1807 letter, again on the subject of the holiness of the Catholic religion and its obligations, Lizana did not hesitate to call to task the problematic habits he perceived among women—tendencies to which he attributed the perdition of men, "transforming [them] into brutes."[45] In his words,

> What do your heads, so superfluously decorated, have to do with Jesus Christ's, so martyred? The immodesty of eyes, liberty of words, ease of step, [and] . . . profanity of your dresses, with the moderation and humility of the divine Savior? And that shameful nudity and softness of your flesh with the mortification of Jesus Christ, whose sheep you profess to be?[46]

Not only did women offend Christ by their objectionable displays of sensuality, they also imperiled their own fate, that of their families, and

41. See also Staples, "Sociabilidad."
42. Lizana y Beaumont, *Carta* (1803), 27–28.
43. Ibid., 28.
44. Lizana y Beaumont, *Carta* (1804), 9–10.
45. Lizana y Beaumont, *Carta* (1807), 20.
46. Ibid.

even of religion itself, which would "transmigrate" elsewhere on account of their offenses: "Disgraceful women! You conspire to your own ruin, to the dishonor of your husbands, to the desolation of your homes: you and all those who foment your lust and caprices conspire to expel our holy religion from this realm."[47] Further elaborating his grievances, Lizana did not hesitate even to accuse women of spiritual suicide and homicide: "We cannot believe that a Christian wife, knowing the damage done by the profanity of her adornments, would be content to be a murderess of her own soul and those of her neighbors[.]"[48]

Lizana, not content to be vague about the scandalousness of women's demeanor and dress, listed among the worst offenses the "indecency" and "tightness" of some dresses as well as the "studied" gait, "wandering" eyes, and "laughing and attractive" countenances of the offending parties.[49] These styles of dress and problematic habits among some women represented for the archbishop not merely occasions of scandal but veritable slaughter, akin to a vicious massacre: "Do not doubt that each of you who adorn yourself provocatively and provoke souls to burn in lasciviousness is crueler than if you mercilessly stabbed tender children, elderly folk, and priests to death."[50] Invoking the biblical story of Cain and Abel, Lizana did not hesitate to conclude, speaking in the voice of God, with the following words of judgment upon the women in question: "Women, the voice of the blood of your neighbor resounds in my ears, the blood of those whom you have led astray with your scandals cries out to me for vengeance."[51]

In the following year, 1808, Lizana published still another document with instructions directed to his flock on proper religious observance, again repeating his disapproval of the "profane and scandalous dresses," "new fashions," and "provocative nudities" he had witnessed in churches.[52] Also in 1808—specifically, in late November, after the unprecedented news of the abdication of Ferdinand VII and the accession of Napoleon's brother Joseph to the Spanish throne had reached New Spain, and therefore underlining once more the intimate connection Lizana perceived between gendered conventions and political and social trends—the archbishop issued a lengthy pastoral instruction exclusively dedicated to the "custom by which wives wear

---

47. Ibid., 21.
48. Ibid., 25.
49. Ibid.
50. Ibid., 25–26.
51. Ibid., 26.
52. See Lizana y Beaumont, *Sentimientos*, 8.

uncovered their chests and arms."[53] Opening his letter with a reference to the desperate nature of the times, Lizana wondered out loud why women, if they refused to dress in clothes of mourning and moderate their spending on "galas and dresses," could not at least cover their bodies and reform the "shameful nudity" with which they presented themselves in public.[54]

Lizana continued by expressing dismay at how members of the "devout sex," regular communicants and penitents in the confessional as they frequently were, could stray so far from divine truth. Professing his desire to clarify the vital importance of dressing appropriately in public, Lizana proceeded to review the theological foundations supporting the virtue of modesty and reasserted the Church's prerogative in punishing those who dared stray from this ideal. Significantly, he then went on to specify that it was not just women who offended God with their scandalous customs. Some men also were failing to conform to gendered expectations, allowing themselves to be seen everywhere with a style of dress "in which the quality of the cut and of the cloth places before the eyes, even if covered, that which modesty cannot permit to be named."[55] Similarly, in another letter, citing biblical precedents, the archbishop lamented how "effeminacy" had provoked God's wrath in the past, leading to societal ruin—a consequence which would also befall New Spain if men too did not resist trends toward "luxury" in their modes of dress. For example, according to Lizana, "[t]he prideful luxury of the daughters of Zion, and the effeminization of the first leaders of the people of God obligated the Lord to abandon them and turn them over as prisoners to their enemies."[56] This "effeminization" could have nefarious consequences, as demonstrated by another biblical king: "[T]he delicacy and delicious life of King Roboam brought him to impiety—and all the kingdom of Judah became idolatrous as it turned effeminate through delights."[57]

For these offenses against modesty and chastity—again betraying the connection he wished to make between gendered conventions and political misfortunes—Lizana blamed the French, "impious" traitors and an "abominable abortion from the abyss," to whom responsibility fell for promoting unbelief and the relaxation and corruption of previously solid moral observance, first in Spain and then in America.[58] Thus, for Lizana as well as for other preachers, some men's behavior was also in need of significant change.

53. Lizana y Beaumont, *Instrucccíon* (1808).
54. Ibid., 1–2.
55. Ibid., 33.
56. Lizana y Beaumont, *Carta* (1803), 29.
57. Ibid., 34.
58. Lizana y Beaumont, *Instrucción* (1808), 35–36.

While women ought to refrain from "galas and dresses," men too needed to avoid "luxury" if they were to preserve the requisite masculinity necessary for proper defense—both spiritual and practical—of the realm.

Similar attitudes emerged in two published sermons offered by Lizana during his term as archbishop. In the first, preached on the night of December 31, 1805 as part of a celebration of thanksgiving for blessings received during the year coming to a close, Lizana made reference to the political troubles already plaguing Spain at the time.[59] For the archbishop the origin of these painful episodes was clear: like the French before them, both peninsular and American Spaniards had sinned and provoked God's wrath. Among other transgressions, such as pridefulness and luxury, Lizana highlighted as especially egregious various offenses committed by women. First, the "lack of shame and modesty" among young women, along with the "license and comfortableness" of married women was problematic. However, worse still were the "horrifying," "daring," and "diabolical" styles of dress among women in general, which had led to numerous other vices.[60] Still more egregious, the perpetuation of these sinful tendencies among the population was responsible not just for social vices or even the worsening political situation; on the contrary, transgressions of this sort could and did provoke manifestations of divine wrath within nature itself. According to Lizana,

> When we sin we commit an abuse of the freedom which God has given us to do either good or bad that is so abominable that in the instant in which we disobey the Creator, all creatures will unite to destroy us, if his powerful hand does not hold them back. The earth, contaminated by so many absurdities (*torpezas*); the earth, weary of suffering so much evil, would shake in the presence of God with terrible movements in order to bury us alive in its entrails . . . as we know it has done, not only in regions far removed from us, but also in those of this new world which we inhabit, in the horrible and appalling earthquake, which did away with the infamous *Villa de Honda* on June 16th of this very year.[61]

Referring to an actual earthquake that had struck earlier that year in the viceroyalty of Nueva Granada (modern Colombia), Lizana characterized natural disasters of this order as manifestations of divine wrath in response to human sinfulness.[62] Specifically, as before, these sins were for the

---

59. Lizana y Beaumont, *Sermón* (1806).
60. Ibid., VI–VII.
61. Ibid., XI–XII.
62. For information on this earthquake, see Ramírez, "Earthquake." According to a

archbishop explicitly gendered transgressions, typified by both "unhappy" women and "effeminate" men.[63] However, as with the citizens of Honda—who, once sobered by the hand of divine justice, reformed their ways and returned to more modest styles of dress—Lizana likewise reminded his own flock that it was God's mercy alone that had thus far stayed the wrath of nature in their own case.[64]

In the second of his published sermons, given in August of 1808 in the midst of the crisis brought on by events in Spain, Lizana again returned to the themes of divine retribution for human sinfulness and the connection between gendered conventions and political events.[65] Referring to the "very particular" valor of Spain's people, Lizana lamented that both in history and now in his own day this courageousness had faded due to the effects of sin. In the case of men, as he explained, "the vices, especially those of the flesh, render effeminate even the strongest; they make our enemies stronger and disperse our armies[.]"[66] Though the responsibility for moral reform fell to all in New Spain, Lizana again singled out women for particular reprehension. According to Lizana, "I see that you are disturbed, sinners; especially you, *señoras*, because I warn you that with your un-moderated lust, with your shameful nudity, with your un-Christian air, steps, and countenance, you enter the church itself to provoke the wrath of God[.]"[67] Nevertheless, Lizana also had some words of encouragement for women, reminding them of the biblical figure Judith, by whose hand, he recalled for his audience, a "numerous army" of idolators had been vanquished.[68] Similarly, in the current time of crisis, Lizana called upon women, who "have a heart so compassionate for feeling the miseries of others," to reach out in pity to "our disgraced nation" through faithful reform of their customs and habits. By doing so, God would relinquish the whip that had been readied to punish sin and finally do away with "that perfidious tyrant" (i.e., Napoleon), thereby securing the inheritance of future generations.[69]

---

study cited by Ramírez, Honda was a significant town before much of it, including the main church and many other buildings, was destroyed by the earthquake and around five hundred people died. See also Walker, *Shaky Colonialism*, which also shows that the Church blamed sinful women in Lima for the 1746 earthquake.

63. Lizana y Beaumont, *Sermon* (1806), XIV–XV.
64. Ibid., XV–XVIII.
65. Lizana y Beaumont, *Sermon* (1808)
66. Ibid., 10–11.
67. Ibid., 20–21.
68. Ibid., 7.
69. Ibid., 20–21.

The French Connection

Sermons and Discourses of Gender and Politics

Like those preached by Lizana, sermons given by other preachers during the period under consideration in this chapter likewise constitute a particularly rich source for historians, as they often reflect some of the tensions and fears latent in the political and social atmosphere that prevailed in the final decades preceding Mexico's wars for independence.[70] Beginning with reverberations from the advent of the French Revolution in 1789, members of the high clergy in Mexico City offered clear evidence in their sermons of the turmoil and uncertainty the Church faced as it attempted to respond to a multiple series of often-unprecedented developments;[71] and, as had been the case in the past, reinvention and reimagining of gendered language provided an important means by which to do so. Amid changing, often chaotic circumstances and because they perceived a close connection between conventions of gender and many of these political and social developments, preachers employed language concerning men and women as a means of shoring up their positions and offering solutions to the various problems and issues at hand. While their visions of masculinity and femininity were not always uniform, they represented a means by which the institution as a whole could address contemporary concerns while also reinforcing its traditional social preeminence and authority.

Masculinity in Sermons

Many sermons continued to advance discourses of masculinity closely associated with military virtue (see chapter 3), though now clearly in response to the events of the French Revolution.[72] For example, offered in the Mexico City cathedral in November of 1791, a sermon by the peninsular Spaniard Juan de Sarria y Alderete suggests the depth of angst felt in the capital upon news of events in France and Europe—trepidation that would only heighten later in the 1790s as Spain's forces were defeated by those of revolutionary France, its ports blockaded by the British, and normal commerce with New Spain

---

70. Ibarra, "De tareas," 345. See also Ibarra's study of the Church in New Spain in the context of 1808: Ibarra, "La crisis."

71. For a study of the increased presence of anti-French sentiments and violent language in sermons see Herrejón Peredo, "Catolicismo." According to Herrejón Peredo, this trend represented a new stage in preaching in New Spain, which culminated in the anti-Napoleonic and anti-insurgent discourses of the first two decades of the nineteenth century.

72. For a study of some aspects of the increased militarism of this period, see García Peña, "El encierro."

severely disrupted.⁷³ Following in the tradition of earlier military-themed sermons, Sarria y Alderete's sermon was a tribute to Spain's military fallen. Characterized by bravery and fortitude, these troops fought courageously for the Spanish monarchy; their "warrior" virtue, "[did] not allow for timid hearts, fearful souls, nor cowardly spirits," but instead required individuals with "great souls" unafraid of difficult challenges.⁷⁴ Introducing what would become a common theme in many sermons during this period, Sarria y Alderete compared the valiant battles engaged in by Spanish troops to those fought by the biblical figure Judas Maccabaeus—a warrior responsible for saving the people of Israel from foreign domination. For the preacher, like Judas in the face of apparently superior forces, Spanish troops had fought bravely and defeated numerous enemies because God was on their side.⁷⁵

On the occasion of a celebration of the Inquisition in 1794, the peninsular Spaniard and Dominican Ramón Casaus Torres delivered a sermon in which he expressed sentiments similar to those of Sarria y Alderete.⁷⁶ According to Casaus Torres, St. Peter of Verona, a fellow Dominican, inquisitor, and the subject of the sermon, showed "manly" courage from an early age, a virtue which had allowed him to rise to the status of a true Christian hero in his service to the Inquisition.⁷⁷ Casaus Torres praised the saint's virtues and called out to his audience, bemoaning the current circumstances in which the Church found itself—especially in light of anti-religious campaigns in France—all of which called for the heroic sort of virtue Peter had exemplified. In Casaus Torres' words:

> What greater praise in the eighteenth century could there be than to say "Hero of the Faith"? Yes, ladies and gentleman, in the eighteenth century. Because, what tears do the highest pastors of Christianity shed! What tumults agitate the richest lands, so fecund also in monstrous errors, in bloody wars! What desolation! What fright!⁷⁸

Offering Peter of Verona as an example, Casaus Torres concluded that all must fight fiercely and bravely for the faith, not giving up until, as in earlier biblical enemies, contemporary opponents were defeated, their "blasphemous tongues torn out," and their "sacrilegious arm[s]" hung before "the temple of

---

73. Brading, "Bourbon Spain," 157; Sarria y Alderete, *Oracion*.
74. Sarria y Alderete, *Oracion*, 9.
75. Ibid., 13.
76. Casaús Torres y Las Plazas, *Sermon* (1794).
77. Ibid., 9.
78. Ibid., 17.

the Lord to serve as an everlasting reminder that there is an omnipotent and justice-seeking God, who castigates and avenges himself in this way against offenses to his divine religion and against his chosen people[.]"[79]

Two years later, in 1796, again on the occasion of celebrations of the Inquisition, Casaus Torres took up similar themes, calling for heroism among believers and emphasizing that there was no room for "weak" and "cowardly" Christians in the fight against the "daring impiety" of those who, as in the anti-religious campaigns of the French Revolution, did not submit themselves to the authority of the "sacrosanct Church."[80] Nevertheless, again like Judas Maccabeus, God would provide for the needs of the people and supply "strong men" to defend the Church.[81] Likewise, almost ten years later, in 1807, Casaus Torres once more took up similar themes, again employing comparisons with Judas Maccabeus and decrying Spain's enemies, now incarnated in the person of Napoleon Bonaparte. According to the preacher, these foes were characterized by an "impudence . . . proper to a dissolute sycophant and an effeminate sybarite"—a memorable description indicative of many preachers' increasing militarism, their heightened emphasis on masculinity and, conversely, their acute aversion to effeminacy in a period in which many were drawing ever closer associations between failures to conform to normative gendered expectations and attacks on the authority and stability of the institutional Church.[82]

Another preacher, the creole José Mariano Beristáin, expressed similarly fierce sentiments of bravery against French perfidy in a 1795 sermon offered in the Mexico City cathedral in honor of Spain's fallen.[83] Opening with a verbal assault on the "barbaric French," Beristáin warned his audience of the dire threat posed by these treacherous enemies:

> Ah, Spaniards: 24 million of those barbarians seek to disturb your peace, alter your customs and, with deceptive flattery, shackle you . . . imprisoning your liberty and leaving you in misery . . . they seek to tear religion from out of your chests, and have already begun to profane your temples, your altars and even your priests.[84]

79. Ibid., 28–29.
80. See Casaús Torres y Las Plazas, *Sermon* (1796), 23.
81. Ibid., 45.
82. Casaús Torres, *Sermon* (1807), 29.
83. Beristáin, *Elogio*. For studies of Beristáin and especially his position as a creole in defending the monarchy during the wars of independence, see the following: Torres Puga, "Beristáin"; Ávila, "La crisis"; Zayas de Lille, "Los sermones."
84. Beristáin, *Elogio*, 7.

To these threats to the very foundations of society Beristáin emphasized that Spanish troops had responded valiantly, expressing his conviction that, "all around I see them engulfed in clouds of smoke and dust, covered with sweat and blood, raising their nervous arms and handing out a thousand deaths with each blow[.]"[85]

Preachers' visions of masculinity did not limit themselves to the arena of military service, however. Daily life could also constitute a kind of battlefield in which ordinary Christians would be called upon to act with heroic virtue and courage in defense of the principles of their faith, again demonstrating the importance of the connection many preachers made between gendered norms and social circumstances. One saint of particular resonance for this vision was Thomas Aquinas, whose renowned virtues served well many preachers' discursive goals. According to one sermon from 1794, Thomas was blessed by God with the honor of receiving a special spiritual "cincture" (a rope or cord tied around liturgical vestments) symbolic of his role as "captain, director and chief of the angelic militia."[86] According to the preacher, Thomas served in the "sacred militia of Jesus Christ" and was renowned for "a type of combat most strange and difficult"—that is, the battles required for resisting temptations against chastity and emerging victorious.[87] It was to this same type of combat, in imitation of actual soldiers, that the preacher emphasized that all Christians were called, "with rectitude and simplicity in all your actions, so that in you might be produced the same offices and effects that the military cincture produces in soldiers[.]"[88] Moreover, as in Lizana's discourses and as other preachers noted in frequent retellings during this period of Spain's ancient history, earlier instances of the abandonment of courage and "manly" virtue had led the nation astray, begetting a population made "effeminate" by "sensualities," "luxury," and "vices."[89] As one preacher put it, "luxury overcame our princes, and with them, as the first exemplars of all the nation, it passed [even] to the strongest of warriors who, being rendered effeminate, no longer manifested that greatness of soul, that heroic intrepidness and ancient valor, which had made Spaniards justly respected in all the world."[90]

85. Ibid., 8.
86. See Flores, *Sermon*, 5–6.
87. Ibid.
88. Ibid., 33.
89. Casaús Torres y Las Plazas, *Sermon* (1805), 11. See chapter 1 for treatment of the medieval Iberian saint and martyr Pelagius (*Pelayo*) and the significance of his legend for Iberian notions of sexuality.
90. Heredia y Sarmiento, *Sermon* (1807), 9. See also Lemoine, *Insurgencia*, 23.

The French Connection

In the context of the events of 1808, the militaristic language often used by preachers came to take on even greater resonance once word of the French invasion of the Iberian peninsula reached New Spain. The shock and horror of the Napoleonic invasion, which resulted in the abdication of both Charles IV and Ferdinand VII in the same year as well as the installation of Joseph Bonaparte on the Spanish throne, clearly resonated in sermons given in Mexico City that year, as preachers expressed sympathy and support for the deposed monarch—a position also reflected in a contemporaneous print whose inscription declared that the "lion" of Spain would never release from its "claws" the "two worlds" (i.e., Spain and America) that belonged by divine right to Ferdinand VII. Among responses offered by preachers, one referred back to the biblical story of the Maccabees, wondering aloud why it was Spain's fate to suffer the indignities that had befallen it.[91] The preacher lamented the lost social order that had followed upon the year's events but insisted that not even the expanse of an ocean could obscure the support of Ferdinand VII's loyal subjects in New Spain for their exiled king.[92] Proclaiming the need for brave and loyal Spaniards to fight back, in another sermon the preacher, as in the above image, compared the Spanish nation to a lion, which, at the first blows from its enemy, would "destroy in its claws the enemies that present themselves before it."[93] Moreover, for the battles to which loyal subjects of Ferdinand VII were called on both sides of the Atlantic, not even distinctions between men and women could excuse individuals from fighting.[94] In the preacher's words, "[t]he nation . . . rises up en masse without distinction of age, class, or sex, with even the elderly, clerics and women taking up arms . . . thus deploying its characteristic valor[.]"[95]

Following subsequent events later that same year, in which local and regional juntas in Spain formed to combat the French and eventually united into a *junta central*, another sermon described the rites of a solemn Mass of thanksgiving offered by Archbishop Lizana in Mexico City's cathedral.[96] In his sermon, the preacher—once again the creole José Mariano Beristáin de Sousa—was explicit in naming the Virgin Mary as the true source for the renewed order represented by the junta's formation. Invoking various other "strong women" from biblical tradition, Beristáin insisted that throughout

91. Jove y Aguiar, *Oracion* (1808), 6.

92. Ibid., 19.

93. Guridi y Alcocer, *Sermon* (1808), 19–20.

94. For another sermon in which women fighters are praised, see Heredia y Sarmiento, *Oracion* (1808).

95. Guridi y Alcocer, *Sermon* (1808), 20.

96. Elliott, *Empires*, 375; Beristáin de Sousa, *Oracion* (1809)

history it had been their matriarchs, and most especially the Virgin Mary, who had saved God's people from their enemies.[97] As this sermon demonstrates, the militant masculinity promoted by preachers in their sermons could also be attributed to the strong moral foundations given to them by their mothers. For example, in one of his sermons already studied above, Beristáin also emphasized that the heroic virtues of the Spanish soldiers he wished to praise, along with their faithfulness, loyalty and obedience to their sovereigns, had as their origin the inheritance of their ancestors' bravery, which they had received through their mothers' milk.[98] Similarly, in a sermon in praise of Santiago, another preacher attributed Spain's recent troubles to "leisure" and "effeminization" while at the same time declaring that motherly values were the origin of the *junta central*.[99]

Femininity in Sermons

Thus, despite the militaristic, hyper-masculine, and sometimes anti-feminine (or at least anti-effeminate) language and imagery in various sermons, many clerics also praised the potential of women to support the efforts of their fellow brave Spaniards, seeking to emphasize the connection between gendered norms and political developments. For these preachers, the key to resolving Spain's (and New Spain's) troubles lay in rediscovering and returning to the metropole's earlier greatness as a nation distinguished for the remarkable bravery of its citizens. To this end, in no way were all feminine attributes to be condemned. Women, especially female saints like the Virgin Mary and others, as observed in the Baroque sermons studied in chapter 2, could act as "strong women" who overcame the weakness of their sex and fought with valor equal or superior to that of men. Embodying the "weakness of their sex" at their worst and yet also constituting a crucial means by which society could be rescued from its current imperilment, women for preachers in this period represented an important referent both for the troubles of the times and for the potential of future renewal. Unlike earlier discourses, however, which, while also employing language about women, had focused mostly on women's spiritual potential to act in "manly" ways at the service of a higher cause, sermonizers in this period turned their attentions increasingly to concrete, practical ways in which women's behavior

---

97. Beristáin, *Oracion* (1809), 16–17.
98. Beristáin, *Elogio*, 15–16.
99. See Carrasco y Enciso, *Sermon* (1809), 30–55. For a study of this and an earlier sermon on Santiago and the importance of the Galician community in Mexico City during this time, see Cardaillac, ed., *Dos sermones*.

The French Connection

had the potential both to threaten and to redeem the social good, depending on the choices women made.

As already observed in the writings of Archbishop Lizana, referring often to "the weak sex," preachers in this period emphasized connections between normative notions of gender and the political consequences they associated with them. For example, many preachers characterized women frequently as lacking in strength or virtue but then often suggested ways in which some women had overcome this trend and achieved great advancements for themselves, their families, society and the Church.[100] Among others, a sermon preached in 1802 by Casaus Torres demonstrates how this narrative functioned.[101] Setting up a comparison between the world and its errors and the courage displayed by the sermon's subject, the early Christian martyr Inés, Casaus Torres challenged his audience to live up to her edifying example:

> Lift up your eyes, cowardly mortal, and look at the world, armed ... with all its loves (*amores*), all its errors, and all its terrors ... which wage the bloodiest of battles against this innocent virgin, weak because of her sex and slight because of her age; and yet, with the grace of the Lord ... this girl triumphs over the world armed with its loves (*amores*), errors, and terrors.[102]

Confounding worldly expectations, Casaus Torres reported that Inés displayed from an early age virtue "superior to her sex," along with "beauty of soul," "candor of innocence," "purity of customs," and "virginal modesty"—traits which allowed her to emerge victorious when put to the test.[103] Thus, Inés' heroic strength allowed her to maintain the honor of her "respectable sex"—something the preacher was not prepared to say regarding many contemporary women. For Casaus Torres, women were gravely threatened by "novels" and "amorous romances," which had begun entering New Spain with increasing frequency during the Bourbon reform period and which, in the eyes of the Church, were linked with the notorious influence of revolutionary France and therefore seriously imperiled established social norms.[104]

100. San Cirilo, *La señora*, 26.
101. Casaús Torres, *Sermon* (1802).
102. Ibid., 4.
103. Ibid., 9.
104. Ibid., 10–11. For studies which account for the opening of New Spain in this period to the influx of new forms of literature and ideas, see Pérez Memén, *El episcopado*; Ampudia, *La Iglesia*. Perceiving them as dangerous, preachers condemned many of these doctrines, which they viewed as a threat both to the good of the faith and the social order. As Casaús Torres stated, addressing contemporary philosophers

Among the ways preachers recommended for overcoming challenges to the faith, women's lives of devotion and piety figured prominently. For example, preached during 1802 as well and also in a conventual setting, the creole Mercedarian priest Melchor Talamantes y Baeza offered a sermon on the virtues of a female saint—Santa Teresa.[105] According to the preacher, Teresa was an exceptional woman "for her sex" and "for her century," not only due to her own merits but also as a result of her origins in Ávila—a city whose women occupied a "very distinguished place among illustrious Spanish matrons" because, in the absence of their husbands and with "manly spirit," they were known to have prepared their city's defenses in cases of military attack.[106] Although, according to the preacher, Teresa should have been "incapable because of her sex" of the virtuous and heroic acts attributed to her, he conceded that she in fact resembled a "strong man" (*varón esforzado*) in the resolve she demonstrated in facing the difficulties associated with her divine calling.[107]

Similarly, in 1804 the creole Oratorian preacher Rafael Antonio Puga y Araujo offered a sermon on the virtues and example of Santa Monica, the long-suffering mother of the early church father St. Augustine.[108] Comparing Monica to the biblical matriarch Judith—renowned for her bravery in beheading an enemy of the people of Israel—the preacher opened by reviewing the heroic deeds of Judith, "one of the most illustrious women ever numbered among the annals of her sex," who, to the "confusion of many men," became "one of the greatest souls" in sacred history.[109] Though Judith distinguished herself for the "manly deed" of defeating an entire army, "cutting off with her delicate hands the head of an enemy," the preacher argued that the "new Judith" he wished to praise—that is, Santa Monica—was even greater.[110] In his words, this new Judith was to be held up as an example for all women: for virgins, as a monument of purity; for married women as the

---

in another sermon: "Who are you, rapacious insects, declared enemies of God, and of men, who are you to lift yourselves up to the starry firmament, and there measure . . . the greatness, the course and the beneficence of this divine star [St. Thomas Aquinas]?" Specifying the writings of Bayle, Voltaire, Rousseau and Diderot, Casaús Torres condemned their "black blasphemies" and "diabolical impieties" as inimical to Christian belief. See Casaús Torres, *Sermon* (1799), 27–30.

105. Talamantes y Baeza, *Panegírico* (1803). Talamantes y Baeza was a creole born in Peru.

106. Ibid., 1–2.

107. Ibid., 19, 23.

108. Puga y Araujo, *La Judit*.

109. Ibid., 1.

110. Ibid., 2–3.

"norm of fidelity"; for widows and for women in general as a "mirror" of modesty, patience, mortification, and "zeal for the interests of God and the good of souls."[111] In contrast to "profane heroes," who ruled with tyranny over peoples and fomented wars and bloodshed, Puga y Araujo praised Monica for exemplifying "the true and solid glory" of souls who spent their days "in holy obscurity," glorifying God "in the retreat of their home[s]," thereby attracting the "admirations of all" and the "blessings of heaven."[112]

The preacher went on to explain that Monica's virtues were not merely valuable for her own salvation. Instead, from the "dawn of her years," the saint easily "confused strong and prideful wise men," thereby earning the respect and admiration of her contemporaries and glorifying God.[113] Addressing the young women of his own time and place—imperiled by the temptations represented by French fashions and social customs—the preacher instructed them to resist temptation and conform their lives to the example of Monica:

> Foolish young women, you who shamefully stain the first rays of youth's dawn with attentions to vanity... you behold nothing in this most prudent virgin that is not a living reprehension of your misguided conduct: She was young like you, dressed in miseries like you, and surrounded also like you with all the flattering objects that fascinate hearts; yet she was a more fervent, vigilant and prudent Christian than you.[114]

In contrast to such foolishness among contemporary young women, the preacher emphasized that Monica strengthened her "manly arm" with the most important of the soul's defenses: "silence, mortification, retreat, [and] continual communication with God."[115] In contrast to contemporary women's habits of attending the theater and indulging in "pomp and vanity," Monica stood out for her fasting and "holy, evangelical abnegation."[116] Moreover, Monica also embodied the virtues of an ideal Christian wife and mother, avoiding the "sinful pride of *señoras*" by recognizing that "the man is the head of the woman" and thus exhibiting the rightful "respect as subjects" of women toward their husbands—virtues the transgression of

111. Ibid., 3.
112. Ibid., 5.
113. Ibid., 5–6.
114. Ibid., 6–7.
115. Ibid., 7–8.
116. Ibid., 8.

which meant "inverting and upsetting the order of God."[117] Thus, despite the "delicacy proper to her sex," Monica rose to the challenges posed to her, not with "prideful contradictions" but with "humble silence," "submissions," "respectful gifts," and "victorious meekness"—these, according to the preacher, were thus the keys both to understanding Monica's greatness and to securing moral improvement and the inculcation of virtue among contemporary women.

In another sermon, on the occasion of a religious profession in a convent in 1806, the peninsular Augustinian friar Dionicio Casado likewise noted the weakness of contemporary women in general, prone as they were to emulating the deleterious example of their French contemporaries.[118] Unlike the nun whose profession was being celebrated, most worldly women were expected to participate in an "inexplicable labyrinth of impertinent ceremonies, noisy dances, indiscretions (*charlanterías*), fashions, vanities, caprices, and other trinkets . . . of [their] age and sex[.]"[119] As members of a "sex idolized by men," women like the professing nun and others who withdrew from worldly temptations were to be commended for resisting the "attractions of luxury, vanity and fashion."[120] Similarly, in another sermon, given following the events of 1808, Casado lamented the "fatal beauty" to which women were attracted.[121] Many women had "misspent" their resources on "devouring luxury," which had ruined their homes and families and become a scandal on which many innocent souls had been "shipwrecked." However, Casado reminded his female audience that the example of other, more virtuous women could serve to edify and inspire them. Not just female saints but exemplary contemporary women were also worthy of imitation—for example, the women of England who had recently demonstrated a particularly "magnanimous generosity" in clothing 4,000 Spanish prisoners and contributing 300,000 pesos for the assistance of Spanish widows in the context of the wars raging in Europe.[122]

As a way of strengthening women in the fight against temptation, the creole priest Juan Ignacio de Heredia y Sarmiento also commended the recent formation by Mexico City's Asturian community of a school for girls, noting that it would serve to promote the "defense and support of the

117. Ibid., 11–12.
118. Casado, *Sermon* (1806).
119. Ibid., 8.
120. Ibid., 1.
121. Casado, *Sermon* (1809).
122. Ibid., 34–35.

youth of the beautiful sex, of that delicate . . . portion of society."[123] The peninsular Augustinian friar Bernardo Antonio González Díaz took up this same subject a year later, emphasizing the school's connection to devotion to the Virgin of Covadonga who, as had occurred earlier in history through the deliverance of Spain from Moorish rule, was without doubt at work in ensuring the virtue and piety of New Spain's young women through the formation of the school.[124] Making explicit this comparison, the preacher offered high praise for the school's benefactors:

> Those furious sectarians [Muslims]—the most lascivious of men—would without doubt have violated the daughters of our fathers, if our distinguished benefactress [the Virgin of Covadonga] had not impeded it; and you, Asturians, grateful for so singular a favor, and in order to liberate your own daughters, and the daughters of your children . . . have erected this college, which you consecrate *to the protectress of the chastity of Asturia's damsels*. Yes, ladies and gentlemen: you have seized these young women from the tempestuous seas of the world, where their innocence would surely shipwreck . . . and have guided them to the secure harbor of this college, eternal monument of your beneficent zeal and your love for religion and *patria*, and an inexhaustible font of public happiness.[125]

There in this school, González Díaz celebrated the lessons that young girls would be taught. Occupied with work proper "to their age, birth, and sex," these young women would learn to be nuns, mothers and wives who, along with husbands "worthy of their illustrious blood and virtue," would contribute to the increase and stature of the Christian population.[126] Having overcome the "weakness of their sex" through the school's intervention, these women would form the vanguard of a new female population in Mexico City prepared to atone for the ill effects of other women's sins and, by their heroic virtue, move society forward in a direction of moral renewal and religious reawakening.

---

123. Heredia y Sarmiento, *Sermon* (1807), 39.
124. González Díaz, *Sermon* (1808).
125. Ibid., 64; emphasis in original.
126. Ibid.

Conclusion

As this chapter has demonstrated, preachers in Mexico City in the final years of the colonial period, led by the discursive examples of Archbishops Núñez de Haro and Lizana, responded to shifting ambient political and social contexts in a variety of ways. Prominent among these responses were multiple gendered discourses, which preachers deployed to promote visions of masculinity and femininity they believed would help ensure social stability and a return to an order either seriously threatened or in imminent danger of collapse—a threat symbolized in the specter of the anti-religious campaigns of revolutionary France. In light of the influx of menacing ideas from "blasphemous" philosophers, pernicious trends of fashion, and the multiple political, economic, and social threats imperiling contemporary society, preachers perceived a need to reaffirm the social and cultural foundations they felt to be under attack and often employed gendered discourses as a privileged means of doing so. Unlike in the Baroque period or even during the age of the Bourbon Reforms, preachers now turned to gender not as an apt vehicle for the celebration of reigning power arrangements or as a way of modeling desired social reforms. Instead, men's and women's behavior and the proper understanding and embodiment of it among contemporaries were now outright, indispensable lynchpins for civilization's survival and telling barometers of its long-term viability. If divinely sanctioned conventions of gender were respected, so the logic went, civilized society would endure the various assaults besieging it; if not, then abject perdition was precipitously imminent.

In the gendered language they directed toward men, preachers called for bravery and virtue among their hearers, attributing historical and present social ills to excessive "luxury," which then led to "effeminization" of previously valiant warriors. With regard to women, preachers called their female congregants to a similar "manly" valor not normally associated with their "weaker sex." However, women's tendency to succumb to "pomp and vanity," along with the fateful social consequences that would ensue as a result, required that female members of the population be particularly vigilant. Women were to return to viewing themselves as "subjects" of their husbands and preferably would remain confined to the home, cultivating silence, contemplation, and obedience to patriarchal authority. In fact, as Archbishop Lizana mentioned in the second of his published sermons and another popular preacher noted elsewhere, if women, as members of the "devout sex," fulfilled the duties proper to their sex—praying, obeying, offering edifying moral examples, and fostering piety—they too, perhaps even more than their husbands and other male counterparts, could help to strengthen and stabilize society.[127] In a context in which church authorities perceived surrounding society as having erred in entertaining and adopting nefarious ideas and customs—which led inexorably to violations of gendered social norms and then, subsequently, to societal decay—those charged with articulating the Church's position in its public discourses began turning to women as key agents in the struggle against such threats. As the next chapters will show, the idea of women as members of the "devout sex" would come to take on increasing importance in the years to follow as preachers continued to seek ways to refashion and rearticulate the Church's vision for society in the context of events leading up to and following from the advent of Mexican independence.

127. Domínguez, *Discursos*, 61–62.

Chapter 5

Delicate Damsels and Perfidious Rebels

Preaching and Gender during the Insurgency

> "Pusillanimous because of their sex, tender in complexion . . . lacking courage or principles for militancy, there was no reason to fear them . . ."[1]

SPOKEN BY A ROYALIST preacher at the height of the decade of insurgency that would eventually usher in Mexico's independence, these potent words made reference to a convent of nuns—symbols for the preacher of a hidden strength to be found in the "weakness" normally associated with women. According to the sermonizer, these women's devotion to God was in fact what had made them strong and to be feared by the insurgents and therefore, despite their status as "tender damsels," they represented the key to confounding the rebellion. For the preacher, as for various others in this period, it was not just women's native "pusillanimousness" but also their inherent tendency toward piety and devoutness that pointed to a way of restoring lost social order and peace.

Ushered in by the public outcry of a parish priest and the popular uprising it inspired, the Wars of Independence in Mexico City were a time of profound crisis for the official Church—a historical moment in which a divided clergy, both insurgent and royalist, saw the need to return to their pulpits with renewed vigor to defend their perceived interests. In the case of the high clergy, sermons, pastoral letters, decrees, and other documents continued to provide a means of shaping official Church positions on unfolding events even while also seeking to quell internal divisions. Though

---

1. San Bartolomé, *El liberalismo*, 8–9.

often focused, as in the preceding decade, on women and gender roles, these official discourses also proved distinct in their often-striking political content and commentary. However, if we look more closely, both telling continuities and important changes emerge in the ways that gendered conventions were used. This chapter studies the use of gender in the new discourses of the era of the insurgency, up to Mexican independence in 1821, and suggests that an important difference from earlier iterations emerged in the increased emphasis starting to be placed on the salvific role of women's piety. As in the case of the sermon mentioned above, women's "pusillanimousness" in this period was gradually turning from a behavioral liability into a devotional asset—a foundational cornerstone for the official Church's discursive strategy during the rebellion and beyond.

Mexico City and Its High Clergy, 1808–1810

Amid the already tense climate of the news of Napoleon's invasion of Spain earlier in the year, in the early hours of September 16, 1808 a coup d'état in Mexico City, improvised with the support of Archbishop Lizana, the high court (*Audiencia*), and the merchant guild, deposed the reigning viceroy.[2] Quickly installing a pliable replacement, this alliance among the mostly peninsular high clergy and viceregal authorities saw to the swift repression of recent creole overtures toward increased local sovereignty for New Spain in the absence of the ruling authority of Ferdinand VII.[3] As David

---

2. Setting a precedent for future political violence, the coup set the stage for the years of insurrection and political instability ahead. For studies that examine aspects of the coup and the larger crisis of 1808, see Rodríguez O., "New Spain"; Elliott, *Empires*, 377; Brading, *First America*, chapter 25; Brading, "La ideología," 369; Villoro, "La revolución."

3. See Ávila, "La crisis," 211–12; Guerra, "La ruptura"; Archer, ed., *Birth of Modern Mexico*, 17–20; Hamill, "Vencer." As Ávila points out, it was not only the fact of the French invasion that provoked a crisis throughout the Hispanic world, including in New Spain, but also what he calls the "irruption of temporality" into politics—the realization that political regimes in fact were not atemporal or permanent but depended on the action of individuals instead of divine sanction—that proved significant. As Guerra also emphasizes—against traditional teleological readings of Latin American independence movements—this rupture from previous understandings of the nature of politics was highly significant in that it left contemporaries with many doubts, uncertainties, and anxieties and, therefore, without a clear sense of how to proceed. Instead of moving decisively and inexorably toward their respective declarations of independence, therefore, Guerra argues that actors in various regions only gradually came together around the "pleiad of dispersed sovereignties" that eventually coalesced into the independent nations of Latin America.

Brading explains, although this suppression of creole interests brought a temporary peace, the years between the coup and Miguel Hidalgo's rebellion witnessed an increasing confidence among many creoles that change would soon come.[4] Possibly seeking to soften the repression and forestall this eventuality, the central *junta* in Spain named Lizana viceroy, investing the archbishop with a new, political authority in addition to his ongoing spiritual duties.[5]

Archbishop Lizana and the Political Context

During his tenure as "archbishop viceroy," Lizana published several dozen decrees in which he passed on instructions and communiqués from Europe and touched on various political and financial matters, including his recommendation that only peninsular Spaniards be approved for high offices and his swift rebuke of a priest who had preached publicly against the Crown.[6] As Brian Connaughton notes, the situation facing the Church itself following the events of 1808 and, subsequently, 1810, was also one of internal divisions and disputes about the most proper way forward.[7] No clear, universal consensus emerged among ecclesiastics and so the Church, along with society, entered into a period of crisis regarding its public posture.[8] Accordingly, despite his political duties—or perhaps because of them, in light of the reigning political instability and uncertainty—Lizana did not abandon his earlier campaign to feminize the anti-religious excesses of revolutionary France by criticizing the frenchified behavior and social

---

4. Brading, *First America*, 562.

5. Lizana was ultimately deposed in May of 1810, leaving the *Audiencia* in control of the viceregal government and thus able to continue repressing proponents of the creole position. Accordingly, as eventually occurred in the insurrection lead by the parish priest Miguel Hidalgo y Costilla, representatives of the creole position realized that legal channels would no longer function as means by which to achieve reform. Instead, alliances with members of the working classes and Indians, along with acts of collective violence, would ultimately be necessary in order to effect necessary political changes. See Brading, *First America*, 562; Schwaller, "Episcopal Succession"; Villoro, "La revolución," 503–4.

6. Brading, *The First America*, 562. For examples of Lizana's writings as archbishop-viceroy see the following: AGN, GD 11 Bandos. Fecha: 1809. Vol. 25, exp. 33, fs. 70; AGN, GD 11 Bandos. Fecha: 1809. Vol. 25, exp. 34, fs. 71; AGN, GD 11 Bandos. Fecha: 1809. Vol. 25, exp. 35, fs. 72; AGN, GD 11 Bandos. Fecha: 1809. Vol. 25, exp. 36, fs. 73; AGN, GD 11 Bandos. Fecha 1809. Vol. 25, exp. 38, fs. 75; AGN, GD 11 Bandos. Fecha: 1809. Vol. 25, exp. 31, fs. 67; AGN GD 11 Bandos. Fecha: 1809. Vol. 25, exp. 32, fs. 69.

7. Connaughton, " Mudanzas," 252–53.

8. Ibid., 253.

customs of New Spanish women. On the contrary, underlining once more the connections he made between gendered conventions, politics, and the Church, the archbishop-viceroy made clear that right behavior among men and women remained of the highest essence in what was, for all of New Spain, a decisive hour.⁹

Moreover, this continued affirmation of careful vigilance over men's and women's behavior occurred within a context of profound crisis for Mexico City itself. Progressively impoverished and indebted over the course of the developing events, the city's residents, including the high clergy, faced an increasingly chaotic civic reality—one which both likely contributed to the Church's sense of alarm and also eventually helped to diminish popular support for Spanish rule.¹⁰ As Timothy E. Anna has demonstrated, living conditions in the city deteriorated significantly during this period: "Throughout the War of Independence vital city services were abandoned or left undone as thousands died in the plagues of 1813, 1814 and 1821, drainage ditches and sewers backed up into homes and convents, packs of wild dogs roamed city streets unchecked, parks and highways deteriorated, crimes increased, market cleanliness declined, [and] medical and educational services were cut[.]"¹¹

Renewed Emphasis on Gender

Amid these harsh circumstances, Lizana and other clergymen set out with all the more determination to enforce religious obedience and proper behavior. Returning to the comportment and morality of contemporary women, for example, in an 1810 decree Lizana called faithful subjects to repentance and proper devotion to Christ in the face of various offenses.¹² Summoning them to the "defense of religion and of the *patria*," the archbishop-viceroy recommended devotion to Christ in the sacrament of the Eucharist as the most propitious way forward:

> Adore him whom the French blaspheme: restore to him with contrite and humbled hearts the sovereign cult, which those

---

9. As Ibarra notes in recent studies of Lizana, the archbishop's actions during this period in favor of the Church and of preserving Spain's dominion were, in contrast to some elements of the traditional historiography, motivated less by fear or weakness than a strategy of considered prudence amid the challenges of the moment. See Ibarra, "De tareas"; Ibarra, "La crisis."

10. Anna, "Finances."

11. Ibid., 74.

12. AGN GD 11 Bandos. Fecha: Abril 12 1810. Vol. 25, exp. 70, fs. 164.

perverse traitors are attempting to seize from him. Prove through your modesty of dress and behavior that you are disciples of the Crucified and not of the fashions and shamelessness of the incredulous philosophers of this age of depravity, whose doctrine you should detest, and whose domination you should loathe. Honor, my children, our immaculate religion with your composure and moderation of dress and manners; we beg this of all for the sake of Jesus Christ, and very particularly of women, to whom already on another occasion we have made the most paternal of warnings about this point in one of our pastorals.[13]

As in his sermons and pastoral letters, once again Lizana, as viceroy, singled out women as "very particularly" responsible for New Spain's moral well being. Similarly, he did so in another document from around the same time, in this case directed to the faithful on the subject of observance of Lent.[14] Among the various offensive customs prohibited during the holy season, Lizana singled out once more those women who "present themselves daringly with indecency and provocative luxury" in churches.[15] For Lizana, this sort of disobedience would surely guarantee the ruin of all; however, women's well-ordered devotion and right behavior could well stay God's righteous anger and secure peace and prosperity once more.

As the year 1810 progressed, Lizana was well aware of the precariousness of Spanish control over America.[16] The situation was delicate and therefore redoubled efforts toward moral rectitude would be necessary on the part of all the faithful, most especially women. In an environment in which lampoons and anonymous broadsides were proliferating against the ruling viceregal regime, priests received instructions to be vigilant against edicts or writings promoting revolutionary violence.[17] As another high-church functionary wrote in a circular letter from April of 1810, the mercies of heaven must have been at work in providing guidance and reassurance despite the many challenges facing the Church.[18] Significantly, the official characterized this divine consolation and assistance as a heavenly affirmation of recent improved behavior on the part of women. Confirming once more that many priests did indeed link women's behavior to the state of current political fortunes, the official wrote that, "without doubt [because

13. There is no pagination within this document.
14. Lizana y Beaumont, *Carta pastoral* (1809).
15. Ibid., 25.
16. Brading, *First America*, 562.
17. Archer, ed., *Birth of Modern Mexico*, 21–22.
18. Sainz de Alfaro y Beaumont, *Circular*.

of] women's devotion as well as the modesty of the dresses with which they have presented themselves in church and their frequent attendance at the most holy sacrament of the altar in this holy week . . . the sacramented Lord has desired to manifest to us his mercies[.]"[19]

Also continuing to refer to female saints and their relevance for contemporary believers through their piety, preachers in the months of 1810 prior to September called on their congregations to renew their devotion and religious observance in hopes of stemming the tide of divine wrath that appeared ready to engulf them. For example, in three different published sermons from those months, preachers highlighted the powerful advocacy of the Virgin of los Remedios and challenged their audiences to live up to her singular example. On July 15 the Dominican creole Luis Carrasco y Enciso praised devotion to Remedios as part of a three-day observance of prayers and supplications for "the triumphs of religion and the fatherland."[20] Invoking the "avenging fire of charity" as part of the title of his sermon, Carrasco y Enciso called down God's ire upon the enemies of Spain—gendered as female in the image of Christ's bride: "Pour out, pour out Lord your wrath, over those who have spilled the blood of Spaniards! May those who have dishonored your bride be erased from the book of life, and never written in the book of the just. May their sight be obscured . . . may their backs be stooped."[21] Three days later the Oratorian creole Juan Bautista Díaz Calvillo expressed similar sentiments.[22] God had grown tired of the lax and scandalous customs of the populace of New Spain, but it was not too late. Díaz Calvillo commended his audience for the forty-eight days of prayer to the Virgin and penitence which they had already undertaken and called for continued vigilance in order to avoid future calamities.[23]

Women especially, as seen in earlier sermons, were to remain particularly vigilant lest their misbehavior and scandalous habits hasten societal downfall, as had already occurred in France. As Díaz Calvillo put it: "To you particularly, ladies, who forget so quickly the repeated entreaties we preachers make to you concerning modesty, for the sake of Jesus and for the love of Mary his worthy mother I beg you to reform your indecency of dress. The sins elicited through these indiscretions are numberless and many are the souls that have been lost through this profanity[.]"[24] Absent reform of these

19. Ibid., 8–9.
20. Carrasco y Enciso, *Sermon* (1810).
21. Ibid., 21–22.
22. Díaz Calvillo, *Sermon* (1810).
23. Ibid., 7.
24. Ibid., 27.

customs, Díaz Calvillo reminded women that, as in France, they too would succumb inexorably to atheism, bringing with them all of their contemporaries.[25] Worse still, if this were permitted to occur in New Spain the very existence of the Church itself would be placed in grave jeopardy:

> You will disgrace Jesus Christ and blaspheme his holy and dignified Mother . . . you will become atheists . . . [However, may] hardships and adversities rain down upon us, may pestilence and hunger come, may water be lacking, may everything including our own lives end, before we see atheism and license come to reign . . . What would become of us then? It can already be said that the Church is reduced solely to the dominions of the Catholic king; and if the faith is uprooted even from them, it will remain hardly anywhere on earth."[26]

Responsible, therefore, for either the heroic salvation or abject downfall of their entire civilization, the role of women amid the current crises was to be a definitive one. As another sermon—given on August 2nd by the peninsular Augustinian friar Bernardo Antonio González Díaz—also made clear, women, insofar as they followed the example of the Virgin, could intervene powerfully on behalf of the cause of the faith.[27] Equating the Virgin with "a formidable army ready for battle," González Díaz emphasized that she was the true "strong woman" of Scripture.[28] Like other holy women in the past such as Deborah, Judith, Esther and Jael, the Virgin and, by implication, contemporary women who followed her example of virtue and right behavior, were the "valorous," "intrepid," and "strong" women whose memory would merit perpetual remembrance.[29]

Little more than a month before the outbreak of Hidalgo's rebellion, it is instructive that one of the final official Church statements prior to September 16th would conclude with an invocation of the Virgin and of the potential of contemporary women to redeem society by following in her footsteps. Evincing the ongoing evolution of the Church's use of various earlier tropes of masculinity and femininity, now that the immense gravity of the surrounding situation had become clearer, prelates were beginning to append to the blanket condemnations of women's behavior of earlier years what amounted to the beginnings of a path to redemption, both for women and for society in general. Though they had sinned in particularly egregious

25. Ibid., 27–28
26. Ibid., 28.
27. González Díaz, *Sermon* (1810).
28. Ibid., 3.
29. Ibid., 6.

ways and committed various excesses due to the "weakness of their sex," women also, as a result of what would come to be increasingly highlighted as their pious tendencies, had the potential to make amends for past misdeeds and steer the course of events, both personal and social, back onto the path of the divine will. Although the Church's official public position would continue to develop during the years leading to independence and would remain often condemnatory toward women during the insurgency, it was this strong belief in the importance of women's piety and right behavior in connection with devotion to the Virgin and other saints that would prove particularly significant as a foundational element of the Church's ongoing public discourses in subsequent decades.

Initial Responses to the Insurgency

Calling out to his parishioners from the steps of his church in the small town of Dolores on the night of September 15, 1810, the parish priest Miguel Hidalgo summoned them to battle against foreign domination under the standard of the Virgin of Guadalupe.[30] Word of Hidalgo's rebellion quickly spread and soon he was joined by a large mass of Indians, *castas*, workers, artisans, and miners, all united by the desire to "expel the Europeans and recover the rights of 'the Mexican nation', and thus end the cruel tyranny of 300 years."[31] Though Hidalgo and a significant number of other priests eventually joined or played a role in leading the rebellion, in Mexico City ecclesiastical authorities reacted with horror and swift condemnation at the news of the unfolding events.[32] Just a few days after the start of the revolt,

---

30. Brading, *Church and State*, chapter 12; Brading, *First America*, 562. For an account of recent trends in the historiography of the insurgency, see Ávila, "Interpretaciones." As Ávila points out, recent historiography has moved beyond the notion that Enlightenment liberalism was the primary source of the independence movement and now takes into account the significance of Catholic traditions, juridical knowledge, and historic notions of constitutionalism. Likewise, there were surprising apparent contradictions present in the intellectual positions of representatives of both the royalist and insurgent sides. For example, the creole royalist preacher José Mariano Berístain envisioned a future for New Spain as a chosen land for Catholicism while José María Morelos expressed a near-medieval vision of society in some of his writings. For specific studies of Hidalgo and his rebellion, see: Terán and Páez, ed., *Miguel Hidalgo*; Herrera Peña, *Hidalgo*; Hamill, *Hidalgo*; Herrejón Peredo, *Hidalgo*.

31. Brading, *First America*, 562.

32. For the question of clerical participation in the insurgency, see Taylor, *Magistrates*, 453–72; Brading, *Church and State*, 239–49; Connaughton, " Mudanzas," 254–60; Victoria Moreno, "La provincia." Regarding clerical involvement, Taylor offers the following conclusions: priests participated in modest numbers—generally smaller

on September 24th the bishop-elect of Valladolid (Morelia), Manuel Abad y Queipo, published a declaration of excommunication against Hidalgo, which was soon affirmed, as well as extended to any who disputed it, by Archbishop Lizana on October 11th.[33]

Lizana Responds

Meanwhile, Lizana himself published an exhortation on September 24th as well, declaring the "martyrdom that oppresses me upon hearing that your brothers are preparing their swift feet . . . in order to spill your blood, not knowing the ruin into which they are heading because they do not follow the paths of peace."[34] Referring directly to the events of just a few days before in Dolores, Lizana offered the following words of warning to his flock:

> I cannot neglect to warn you of the risk you run for your souls, and the ruin which threatens your persons, if you do not shut your ears to the tumultuous voice, which has raised itself up in these days in the towns of Dolores and San Miguel el Grande, and has reached to the city of Querétaro. Some unruly persons, among whom I hear with pain in my soul the name of a priest worthy of pity . . . appear to be the principal authors of the rebelliousness.[35]

---

than some secular scholars have imagined and larger than church officials did; priest insurgents were not usually young radicals in line with French or British liberal ideals but instead "[m]ore, in fact, were men of modest learning in mid-career who had not been conspicuous in the politics of self-promotion or protest before 1810 and seem to have been dedicated pastors" (*Magistrates*, 455); most insurgent priests were not dissolute and, in terms of their loyalties, often remained neutral, not acting until there occurred "a sense of a traditional and proper role in public life being wrenched from them, a sense that order and the conditions for salvation were disappearing" (ibid., 459). According to Ibarra, there is evidence that some cathedral chapter members in Mexico City and other dioceses did support independence, though not as an identifiable group. Rather, as Victoria Moreno points out, ecclesiastics evolved politically in a variety of ways in light of their own loyalties along with the changing surrounding circumstances. For some—especially bishops—this meant invoking just war theology as a justification for inciting priests and the faithful to defend the monarchy.

33. AGN GD 11 Bandos. Fecha: Octubre 11 de 1810. Vol. 25, exp. 115, fs. 318. For an account of the royalist ideological campaign in Mexico City following Hidalgo's rebellion and the Church's role in it, see Herrero Bervera, *Revuelta*, 222–28.

34. Lizana y Beaumont, *Exhortación* (1810), 1.

35. Ibid., 2.

Addressing Hidalgo directly, Lizana asked how the priest could have dared commit so bold and egregious a betrayal of his divine calling:

> Tell me, poor one, deceived by the malignant spirit, you who shone before as a bright star on account of your knowledge, how is it that you have fallen like another Lucifer by your sinful pride? Miserable one! Do you not know that my angels (thus Scripture refers to priests) go behind you like that multitude which seized the head angel of the apostates in heaven: all will fight with the purpose of the ecclesiastical militia, and your name shall never again be heard in this divine kingdom, except as the subject of eternal anathemas.[36]

According to Lizana, the key to victory over Hidalgo's rebelliousness was once again a gendered solution—namely, the reaffirmation of the need for all believers to fight as part of the "ecclesiastical militia."[37] In other words, like the other militant "battles" to which Lizana and other clerics had called the faithful in the previous decade, the need for "manly" and courageous responses to ongoing displays of pridefulness and disorder would continue, albeit now with much greater intensity.[38] Hinting at how best to engage in this "combat"—and in wake of a special mass held in the cathedral on November 1st attended by thousands of Mexico City residents—in another decree dated November 3rd Lizana called for renewed devotion to the Virgin of Remedios and to the sacraments as means of regaining God's favor.[39] Directing his comments to "valorous Mexicans," he called upon his flock to unite with the Virgin "to take away sins." If all returned to the sacraments and performed the devotions of a special mission program, which included a series of talks and devotional exercises to be held before the image of Remedios, there would be nothing to fear: all enemies would be swiftly defeated and past tranquility and peace would return to Mexico.[40]

---

36. Ibid., 3.

37. For an account of how Lizana and other bishops adopted militaristic standpoints in their discourses, often grounding them in traditional theological theory of just war, see Ibarra, "Los problemas," 176.

38. Lizana confirmed this assessment in another letter, from October 18th, in which he disputed many of the claims made by Hidalgo and reaffirmed his call to obedience of the Church hierarchy. See Lizana y Beaumont, *Nos* (1810).

39. Herrero Bervera, *Revuelta*, 227. See also Lizana y Beaumont, *Nos* (1810).

40. Lizana y Beaumont, *Nos* (1810).

Other Clerical Responses

Though Lizana did not live long after the publication of this last decree, his response to the events of 1810, including condemnation of the disobedience and betrayal of Hidalgo and gendered recommendations of a "valorous" return to piety, also characterized the positions taken by other members of the high clergy in Mexico City throughout most of the remaining years prior to independence.[41] As Eric Van Young points out regarding popular culture in this period, so too within elite clerical culture in Mexico City in the decade of the insurgency, perceived threats to the reigning system called for decisive public, discursive responses on the part of the clergy.[42] In Van Young's words, "what [was] at stake [was] the defense or reequilibration of . . . a moral universe—of a cohesive . . . system of ideas for explaining authority [and] legitimacy[.]"[43] Though Van Young is referring primarily to peasant responses to insurgent movements, a similar dynamic is observable in the development of official church discourses—fashioned likewise to shore up the "coherence and legitimacy" of their own particular system of authority. For example, mourning Lizana's death, the Mexico City cathedral *cabildo* published a decree on March 28, 1811 in which it praised the late archbishop's virtues and echoed his words of condemnation for Hidalgo's movement.[44]

Repeating similar condemnations later that year in September, the *cabildo* also addressed questions that had begun to arise over ecclesiastical immunity.[45] Specifically, despite earlier protests on the part of the Church over attempts by the Crown to chip away at clerical immunity to civil legal authority, in light of Hidalgo's movement, the *cabildo* expressed a position strongly in favor of submitting priests to the jurisdiction of the law.[46] Like Lizana, the *cabildo* also recommended a return to piety and proper comportment in church as especially crucial to the Church's efforts to counter the evils unleashed by Hidalgo's movement.[47] According to the *cabildo*'s decree, "contempt" and "irreverence" on the part of the faithful in church "irritated" God and therefore the current "calamities" were punishments sent

---

41. Lizana died on March 6, 1811. See Schwaller, "Episcopal Succession," 210; *Nos el Presidente* (1811). For studies of clerical discourses—including those of insurgent clergy—during the insurgency see Herrejón Peredo, *Del sermón*, chapter 10; Villoro, *El proceso*.

42. Van Young, *Other Rebellion*.

43. Ibid., 16.

44. *Nos el Presidente* (1811), 9–10.

45. *Carta pastoral*, (1811).

46. Ibid., 5.

47. *Nos el Presidente* (1811).

"in revenge" for such sinfulness.[48] Those who entered churches in particularly egregious ways—mostly women—"indecent in their mode of dress, nakedness, or immodesty of actions," would therefore suffer the "anathema of the avenging blood of Jesus Christ."[49]

Gender and Anti-insurgent Sermons

As Carlos Herrejón Peredo and Brian Connaughton explain in recent studies of sermons from this period, preachers too echoed the condemnatory themes heralded by Lizana and ecclesiastical leadership.[50] Both authors note the predominance during these years of what Connaughton labels "the language of passions"—a reference to the considerable emotional stake many priests felt in the progress and outcome of the war and its implications for the Church, along with ongoing internal divisions within the institution.[51] Matthew O'Hara has also recently suggested intriguing connections between the emotions called forth by and reflected in sermons—especially, given the uncertainties and various calamities of this period, anxiety—and surrounding historical developments.[52] As Herrejón Peredo likewise explains, many anti-insurgent sermons were offered in the form of diatribe, where political questions were given special prominenece—for example, in the case of one particularly impassioned preacher, the sermon, given outdoors and later repeated for the viceroy, high court and other authorities, lasted no fewer than three hours.[53] As Alfredo Ávila has also pointed out, discourses from both sides depended for their efficacy less on their own internal logic than on the persuasive, visceral ways in which they were formulated and articulated—in the case of royalist sermons, for instance, through the conventions of gender studied in this chapter.[54] For example, given in the Convento Grande de San Francisco on September 28, 1811, a sermon by the royalist creole priest José Mariano Beristáin de Souza attempted to reclaim devotion to the Virgin of

48. Ibid..

49. Ibid..

50. Herrejón Peredo, *Del sermón*; Connaughton, "Politización." Both Herrejón Peredo and Connaughton follow the development of sermons over the course of the insurgency, noting the continuing presence of anti-Napoleonic discourses, the development of a providential vision of Mexican identity, negotiation of divisions among members of the clergy, and ongoing moral exhortation of audiences.

51. Connaughton, "Mudanzas," 255–60.

52. O'Hara, "Visions."

53. Herrejón Peredo, *Del sermón*, 288–307.

54. Ávila, "Interpretaciones," 29–30; Herrejón Peredo, *Del sermón*, 287.

Guadalupe for the royalist side.⁵⁵ According to Beristáin, the invocation of the Virgin of Guadalupe by the rebels constituted an insult to Mary herself, as her apparition "authorizes [the current] order and the subordination of the Indians to Catholic Spain."⁵⁶ To restore order, Beristáin recommended a return to piety and proper devotion, expressed through "the fundamental precepts of the law of God, which are charity and love."⁵⁷

Gendered Piety and Social Order

Proper social order was also of singular importance for the creole Oratorian Juan Bautista Díaz Calvillo, who dedicated a sermon in the Mexico City cathedral to the Virgin of Remedios on October 30, 1811, in commemoration of the victory of royalist forces over rebel forces at Monte de las Cruces.⁵⁸ Praising what he called the exceptional courage of the royalist troops, Díaz Calvillo commended the "virtuous Spanish heroes" who "neither grew intimidated at the sight of danger, nor fled from the presence of a formidable army, nor vacillated in the midst of fierce and obstinate combat, nor fainted out of hunger or fatigue[.]"⁵⁹ Along with this praise for the troops' mascu-

---

55. For studies of Beristáin, see Ávila, "La crisis"; Torres Puga, "Beristáin"; Zayas de Lille, "Los sermones." As these authors point out, the traditional historiographical portrayal of Beristáin and other like-minded creoles as traitors to creole nationalism due to their support for the royalist cause is in need of updating. Beristáin and other creole royalist preachers feared French political and cultural influences, but, instead of seeking the separation of New Spain from the embattled *patria*, expressed their own understanding of creole identity, along with confidence in the divine, providential plan which, for them, guided history and therefore would in due time bring about the defeat of Napoleon and the restoration of the monarchy. Also significant for Beristáin and others was the consummation of an earlier strain of ecclesiastical discourses, discussed in chapter 2, in which Mexico, especially because of the singular privilege of the apparition of the Virgin of Guadalupe, was viewed as the site of the New Jerusalem prophesied in the biblical book of Revelation. According to this narrative, it was to Mexico that the pope and Spain's monarchs would ultimately alight following the defeat of Napoleon's forces. However, the advent of Hidalgo's rebellion threatened to dash Beristáin's and others' hopes for such an eventuality and therefore provoked his and other preachers' visceral sense of disappointment and hostility toward the insurgency.

56. For a study of some of the continuities and changes in Guadalupan sermons from the late colonial period through the wars of independence, see Traslosheros Hernández, "Santa María." For an analysis of how both royalist and insurgent leaders shared common cultural understandings from which they devised alternate solutions to the crisis at hand, see Ávila, "La crisis," 218–21.

57. Beristáin, *Declamacion*, 24.

58. Díaz Calvillo, *Sermon* (1811).

59. Ibid., 8–9.

line, militaristic bravery, Díaz Calvillo also celebrated the courage of the people of Mexico City—gendered in his account as female (*la feliz y dichosa México*)—who impeded the rebels' progress.[60] Though referring to military prowess as well, Díaz Calvillo seemed to favor the prayers and devotion of Mexico City's residents as particularly instrumental in achieving the desired outcome. For example, Díaz Calvillo described how the Virgin, "pestered" (*importunada*) by the "fervent sighs" of the faithful and honored by the devotion her image had received, decided to intervene on behalf of restoring order and tranquility.[61]

One concrete example of how the power especially of women's devotion manifested itself around the same time as Díaz Calvillo's sermon emerges in the story of an enthusiastic female devotée of the Virgin of Remedios, doña Ana María de Yraeta, a peninsular Spaniard and widow of a late high court official.[62] As William Taylor has demonstrated, Yraeta campaigned actively in early 1811 on behalf of devotion to Remedios, petitioning the city government that the Virgin under this particular advocation be declared "la Generala"—that is, the supreme commander of royal forces in their efforts to quell the rebellion. Though her request was eventually denied, Yraeta remained indefatigable in her determination to promote the Virgin in this manner, submitting another petition in 1818, and continuing to promote and engage in devotion to Remedios even after the ultimate defeat of the devotion's erstwhile royalist beneficaries in 1821.[63]

Thus, for Díaz Calvillo and other royalist preachers—as in some earlier sermons from before the rebellion but now with even greater urgency—it was crucial to commend the cultivation of masculine, militaristic virtues in their listeners while at the same time increasingly arguing that the most appropriate means of embodying such virtues—especially for women like doña Ana María Yraeta, but for men as well—was through renewed piety and moral virtue. This combined vision of militarized masculinity and devout femininity found ideal expression for Díaz Calvillo in the image of Remedios, the "strong woman" whom he credited with the victory his sermon commemorated. For him, Mary was the one who, "not disdaining to take on personally the role of army general," ultimately led the royalist forces to victory.[64] In contrast, as he revealed in a supplementary document, published with his sermon, on the history of local devotion to Remedios between

60. Ibid., 8.
61. Ibid., 43.
62. See Taylor, "La Virgen."
63. Ibid., 233–34.
64. Díaz Calvillo, *Sermon* (1811), 31–34.

1808 and 1812, Díaz Calvillo insisted that the gendered social order had deteriorated among rebel forces, with women, "in order to free themselves from all burdens, [throwing] their own most tender children, exhausted by hunger, to the ground," in order to follow insurgent leaders.[65]

Contemporary evidence confirms that women were recruited by insurgent leaders and encouraged to fight.[66] For Díaz Calvillo, such flagrant violations of gendered norms had already yielded social chaos in France and were now well on their way to infiltrating Mexican society as well. Therefore, only by promoting activities that encouraged women to continue assuming their assigned "burdens"—for example, the recent establishment of a *vela* to the Virgin of Remedios among members of "the devout sex," which he commended—would proper order be restored.[67] Reflecting a similar perspective on gendered roles, the peninsular priest Manuel Alcayde y Gil offered a sermon in the Mexico City cathedral toward the end of 1811 in which he expressed "horror" at the current state of social disorder and the need to implement a "reform of customs" in order to stay God's impending vengeance.[68] Otherwise, as had occurred in France, all the consolations and sacred rites of religion, as they had been known, would be replaced by "indecent songs" and the worship, as seen in Paris' Notre Dame Cathedral during the French Revolution, of an "infamous prostitute" dressed as the goddess of reason.[69]

Men, too, according to preachers, could stray from norms assigned to them, thereby jeopardizing the fate of their contemporaries—but the danger was particularly great for effeminate men. For example, in a sermon from 1813 the creole Diego Miguel Bringas y Encinas continued to warn of the dangers of "effeminate" men who exhibited "criminal indifference" to established laws and customs.[70] In contrast to this pernicious influence, Mexico City's residents, both male and female, had the duty to "disarm the omnipotent arm" of God's wrath with "humiliation and repentance"—a method he described as the most efficacious means for securing temporal peace and eternal happiness.[71] Likewise, according to a *cabildo* decree also from 1813, the custom of admitting "profane" and "effeminate" music into

65. Díaz Calvillo, *Noticias*, 189.

66. AGN, Operaciones de Guerra, vol. 406, fol. 195. See also Arrom, *Women*, 36.

67. For an extensive account by Díaz Calvillo of the foundation of this *vela*, see Díaz Calvillo, *Noticias*, 150–152.

68. Alcayde y Gil, *Oracion* (1812), 32.

69. White, *Roman Catholic Worship*, 53; Alcayde y Gil, *Oracion* (1812), 27.

70. Bringas y Encinas, *Sermón* (1813), 44.

71. Ibid.

church services was impeding "pure and pious movements of the human heart toward God" and instead reminded them of the latest dances and scenes from the theater.[72]

Specific Visions of Gender Roles

As in the case of references to women already mentioned, the message of many preachers for both men and women was twofold: first, strictly defined gender roles had to be followed lest social decay ensue; second, the surest means of recovering lost order and discipline was by returning to the exercise of piety and moral virtue. According to preachers, all "Spaniards," whether men or women, were called to defend valiantly the cause of their *patria*—now united into a single reign in both Spain and America by the Constitution of Cádiz 1812.[73] For example, the Dominican friar Juan González noted the recent bravery of contemporary women who, "forgetting their sex," joined with other citizens in calling for "revenge against the enemies of God and of Spain."[74] For some women this might have included actual combat but for all it would certainly have meant right devotion, as "the devout sex," to the "God of armies," who alone could restore order and grant peace.[75] According to this preacher, it was the "electric machine" (*máquina eléctrica*) of the combined love of God and fidelity to the king that would ultimately save the day and secure victory for Spain, both on the Iberian Peninsula and in America.[76]

Similarly, in another sermon from the same year, González emphasized how the example of the early Christian martyr Santa Inés ought to speak forcefully to all believers, whether men or women.[77] Unlike the sermon on Inés from the Baroque period examined in chapter 2, in this sermon Inés was not simply a heroic figure to behold with wonder but rather an example to be explicitly emulated.[78] For example, the "manly soul" which Inés displayed was not merely to be admired but imitated in specific ways.[79] Though the preacher noted that men should also follow Inés' example, he

72. *Nos el Presidente* (1813).

73. For studies of the significance of the Constitution of Cádiz in this context, see the following studies by Vázquez: "El liberalismo"; "De la crisis."

74. González, *Sermon* (1816), 35–36. The place of González's birth is not known.

75. Ibid., 38–39.

76. Ibid., 56–57.

77. González, *Sermon panegirico de Santa Ines*.

78. Ibid., 12–13.

79. Ibid., 24.

emphasized her special importance for women. Specifically, young women needed to follow her lead and abandon putatively enlightened "passions for dresses," "fallacious and artificial language," and "secret bonds" (*secretos lazos*).[80] Likewise, married women had to learn to "perfect themselves in their state," especially in light of the "many responsibilities" (*muchos cargos*) for which they would be held accountable by God.[81]

Another sermon that touched on similar themes, albeit in a significantly different way, merits extended consideration as an example of how the Mexico City high clergy's understanding and use of gendered language and ideas continued to develop over the course of the insurgency. Given in May, 1816 in the Convent of Santa Teresa, the sermon's author—the peninsular Carmelite friar José de San Bartolomé—entitled his reflections, significantly, *Liberalism and the Rebellion, Confounded by a Tender and Delicate Damsel*.[82] Opening with a strong affirmation of the role of women in defending the Church, San Bartolomé characterized the professing nuns he was addressing as "new soldiers" for the "celestial squadrons" of convent life.[83] However, San Bartolomé did not wish to address only nuns. Invoking the creation narratives of the biblical Book of Genesis, San Bartolomé reminded his audience that all women, the same as men, were "equally individuals of the human species" and that therefore they too "enter into the plan of religion."[84] Created from the biblical Adam's side rather than either his head or his feet, women were "neither slaves nor rulers of men, but intimate life companions [and] help[ers]."[85] However, because of sin, both men and women tended to forget each other's dignity; in the case of men, they often viewed women with disregard and saw them as all but useless; for women, their tendency was to "elevate themselves above men" in order to attempt to govern and command them, failing to remember that "their influence is only to help" or, at the most, "to make up for [men's] faults where they may be defective or lacking."[86]

Hinting at how some men had in fact recently proven both defective and lacking, San Bartolomé pointed to verbal and physical attacks against nuns witnessed in recent years and concluded that the nuns in truth constituted a reflection of the Church's triumph over social disorder and rebellion

80. Ibid., 32.
81. Ibid.
82. San Bartolomé, *El liberalismo*.
83. Ibid., 3–4.
84. Ibid., 4–5.
85. Ibid.
86. Ibid.

by means of their piety. Why else, the preacher wondered, would the attackers have felt compelled to attack women—who were "pusillanimous because of their sex" and therefore could not possibly represent a threat—if not because of the strength of their religious devotion? In truth, for San Bartolomé, such persons did in fact fear women, not because of their superior military strength but as a result of their faith in God and their loyalty to the *patria*—the twin, "most strong" columns, in his words, that would frustrate the realization of their perfidious schemes.[87] Also crucial for resisting such ideas, San Bartolomé mentioned the importance of the revival of religious life, both male and female, especially as reflected in the return of the Jesuit order to Mexico.[88] The restoration of proper religious devotion, as manifested in stronger, more abundant conventual life—rendered as a "tender damsel"—would secure both temporal and eternal salvation, and guarantee the downfall of "effeminate and seductive" values, along with the restitution of proper "Spanish character."[89] Thus, although related to earlier anti-insurgent gendered discourses, San Bartolomé's sermon signals the beginnings of something new. Still couched in gendered assumptions about female "weakness" and the need for men to avoid "effeminacy," what was nevertheless different about this sermon was its conviction that ultimate victory would come not through military might but, paradoxically, through the deceptive "pusillanimousness" of women's piety and devotion.

New Leadership, New Directions

Something of this emphasis on strength through piety also manifested itself in Mexico City's new archbishop-designate in this period, Antonio Bergosa y Jordán. Appointed to the office of archbishop in 1811, Bergosa y Jordán— the bishop of Oaxaca and a relatively moderate episcopal voice, who favored initiatives to abolish the Inquisition and approved of the Constitution of Cádiz—articulated his opposition to the insurgency in gendered terms

87. Ibid., 8–9.

88. Ibid., 22. The return of the Jesuits to Mexico occasioned a number of celebrations and printed commentaries. For example, see Castañiza González de Aguero, *Relación*; José Manuel Sartorio, Untitled document, 1822 (California State Library, Sutro Collection, PM 214). For a study of this development and its significance for religious devotions in independent Mexico see Correa Etchegaray, "El rescate." See also the following sermon given on the ocassion of the profession of two new Jesuits following the order's return to Mexico: Lerdo de Texada, *Discurso*. For other sermons in which the return of the Jesuits is invoked see Díaz Pérez y Calvillo, *Elogio*; Ruiz de Alarcón, *Sermon*.

89. San Bartolomé, *El liberalismo*, 25, 33–34.

similar to though at times more favorable toward women than those of his predecessor, Lizana.[90] For example, in a pastoral letter from June 1814, the archbishop compared the Church to an army always at watch against its enemies.[91] However, women were not to be discounted as part of this "army." Referring back to the heroic deeds of the biblical Maccabees, Bergosa y Jordán likened the Church's own struggles to theirs, highlighting "the purity of their consciences and customs, the efficacy of their prayers, and [their] indispensible observance of the precepts of the law"—virtues most ideally embodied, significantly, by the heroic women of the time.[92] According to Bergosa y Jordán, God himself had offered the women as models, demonstrating how all were to act under similar circumstances, such as those experienced by Mexico City's population in battling the insurgency. Again, as Bergosa y Jordán also emphasized in a sermon offered in the Mexico City cathedral in celebration of news of the return of Ferdinand VII to the throne in 1814—news he would soon welcome less enthusiastically once the restored king refused to accept his nomination as Mexico City's archbishop and ordered him to return to Oaxaca—devotion to the Virgin, especially under the title of the Immaculate Conception, provided a key for restoring lost order.[93] Calling her both "valorous" and "beautiful," Bergosa y Jordán praised the Virgin as another Judith who had triumphed against the sinful pride of France.[94] Although deceitful forces, including agents of France who employed "a herd of women, or better yet enchanting sirens of various nations" and other "monsters of irreligion," attacked the forces of the Crown, all had been restored to right (gendered) order through the Virgin's intercession.[95] Similarly, in New Spain the archbishop recommended that proper devotion to the Virgin and careful emulation of her both "valorous" and

90. For Bergosa y Jordán and his association with the Constitution of Cádiz and its criticisms of some ecclesiastical traditions, see Hamnett, "Antonio"; Connaughton, "Politización"; Connaughton, "Los lindes."

91. Bergosa y Jordán, *Nos* (1814).

92. Ibid., 9–10.

93. Bergosa y Jordán, *Sermon* (1814). See also Hamnett, "Antonio," 119, 125–26. Hamnett suggests that, despite Bergosa y Jordán's strong record of support for Ferdinand VII, royal officials in Madrid may have had concerns about the bishop's ideological purity, stemming from his support for the abolition of the Inquisition and his favorable attitude toward the Constitution of 1812—both of which Ferdinand VII annulled upon his return.

94. Bergosa y Jordán, *Sermon* (1814), 5.

95. Ibid., 20.

Delicate Damsels and Perfidious Rebels

"beautiful" virtues would secure the return of appropriate balance among "religion, king, and *patria*."[96]

Also celebrating the return of Ferdinand VII, other preachers praised the famed bravery of Spain's soldiers—the "sons of Iberia" and "strong and intrepid men" who had always come to the aid of Spain in time of need.[97] Numbering Ferdinand VII among such heroes, one preacher pointed out that one of the king's strongest virtues consisted of his devotion to the Eucharist. Against those the preacher labeled, in gendered terms, as "prostituted" and "seductress-like," the devotion of the king in the face of adversities, "before the throne of the sacramented Jesus"—in which he "paid tribute and pure homages from his soul" to the Eucharist and defended its proper cult—was without doubt the key to his ultimate restoration.[98]

Movement Toward Independence

Following Ferdinand VII's return in 1814 and the subsequent accession of a new archbishop and a new viceroy in Mexico City—Pedro de Fonte and Juan Ruiz de Apodaca, respectively—a redoubled campaign against the insurgency commenced.[99] First, offers of pardon were extended on behalf of the Church toward insurgents and, second, a fresh military campaign began, leaving only a few isolated remnants of rebellion.[100] However, although the popular insurgency was all but defeated, events soon transpired which would lead

96. Ibid., 34.

97. See the following: Carrasco y Enciso, *Oracion* (1815); Carrasco y Enciso, *Oración* (1814), 27–28; González Díaz, *Sermon* (1815), 6–7; Roxas y Andrade, *Sermon* (1815), 5.

98. Roxas y Andrade, *Sermon* (1815), 11.

99. See Lynch, *Latin America*, 127–32; Green, *Mexican Republic*, 78; Bravo Ugarte, *Diócesis*, 64; Pérez Memén, *El episcopado*, 173; Staples, *La iglesia*, 74; Schwaller, "Episcopal Succession," 210–211; Villoro, "La revolución," 515. Fonte did not remain in Mexico long, abandoning his see over objections to the coronation of Agustín Iturbide in 1823. Despite requests to do so, Fonte never returned to Mexico, though his resignation as archbishop was not accepted by the Holy See until 1837. Mexican Church leaders' opposition to the insurgency was also bolstered in this period by the papal encyclical *Etsi longissimo*, in which Pius VII counseled opposition to the rebellion along with loyalty to Ferdinand VII.

100. See AHAM, Base Colonial, Caja 166, exp. 46, fs. 2. Fondo: Episcopal, Sección: Secretaría Arzobispal, Serie: Edictos. Año: 1816. *Edicto pastoral del arzobispo Pedro de Fonte sobre la excomunión a los insurgentes*. In his edict, the archbishop affirms the ability of priests to absolve insurgents of their "past crimes," on the condition that they turn in any "sediciuos papers" that may be in their possession and denounce insurgent leaders.

eventually to Mexico's declaration of independence from Spain. First, resentment was growing among creole army officers against ongoing Spanish efforts to prevent them from assuming higher positions of leadership, while many soldiers had grown weary from the long anti-insurgent campaign. Then, in 1820 Ferdinand VII was forced by a rebellion in Spain once more to recognize the Constitution of Cádiz of 1812, including some provisions potentially threatening to Church wealth and privileges.[101] By 1820, therefore, the situation had become intolerable, such that many creoles, members of the high clergy, and army officers all were now disposed to a change in governance.[102] In response, creoles under the leadership of Agustín de Iturbide fashioned a three-part plan (*tres garantías*) for independence in which Catholicism was proclaimed as the state religion, the secular and regular clergy's traditional prominence and privileges were preserved, and monarchy was retained as the form of government.[103] Uniting the creole oligarchy, including the high clergy, Iturbide's plan succeeded and in a short time his army secured the loyalty of Mexico's principal cities and he entered peacefully into Mexico City on September 27, 1821, having secured independence in a short period of just seven months and at the cost of only 150 lives.[104]

The Church and the Consumation of Independence

Despite ten years of rebellion, however, Mexican independence represented a victory for the conservative forces—and the gendered arguments and visions they frequently articulated—that had originally opposed Hidalgo, Morelos, and the other insurgent leaders. Defending the Church against threats to its traditional privileges and the "contamination" of liberal philosophy, the mode of independence secured by Iturbide quickly won the approval and backing of the high clergy, threatened by declining revenues and reduced numbers of clerical personnel.[105] For example, in June of

101. See Connaughton, "Politización," 197–99.

102. For studies of the Church's involvement in moves toward independence, see Ibarra, *El clero*; del Arenal Fenochio, "El Plan"; del Valle Pavón, "El apoyo." According to Ibarra and del Arenal Fenochio, the Plan of Iguala was less conservative and reactionary than traditional histories have claimed, as it represented, at least initially, an effective means of providing for both social unity and continuity in the Church's traditional privileges. In her own study, del Valle Pavón demonstrates how members of the high clergy supported Iturbide both discursively and financially.

103. Bazant, "From Independence," 1; Vázquez, "De la crisis," 29–31; Villoro, "La revolución," 518–19.

104. Anna, "Agustín de Iturbide and the Process of Consensus," 188.

105. Bazant, "From Independence," 3; Villoro, "La revolución," 520.

1820 the creole priest José Miguel Guridi y Alcocer offered a sermon in the Mexico City cathedral parish *sagrario* in which he praised provisions from Iturbide's impending arrangement—most especially its guarantee of Catholicism as the official state religion of the new independent Mexican nation.[106] Likewise, on September 28, 1821—the day immediately following Iturbide's triumphal arrival in Mexico City—the creole priest José Manuel Sartorio offered a sermon in the cathedral in which he celebrated Mexico's newly confirmed independence as the work of God.[107] Although it had been long in coming, independence was to be attributed to the (masculine) "God of armies," who had placed his omnipotent hand upon the nascent Mexican state.[108] Above all, however, the new regime's preservation of the traditions and preeminence of the Church was what most merited loyalty to it on the part of believers, a sentiment echoed a year later in a sermon offered at the sanctuary of the Virgin of Guadalupe in which the preacher, the creole priest José Julio García de Torres, associated the downfall of Spain with its renunciation of right religious belief and practices.[109] Outlining a position that would appear regularly in the discourses of the high clergy in subsequent decades, García de Torres pointed to the importance of the Catholic religion and its ministers as foundational for society.[110]

Similar sentiments found echo in other sermons, as in one also given in 1821 in which the Franciscan friar José María de Jesús Belaunzaran cited the biblical figures Moses and Solomon, invoking the latter in comparison to the Mexican empire's "most serene leader" and outlining the Church's most essential work as that of defending "the most holy rights of the religion of Jesus Christ" and the preservation of its societal prominence.[111] In pursuit of his goals, Iturbide soon had himself crowned emperor of Mexico on July 21, 1822, an occasion which elicited great pomp and solemnity and for which the bishop of Puebla, Antonio Joaquín Pérez Martínez offered the official sermon in Mexico City's cathedral.[112] Calling Iturbide a "gift from the Omnipotent," Pérez Martínez affirmed the appropriateness of his coronation and offered thanks that the new emperor's reign promised security and benefits for the Church and its ministers, although the relationship of

106. Guridi y Alcocer, *Exortacion* (1820), 2–3.
107. Sartorio, *Gozo*.
108. Ibid., 4.
109. See ibid., 9–10; García de Torres, *Sermon* (1821), 11–12.
110. García de Torres, *Sermon* (1821), 13–14.
111. Belaunzaran, *Discurso panegirico*, 4. Belaunzaran's place of birth is not known.
112. For studies of Iturbide's empire, see Landavazo and Sánchez Andrés, "La opción"; Bazant, "From Independence," 4–5. See also Pérez Martínez, *Sermon*.

the Church with Iturbide was also characterized by some conflicts[113]—for example, regarding the status of the *patronato real*, which had previously governed the filling of vacant episcopacies, among other matters.[114]

Later that same year, just weeks before the January 1, 1823 start to the process, led by Antonio López de Santa Anna, that would usher in the downfall of Iturbide's regime, another preacher offered what was to be the final sermon preserved in printed from the period of Mexico's first empire.[115] Calling Iturbide a (masculine) "religious hero," the preacher celebrated the emperor's defense of religion and the Church—attributes which would assure the stability of his reign since religion constituted the foundation for any society's stability and success, without which it would inevitably come undone.[116] Thankfully, however, Mexico's fate was secure since, in the preacher's words, "we live, by the grace of God, in the most Catholic country in the world"—a nation saved from the disgrace of the apostasy of the "old continent" but nevertheless still in need of "vigilant sentinels" to ward off the attacks of "peccaries" in the form of "venomous foreign books" and "national writers," the "flowers of whose eloquence," hid the "asp of unbelief."[117] Iturbide's secure reign and the (gendered) religious heroism he inspired would ensure tranquility and prosperity for the Church's mission and confirm its privileged status as one of the central pillars of the nascent Mexican empire.

---

113. See Pérez Martínez, *Sermon*, 10–11. See also García Ugarte, "Provisión"; Connaughton, "República; Connaughton, "Una república"; Connaughton, "El ocaso." As García Ugarte points out, the question of the continuance of the *patronato real* (in which the papacy had conceded to the monarchs of Spain the privilege of appointing bishops in America) in the post-independence period was a contested one. Against the wishes of Iturbide's government, the then-archbishop of Mexico Pedro José de Fonte concluded that in fact the *patronato* had ended with the advent of Mexico's independence from Spanish monarchical rule. Nevertheless, as Brian Connaughton has pointed out, the *patronato* did not consist just of civil nominations for Church positions but a number of other issues, including the nature of the Church itself and its governance—something that could, for some at least, even be conceived in federalist terms.

114. See also Costeloe, *Church and State*; Ampudia, *La Iglesia*, 241–42; Ramos, "Documentos," 18–20; Green, *Mexican Republic*, 79–80, 178–80; Morales, *Clero*, 99–124; Staples, *La Iglesia*, 37–54.

115. For accounts of the unraveling of Iturbide's empire, see Rodríguez O., "Struggle"; Bazant, "From Independence," 5–6; Villoro, "La revolución," 523. See also de la Bárcena, *Sermon*.

116. de la Bárcena, *Sermon*, 9. For studies of this preacher, Manuel de la Bárcena, see Connaughton, *Dimensiones*; Ávila, "El cristiano."

117. de la Bárcena, *Sermón*, 10.

Conclusion

Despite Mexico's "most Catholic" status, however, the attacks of various "peccaries" and "asps" would prove more difficult for the Church to uproot than preachers during Iturbide's empire could have anticipated. Over the course of the insurgency, preachers had developed discourses often highly militaristic and even violent, rooted in notions of masculine power and valor. Against these values, women's misbehavior and the "luxuries" of "effeminiate" men remained threats. Femininity could also be redeemed, however, provided that women dedicated themselves to traditional piety, as some laywomen did with notable enthusiasm and alacrity. Moreover, by the end of the insurgency, and in light of Iturbide's favorable arrangement for independence, it appeared that the principle objectives of the earlier strategies had indeed been achieved. Mexico was now independent from apostasizing, liberal Spain and free to pursue its status as a "most Catholic" nation.

However, this was to be a fleeting, illusory victory for the Church. In the wake of Iturbide's fall and the advent of a republic, the institution would have to adapt to an unprecedented reality—namely, that of a polity in which the unassailable security of its hegemonic standing was no longer a foregone conclusion. Amid proliferating alternate discourses dispensed by a variety of groups and factions, the Church would once more need to adapt its own discourses to the exigencies of the day if it were to survive and ultimately regain its social standing. To this challenging task the purveyors of official church discourses would thus turn in the years to follow. Appropriating and reimagining some of the more positive strains of language used to characterize women's piety during the insurgency, the high clergy would look once more to the rhetorical potential of gendered language and conventions as a privileged means of articulating and defending its own vision for Mexican society in the years and decades ahead.

Chapter 6

Pious Women and New Foundations

Post-Independence Church Discourses

"Devout sex, interesting sex: give to the world a testimony of your piety, your zeal, and your religious devotion."[1]

FOLLOWING THE DEPARTURE OF Agustín de Iturbide and the fall of his imperial regime, Mexico entered into its first period of republican government and the beginnings of a long period of national debate and contestation surrounding the nature and governance of the nascent republic. By no means unaware of the significance of this transition, the Church actively and energetically responded to the ensuing political and social changes, seeking ways to retain its traditional privileges and place of prominence under the new circumstances. As reflected in the above excerpt of an officially approved document from the mid 1820s, the Church in this period was turning once more to language and conventions of gender as an important part of its response to the political and social developments that followed in the wake of independence. However, whereas in the immediately-preceding decades the Church had frequently scolded women and some men for their moral laxity and misguided social customs, increasingly after independence the institution turned its attention to a more positive aspect of women's behavior—their purported status as "the devout sex." Likewise, men too were called to new gendered ideals, still normatively masculine but now founded more in pious devotion than in military prowess. Rising to the challenges of the age, the Church shaped gendered discourses in this period as an important aspect of the new foundations, anchored in the devotion of the faithful, which it sought to propose for Mexican society.

1. *Estatutos* (1825), 9–10.

The Context for Post-Iturbide Church Discourses

As noted at the end of chapter 5, even during the brief imperial interlude of Iturbide, preachers in Mexico City were beginning to emphasize the need to guarantee the Church's central place in the life of the newly independent Mexican nation. Though theoretically guaranteed such a place under Iturbide's arrangement, it was apparent even then that not all public voices spoke unequivocally in support of the continuance of the Church's traditional privileges and prerogatives. All the more so after the fall of the Iturbide regime, officially endorsed preachers in the early years of the Republic soon realized that they would be vying with a multitude of competing voices and interests for the loyalties and affections of the Mexican populace. As before Independence but now in a different way, many of these preachers turned to gendered language and norms as an important vehicle for making their case in the nascent Mexican public sphere.

An Opening Example

The first sermon published in Mexico City following Iturbide's departure and the establishment of a republic was one in which themes of gender figured prominently.[2] Given in Mexico City's cathedral in August of 1823 on the subject of the early colonial saint Rose of Lima, the sermon—offered by Miguel de Talavera, the prior of the local Convent of Santo Domingo—opened with a lament concerning the difficulties of exercising the "holy ministry of the word" (i.e., preaching) in the current age. The preacher noted that the Church's enemies had made recourse to satire, criticism, spoofing, sarcasm and sophisms in their attacks on sacred doctrine, eliciting on the part of the "ministers of the sanctuary" the "greatest bitterness of their souls."[3] However, all was not lost. Despite the challenges posed to the Church by such impudent attacks, Talavera pointed out that hope remained in the form of "an innocent virgin" known for her "singular feats" and "heroic virtues"—Saint Rose of Lima.[4] By praising Rose's incomparable virtues, Talavera expressed the hope that something of her merits might come to take root amid unhappy contemporary circumstances. Likewise, he clarified that, like Rose, he would not attempt to refute the Church's enemies directly

---

2. See *Sumaria* (1824). For a treatment of Talavera's sermon see Connaughton, "Religión."

3. *Sumaria*, 1–2.

4. Ibid., 2.

since "the disciples of the cross do not need such persuasion." Like Rose, for the faithful of Mexico City, "the mere name of divine authority is enough."[5]

Reviewing the course of Rose's life, Talavera noted first that the eventual saint was known to display the fortitude of "strong men" in the midst of "incredible suffering."[6] Invoking such "manly" strength, Talavera implied that it was direly needed under the current circumstances in which "nothing is heard in our capital except invectives against the sacrosanct religion of Jesus Christ."[7] Against such effrontery, the preacher expressed his hope that "heroes of solid and true virtue" might be formed to combat attacks against the Church.[8] Returning to Rose as an exemplar of such virtue, Talavera noted that what had made the saint extraordinary was the way in which, by the guidance of "an invisible and omnipotent hand," she overcame the "weakness of her sex."[9] For example, having perceived such "weakness" as a child in the behavior of her own mother who, seeking social advancement, ordered that her attractive daughter be adorned with a crown of flowers, Rose responded by placing a thick safety pin within the crown and allowing it "with unspeakable pain to pass through her skull," such that it could not be removed except by the operation of a surgeon.[10] Calling on the members of his audience and the faithful in general—that is, "Catholic Americans, who glory in being children of the Roman Church"—to take inspiration from Rose's example, Talavera denounced the "seductive spirit" of others who, like "the woman of Babylon," offered to their compatriots the "venom of irreligion." Against such perfidy, the preacher counseled resolute loyalty to the faith. Imitating Rose in their own battles against "desolation and seduction," the faithful would emerge triumphant and secure their eternal happiness.[11]

Reviving numerous tropes from earlier sermons and discourses, this sermon is particularly significant for the way in which it refers back both to some of the conventions of Baroque sermons—including emphasis on the extreme, utterly extraordinary holiness of saints—as well as more recent conventions, including the importance of close imitation of holy

---

5. Ibid., 10. See also Connaughton, *Clerical*, 117, 196. As Connaughton points out, invocations of the unquestionable, divine authority associated with the Church started to increase following independence as the Church needed increasingly to compete with purveyors of alternate visions for Mexico's future.

6. *Sumaria*, 8.

7. Ibid., 10.

8. Ibid.

9. Ibid., 14.

10. Ibid., 11.

11. Ibid., 15–16.

figures and the inculcation of virtue as means of overcoming women's innate "weakness." Combining these two streams and hinting at other, additional strategies—for example, the unassailability of ecclesiastical authority and the primacy of Rome—Talavera's sermon provides an example of how the Church's public discourses would continue to develop in the opening years of independence.

Talavera's sermon, though grounded in common tropes, was quite controversial. Some audience members complained to church authorities that the sermon had been too extreme and graphic in the language about rigorous penances that it had employed and that it contained elements excessively critical and even seditious toward the nascent republican government.[12] Church authorities evidently felt the need to come to Talavera's defense, giving their approval for the publication of the sermon and providing along with it the testimony of witnesses who had both heard the sermon in person and read carefully its printed version. Concurring resolutely with Talavera's principal points, one witness emphasized that the defense of religion and the state against "consummately resolute and seditious sectarians" ought to be "ardent, manly and vigorous."[13] The commentator noted that despite the complaints of some who were offended by the sermon's strong language, "it is not only permitted, but necessary in certain circumstances to use words and actions that excite in the souls of those who hear them movements of disdain, hate, and indignation against error."[14] Another witness, testifying against those who would slander Talavera for purportedly pronouncing an invective or satire against the government, insisted that the preacher spoke with "sweet strength," "agreeable anointing," and "animated fire" the "solid, certain and infallible" truths of his discourse.[15] Church leaders apparently agreed with this assessment, as reflected in the official approval they extended for the sermon's publication.[16]

---

12. Connaughton, "Religión," 329–32. As Connaughton points out, the disagreements over Talavera's sermon were held on all sides by Catholics, whatever their political leanings—an important point to consider in seeking to understand the high clergy's public discourses and its efforts to regulate definitions of normative Catholicism following independence.

13. *Sumaria*, 32.

14. Ibid.

15. Ibid., 33–34.

16. Ibid., 35.

A Difficult Surrounding Context

For that reason, despite the controversy it had occasioned—or, perhaps, precisely because of it—the institutional Church saw the printing and distribution of this sermon as an important task to be taken up in the immediate aftermath of the transition of Mexico's government from empire to republic. Whereas in earlier times the sermon's graphic language likely would have gone unremarked and the Church itself may not have felt compelled to print the document, circumstances by the early 1820s had changed significantly. As alluded to in the sermon's references to surrounding satire and criticism of the Church, at the time of the controversy over Talavera's discourse the church was under pressure on many different fronts, engaged in desperate efforts to preserve its economic and political power not just in the discursive arena but the legal, political and economic spheres as well. The continuance of the *patronato real* concerning the appointment of bishops was at stake, for example, which for the Church was significant as it represented an opportunity for the institution to free itself from some of the effects of the Bourbon reforms, thereby potentially achieving even greater independence from the state than it had enjoyed in the colonial period.[17]

Also significant was the status of Church property and traditional clerical privileges such as the training of clergy in seminaries.[18] With many seminaries closed and in the effective absence of episcopal leadership—all of Mexico's bishops had either died or fled into exile by 1829—the Church struggled to maintain both its position of social authority as well as its own internal institutional cohesion.[19] Meanwhile, the Church found its material interests threatened both as the value of its properties declined amid larger economic difficulties facing Mexico after independence and its ability to rely on income from tithes was abolished.[20] However, as

---

17. See García Ugarte, *Poder*, chapter 1; Costeloe, *Church and State*, 7–8; Staples, *La iglesia*, 35–73; Stevens, *Origins*, 32–33; Casillas, "La discusión"; Green, *Mexican*.

18. For studies of the larger economic, political and social realities facing the Church following independence see Chowning, "Management"; Bazant, *Alienation*. See also Costeloe, *Church Wealth*; Costeloe, *Central Republic*.

19. Lynch, *Latin America*, 132; Staples, *La iglesia*, 18–31; Stevens, *Origins*, 32; Green, *Mexican Republic*, 75–78; Shiels, "Church and State." Lynch reports that the Church had lost up to half its secular clergy and even more regular clergy by the 1830s. Additionally, for discussion of some of the internal divisions within the Church itself, including some clerical support for liberalism—for example, from the prominent cleric and political figure Servando Teresa de Mier—see Bazant, "From Independence," 4–5; Casillas, "La discusión."

20. Staples, *La iglesia*, 97–126; Stevens, *Origins*, 33; Costeloe, "Administration"; Macune, "Impact."

Margaret Chowning and Jan Bazant have pointed out, the Church did not take these threats lightly, responding vigorously in defense of its economic interests and, in general, largely succeeding in retaining most of its wealth in the years prior to the Reform.[21]

Likewise important, as evident in Talavera's sermon and as Carlos Herrejón Peredo, Brian Connaughton and Mariana Terán Fuentes have pointed out, was the expanded publication of civic oratory and speeches following independence—giving rise to a new genre of published discourse beyond the sermons that had almost completely dominated during the colonial period.[22] By the early 1820s laymen such as José Joaquín Fernández de Lizardi and others were making greater inroads into the realm of public speaking and publishing, sometimes—though not always—in ways inimical to the priorities and vision of the Church hierarchy.[23] Likewise, many of these authors were publishing novels and making use of greater freedoms afforded the press, as witnessed in the rise of thousands of broadsides and pamphlets as well as regularly published newspapers, all of which had the potential to serve as mouthpieces for ideas inimical to the priorities of Church.[24]

Also worrisome for church authorities was the expansion of politics beyond the former dominance of the alliance between the Church and Crown.[25] As Brian Connaughton and other scholars have shown, as liberals and non-church officials began to use ecclesiastical imagery—for example, the body or collective of believers—in order to try to build ideas of the nation, the Church responded with images of the nation (the Catholic nation) and other new ideas in order to press its own case.[26] In this way, Connaughton emphasizes how prelates, through their discourses, shaped a distinctive clerical space in which they could manage the Church's own transition from the *ancien régime* to circumstances following independence.

---

21. Chowning, "Church Wealth," 461. See also Bazant's introductory chapter in his study of church wealth in the Reform period, *Alienation of Church Wealth*; and Morales, "La distribución."

22. Herrejón Peredo, *Del sermón*, 343. For studies of the evolution of secular discourses following independence and their relationship with clerical discourses, see also Connaughton, "La sacralización"; Terán Fuentes, "Recordar."

23. Ávila, "Interpretaciones," 38; Connaughton, " Mudanzas," 266–67.

24. Costeloe, *Central Republic*, 12–13. See also Clark de Lara and Speckman Guerra's recent three-volume edited study on various manifestations of literary culture in nineteenth-century Mexico, *La república*.

25. Costeloe, *Central Republic*, 13.

26. See Connaughton, *Clerical Ideology*. In addition to the studies by Staples, Ávila, and Pani cited above, see also the following additional studies by Connaughton: "Conjuring"; *Dimensiones*; "Entre"; "El cura"; "Los curas"; "El ajedrez."

While generally conservative in the sense of seeking to "combin[e] ideology with the desire to preserve the status quo, while admitting the fewest possible changes," Church discourses were not static. Rather, clerical discourses can be seen as constituting a "creative updating [of church traditions] with an eye to [current] dilemmas" and therefore served "as an expression of the tensions between inherited ideology and the demands of the moment."[27] As Erika Pani has also pointed out, in the various forms of its public discourses, the Church did not wish to put forward a rigid, inflexible position but rather sought to adjust its message in order to participate in and shape contemporary debates.[28] Though now in competition with various civic discourses, official church discourses in Mexico City thus continued to represent a supple, adaptable means by which the Church could both articulate its public position on contemporary issues and adjust its approach in light of ongoing political, economic, and social developments.[29]

Gender and New Directions for Church Discourses

The remainder of this chapter, therefore, seeks to contribute to scholarship on the Church's post-independence discourses by positing that, in addition to elements such as political content and economic concerns pointed to by other scholars, another essential aspect of these discourses centered around the gendered imagery and language employed within them. As evident in Talavera's sermon and the responses that it elicited, the Church would return in this period to earlier gendered strains in its discourses, emphasizing reinvigorated piety in the form of devotion to saints and the emulation of many of their devout practices by the faithful. However, unlike in previous times—when either men and women were praised for embodying traits of the opposite sex or emphasis was placed on the development of "manly"

---

27. Connaughton, *Clerical Ideology*, 41–42. For further summary of the positions of the high clergy and its allies after independence, see Staples, *La iglesia*, 16–17; Connaughton, *Dimensiones*; Nesvig, ed., *Religious Culture*; *Memoria*, ed. Ramos Medina; *Iglesia*, ed. del Pilar Martínez López-Cano; *Hacia*, ed. Puente Lutteroth.

28. Pani, "Para difundir," 121. See also *Poder*, ed. Connaughton; Connaughton, *Clerical Ideology*, 7; Connaughton, "El clero," 360; Ávila, "Interpretaciones," 32. In the ongoing development of its discourses following independence, Connaughton shows how the Church gradually appropriated aspects and elements of secular, even liberal discourses for its own purposes.

29. See Danés Rojas, *Noticias*, 25. For further elaboration of the diversity of opinions and political approaches among Church leaders, see Staples, *La Iglesia*, 161–62; Connaughton, "El clero," 353–55; Connaughton, "Conjuring"; Connaughton, "Enemy Within," 185.

virtues in both sexes in response to contemporaneous threats—the order of the day now was resistance to the "venomous seduction" of the forces of "irreligion" by means of renewed piety. Though the sort of virtue required for such spiritual warfare could be labeled "manly," it was masculine in a specific sense. Whereas during the period of the insurgency and the years immediately preceding it there had been two distinct, though related, visions of idealized gender identity enshrined in sermons—namely, that of virtuous, militarized male warriors and their heroic, devout, stay-at-home female companions—now, after independence, an adaptation of the latter vision came to take on greater discursive importance.

Though still couched in terms of the dominant patriarchal system in which men were the normative reference point and still directed toward male believers as well, "masculinity" in post-independence official Church discourses—that is, the normative vision of gender the Church promoted—began to take something of a feminine turn as preachers came down increasingly less on the side of promoting militancy and more on what they would come to label the "sweetness" and "tenderness" of religion.[30] Though this tendency would grow more marked toward the middle decades of the century, the transition in gendered language is evident in many of the sermons studied in this chapter. Specifically, the message was that, like Saint Rose of Lima, both men and women in post-independence Mexico City were still called by the Church's official representatives to "ardent, manly and vigorous" resistance to trends perceived to threaten sacred doctrine and the Church's traditional place of societal prominence; however, they were invited to do so increasingly in ways that formerly would have been more closely associated discursively with women—that is, by confronting the Church's opponents less directly, and instead taking refuge in "holy piety" and relying on the "tenderness" of religion and the weight of "divine authority" as the most effective means of neutralizing opposition. Acting in "manly" ways precisely by imitating St. Rose—a rigorously pious woman—Mexico City's faithful were to secure the Church's status as a pillar of social stability, thereby confirming the future prosperity of their emerging nation and assuring the status of their own eternal salvation.[31] Amid the array of

---

30. See Connaughton, *Clerical Ideology*, 93.

31. For the importance of piety as a topic in the development of the Church's discourses, see ibid., 65. For another scholarly study in which the author observes a similar transition in Latin American Church discourses on women and gender in the late eighteenth and early nineteenth centuries see Barcelo Miller, "De la Polilla." Barcelo Miller uses church authorities' correspondence to argue that the Church's discursive understanding of women changed from an image of sexual depravity to one of virtue in this period.

issues and questions facing Mexican society, including the nature of governance in the nascent republic and the question of the role of religion within it, the Church too had to discern its way. As emerged in Talavera's sermon, the official Church in the years and decades following independence would once again need to find its public voice—a compelling, national presence through which to articulate its positions on the contentious issues and questions of the day. It is the argument of this chapter that one important way in which the Church accomplished this task was through the gendered discourses of piety it developed and promoted throughout the 1820s, 30s, and beyond.

Women in the Aftermath of Independence

Of importance to consider, in light of the gendered language and imagery present in church discourses following independence, is the context of gender relations in which contemporary men and women found themselves. In her study of changes in marriage relationships during the period of transition between the colony and independence, Sonya Lipsett-Rivera points to an increase in the number of women working outside the home.[32] As Anne Staples also notes, occupations such as that of *estanquillera* (female cigar shop worker) were increasingly common for women following independence, allowing them to transcend some of the normal daily restrictions of the home and interact with other women.[33]

As Silvia Arrom also explains, new intellectual trends as well as changes in royal policies had produced alterations of laws governing guilds in the late colonial period, therefore allowing more women to enter into professions, though sometimes upsetting the balance of gender roles and male authority as a result.[34] As this development occurred, Lipsett-Rivera notes an increased tendency around the time of independence and following among women seeking divorces to claim that they had assumed the role of primary provider for themselves and their children.[35] Emerging from reforms in the Bourbon period in which women's education was increasingly advocated as a means of improving the welfare of the state, by the time of independence and in subsequent decades women's roles as, potentially, the heads of their

---

32. Lipsett-Rivera, "Marriage," 127.
33. See the following by Staples: "Sociabilidad," 106–8; "Mujeres."
34. See Arrom, *Women*, 26–32; Lipsett-Rivera, "Marriage," 130; Green, *Mexican Republic*, 58.
35. Lipsett-Rivera, "Marriage," 138.

Pious Women and New Foundations

own families, also changed their social status.[36] No longer necessarily strictly subservient to their husbands, women now had an important social role to play "for both religious and civic education and for inculcating patriotism in their offspring"—a reality sometimes reflected, with varying degrees of enthusiasm, in the contemporary literature of the period.[37]

Although, as Erika Pani has demonstrated, women's systematic exclusion from political activity was an important dimension of the beginnings of republican citizenship in Mexico, women did occasionally intervene in the public arena on behalf of their husbands and families.[38] In the late 1820s one group of women managed to secure publication of a document of significant importance to them—a petition directed to president-elect Vicente Guerrero on behalf of their peninsular-born husbands who faced imminent expulsion from Mexico.[39] Calling themselves a "disgraced portion of American wives and mothers," the women entreated Guerrero to overrule the law and allow their husbands to stay. Otherwise, prostitution would be their only recourse and their children, left without fathers, would become "so many monsters that will plague the beautiful soil of Anahuac[.]"[40] Emphasizing the growing emphasis on women's role in the education of their children in the nineteenth century, the group asked why provision had been made for the children of Americans born overseas, including in Spain, but not for the needs of women who had given birth to the American children of Spanish fathers.[41] Signed by dozens of women, each of whose names were listed along with the number of their children, the document noted that a delegation of *señoras* personally delivered the manifest to Guerrero. One

---

36. For a study of female-headed households in Mexico for this period, see Kuznesof, "Gender." Kuznesof concurs with Lipsett-Rivera concerning the expansion of employment opportunities for women in this period as well as their ability to serve as heads of households but points to larger economic realities as more determinative of women's overall quality of life.

37. Lipsett-Rivera, "Marriage," 138–39. See also Raffi-Béroud, *En torno*, 183–86; Mora Escalante, *De la sujeción*; Fernández de Lizardi, *Itching Parrot*. As evident in the first chapter of *El periquillo*, with its implicit critique of the superstition of old women's piety, Lizardi along with other contemporaries expressed ambivalence in their writings toward the virtues of women's piety that preachers emphasized frequently in their sermons in this period. Still, as Raffi-Béroud points out in her study, this did not signify complete opposition on the part of Lizardi and other liberal reformers to some of the traditional religious values associated with women, especially motherhood as embodied in the Virgin Mary.

38. Pani, "Ciudadana."

39. *Esposicion* (1829).

40. Ibid., 1–2.

41. Ibid., 4.

of their number, doña Mariana Cervantes, spoke as a representative for all, acquitting herself with "reasoning full of sensibility and tenderness, [which] pleased all who heard."[42]

Nevertheless, despite the successful entrance into the public sphere by some women, as a recent study by Ana Lidia García Peña has shown, attempts to control and even imprison women were also on the rise around the time of independence.[43] With the rapid militarization of society during the turbulent opening decades of the nineteenth century in Mexico, police actions—often in the form of initiatives taken by local, non-professional *alcaldes de barrio*—grew increasingly more vigilant against women, at times even detaining them indefinitely under house arrest for perceived offenses.[44] As García Peña explains, in a context of ongoing threats of uprising and war as well as economic difficulty and industrial and agricultural stagnation, military and police control over the city's inhabitants increased, manifesting itself especially in vigilance over women's behavior.[45] As a result, women could be subject to arrest, detention and even violence, often based on scant evidence.[46]

Thus, although opportunities for some degree of autonomy had opened up to women after independence, efforts to confine and limit their visibility and mobility remained influential.[47] Intriguingly, in the case of the Church—as will emerge through study of sermons and other discourses in this chapter—the message of the institution both toward women and about them, while still nominally patriarchal, did not parallel secular efforts at containment and surveillance. Instead, through the gendered vision it promoted in its official discourses, the Church showed itself increasingly optimistic and supportive of the ways in which women's nature as "the devout sex" could prove instrumental in redeeming both themselves and society at large.

Gender in Church Discourses

As in the case of Talavera's sermon, other preachers in the opening years of the republic turned with frequency to the importance of piety, both in the lives of the saints and as an essential virtue to be imitated by the faithful.

42. Ibid., 8.
43. García Peña, "El encierro."
44. Ibid., 108–20.
45. Ibid., 105–6.
46. Ibid., 116–22.
47. Lipsett-Rivera, "Marriage," 140; García Peña, "El encierro," 129–31.

Though often still articulated in terms of normative "manliness," the language in these sermons started in this period to take on more feminized overtones as preachers made increasingly emotional appeals to their audiences and portrayed the most heroic sort of bravery as that embodied by practices which many of their predecessors had associated discursively with women. For example, in a sermon from the year after Talavera's, for the occasion of a bishop's funeral, the preacher—Carmelite friar José Manuel de Jesús—noted the importance of a type of virtue which only religious devotion could provide.[48] According to this preacher, "religion alone can give us clear and simple knowledge of virtue." Without "lifting our eyes to heaven" and following in the "rugged" and difficult path of the "works and rigors of penitence," no one could know the true depths and origins of virtue. Instead, those who lacked proper religious devotion occupied themselves solely with vanity, following the "sonorous voice of fame" and adulation rather than the authentic path to true happiness.[49] While such language could also have been heard from Mexico City's high clergy in the first or second decades of the nineteenth century, what was different now was the absence of a differentiation between men's and women's right behavior. Whereas before men were to be brave, albeit devout, soldiers and women were to "fight" through their piety, now everyone was called to the type of spiritual combat taken up more specifically by women in earlier decades.

According to the Mercedarian priest Félix María Somellera, the piety to which priests referred in their sermons was not to be divorced from the political realm.[50] Responding to critics who would seek to separate religion from the affairs of the state, the preacher made clear that such ideas represented a type of "perversity" opposed to the truths of Christ.[51] Tellingly, however, as Talavera had also done, the preacher declined to challenge such "false patriots" directly, declining to actively dismantle their arguments. Instead, leaving such efforts to "better talents"—and thereby departing significantly from the example of earlier preachers who did not hesitate to counter their opponents' arguments with frequently acrid responses of their own devising—the preacher asserted that any pious believer who loved both his country and "Christian liberty" would be satisfied with the Church's stance on the "false patriots" and therefore would dismiss their conclusions outright, accepting instead those of the Church. Offering an emotional appeal to his audience's devotion to the Virgin Mary, the preacher pointed out that

48. de Jesús, *Sermon* (1825).
49. Ibid., 5.
50. Somellera, *Panegírico*.
51. Ibid., 19.

the Virgin had not forgotten the "miseries of the *patria*" and would soon come to its aid.[52] In other words, as study of additional sermons will also show, as officially endorsed preachers confronted the rebellious, secularizing tendencies of some fellow citizens, which largely opposed the Church's own vision for Mexican society in this period, one important rhetorical strategy which they developed involved emotional appeals founded on references to pious devotions and traditions. Insofar as such appeals grew increasingly emotive and invoked devotional practices often performed by or associated with women, preachers can accurately be said to have initiated a new phase in the preaching of the high clergy in Mexico City—one in which official religious discourses, though still couched in the language of "manly" virtue, took on a distinctly feminized tone.

Another example of this gradual feminization through emotional appeals to piety appears in a sermon given in 1829 in celebration of the Immaculate Conception.[53] Lamenting what he saw as the "horrors" and "sad state" of current events, including persecutions of the Church, the Franciscan friar Manuel María Domingo wondered out loud how it could be that God's wrath had not yet obliterated practitioners of the "general relaxation," "horrible prostitution," and "abominable corruption" which surrounded the Church.[54] Like the "impetuous torrent of an enormous river," God's ire could strike at any moment, the preacher explained, were it not for the intercession of the Virgin.[55] Once more confirming the crucial importance of pious devotion for current times, the preacher noted that, particularly under the advocation of the Immaculate Conception, the Virgin remained a powerful intercessor before God.[56] As other preachers had noted earlier, the surest, most effective means of fighting back against affronts to the Church was to be found less in descending to the level of opponents by responding directly to their arguments than in "lifting eyes toward heaven" and engaging in the practices of devotion—in this case to the Virgin as the Immaculate Conception—which alone would ultimately secure victory for the interests and priorities of the Church.

Similar messages appeared in other sermons published in the same year. Preached by the Mercedarian Juan de Aguirre in honor of the medieval Hungarian king and saint Ladislaus, one sermon praised the holy monarch's

52. Ibid., 20.
53. Domingo, *Sermon* (1829).
54. Ibid., 16.
55. Ibid., 9–10.
56. Ibid., 16.

virtues as those to which all Christians should aspire.⁵⁷ Eschewing worldly honors and pleasures and displaying a consistent spirit of religious fervor, Ladislaus overcame the base passions of the flesh through "ardent sighs" borne of the "abundant tears and blood" he shed through rigorous penitential practices.⁵⁸ Though a warrior king and a famed conqueror, the preacher emphasized that Ladislaus succeeded not by his own strength but through his devotion to God—an attitude manifested especially in his "pacific and meek" demeanor and his "timid and delicate" conscience. A "man of tears and sobs," characterized by mortifications and "covered with ash and cilice," the secret of the king's success lay with the vigorous religious devotion he displayed, which allowed him to balance admirably the many requirements of a just and wise ruler.⁵⁹ As a true "Christian hero," Ladislaus triumphed over worldly temptations and displayed virtue sufficient to make him appear "even on earth, equal to the angels."⁶⁰ As in other sermons, here too the virtues of piety and vigorous religious devotion—again couched in terms often associated with femininity, such as "pacific and meek" and "timid and delicate"—received special praise and were suggested as the most efficacious means by which the Church, whether in heroic leaders like Ladislaus or among believers more generally, could face and defeat its enemies.

Another set of sermons from 1829 also offers still further important indications regarding the development of Church discourses in favor of gendered notions of piety. Sponsored by the archconfraternity of the parish of la Santa Veracruz in central Mexico City, the published sermons commemorated two recently deceased and well-remembered figures—the priest José Manuel Sartorio and the military leader Ignacio Paz de Tagle.⁶¹ Although scholarship on *cofradías* in this period has demonstrated a decline in their membership, it nevertheless does not conclude that the groups stopped functioning.⁶² Indeed, despite increasing emphasis in Church discourses on attitudes of devotional piety often associated with women, the actions of the lay leaders in this case demonstrate that the turn toward piety was inclusive of men as well.⁶³ For example, organized at one of the group's meetings,

57. Aguirre, *Panegirico*.

58. Ibid., 2.

59. Ibid., 14.

60. Ibid., 15.

61. *Solemnes honras* (1829).

62. See Pescador, *De bautizados*; Chowning, "Laywomen"; Chowning, "La feminización."

63. One indication of the active participation of men in the archconfraternity's affairs is a document from the same period, which records signatures from several

the effort to sponsor the memorial grew from the initiative of the organization's lay male leadership.⁶⁴ Moreover, the *cofradía*'s statutes for its female members indicate that feminized pious language could be used comfortably within a public religious institute that also included men. According to the statutes, women, as members of the "devout sex" and the "interesting sex" were called to offer an edifying example in society with the "glorious fatigues" of their piety and religious zeal; their good works, done with proper devotion, could embody the goodness of God, the "loving father of mercies" and secure their place among the blessed in heaven.⁶⁵

In the two sermons commissioned in honor of Paz y Tagle and Sartorio, similar sentiments emerged. Confirming the continuing importance of masculinity as a value to be upheld, the first preacher gave thanks that the young Paz y Tagle had not gone the way of many others, who "run wild" in pursuit of "delights which render them effeminate."⁶⁶ Significantly, in the subsequent sermon in honor of Sartorio, the preacher likewise celebrated how the late priest, almost uniquely among other high clergy during the insurgency period—had spoken boldly and courageously in favor of Mexico's independence. In contrast to what many by the late 1820s, according to the preacher, now looked back on as an "aristocratic and servile" class of clerical leaders which, during the insurgency, had pursued its own "particular interests" more than those of the *patria*, Sartorio stood as a beacon of notably courageous virtue.⁶⁷

---

dozen male archconfraternity members in support of one of the church of Santa Veracruz's priests, who had been accused of "fanaticism" by "mistaken" parties. The group's members responded decisively to the accusations, assuring readers of the priest's personal holiness and devotion to his sacred duties. See *Manifiesto* (1828), 1. Nevertheless, see also Chowning, "Laywomen," and "La feminización." Chowning has studied confraternities in Mexico's center-west region following independence and has found evidence to suggest that some men were in fact dropping out, at least from cofradía membership. Among contributing factors, Chowning cites economic problems that plagued many confraternities, which discouraged male leadership, as well as the appearance both of new civic associations (e.g., Masonic lodges, social clubs, and scientific societies) and new discourses of (mostly male) citizenship—both of which gave men alternate social and political opportunities. Nevertheless, for Mexico City there have not yet been studies to show whether men left or stopped participating in the church in this period. Working from the available evidence I have studied from the discursive realm, it does not appear that preachers were as yet concerned in the 1820s and 30s with decreased male participation. See also Pani, "Ciudadana," 13–14.

64. *Solemnes honras* (1829) 1–3.

65. *Estatutos* (1825), 9–10.

66. *Solemnes honras* (1829), 8.

67. Ibid., 15–20. Describing his efforts, the preacher noted that Sartorio was often consulted by the "new Maccabees" (i.e., insurgents) for advice, as well as by many

As these sentiments demonstrate, conventions within official Church discourses—including gendered language—were continuing to change in the years following Mexico's independence. Couched in language of piety and devotion, it was now even acceptable for preachers who published their sermons with official ecclesiastical sanction to refer back to earlier bishops and clerics from the period of the insurgency with disapproval and criticism. Though they shared with those earlier predecessors some of the same discursive conventions which appeared in previous sermons—including the trope of "effeminization" caused by lack of proper moral virtue—preachers were now in a sense turning the tables on the earlier exponents of those positions, naming *them* as those who had failed to act properly. By implication, in other words, those citizens and members of the clergy (e.g., previous archbishops, etc.) who had neglected to act in ways similar to Paz y Tagle and Sartorio were in fact the ones who had truly been "rendered effeminate," lacking in the moral virtues that flowed from authentic piety and thus failing to act in the "manly" ways required by the difficult circumstances leading to Mexico's independence. In contrast to such "effeminization," the preachers and their enthusiastic supporters and benefactors in the archconfraternity offered the edifying examples of Paz y Tagle and Sartorio. What was their secret? How had they resisted the "effeminizing" wiles of the age? For the preachers and archconfraternity members it was clear that the answer lay with the two deceased men's ardent religious devotion. Though often associated with women, in the years following independence in Mexico City, therefore, such virtues came to resonate in new ways as well with men—both clerical and lay—who, like their female compatriots and fellow believers, could now look to reinvigorated religious devotion as an essential means by which to renew and strengthen both Church and society.

Reinvigorated Piety

By the 1830s, the importance for both men and women of the gendered vision of piety described above had grown so significant in the Church's official discourses that in some sermons preachers did not even feel the need to make explicit reference to current political and social circumstances.

---

members of the clergy, who sought a way to remain faithful to the "*patria* that implore[d] their help" without occasioning "the anathema of the Church, of which they [were] ministers." In spite of the calumnies of royalists, whom the preacher described as having denounced Sartorio falsely as a drunkard, and efforts by the viceroy Calleja to enlist the archbishop in punishing him, this "rebel priest" succeeded in helping unite his people through the combination of "innocence of customs," "humility and poverty of spirit," "love for his *patria*," and the "ardent charity" he displayed on behalf of all.

Preaching Power

Retreating into "holy piety" and "true devotion," these preachers emphasized the importance of cultivating spiritual relationships with God and the saints and practicing acts of sincere religious feeling as solutions to current social problems—a strategy that Brian Connaughton associates with a turn in Church discourses toward piety as a key foundation for the ideals the nation professed to espouse.[68]

Preaching Devotion

An instructive example of the renewed emphasis on piety in official church discourses emerges in a sermon given at the sanctuary of the Virgin of Guadalupe in late 1830 in the presence of the vice president of the republic, Anastasio Bustamante. Offered by the secular priest Tomás Francisco López Rodríguez de Figueredo, the sermon is dedicated almost exclusively to praising the wonders of the Guadalupan image.[69] Saving his brief but pointed political remarks for the conclusion, the preacher addressed Bustamante and the other secular leaders in attendance directly, invoking the Church's fresh emphasis on piety and reminding them that the best nations were those "whose superiors base the happiness of the state on devout practices."[70]

In a similar way, another preacher—Lázaro de la Garza y Ballesteros, later the archbishop of Mexico City—in a sermon from 1833 stressed the importance of piety among the faithful and obedience to legitimate authorities.[71] According to Garza y Ballesteros, without such proper religious devotion and observance it was no wonder that "disgraces one after the other" continued to afflict Mexico. Instead of following the gospel of Christ and thus assuring their status as good public citizens, the people of Mexico had strayed and given in to "corruption and ignorance" as a result of the "multitude of books" to which they had been exposed.[72] In contrast to such decadence, the future archbishop recommended a return to the fundamentals of religious devotion, which would assure proper order and prosperity for society.

---

68. See Connaughton, *Clerical Ideology*, 124. As Connaughton points out, by the 1830s a clear transition is apparent in the Church's official discourses as it turned increasingly to the promotion of piety as an essential means of strengthening its place in society.

69. López Rodríguez de Figueredo, *Oración panegírica*.

70. Ibid., 10.

71. See Garza y Ballesteros, *Sermones*, 8.

72. Ibid., 10–11.

Pointing to the evolving gendered conventions that undergirded the piety being promoted in sermons, discourses in the 1830s not only emphasized the importance of devotion but also gave indications of how notions of gender should support it. One sermon, for example—offered in Mexico City's cathedral in 1833—returned to a theme seen in earlier baroque sermons: the feast of the wedding of Mary and Joseph.[73] As in the earlier sermons, the preacher alluded to the greatness of Joseph's virginity—an attribute which, in the predominant discourse of the Baroque, rendered him like a mother to Jesus. However, although the preacher referred to how Joseph "made himself similar to Mary," he lost no time in emphasizing that it was Joseph's fatherhood that truly distinguished him.[74] Describing fatherhood in general as "a perfection and a true joy," the preacher noted that Joseph's fatherhood was all the more remarkable for two reasons: first, because, by a special grace, he was permitted to share in the fatherhood of God; second, because he was a father "adorned with all faith."[75] According to the preacher, all who were "pious and Christian" would recognize without doubt this truth. However, "the darkness that calls itself light" of the "present age" had with "unheard-of pride" dared to question the historical veracity of Joseph's and Mary's virginity.[76] For that reason, the preacher recommended a return to the essentials of religious devotion, as embodied in Joseph's own example. In other words, for men as for women, the "pride of the age" was entirely too much. Rather than directly confronting it, the faithful were to take refuge in the spiritual authority of the Church. To do so, as suggested in this sermon, for men this meant not a renunciation of masculinity or fatherhood but rather a particular reimagining of both that would be rooted in pious practices and obedience to the Church. Amid a "furious ocean of passions," believers—emboldened by "that divine fervor which religion inspires"—would emerge victorious and secure happiness and peace for both themselves and society.[77]

Piety in Daily Life

Regarding gendered language about women in sermons, an important aspect of the surrounding context for consideration is the participation of women in pious activities. As William Taylor demonstrates in a recent

73. *Sermon pronunciado* (1833).
74. Ibid., 8.
75. Ibid., 11.
76. Ibid., 9.
77. Ibid., 12.

study of the rise of religious devotions and shrines following independence, although the Church, lacking in episcopal leadership through the first two decades of independence, found itself comparatively weak institutionally, popular devotions and lay piety—manifested especially in shrines, miracle stories, and ex-voto paintings—grew in strength and popularity in this period.[78] As Taylor notes and as also witnessed in contemporary sermons, some of the language used in these materials grew more feminized, highlighting values such as "tenderness" and "affection" as key.[79]

This generalized sense of the importance of piety for daily life, while important in official ecclesiastical discourses as well, grew gradually more popularized over the 1830s and 40s with the advent of publications directed primarily toward women. Intriguingly, given the circumstances of the years immediately preceding its appearance—in which the Church had found its interests jeopardized by liberalizing reforms—the first of these publications I was able to find comes from 1835.[80] While not explicitly directed toward women, the document's title—*The Christian Year, or Devout Exercises for All the Days of the Year*—invoked the importance of daily devout exercises of the sort that, as demonstrated by contemporaneous sermons, would have been associated with women in the public mind.[81] For example, daily devotions to various saints included meditations on subjects that would have been familiar as part of nuns' vows and many women's aspirations to imitate them, such as overcoming "self love," "prompt obedience to the voice of God," and "Christian charity." With additional content including "moral reflections" and an "explanation of the truths of religion," the calendar provided daily information about the lives of various saints and included moral messages meant to edify, encourage and preserve the devout on the right path.[82]

---

78. Taylor, "Santuarios."

79. For an example of one such sermon, see Sánchez de Espinosa, *Himno*. In his introductory note, one supporter of the work praised its "tender production." Likewise, the author himself invoked tenderness in addressing Christ.

80. Liberalizing civic reforms under President Valentín Gómez Farías, which had been affecting the Church in the early 1830s, were temporarily abrogated by Antonio López de Santa Anna upon his seizure of control of the government not long before the publication of this document. For an account of some of Gómez Farías' reforms, including the lifting of both the obligation to pay tithes and the civil enforcement of religious vows and other provisions affecting the Church's finances, see Ampudia, *La Iglesia*, 247; García Ugarte, *Poder político*, chapter 2; Bazant, "From Independence," 14–15.

81. See *Año crisitano*, (1835).

82. See also *Diario de los niños* (1840).

Pious Women and New Foundations

Following the publication that same year of another calendar with daily devotions, in 1838 the first in a series of multiple calendars and magazines directed specifically to women was printed.[83] Dedicated to Mexico's *señoritas*, the calendars' introductions described the women in glowing terms, noting not just their physical beauty but the character of their souls. According to one author, "in Europe their spirits are more cultivated, but in Mexico their hearts are kinder. Here they are not just sentimental, but tender; not just soft but virtuous . . . Rarely are their passions tempestuous, and, even when they ignite, they extinguish themselves easily; but normally they emit a peaceful light, similar to the bright star of Venus. Decency is painted in their eyes, and modesty is the greatest and most beautiful enchantment of their souls." Mexican women were thus destined, "by their multiplied virtues, to serve as a support to [men] in traversing the sad desert of life."[84] Among the women's "multiplied virtues," the calendars made clear that some of the most important were those associated with their piety, as evinced by sections on saints days, pious stories, and forthcoming church events.

Gendered Piety in Sermons

Additional sermons from the 1830s continued to highlight the importance of gendered notions of piety and renewed devotion to Catholic traditions, including one from 1835 in which the preacher celebrated the virtues of St. Thomas Aquinas in contrast to the errors of modern philosophy and warned his listeners of the dangers of "voluptuousness."[85] However, as this and other sermons studied above demonstrate, in comparison to their predecessors from before independence, preachers in this period placed much less emphasis on blaming women in general for such "dangers." Instead, both men and women were charged with living out ardently in their lives the pious practices and devotions often associated with "the devout sex." In fact, if anything, preachers' esteem toward women and their celebration of devotional practices among them appear to have grown during this period. One sermonizer spoke with gratitude of the Virgin Mary's closeness to those devoted to her "through her sex," while another praised a recently beatified Oratorian priest for the "modesty he observed," along with the "pause and order of his walk" and the "meditation and composure of his senses"—virtues which inspired those who observed him, presum-

83. See Gómez Marín, *Meditaciones*; *Calendario* (1838); *Calendario* (1839); *Calendario*, (1840).

84. *Calendario* (1838), 6.

85. See Barajas, *Sermon panegírico*, 1–2, 9–10.

ably many among whom were women, to "embrace virtue" and to abhor "dances and foolish diversions."[86]

Similarly, other preachers emphasized the importance of piety and right living in general, which, by promoting the "sweetness" and "divinity" of religion, would assure "constant friendship" and "perpetual peace" in society—traits no longer associated with the hyper masculine religiosity of earlier discourses but instead now with a softened, more "tender" and "sweet" vision of religion.[87] Still others praised the virtues and other-worldiness of saints like Luis Gonzaga, whose example called all to the "constancy of his piety," the "fervor of his abnegation," and the "rigors of his penitence."[88] Likewise, a sermon from 1839 in praise of a celebrated image of the crucified Christ—unlike sermons from earlier decades which lauded the military vigor of the "God of armies"—portrayed Christ as the "one sent from God" who arrived "without riches, without armies, without magnificence."[89] According to the preacher, this God was one whose "coming is peaceful," whose "thoughts [are] of peace" whose "mission [is] the precious fruit of the most ardent charity" and who therefore represented "the excess of divine love."[90]

Again, unlike earlier sermons from before independence, by the 1820s and 30s preachers who secured official Church approval for their sermons in Mexico City were offering a message tied less to the cultivation of military virtues and more to the inculcation of habits of devotion and piety which, in their view, would help to strengthen the Church against the attacks of its enemies. Still articulated within a normatively patriarchal social and ecclesiastical system and still retaining many male adherents, the "manly" (i.e., good or positive) virtues sermonizers now preached nevertheless took on a distinctly feminized character as they came to be associated with traits and practices often traditionally identified with women. In the context and circumstances of the mid-nineteenth century studied in the next chapter, this tendency in sermons toward celebrating the power of religious devotion in often feminized language would only increase in importance as the Church faced renewed challenges to its authority and privileges and sought ways to respond and regroup.

86. See de San Juan Crisóstomo, *Sermon* (1836), 11–12. See also Gómez Marín, *Oracion panegírica*, 9.
87. Pinzón, *Sermon* (1837), 8–12.
88. Moreno y Jove, *Sermon* (1839), 15.
89. López Rodríguez de Figueredo, *Sermon* (1839), 1.
90. Ibid., 1–2.

Conclusion

As the sermons studied in this chapter demonstrate, one of the priorities of Mexico City's high clergy following independence was to respond decisively to what they perceived to be increasing attacks on the Church. However, unlike in earlier times—when they frequently called their audiences to militaristic attacks on the Church's enemies—preachers by the 1820s and 30s had begun to pursue a different strategy. Still couched in patriarchal terms, what was different about official Church discourses in this period was that preachers now effectively were equating the "manly" duty to which they called their audiences with the mindset and practices of pious devotion, traditionally associated with women. In other words, the "virile" answer to "effeminizing" intellectual and social trends was no longer to be found necessarily through recourse to militaristic "battles" waged against the Church's enemies. Rather, the authentic solution now rested with retreating from engagement with "the pride of the age" and securing victory for the Church's position by way of strengthening its foundations in the pious belief and sincere devotional practices of the faithful. Far from resisting *feminization*, therefore, the Church now emphasized that the surest means of avoiding that worst of all possible fates in a patriarchal system—i.e., "effeminization"—lay, paradoxically, with encouraging "manly" responses to reigning importunities precisely through celebration of virtues traditionally associated with women—that is, by way of renewed participation by both men and women in the pious devotional practices frequently associated with members of "the devout sex."

Chapter 7

Gendering Reform

Mid-Nineteenth Century Church Discourses

"A representative stated that their testimony should not be taken into account because, 'Women are not persons, but simply things'— an impudent vilification of so worthy a portion of society."[1]

COMMENT OF ARCHBISHOP LÁZARO DE LA GARZA Y BALLESTEROS, MEXICO CITY, 1859, REGARDING RECENT REMARKS BY A LIBERAL CONGRESSIONAL REPRESENTATIVE.

RESPONDING TO ONGOING ATTACKS on church privileges set in motion by the Reform Laws of the 1850s, Mexico City's archbishop, Lázaro de la Garza y Ballesteros, published a series of pastoral letters in which he laid out the Church's position that rather than representing an obstacle or hindrance to social happiness, the Church in fact was the only authentic foundation on which social order could rest. One sign of the dangers of liberalism, in the archbishop's view, was their dismissiveness toward women. According to Garza y Ballesteros, a number of "the most noble Mexican *señoras*" had sent "representations" to the contitutent congress in 1855 in order to testify against legislation favoring religious tolerance—a circumstance that, as referenced above, elicited the disdain of liberal delegates, one of whom asserted that "Women are not persons, but simply things." For Garza y Ballesteros, such deplorable disdain for "so worthy a portion of society," constituted an important reason for distrust of liberal initiatives and confirmed that much more decisively the Church's own position.

1. Garza y Ballesteros, *Cuarta carta*, 6.

Gendering Reform

As is evident in Garza y Ballesteros' letter, official ecclesiastical discourses continued to respond to contemporary political and social developments in mid-nineteenth-century Mexico City, including the years leading up to and following the Reform. As in the 1820s and 30s, these official formulations often included gendered references both to idealized male and female saints and to piety among contemporary men and women. Even more than in the previous two decades, however, men and especially women in this period came increasingly to stand in for what was good and stable in society and therefore what needed to be both defended and perpetuated. Specifically, it was piety and devoutness, especially as embodied by women and the institution of motherhood, that was to be celebrated and encouraged. As in Garza y Ballesteros' letter, although traditional piety might be mocked and ridiculed by the Church's enemies, it was the practice of the virtues associated with it that would lead society back to its divinely ordained path. However, as also emerges in the archbishop's letter, another important difference from the previous decades was the presence now of a reinvigorated episcopacy, prepared once more to exercise spiritual leadership over its flock. In contrast to the effective absence of bishops in Mexico City and most other areas of the country for over a decade after independence, the 1840s and subsequent decades witnessed the arrival of new leaders ready to resume the struggle to defend the Church's rights and prerogatives in the face of ongoing challenges.

As difficulties mounted in this period, evidence from the Church's official discourses demonstrates that the new leadership once again, as at the beginning of the nineteenth century, assumed a defensive posture toward what it perceived as increasingly brazen attacks on its rights and prerogatives, once more employing gendered language in its efforts to do so. However, in contrast to their predecessors' condemnations of women's behavior, bishops and other officially endorsed clerics in this period took a more favorable tack toward members of their flocks, both male and female. Albeit mostly unconsciously, prelates shifted their approach as they began to perceive that, especially in the case of women, recruiting believers to their side—thereby buttressing the Church's own inernal cohesion—was a more effective strategy than laying fault with the faithful for the country's problems. In making this rhetorical shift, prelates were switching the locus of blame for the crises facing the nation. Rather than originating among misbehaving (mostly female) members from within the body of believers, the country's problems were rather to be attributed to "daring," "diabolical" forces outside the sacred boundaries of the community of faith. In other words, although prelates in this period would never explicitly renounce their goal of restoring the Church's centrality to Mexico's national life, their strategies reveal a growing implicit recognition that, ultimately, it was the Church's own survival as an institution that was most important.

Thus, in sensing a need to regroup internally and strengthen the Church against its foes, bishops and other clerics turned their criticisms outward, toward external enemies, and focused energies internally on reinvigorating practices and attitudes of piety and devotion central to the institution's mission. Crucially, as seen in each period examined in this study, one important way in which the Church accomplished this task was through gendered language. As they had in the 1820s and 30s but now with greater intensity, preachers and other purveyors of church discourses now spoke, often in increasingly feminized terms, in praise of piety and devoutness as an essential part of the answer to reigning assaults on the faith. Although the Church's adversaries would also need to be challenged, this mission would never succeed if the institution's own internal strength and legitimacy were not reinvested with the (gendered) spiritual power of the people's belief.

This chapter, therefore, will examine the development of official church discourses between the 1840s and the early 1870s as a means of studying in greater depth the nature of the Church's role in the ongoing struggle to determine Mexico's future course during the mid nineteenth century. The chapter examines a number of sermons and other examples of public discourses and suggests how language and concepts of gender continued to shape both the Church's response to the crises of the period and the eventual sense of a working resolution achieved in the years immediately preceding the opening of the *Porfiriato* and the beginnings of a new chapter in Mexican national and ecclesiastical history.

Reinvigorated Church Leadership

By the end of the 1830s, it had been almost two decades since Mexico City's still-nominal archbishop, Pedro de Fonte, fled abruptly for Spain, never returning to his see despite orders to do so from Rome.[2] This situation persisted, leaving the Mexican church with few bishops, until an accord between Mexico and the Vatican was finally reached in the late 1830s, allowing for the appointment of a new archbishop, Manuel Posada y Garduño, and his formal consecration on May 31, 1840.[3] Generally well regarded within the Church and later remembered for his pastoral manner, Mexico City's first non-peninsular

2. See chapter 5 for more details on Fonte's departure.

3. See Bravo Rubio, "La gestión"; Valverde Tellez, *Bio-Bibliografía*; Bravo Ugarte, *Diócesis*, 64; Murray, "Fray José"; Schwaller, "Episcopal"; Lynch, *Latin America*, 132; Green, *Mexican Republic*, 78.

archbishop wasted little time in addressing his flock upon assuming leadership, expressing the importance of perseverance in the faith during "dangerous times."[4] For the archbishop, despite the best efforts of malevolent forces to impose upon Mexico both impiety and "total apostasy" through "erroneous doctrines," "malignant books," "obscene paintings," and "dreadful customs," a "special providence" from God had preserved believers' faith both "pure and unalterable"—like a "firm rock amid the numbing waves."[5]

The rock of faith, however, could not retain its strength in isolation. Rather, Posada y Garduño pointed out that faith would have to be rooted in each believer's heart and accompanied by the practice of virtue in order to endure in the long-term.[6] When practiced in this way, faith could lend to men and women an "indefectible certitude" and abundant consolation, provided that each person avoided "vain curiosity" about things beyond their understanding.[7] Rather than relying on their own inventiveness, human beings needed instead to practice humility and respect for the "weight of authority" if they wished to reinvigorate their faith and resist temptation.[8] By "resting in the doctrine of your Mother, the Church," the faithful could free themselves from "worries and questions" and attain the certitude of unassailable belief.[9] As a result, the faithful were to avoid contact with "philosophers of the day"—arrogant proponents of "daring opinions," "erroneous maxims," and "false doctrines" concerning the respect owed properly both to God and the Church.[10] In order to preserve their faith unharmed, believers had to eschew the reigning "fashionable enlightenment," content with remaining "obedient to the Church, your Mother."[11]

Clues to the significance of Posada y Garduño's letter emerge in accompanying documents, which related instructions from the archbishop for the reading of the letter at Sunday masses.[12] Here the archbishop commended his fellow priests and preachers for their devotion to the common flock which they were to shepherd and called them to continue to preach and combat together the "opposing forces of the abyss." Similarly, in an 1845 pastoral ad-

---

4. Posada y Garduño, *Pastoral* (1841), 4. See also Valverde Tellez, *Bio-Bibliografía*, 252.

5. Posada y Garduño, *Pastoral* (1841), 4.

6. Ibid., 4–5.

7. Ibid., 6–7.

8. Ibid., 8.

9. Ibid.

10. Ibid., 9.

11. Ibid., 10.

12. AGN, GD 118 Justicia, vol. 255, exp. 24, fs. 271–82. Año: 1841.

dressed to priests, the archbishop lamented the reigning "persecution of the clergy," and recommended unity through a common spirit of charity as the most effective means of combating the "corruption of the age."[13] As made clear in his letter, Posada y Garduño recommended both to fellow clergymen and the faithful renewed commitment to faith and virtue—qualities best expressed in his view through obedience to the Church. As other prelates would continue to do in subsequent years and decades, the archbishop emphasized the importance of the institutional Church and its authority—and, increasingly, that of the pope—in shoring up and securing the unity of believers and the steadfastness of their faith in the face of "the abyss."

One manifestation of "the abyss" with which parishioners in Mexico City would doubtless have been painfully familiar in the 1840s were the events preceding and following from war between the United States and Mexico, including the former's eventual annexation of a large portion of Mexican national territory.[14] In August of 1847, during the most volatile days of the war, another archbishop, Juan Manuel Irizarri y Peralta—a member of Mexico City's clerical elite and a former congressional representative—published a pastoral letter in which he attributed Mexico's difficulties in the war, despite the injustice of the American invasion, to its own sins.[15] Like Spain in its eighth-century losses to Moorish forces, punished for its transgressions against God—which, as earlier preachers had noted, included the "effeminization" of formerly brave warriors—so too Mexico, because of its internal divisions and "inconstant governments" was now the recipient of God's avenging justice.[16] However, all was not yet fully lost. Addressing all "pious Mexicans," Irizarri y Peralta called upon his audience to support and defend the Church—the only authentic source of unity for the country. If not, the archbishop pointed out that the United States invasion would fully succeed and "our sacrosanct religion, the only one that is true" would suffer the "unspeakably abominable disgrace" (*desgracia infanda*) of having to tolerate other religions.[17] In other words, as other preachers would

13. AHAM, Base Siglo XIX, Caja 69, exp. 74. Fondo: Episcopal, Sección: Secretaría arzobispal, Serie: carta pastoral. Año: 1845. Carta pastoral del arzobispo Manuel Posada y Garduño a los venerables curas, parrócos, jueces eclesiásticos y vicarios foráneos de esta diócesis, sobre la desición del cabildo de compartir el diezmo (4 ejemplares). Fs. 8.

14. For the question of the Church, politics, and religion during the war with the United States, see García Ugarte, *Poder politico*, chapter 4; Connaughton and Ruiz Medrano, ed., *Dios, religion*; Connaughton, "El catolicismo."

15. For Irizarri y Peralta's career, including his congressional service, see Staples, "La participación," 342–43. See also Irizarri y Peralta, *Pastoral*.

16. Irizarri y Peralta, *Pastoral*.

17. Ibid..

also stress, the key to overcoming the many nefarious threats to internal Mexican political unity lay principally with a return on the part of all to sincere piety as a means of defending and strengthening the only authentic arbiter of social harmony: the Church.[18] No longer able to tolerate the excesses and betrayals of "the age," by the late 1840s it had become increasingly clear to Church leaders that nothing short of what Brian Connaughton has termed a "resacralization" of society would suffice to redeem it from imminent perdition.[19]

Indications of how this resacralization would work emerged in the pastoral letters of Mexico City's new archbishop in the 1850s, Lázaro de la Garza y Ballesteros. Having spent time as a bishop in Sonora, where he developed a reputation for his own personal piety, Garza y Ballesteros came to Mexico City with a desire to renew his flock's devotion to traditional beliefs and pious practices while also solidifying the Church's position vis-à-vis the national government.[20] However, unlike predecessors who had singled out members of the flock—especially women—for particularly severe berating, a shift in approach is evident in Garza y Ballesteros' discourses. Specifically, instead of excoriating his flock and blaming them for the current troubles, the archbishop, while stern concerning necessary improvements, reserved his most biting critiques for forces outside the Church.

One example of this approach emerges in a series of letters published by Garza y Ballesteros in the early part of the 1850s. While the archbishop focused in the letters on the "most sad state" in which he found the "morality of customs," he made clear that he was referring less to the problematic behavior of individuals within the Church and more to the corruption of

18. Connaughton notes that the period of the U.S. intervention and its aftermath marks another watershed in Mexican clerical discourses. Whereas in the decades following independence the Church had labored to adjust its discourses to the needs of the times, now was the time for "the age," especially as manifested in the ideas of Mexican liberals, to adjust to the requirements of the Church. See Connaughton, "El clero," 367.

19. Ibid., 366–67.

20. See Connaughton, "Una ruptura," 27–28. For examples of Garza y Ballesteros' writings from Sonora, see Garza y Ballesteros, *Varias cartas*; Bazant, "From Independence," 33. In this series of pastoral letters—reprinted in Mexico City upon the archbishop's arrival—Garza y Ballesteros expounded on the importance of morality and the regulation of church life, including for members of the clergy. One of Garza y Ballestero's fellow bishops, Pelagio Antonio de Labastida y Dávalos in Puebla, was another Church leader who experienced conflict with the civil government in the 1850s, clashing, for example, with President Ignacio Comonfort. Nevertheless, not all liberals, including Comonfort, were fully or radically opposed to collaborating or seeking compromise with the Church. For a study of moderate liberals, see Villegas Revueltas, *El liberalismo*.

society in general.[21] Without the foundational morality provided to society by religion, Garza y Ballesteros wondered out loud, what would become of the nation? The good of society was, in the archbishop's words, "inseparable" from that of religion and, by extension, the Church; without faith in God there could be no hope for the future.[22] As other clerics would also emphasize in their sermons, for Garza y Ballesteros the importance of a return on the part of all to pious devotion to God was, therefore, essential.[23]

However, as the 1850s progressed, increasingly Garza y Ballesteros and other prelates began to realize that what was different now was the gravity of increasing attacks on the Church from forces the archbishop and other clerics saw increasingly as beyond the pale. Now that the Church and religion itself were under attack, strong counter measures were called for, which, in proportion to the gravity of the situation, would need to originate from the deepest core of the Church's essence—that is, the authenticity and sincerity of the piety and devotion of its members. Consequently, because piety was perceived as central to reviving the Church's fortunes and because conventions of gender were deeply ingrained within notions of piety, it would frequently be through gendered language and imagery that clerics in this period would attempt to defend the institution's interests. Often turning to feminized language at the service of their discursive goals, bishops and other preachers looked increasingly to visions of moral virtue and pious devotion associated with women and motherhood as essential means of shoring up the Church's defenses and assuring its ongoing institutional viability.

Women's Education and Piety

Before turning to closer study of feminized language and imagery in sermons and other church discourses, it is important to provide a sense of the context in which actual women found themselves in mid-nineteenth-century Mexico City. Recent scholarship has demonstrated that many women in this period remained devoted to traditional piety while also finding ways of combining their religious practices with more practical concerns, such as keeping up with styles and fashions in order to appear at their best for

---

21. Garza y Ballesteros, *Edicto* (1852), 12–13.
22. Ibid., 13–14. See also Garza y Ballesteros, *Pastoral* (1852), 7.
23. Nevertheless, this did not necessarily mean a blanket condemnation of liberalism on the part of Garza y Ballesteros—in fact, the archbishop shared common values with liberals and, at least in the first part of the 1850s, sought to promote both elements of republicanism and the Church's interests simultaneously. See Connaughton, "Una ruptura," 34–36.

Gendering Reform

religious holidays and social events.[24] While some evidence points to an increasing secularization of women's activities in this period—including a decline in cloistered convent professions—other indications suggest that women were also finding new ways to combine traditional religiosity with fresh opportunities to expand beyond the confines of the home.[25]

Among examples of this phenomenon, increasingly in the 1840s one way for women to meet together and participate in outside activities was through collective works of charity and piety.[26] In one document commissioned by the Mexico City cathedral chapter (*cabildo*), for instance, a group of female leaders provided an explanation of the purpose and functioning of the organization they ran for orphaned children, while another religious pamphlet promoted devotion to the Divina Infantita—a particular advocation of the Virgin—thanks to the sponsorship of "two loving *esclavas* and daughters of the Immaculate Conception of this divine girl."[27] In a similar way, in a recent study Margaret Chowning has documented over 80 foundations of a new organization of lay women who came together in this period to organize ongoing vigils (*vela perpétua*) in devotion to the Eucharistic sacrament.[28] Likewise, in 1845 a biography of St. Vincent de Paul appeared in honor of the special monetary contributions of one female donor toward the establishment of the new female religious order of the Sisters of Charity (*Hermanas de Caridad*) in Mexico—characterized by its unique requirement of only yearly, renewable vows and a lack of claustration of its members.[29] As Anne Staples puts it in her study of women in this period: "For the first time in their history, Mexicans saw these women, unmistakable with their wide-winged veils, [no longer confined to the convent], coming and going in the street to hospitals and later to the schools they administered."[30]

Regarding schools and education, this period also saw the rise of support for greater education of women and girls, often articulated as a means both of eradicating prostitution among women of lower social classes and, for elite women, of ensuring the preservation of social values and norms.[31]

---

24. Staples, "Sociabilidad," 106–10.

25. Arrom, *Women*, 47–49; Chowning, *Rebellious Nuns*, chapter 6. As Chowning notes, declining professions in this period could also be attributed to other factors such as complications in obtainnng licenses to admit novices.

26. Staples, "Sociabilidad," 110–111.

27. *Esposición* (1840); *Exaltacion* (1843).

28. Chowning, "Laywomen."

29. *Vida de S. Vicente de Paul*. See also Staples, "Sociabilidad," 111.

30. Staples, "Sociablidad," 111; Arrom, *Women*, 48–49.

31. Carner, "Estereotipos," 104; Sánchez Korrol, "Women," 74.

Preaching Power

As scholars have demonstrated, by the early 1840s, acceptance of women's education was a commonplace, receiving legislative enshrinement in Mexico City in 1842—albeit with little practical enforcement—and, by the end of the 1860s, resulting in the founding of schools exclusively for girls.[32] As one contemporary document argued, women's education would lead not only to their own betterment but to the edification of society in general:

> The woman whose intelligence has been developed through studies and arts appropriate to her sex, will be neither frivolous nor dissipate, and she who has practiced constant exercise of her faculty of thought will never be indiscreet, careless or imprudent. Habituated to meditate and to reflect on her actions, she will easily disdain vain words and useless conversations, which are always the unequivocal sign of an empty mind and whose ideas and thoughts are in perpetual disorder.[33]

Proclaiming the promotion of this type of education for women as its most significant purpose and yet not divorcing this endeavor from the importance of women's ongoing devotion to religion, the magazine's editors provided their readers with articles and features on various topics, including natural history, geography, physics, astronomy, literature and, significantly, religion. Emphasizing the importance of religion in women's lives, including devotional feasts such as Corpus Christi and the Assumption of the Virgin, the calendar's editors evinced a conviction that the type of education for women that they were advocating was not at all in conflict with or opposed to the style of piety and devotion being promoted by Church officials in the same period.[34] Meanwhile, in the case of men, evidence at least from the church discourses studied here does not indicate significant clerical concern with decreased male participation in religious services and devotional practices, at least in the first part of the period studied in this chapter.[35]

32. Arrom, *Women,* 19–20; Sánchez Korrol, "Women," 74–75.

33. *Semanario* (1841), IV.

34. In a similar publication in 1842, the same publisher offered another magazine entitled *Panorama de las señoritas,* likewise dedicated to the virtues of "the beautiful sex" and "the enchanting sex," as well as the advantages of women's education. See *Panorama* (1847).

35. Regarding men's devotion and public involvement with the Church, the 1840s saw the ongoing publication of Catholic magazines, some of which featured stories and articles appealing to women, but which displayed clear evidence of being directed at male audiences as well. Likewise, various laymen manifested their opposition to initiatives favoring religious tolerance and also organized petitions on behalf of the Jesuit order. See *Defensa de la petición*; *Defensa de la Compañía*; Suárez y Navarro, *Juicio crítico*; *Semanario* (1843); *El Ilustrador* (1847); *Carta de un amigo*; de la Vega,

Gendered Language in Sermons

As preached in sermons in the late 1840s and 50s, notions of piety and devotion were now even more crucial amidst a series of crises including variations between liberal and conservative governments, the debacle of the U.S. invasion and seizure of national territory, further appropriations of Church assets, and the introduction of proposals for religious tolerance.[36] Revealing how the language of piety became gendered in many of these discourses, in one anti-Protestant sermon from 1849 the preacher, José Cayetano Orozco, noted that priests formed a crucial foundation for Mexican society and provided a distinct advantage as spiritual guides since, unlike the "protestant priesthood," they avoided the pitfalls of "living with a woman" and therefore of becoming "solicitous of worldly vanities" in order to "please their wives."[37] On the contrary, the Catholic priesthood, unencumbered by women's "vanities," professed an "essentially intolerant religion"—one in which there was "only one Jesus Christ." This divine foundation for society could not be sacrificed or altered since it constituted the authentic expression of God's will and remained the sole source of true consolation amid the vicissitudes of life. As the preacher put it: "Oh divine priesthood; even if the wisdom of the age should change like the times, the victim that you offer is the same! If there are revolutions among empires, there is no variation in your sublime offering! If mundane philosophy remains complacent in its versatile systems, your sacrifice is immutable, like God himself[.]"[38] In other words, although the sermon revived earlier tropes of women's vanity and the threat it could pose to society, the focus now was no longer on problematic women within the Church itself. Instead, it was now Protestant women and their interloping clerical husbands who were imperiling society. In contrast to these threats, the Catholic priesthood, the Eucharist, and other traditional attitudes and

---

Opúsculo (1849); Canseco, *Esplicación*; *Representación que la Congregación*; *Representación que han elevado*; AGN, GD 120, Justicia Eclesiástica, Vol. 161, fs. 29–59.

36. By the 1840s the idea of religious tolerance had been at play already in Mexico for several decades. For studies of the development of ideas in favor of tolerance, see Ruiz Guerra, "La aceptación"; Ruiz Guerra, "La libertad"; Santillán, "La secularización"; Bazant, "From Independence," 17–26. See also Hale, *Mexican Liberalism*, 35–36. Hale emphasizes that despite concerns on the part of church leaders regarding their intentions, not all liberals were virulently anti-clerical.

37. Orozco, *Sermon* (1849), 16–17. These sentiments may also represent a response on the part of the Church to liberal emphasis on marriage and family. See Silvia Arrom's analysis of novelist Manuel Payno and other liberals' disdain and even hatred for spinsters. Arrom, *Women*, 138–39.

38. Orozco, *Sermón* (1849), 22–23.

practices of devotion were now the safe, "immutable" harbor in which the interests of the Church and of the nation could take rest.

Wedding Femininty and Religion

In support of these devotional practices and traditions, preachers' language grew increasingly feminized in this period as they turned with greater frequency to traditional attributes of women and motherhood and their positive associations with religion. For instance, following a cholera outbreak in Mexico City in 1850, the Carmelite preacher Pablo Antonio del Niño Jesús noted, in distinctly feminized terms, the importance of religion for society in alleviating despair and instilling hope.[39] Like a "solicitous mother" who suspended her children from her "abundant breast" and fed them with "a milk that cures all their sorrows," religious faith was the sole authentic foundation for a healthy and prosperous society. Providing "sweet consolations," "robust support," and a "soft and efficacious balsam" for its ills, religion in fact represented the essence of society. In the words of the preacher, "it is not possible to conceive of society without religion."[40] Just as Mexico had suffered terribly during the recent outbreak, so it was also suffering spiritually under even graver threats. Indeed, the "horrible specter" of the cholera outbreak was, in an important sense, a metaphor for how Mexico needed to return to its religious foundations in order to prosper once more as a society. Therefore, as in the case of the outbreak, against the equally horrifying and "ferocious shout" of those who dared seek an "impious tolerance" for other religions while ignoring the "exclusive sovereignty" of God, it was the intercession of the Virgin alone that would spare the country from a fate far worse than the plague.[41] Staving off the "total destruction" of the "ungrateful and sinful Mexican people," it was "Mary and Mary alone" who, with "almost omnipotent pleas," would gain for Mexico the pardon of its sins, the suspension of its punishment, and the prolongation of its life as a nation.[42] To this "strong woman" alone—this "Mother of pieties"—belonged thanks not only for the diminishment of the cholera outbreak but, by implication, any future moral, social, or political cohesion in Mexico.[43]

As is evident in this sermon, by the early 1850s, amid various social and political crises, preachers once more began to single out what they viewed

39. del Niño Jesús, *Sermón* (1850).
40. Ibid., 7–8.
41. Ibid., 9–12.
42. Ibid., 14–15.
43. Ibid., 17.

as problematic behavior on the part of individuals and groups in society, often employing gendered language to do so.[44] For example, also responding to the 1850 cholera outbreak, another preacher invoked the intercession of the Virgin Mary as instrumental in staying the plague's effects.[45] According to this sermonizer, although the "terrible sword" of the "God of vengeances" had struck down upon Mexico City in the form of the recent plague, all was not lost, because of the intercession of the Virgin.[46] However, dangers remained, especially insofar as the people of the city had not repented of their sinful, scandalous ways. In particular, the "luxury," "vanity," "looseness" (*desenvoltura*) and "immodesty" of dresses among some, the "scandalous liberty" and "abominable dissolution" found in the facial expressions, gait (*paseos*) and attendance at theaters among others, and the disdain for images of Christ and "profanation of temples and holy days," among still other offenses, all represented ongoing threats which at any moment could provoke the "trembling of the earth" and God's "eternal indignation."[47]

However, despite occasional passages like these—which contrast to their far greater frequency earlier in the nineteenth century—clerical discourses in this period are striking for their overall lack of invective against women. With a few exceptions like the passages cited above and one document from 1850—published anonymously under the title "Sermon of Men Against Women," which rehearsed earlier notions about women—most sermons and other published church documents spoke favorably of feminine virtues such as motherhood and women's devotion to the Church.[48] For example, additional calendars and magazines were published in the 1850s and subsequent decades, which extolled women's virtues and, specifically, their unique potential to regenerate society,[49] while one like-minded

44. Connaughton describes the environment of the 1850s as one of increasing polarization and confrontation between church and state. See Connaughton, "Enemy Within," 195–97. Nevertheless, Connaughton also points out that even during this period and subsequently there still existed significant diversity among Catholic leaders, and individual Catholics as well, concerning the merits of liberalism. For this reason, Connaughton advocates use of the plural term "Catholics" rather than the singular "Catholic" as a means of reflecting the diversity of opinion among believers.

45. Abogado, *Sermón* (1850).

46. Ibid., 1–4.

47. Ibid., 7.

48. *Sermón de los hombres* (1850). Perhaps reflecting the growing tension between the Church and liberal government officials in the 1850s, the document, with its emphasis on the purported vices and weaknesses of women, may represent an expression of how gender remained an important site of contestation within ongoing cultural and political battles.

49. See *Diccionario* (1851); *Primer calendario* (1851); *La Semana* (1851); *La*

clerical pamphlet went even further, dedicating its entire content to providing an account of the opposing natures of men and women and suggesting women's fundamental role in supporting a strong Catholic society by means of the positive influence of their piety on their husbands and families.[50]

Gendering Devotion

Also important in this period was the continuing publication of devotional materials often dedicated to women or associated with their pious practices. For instance, one devotional booklet from 1851 took the form of a dialogue or "colloquium" between Jesus—characterized as "most sweet"—and "the soul, his wife," while other materials related miraculous apparitions and prophecies, promoted the cult of saints, and reported on contemporary religious events.[51] Likewise, books on women's morality and religious devotion originally published in Europe also appeared in Mexico in translation in this period.[52] As mentioned at the beginning of this chapter, women also continued to intervene publicly in favor of the Church, as occurred in the mid-1850s when groups of women wrote to the constituent congress in opposition to a proposal for tolerance of other religions.[53] Also significant was the establishment of various women's societies dedicated to the promotion of piety and religious good works, including the *Sociedad de la Purísima Concepción*, the *Sociedad de San Vicente de Paul*, the *Señoras de la Caridad*, and the *Sociedad Católica de Señoras*.[54] As Erika Pani has also pointed out, these interventions by women

---

Camelia (1853); *Noveno calendario* (1859); *Calendario* (1864); *Calendario* (1866); *Primer calendario* (1871); *Segundo calendario* (1872); *Tercer calendario* (1873); *Quinto calendario* (1875); *Calendario* (1878).

50. *El fin del hombre*.

51. See *El camino verdadero*; *Profecías de Matiana*; *Aparición milagrosa*; *Asociación* (1874); *Apuntes biográficos*. For examples of additional ways in which Church officials sought to promote and reward this type of piety, see the following: AHAM, Base Siglo XIX, Caja 89, exp. 40. Fondo: Episcopal, Sección: Provisorato, Serie: conferencias morales. Año: 1852. Expediente relativo a las conferencias morales establecidas por la pastoral del Ilustrisímo señor arzobispo, parroquia de Santa Anna. Fs. 9; AGN, GD 14, Bienes Nacionales. Año: 1852. Vol. 1524, exp. 35. Concesión de indulgencia plenaria para la devoción de las cuarenta horas. México.

52. For example, see the following: *Virginia, la doncella*; *La doncella cristiana*; *La mujer cristiana*.

53. See *Representación que varias señoras*; *Representación que algunas señoras*.

54. See *Reglamento* (1860); *Primer calendario* (1858); *Sociedad* (1862); *Reglamento* (1863); *Memoria* (1865); *Reglamento* (1870); AHAM, Base de Pelagio Antonio de Labastida y Dávalos, Caja 55, exp. 45. Sección: Secretaría Arzobispal, Serie: Asociaciones piadosas. Año: 1870. Sociedad Católica. Con relación a la Sociedad de señoras. Fs. 4.

Gendering Reform

in favor of the Church and examples of their support for pious societies and activities played an important role in the increased recourse preachers and other official church representatives were starting to make to idealized concepts of women and femininity in this period.[55]

Evidence from the 1850s of interactions and occasional disputes between male-dominated confraternities and priests likewise shows that religious associations continued to matter to men.[56] Similarly, as in the 1840s, laymen again intervened publicly on behalf of the Church against the possibility of religious tolerance and evidence of membership in groups such as the *Sociedad Católica* indicates strong ongoing male support within them at least through the late 1860s.[57] Some lay men also continued to participate in pious devotions, including the promotion of Eucharistic adoration in Mexico City in the late 1860s, practices of pilgrimage in the 1870s, and leadership and participation in organizations such as the *Sociedad Católica*.[58] Other Catholic periodicals from this period likewise

---

55. Pani, "Una ventana."

56. For example, one series of documents from the archives of the Archdiocese of Mexico City describes efforts on the part of members of the Archconfraternity of la Santa Veracruz to adjudicate a dispute with a local priest, another published document on devotion to the Virgin makes note of how leaders of a lay group petitioned church leaders for indulgences associated with pious practices, and other documents describe a commission sought by Mexico City officials for a novena to the Virgin of Remedios, the collaboration of a lay leader of the *Sociedad de San Vicente de Paul* with its clerical leader, and a visit to another *archicofradía*. See AHAM, Base Siglo XIX, Caja 81, exp. 56. Año: 1850. Expediente sobre visita a la archicofradía de San Ignacio de la parroquia de Santa Catarina Martir formado a pedimento de Manuel Falcón, mayordomo de la fábrica espiritual y material. Fs. 22; *Tiernos coloquios*; *Sociedad de S. Vicente*; *Noticia* (1869); *Noticias* (1870); *Noticia* (1871); AHAM, Base Siglo XIX, Caja 111, exp. 99. Fondo: Cabildo, Sección: Haceduría, Serie: Jueces hacedores. Año: 1854. Manuel Elizalde sobre contribución para celebrar un solemne novenario a Nuestra Señora de los Remedios por las necesidades públicas. Fs. 2; AHAM, Base Siglo XIX, Caja 96, exp. 9. Fondo: Episcopal, Sección: secretaría arzobispal, Serie: visita pastoral. Año: 1858. Visita a la ilustre Archicofradía del Santísimo y Santa Catarina Virgen y Martir de México.

57. For example, see *Representación contra* (1856). This document, which features the signatures of some hundreds of men who expressed their support for its contents, expresses the belief that supporters of the Church's position were in the majority against the betrayal of "a few dozen political visionaries" (ibid., 1–2). See also *Representación que los habitantes de Zamora* (1856); *Representación que elevan al Soberano* (1856). For petitions from various places throughout Mexico in favor of the Church's position, see also AGN, GD 120, Justicia Eclesiástica, Vol. 187, fs. 248–60. For the *Sociedad Católica* see *La Sociedad Católica* (1869); *Reglamento provisional* (1869).

58. See *Obra de la esposición*; *Adoración nocturna*. The first of these pamphlets includes the names of ten male leaders of the society devoted to the promotion of eucharistic devotion. See also *Itinerario* (1874); *Comunicación* (1875).

featured stories that integrated religious news and pious devotions with practical, scientific areas of knowledge and contemporary politics and business subjects—all likely aimed at a predominantly male audience.[59] It was only toward the end of this period that possible indications emerged that men may have begun to attend church less frequently—perhaps an affirmation that, for much of the time under consideration here, the struggle had been precisely inside and within Catholicism to determine the direction of policy, links with liberalism, and change.[60]

Marian Piety, Rome, and the Feminization of Religion

Even as sermons and the devotional language they promoted grew more feminized through associations with positive purported aspects of femininity, another impetus toward the feminization of religion emerged in a series of developments that bound devotion to the Virgin and loyalty to the Holy See ever more closely together. Important indications of this trend can be observed in sermons in praise of the Virgin beginning in the early 1850s.[61] According to one sermonizer, the Mercedarian Ramón Dávila, God was to be thought of as both vengeful and compassionate at the same time. Despite the need to correct and punish sinners, God also provided a means for curing their "sorrowful wounds" precisely through the "divine Judith" who "descends from the sky" in order to dry the people's tears and grant them liberty "for the glory of the sanctuary."[62] In a sermon from 1852 in praise of the Virgin of Guadalupe, another preacher, the priest Francisco Javier Miranda, referred to the Virgin's sanctuary as a "meeting point" (*punto de reunión*) for all Mexicans—the only tie that bound their affections and the sole principle of unity

---

59. See *La Regeneración Social* (1869); *Revista universal* (1869); *El Mensajero* (1875). For an example of a tract written (at least according to the published accompanying information) by a Catholic layman in the 1870s against liberalism, see *Las Hermanas* (1874).

60. See AHAM – Base Siglo XIX, Caja 124, exp. 2. This series of files recounts a controversy that emerged in the 1860s and 1870s surrounding women's participation in church music. Petitioning to sing during mass, women's requests were usually turned down by church officials due to the purported threat the sound of their voices could pose to public morality. However, the fact that one of the justifications cited by the women in favor of their requests was the increasing lack of sufficient numbers of male musicians points to the possibility that men's pariticipation in church may have started to decline by the second half of the nineteenth century.

61. For example, see Dávila, *Panegirico* (1850).

62. Dávila, *Panegirico* (1850), 4–5.

and strength capable forging the people into a unified nation.⁶³ Intriguingly, the preacher extended this comparison to recent attacks on the authority of the papacy, making a similar argument that, as the "center of the Christian nations," the "rector of the Church of Jesus Christ," and the "foundation of Catholic unity," the pope and the papacy, like the Virgin of Guadalupe for the people of Mexico, constituted the sole authentic source of unity for the otherwise disparate, centrifugal collective body of the Church.⁶⁴

Papal Affirmation of the Immaculate Conception

This move toward closer association between the Virgin and the papacy in church discourses intensified in 1855 and 1856 with celebrations of the official papal declaration of the doctrine of the Immaculate Conception.⁶⁵ Giving thanks for the official proclamation of a doctrine that had long enjoyed widespread credence and devotion among the faithful in Mexico and support within New Spanish and Mexican sermons, the preachers who reflected on the event did not hesitate to comment on the significance of the moment.⁶⁶ Among these preachers, archbishop Lázaro de la Garza y Ballesteros himself enthusiastically greeted the news in his own published sermon.⁶⁷ For Garza y Ballesteros, the authenticity and truth of the doctrine of the Immaculate Conception had never been in doubt. The Virgin Mary indeed "unites the glory

63. Miranda, *Sermon* (1853), 15–16.

64. For another sermon which mentions the importance of the papacy and unity and peace in Mexico, see Covarrubias, *Sermon* (1853).

65. To highlight the significance of this proclamation a lengthy document on the doctrine of the Immaculate Conception, along with a description of the ceremonies accompanying its proclamation in Rome, was published in 1855. See *Homenaje* (1855). A novena booklet on devotion to the Immaculate Conception also appeared the following year. See *Novena* (1856). For examples of the ceremonies and celebrations held in Mexico City in honor of the proclamation, see California State Library, Sutro Collection, pamphlets 266:7999 and 266:8000.

66. As mentioned in chapter 2, one of the most popular tropes found in Baroque sermons on the Immaculate Conception and the Virgin of Guadalupe included belief that devotion on the part of the people of New Spain to the Guadalupan image would eventually result in an official papal declaration of the Immaculate Conception, along with a possible transmigration of the papacy to Mexico—an event that would signify the imminent end of the world. Therefore, as demonstrated in the sermons studied in this chapter, Pius IX's official declaration of the doctrine of the Immaculate Conception in 1855 had a particularly strong resonance in Mexico, especially in light of the ongoing struggles facing both the embattled Mexican Church and the papacy at the time.

67. Garza y Ballesteros, *Sermon* (1855).

of virginity with the dignity of mother[hood]" and was therefore to be recognized for her exceptional holiness.[68] However, even more crucially, as a result of Pius IX's declaration, the piety of the Mexican people would now grow that much stronger, both in their veneration and respect for the Virgin as well as their overall religious devotion.[69] Significantly, one year prior to his sermon Garza y Ballesteros himself had published an extensive pamphlet on the topic of the pope's apostolic authority.[70] Defending the authority of the successor of Peter, Garza y Ballesteros emphasized that "in all parts [of the world] Peter [i.e., the pope] should be heard and obeyed[.]"[71] By "divine right," the Roman Pontiff enjoyed the privilege, bestowed by Christ himself, of receiving unquestioning obedience—a doctrine always and everywhere true throughout all of history, "without the least contradiction."[72] This authority, therefore, as the source of the declaration of the Virgin's Immaculate Conception, not only affirmed and enshrined a popular religious devotion but did so in a way not subject to the vagaries of passing political and social circumstances that were afflicting the Church both in Mexico and in Europe.[73]

Other preachers celebrated the news of the papal declaration with similar, often feminized language and sentiments, emphasizing especially the aid that the new doctrine would provide in fomenting religious devotion in society. According to the Oratorian preacher Felipe Villarello, religion was the strongest tie that bound society together and therefore required of all believers and citizens the unabashed profession of their beliefs both in word and in deed.[74] To this end, it would be necessary to awaken the "sleeping piety" of Mexico's citizens, renewing them in the most essential dogmas of their "adorable religion," so that all would unite behind the authority of the pope. Thankfully, according to Villarello, precisely such a summons had arrived in the form of the papal declaration of the Immaculate Conception—a doctrine which would offer to "devout souls" a "new and most sweet sentiment" of "most fervent devotion."[75] For the Jesuit priest Ignacio María Lerdo, this

68. Ibid., 19.
69. Ibid., 21–22.
70. Garza y Ballesteros, *Opusculo* (1854).
71. Ibid., 7.
72. Ibid., 9.
73. See the discussion below of the rise of ultramontanism in this period and its connections to the doctrine of the Immaculate Conception, the 1864 Syllabus of Errors, and the doctrine of papal infallibility.
74. See Villarello, *Sermon* (1855), 7–8.
75. Ibid., 8–9.

spiritual reawakening could not have come at a more opportune moment.[76] According to Lerdo, the Church and society currently found themselves amid the "most anguishing" of times. A veritable "crowd of seducers" and a "swarm of trouble makers" (*perturbadores*) were agitating and devastating society, seeking its "complete dissolution."[77] However, all was not lost as devotion to the Virgin Mary had always served as the refuge of the Church and would continue to do so in the present age—specifically, by staying the forces of social dissolution and restoring lost (religion-based) unity.[78]

Refashioning the Church as Mother

Whether in society or among believers, unity was a virtue increasingly likened and attributed in this period to the virtues of motherhood. In fact, as the Oratorian preacher Gil Alamán pointed out, in strikingly gendered terms, it was in truth maternal love itself—as manifested in the Virgin Mary but also among everyday women and mothers—that would rescue society and the Church from present dangers.[79] In the preacher's words, maternal love was the most pure and perfect affect of the human heart; its strivings were "heroic," its sacrifices immense, its tenderness "inextinguishable." Always constant, solicitous and swift to help, motherly love dedicated itself to the needs of its children and could never abandon them.[80] In fact, the preacher insisted, motherly love was the most fitting image for the love that the Church itself—by which he specified that he meant its "legitimate prelates," especially the "Supreme Pontiff," its "visible head"—expressed toward its own spiritual children, the faithful.[81] Caring for and seeing after the "security," "conservation" and "happiness" of these "children," the Church, like a solicitous mother, defended its own against the "sad and disastrous" surrounding climate by feeding them with the "sublime truths" of its dogmas.[82]

One such dogma was the Immaculate Conception but, as Alamán noted, what was even more essential were the power and authority behind the declaration—the unassailable spiritual supremacy of the "legitimate

76. Lerdo, *Sermon* (1855).

77. Ibid., 22.

78. Ibid., 24. See also *Diario de los niños* (1840).

79. Alamán, *Sermón* (1856). For additional sermons celebrating the papal declaration of the Immaculate Conception, see Moreno, *Sermon* (1855); Diez de Sollano, *Sermon* (1855).

80. Alamán, *Sermón* (1856), 31.

81. Ibid.

82. Ibid., 27.

vicar of Jesus Christ," the pope.[83] Against the "diversity of opinions" and "insubordination" of society, the pope represented concretely the maternal love and solicitude of the Church toward its "children." In other words, the pope was to be thought of as a kind of spiritual "mother" who also happened to be male. He was to be revered as the supreme leader of an institution founded on patriarchal authority but also characterized by what preachers labeled the "tenderness" and "affection" of its maternal love. This unique, gendered authority, and it alone, possessed the capacity to unite everyone into a "docile flock" under the pope's teachings, therefore affording him an "immense sphere" of jurisdiction over spiritual and religious matters.[84]

Significantly, in contrast to sermons from the late eighteenth century which rarely mentioned the pope and frequently celebrated the authority of the reformist Bourbon state, by the mid nineteenth century, both in Mexico in the documents under consideration in this chapter and elsewhere in Latin America and Europe, surrounding circumstances had changed sufficiently such that the office of the papacy now represented for preachers an idealized bulwark on which the enduring strength of the Church could securely rest.[85] As demonstrated in the Mexican case, the nature of this absolute ecclesiastical authority had also taken on a distinctly gendered tone. No longer simply a bishop or administrator, the pope and the hierarchy of other bishops under him now formed the basis for a kind of spiritual matriarchy—an unmistakably patriarchal system now couched in feminized, maternal terms as a means of shoring up the Church's spiritual authority and the unity it had the capacity to promote in society.

With this increased focus on the importance of the papacy for the life of the Church, Mexican prelates formed part of a larger context in which the revival of Catholicism in the nineteenth century came into frequent conflict with the maturation of liberal political projects both in Europe and America. As one scholar has put it, this was a "clash of cultures," originating in the period of the French Revolution and intensifying throughout the nineteenth century, though not always in contrasts as marked as traditional narratives have tended to portray.[86] Ultramontanism, as this phenomenon came to be known, with its attendant conservative, Rome-centered discursive tendencies, shaped church discourses throughout the Catholic world in increasing ways

---

83. Ibid., 40–41.

84. Ibid., 37–42.

85. For the rise of ultramontane loyalties in nineteenth-century Catholicism, see Anderson, "Divisions," 25–26.

86. See See McMillan, "Religion," 45. See also Ivereigh, ed., *Politics of Religion*, 3–4.

Gendering Reform

over the course of the nineteenth century.[87] Roughly corresponding to a continuum of liberal opposition and mostly conservative ecclesiastical reaction, this phenomenon has been described by one scholar as "a correlation between hostility towards the Church by the Liberal State, on the one hand, and the reactionary discourse of ultramontanism, on the other."[88]

As the evidence studied in this chapter from Mexico also demonstrates, church discoure had changed in significant ways by the mid nineteenth century. Still articulated in the context of patriarchal authority, purveyors of these discourses certainly had not given up on the potential of either men or women to return to the essentials of the faith. However, what was different was the way in which Church leaders understood and articulated the nature of religious faith itself. Rather than as an aspect of societal cohesion to be taken largely for granted as foundational, by the middle of the nineteenth century Mexican prelates were starting to realize that they would now have to fight for the Church's place in society. No longer enjoying a guaranteed role as the privileged counterpart of secular authority, the Church now needed to reassert and rebuild its place in Mexican society, starting from the ground up—that is, by encouraging renewed zeal and religious fervor among the faithful. To do so, it discovered that new discourses of femininity, in which the virtues of motherhood and piety were associated both with actual women as well as with the Church itself and its leaders, would provide consolations to the faithful amid the tribulations of the age, even while reaffirming and securing the institution's patriarchal authority as the sole, indispensable source of authentic social cohesion.[89]

---

87. For a recent study of the phenomenon of ultramontanism in nineteenth-century Catholicism, see Atkin and Tallett, *Priests*. For ultramontanism in Mexico, see Connaughton, "Voces"; Brading, "Ultramontane." In his study, Brading cites the figure and public discourses of Clemente de Jesús Munguía—bishop and later archbishop of Michoacán—as decisive in moving the Mexican Church in ultramontane directions. For an alternate view on Bishop Munguía—in which the author argues that Munguía in fact promoted the independence of the Church from the State rather than strict opposition to it—see Mijangos y González, "Lawyer."

88. Ivereigh, ed., *Politics of Religion*, 7. As Ivereigh also explains, where hostility to the Church was less pronounced so too were the Church's discursive reactions.

89. See Connaughton, *Clerical Ideology*, 153. As Connaughton points out, the self-remaking the Church engaged in through its discourses not only involved responding to perceived attacks but also recruiting new sources of support—for example, female believers and the piety associated with them. See also commentary on the significance of religion for social order in the following sermons: del Barrio y Rengel, *Sermon* (1857), 21; del Niño Jesús, *Sermon* (1857), 5–6.

Gendered Discourses and the Reform

Even as preachers were invoking the Virgin Mary and gendered notions of church authority and piety as a response to contemporary events, a new challenge was soon to manifest itself in the late 1850s in the guise of the Reform—a series of initiatives undertaken by the liberal government that posed a significant threat to traditional church rights and privileges. In response to provisions of the Reform—including the Constitution of 1857 and the Juárez and Lerdo laws, which affected clerical civil immunity and church property—prelates once again responded forcefully through their published discourses, often invoking gendered language to do so.[90]

Not content to stand idly by, Garza y Ballesteros himself intervened repeatedly during the years of the Reform with a series of impassioned pastoral letters.[91] In one pastoral from 1858, following the advent of war earlier that year, the archbishop highlighted the importance of morality for public peace, noting that the "public decadence of the nation" and its "continuing discords" stemmed from nothing other than "public and scandalous" sins.[92] Then, in a series of five letters in 1859—another significant year, given the promulgation by the liberal government of an additional series of laws af-

---

90. For treatments of church-state conflicts in this period, see García Ugarte, *Poder político*, chapters 7–10; Ceballos Ramírez, "Un siglo," 380–384; Enríquez Perea, "La república"; Connaughton, *Clerical Ideology*, 212; Ampudia, *La Iglesia*, 249; Bazant, "From Independence," 32–33. In addition to the Lerdo and Juárez laws, other laws also promulgated in 1856 and 1857 pertained to the civil enforcement of religious vows, the banning of the Jesuit order, the exclusion of Church censors from the press, and clerical control of cemeteries and parish fees. The most controversial element of the Constitution of 1857 was its Article 15, which, though it did not successfully pass, provided for religious freedom and tolerance.

91. Though Church officials often perceived themselves to be under attack from civil authorities, not all of these authorities were openly hostile to the Church. In fact, many were Catholics themselves and, as Brian Connaughton has argued, were likewise seeking to promote the values they had learned in their own religious upbringing. See Connaughton, "La religiosidad," 70–76; Connaughton, "Soberanía." Significantly, Connaughton highlights differences between Puebla's bishop Pelagio Antonio de Labastida y Dávalos in 1857 and the liberal Francisco Zarco over the propriety of political and social changes from nearly a century before—from the reign of the Bourbon reforming monarch Charles III. Referring even further back in history, Zarco also criticized the strain of Catholicism that Spain itself had brought with it in the conquest of Mexico. In contrast to such a style of Catholicism, the sort practiced in the United States proved attractive to Zarco—and also to another contemporary bishop, Pedro Espinosa y Dávalos of Guadalajara, who was exiled to the US in 1861—as, in these figures' view, the enjoyment of religious freedom there allowed the Church to pursue its pastoral and doctrinal mission without the corrupting influence of political involvement.

92. Garza y Ballesteros, *Carta* (1858), 5. See also Ampudia, *La Iglesia*, 250.

firming the separation of church and state, freedom of religion, and various other anticlerical provisions—the archbishop outlined his vision of where the Reform had erred in its attacks on the Church and how the community of believers ought to respond.[93]

Significantly, as noted earlier in this chapter, one encouraging way in which Catholics had already begun to respond came in the form of women's initiative. As the archbishop himself noted, despite the adverse effects of provisions of the Reform on female religious life, Mexican young women retained a "true spirit of piety"—something clearly lacking among members of Juárez's party, whom Garza y Ballesteros accused of declaring that "women are not persons, but simply things." The archbishop explained that many of "the most noble Mexican *señoras*" had submitted written testimonies (*representaciones*) to the national congress of 1855 in opposition to religious tolerance and that the liberals had responded with contempt for the women's piety, using the expression against them which Garza y Ballesteros cited.[94] Expressing disdain for such a contemptuous affront to "this part of society most worthy of consideration" (i.e., women), the archbishop's comments demonstrate how, by the 1850s, representatives of the official Church had begun to reconsider the virtues of "the devout sex" in their discourses, restyling the institution as both a defender of women and a proponent of the virtues most closely associated with them—namely, affective piety and sincere religious devotion.

Although some official Church discourses during the Reform also recommended a return to something of the militaristic attitude observed in sermons from the first decades of the nineteenth century, overall the trend was toward engagement with the enemy less through military victories than through pious devotion.[95] Even as prelates expressed distress in trying to

---

93. See Ampudia, *La Iglesia*, 251–52; Danés Rojas, *Noticias*, 28–29. Among the provisions of the laws which the Church found problematic, both in 1859 and in subsequent years, Ampudia and Danés Rojas cite the following: equal protection for all religions; non-involvement of the state in the adjudication of church fees; prohibition of real estate donations to the Church; nationalization of Church properties; suppression of monastic orders; confiscation of books and art; prohibition of the wearing of clerical garb in public; civil marriage; civil registration for births, marriages, and deaths; reduction of religious holidays; prohibition of public religious celebrations without prior authorization; prohibition of attendance at church functions by civil officials; civil control of institutions of charity and assistance; expulsion of the Roman apostolic delegate and several bishops; suppressions of convents; prohibition of the public use of religious insignia.

94. Garza y Ballesteros, *Cuarta carta*, 6.

95. For examples of more militaristic sermons, see Cordero, *Sermon* (1859); Sánchez, *Sermon* (1859). See also the common distress expressed by many of Mexico's

adjust to the various challenges they faced—including, in early 1861, the expulsion by the liberal government of the papal apostolic delegate and five bishops, among them Garza y Ballesteros and Michoacán's Clemente de Jesús Munguía—they also remained convinced that the feminized language of piety described above would be an essential part of any effective response.[96] For example, preaching at the end of a three-day solemnity of prayer offered at the *colegiata nacional* of Guadalupe for "present needs," just a few months before the expulsion, Munguía recommended avoidance of more fighting and instead a return to the cultivation of religiously-inspired virtue, which would secure triumphs of a "more elevated character."[97] Religious unity was the sole authentic source of unity for Mexico, and therefore the only way forward remained to renew patriotism and "social morality" by fomenting Mexico's "religious spirit" against the forces of "material power."[98] In doing so, the nation would avoid the "triple death" of its religious spirit, moral practices and patriotism and therefore would find, in religious practice, the only authentic solution to its many problems.[99] Again, the key for Munguía, as for other prelates, was to encourage a return by the faithful to renewed piety and religious devotion—that is, to the cultivation by both men and women of the "tender" and "motherly" virtues promoted in church discourses—in order to solidify the Church's foundations in the solid practices of the faithful and to strengthen its enduring resolve.[100]

Another telling endorsement of these discourses—in this case lifting up the greatness of motherhood—emerged in a sermon from 1862 in celebration of the Virgin of Guadalupe, in which the preacher, José María Sainz Herosa, confessed that "there is nothing softer, sweeter, nor more ineffable than the relations of motherhood."[101] The effects motherhood produced in "sensitive souls" caused "indefinable joy" and were beyond praise.[102] Therefore, the motherhood of the Virgin as exercised through the adovcation of

---

bishops in a joint 1859 pastoral, *Manifestación*. For annotated studies and commentaries on this letter, see Romero Galván, "La manifestación"; Alcalá and Olimón, *Episcopado*; Connaughton, "Una ruptura," 51–53.

96. See Bravo Ugarte, *Bio-bibliografía*, 148. See also Puente Lutteroth, "'No es justo,'" 299.

97. Munguía, *Sermon* (1860), 30–31.

98. Ibid., 51.

99. Ibid., 61–62.

100. Munguía himself again confirmed these sentiments in another sermon from 1860, given in Mexico City, in which he praised the virtues and especially the humility of St. Vincent de Paul: Munguía, *Panegírico* (1860), 60–61.

101. Sainz Herosa, *Sermon* (1862).

102. Ibid., 3.

Guadalupe continued to benefit the Mexican nation as the Virgin promoted the "sanctification of souls," "true happiness" and the "admirable exercise of mercies"—all virtues associated with her own motherhood and, by implication, to be inculcated in all of her children in Mexico, both male and female. Similarly, in a sermon from 1863, José María Cayetano Orozco noted the importance of the Virgin in demonstrating that all authentic sovereignty belonged to God alone and therefore that the "bloody consorting" (*sangriento consorcio*) of democracy and impiety was in vain.[103] Instead, the solution to Mexico's problems lay with a return by all to the virtues and ideals embodied in the feminized notions of motherhood and piety espoused in the Church's official discourses—an action that, it was hoped, would restore religion's proper and essential role as the foundation of national unity.[104]

Empire, Republic, and New Discursive Directions

Committed to the ideal of religious piety as the foundation for social welfare, the Church during the years of the Reform had not renounced its claim to the place of prominence it had traditionally enjoyed in society. For that reason, the advent of the French intervention in Mexico and the installation of a new emperor was well received in many quarters within the Church as it held the potential to restore something of the institution's erstwhile social authority and prominence.

Advocating the imperial and monarchical form of government of the new emperor, Maximilian von Habsburg, in 1863 the Carmelite Pablo Antonio del Niño Jesús attributed the triumph of the new government, and of the Church along with it, to the Virgin's intercession.[105] Likewise, the bishops of Mexico addressed the new emperor in an 1864 pastoral letter in which they expressed regret for the ways in which Mexico's sins had resulted in the turbulence of the Reform era while also sharing their enthusiasim for how hope had now been restored in the form of Maximilian.[106] In the bishops' words, providence had, with the advent of the new empire, "desired to favor

103. Ibid., 5. See also Orozco, *Sermon* (1863).

104. For treatments of the question of the Church's perceived role in promoting national unity, see the following studies by Connaughton: "Nación"; "Modernización"; "Los curas."

105. del Niño Jesus, *Sermon* (1863).

106. *Carta pastoral* (1864). Despite the support of these bishops for this position, it is important to note that not all of Mexico's bishops favored the French intervention. For example, contemporary correspondence from the bishops of Guadalajara and San Luis Potosí demonstrates that these two bishops did not support what they saw as a foreign invasion. See Ramos, "Documentos," 23–24.

us with a grace which, if well utilized and afforded a faithful response, will suffice to consolidate in every way our social happiness."[107]

Such "social happiness," at least as the bishops envisioned it, was not to be, however, even during the period of the Second Empire.[108] Following the rapid failure of the imperial regime and the restoration of the Juárez government, and as a result of its own significantly weakened position, the Church printed fewer sermons during the remainder of the 1860s and most of the 1870s.[109] It did, however, continue to publish pastoral letters—including from the newly appointed archbishop of Mexico City, Pelagio Antonio de Labastida y Dávalos—embarking in this way on an effort to reform the Mexican Church, once again frequently in gendered terms, from within.[110] For instance, in a letter from 1863 the newly appointed archbishop lamented what he characterized as the "horrendous fruits" of the "tenebrous and active labor of progress," including its attacks on the Church and its ministers, Catholic beliefs, and public morality, all of which had produced the "disgusting mud of crimes, misery and humiliation" into which Mexican society had descended.[111] Likewise, in another letter, from 1866, Labastida y

---

107. See *Carta pastoral* (1864), 4–5. For reproductions of some of the correspondence of Mexico City's archbishop Labastida y Dávalos concerning the advent of the second empire, see Ramos, ed., *Del archivo*, Documents 49–52. Additionally, for a study of the development of support for monarchy in Mexico following independence, see Pérez Vejo, "Las encrucijadas."

108. For an account of some of the ways in which Maximilian actually proved disappointing to some church leaders, including the papal nuncio, see Galeana de Valadés; Gómez-Pérez, "El emperador"; Ramos, "Relaciones," 24–26. For accounts of the second empire, including its internal political *imaginnaire*, see Bazant, "From Independence," 44–47; Pani, *Para mexicanizar*; Ampudia, *La Iglesia*, 252–53; Puente Lutteroth, "No es justo," 299. As Puente Lutteroth points out, it was in fact Maximilian himself who in 1865 came into conflict with Michoacán's newly installed archbishop—Clemente de Jesús Munguía—over his opposition to the emperor's continuance of liberal policies, including the alienation of church wealth.

109. For a summary of the Church's position in the wake of the liberal victory against the French occupation, see Katz, "Liberal Republic," 55–56. According to Katz, although the Church never fully returned to its pre-1857 levels of legal privilege, official status, or influence in education, it nevertheless recuperated relatively quickly through donations as well as improved relations with significant portions of the rural population, for whom it was no longer a creditor. See also Danés Rojas, *Noticias*, 29.

110. For Labastida y Dávalos' early life and tenure in Puebla and Mexico City, see García Ugarte, *Poder político*, chapters 2, 6, 11–15; For a study of internal church reform in the decades following the downfall of the second empire, see Olimón Nolasco, "Proyecto." For example, Olimón Nolasco points out that in an 1866 pastoral letter the Mexican bishops promoted internal Church reform, including of religious life.

111. See Labastida y Dávalos, *Carta* (1863), 12–13.

Gendering Reform

Dávalos bemoaned the "irreparable damage" done to society by recent wars and social unrest.[112] However, he resolved to begin the process of healing and renewal by promoting religious devotion in proposed pastoral visits—a process that corresponded to the Church's recovery and expansion in the late 1860s and 1870s.[113]

In seeking internal reform, Labastida y Dávalos and other bishops in the 1860s looked increasingly to lay devotional organizations, made up of both men and women, which represented alternative spaces for the construction of new mentalities and practices in support of ecclesiastical authority—for example, in organizations such as the *Señoras de la Caridad*, whose motto, "Charity compels us," appeared prominently in the group's literature.[114] As Manuel Ceballos Ramírez has pointed out, organizations such as the *Sociedad Católica*, whose full name included the words "of the Mexican nation," formed the beginnings of a larger movement in this period among lay Catholics and the church hierarchy—one which, in competition with the liberal state, attempted to fashion and perpetuate a parallel society or nation loyal to the principles of the Church.[115] In their efforts, the bishops were also responding to larger transnational movements in the Catholic world, including the publication by Pope Pius IX in 1864 of the *Syllabus of Errors*, with its condemnations of various modern political and social positions and ideas, and the advent of the First Vatican Council in 1868.[116]

As one study of Mexico's participation in the Council has demonstrated, it is evident that Mexican bishops adhered closely to the position of the papacy, including on the doctrine of papal infallibility—a position likewise reflected in images featured in publications from the years following the declaration, such as those of the Catholic newpaper *La Regeneración Social* in 1869 and the *Sociedad Católica de México* in 1870, which referred to Pius IX as "the immortal Pontiff."[117] Accordingly, as mentioned earlier with regard to preachers' increased tendency to look to Rome and the papacy as solutions to the Church's difficulties, some scholars have begun to refer to a "Romanization" of the Mexican Church over the course of the nineteenth century.[118] In

112. See Labastida y Dávalos, *Edicto* (1866), 3–4.

113. See Katz, "Liberal Republic," 55–56; Ceballos Ramírez, "Un siglo," 386–87; Puente Lutteroth, "No es justo"; García Ugarte, *Poder político*, chapter 15.

114. Puente Lutteroth, "No es justo," 298–301. See also *Memoria* (1865).

115. See Ceballos Ramírez, "Un siglo," 384; Emilio Portes, *La lucha*, 108.

116. Puente Lutteroth, "No es justo," 302–15; Atkin and Tallett, *Priests*, 137–41.

117. Puente Lutteroth, "No es justo," 314; Ramos, "Relaciones," 60–61. See also *Primer calendario* (1871); *La Regeneración* (1869).

118. Bautista, "Hacia la romanización"; Lida, "La iglesia"; Puente Lutteroth, "No es justo," 321–22; Meyer, *Historia de los cristianos*.

other words, as the Church gradually lost ground in its efforts to retain its traditional political and economic power and authority, it adapted by adopting new discursive strategies—including references to papal authority and infallibility often articulated in gendered, "motherly" terms—to strengthen and solidify its social power.[119] As one scholar explains: "The multiple actions with which believers manifested their faith, the ways in which religious practice was made evident, the circumstances which permitted their subjectivity to be objectified, constituted something of an 'occult power' which permitted the Catholic Church to remain present, regroup and remain the hegemonic faith of Mexico in spite of the liberal reform."[120]

Ongoing manifestations of this "occult power" continued through the last years under consideration in this study, as evident in a joint pastoral letter of number of Mexico's bishops published in 1875. Written in response to initiaives undertaken during the presidency of Sebastián Lerdo de Tejada toward further codifying the separation of church and state, the archbishops of Mexico City, Michoacán, and Guadalajara offered a position similar to that of their predecessors in earlier pastoral letters. The document's invocation of gendered language, however, was now even more specific in its emphasis on the crucial role women were to play in combating contemporary political and social ills by promoting renewal, starting from within the community of believers.[121] Specifically, the archbishops lamented the current state of affairs, in which the Church now found itself despoiled of the resources it needed to serve the poor and unable to provide for the support and continuing development of its clergy.[122] Abandoned and persecuted by the government, the institution's only support was now the income it received from the lay faithful, whose "piety and charity" had helped assuage somewhat the difficulties posed by the governmental persecution.[123] Although it seemed

119. See Villaneda, "Periodismo," 325. For an example of a contemporary publication in honor of the convocation of the Council, see *Artículos* (1869). For a contemporary pastoral letter in support of the newly proclaimed doctrine of papal infallibility, see *Opúsculos* (1870).

120. Villaneda, "Periodismo," 325–26. As Villaneda explains, among the various strategies with which the Church sought to confirm and strengthen its social authority, including in the traditional forms of sermons and pastoral letters, the use of the press represented a means of growing significance—in the author's words, it was "one of the thickest threads in the Church's web of social power."

121. See Olimón Nolasco, "Proyecto," 281–83; *Instrucción* (1875). As Olimón Nolasco points out, the letter is not directed to the government in general or to government figures. Instead, it addresses the clergy and the faithful, seeking to promote reform from the inside out, starting from within the community.

122. *Instrucción* (1875), 34.

123. Ibid.

likely that within "a very few years" the majority of Mexico's churches would be in ruins—turned into "common residences" or, "truly horrible," houses of "license and prostitution"—all was not yet lost. If the "religion and piety" of the people could be renewed, there remained some degree of hope.[124]

Singling out women in particular as the special embodiment of this hope, the archbishops commended the "heroic" efforts of the Sisters of Charity (*Hermanas de Caridad*), referenced earlier in this chapter, who had recently abandoned Mexico rather than submit to the requirements of anti-clerical laws that they disband and return to the lay state.[125] Citing the witness of the nuns but then extending the praise of their virtue to Mexico's abundance of devout Catholic lay women, the bishops expressed their vision of the crucial importance of women's devotion in the context of the reigning social circumstances in which the Church found itself:

> But if the Mexican Church has been able to give to the world that edifying and moving example in more than three hundred of its daughters [the Sisters of Charity], its fecundity has not been exhausted, but instead there remain in the country some thousands of Catholic *señoras*, in whom . . . [God] inspires thoughts and resolutions similar to those of their sisters, as regards the service of the poor and the helpless.[126]

Extending their praises for women even further, the archbishops noted that "the whole world recognizes as a fact beyond doubt that [women] are gifted with an instinct of faith much livelier than that of men."[127] Due to the divine "providential order," women were created as the "first apostles" for their families and graced with an "exquisite sense" (*sentido exquisito*) of the faith, educating their children in the doctrinal and moral teachings of the Church and thereby ensuring its continued perpetuation.[128] Not limited just to Mexico, the archbishops highlighted similar displays of piety among Catholic women in Europe and the United States and encouraged Mexico's women to heed their example.[129] If Mexico's women also followed in this "exquisite" way of piety and devotion, they too could help renew the Church from within and bolster its sacred authority and mission for many years to come—even while they also confirmed the growing need for unquestioning loyalty to ecclesiastical authority.

124. Ibid., 36.
125. Ibid., 42–43.
126. Ibid., 45.
127. Ibid., 47.
128. Ibid.
129. Ibid., 52.

Conclusion

As this chapter has demonstrated, by the second half of the nineteenth century, purveyors of official Church discourses in Mexico City had come to place special emphasis in their sermons and pastoral letters on virtues and acts of traditional piety, usually associated mostly with women but now essential for all believers, both male and female. Employing this increasingly feminized language as an important aspect of its response to reigning social and political threats to its institutional integrity, the Church came to portray itself increasingly as a loyal defender of women and an embodiment of the virtues of femininity and motherhood. Though still fundamentally patriarchal in its institutional makeup, the Church now viewed both itself and Catholic women in the positive light of the feminized language of piety and motherhood it had developed over the course of the century—a language it then used as a means of reinforcing the crucial importance of religion's public prominence as the foundation of social good.

In other words, by the latter decades of the nineteenth century, Mexico City's high clergy were encouraging believers, both men and women alike, to unite in shared devotional practices and beliefs anchored in feminized ideals of piety. Retreating to the "tenderness" of religion, believers were to model virtue to their contemporaries and, in the process, redeem society from the corruption to which it had descended. However, although it was not yet explicit, there was something of another change at work in these discourses. Recognizing, at least implicitly, that there were now forces within Mexico at odds with the Church and not likely soon to alter their stance, official representatives of the institution were gradually constructing fresh discourses for a new age. Styling themselves as representatives of a benevolent and motherly institution, these clerics were starting to recognize that the Church itself, and not the polity for which it had formerly served as a privileged arbiter of morals and customs, was now something of its own, independent entity. Although the moral turpitude of surrounding society would remain a consideration, it was now a concern less of the sort intent on restoring the institution's former official political sway than with preserving its privileged influence over the hearts and minds of the faithful. As recent scholarship on this period has noted, by no means was the Church retreating from its desire to transform society and retain its position of hegemonic prominence.[130] Rather, the change in discursive approach outlined in this chapter marks a transition from a defensive stance against secular attacks—predicated on the assumption that the Church and society were

---

130. See Lida, "La iglesia," 1404–5.

effectively one—to an approach in which the Church, no longer coterminous with a corrupt national polity and newly reinvigorated from within, began to take the offensive, capitalizing on the dynamism of its campaigns for internal renewal through revitalized piety and devotion. This transition in church discourses would take time to develop, but its impetus, founded on the feminized language of piety and motherhood that developed in the nineteenth century, would carry the institution forward well into the twentieth century and beyond.

Conclusion

Gendered Church Discourses Come Full Circle

"Jesus! What an august name, oh Catholics and beloved children! How sweet it is to recall this name . . . which exceeds oil in its softness and honey in its sweetness[.]"[1]

"The triumphs of the [faith] . . . are and always will be the result of the constancy of its Pontiffs . . . in sustaining the never-ending struggle[.]"[2]

TWO STATEMENTS OF ARCHBISHOP PELAGIO ANTONIO DE LA-BASTIDA Y DÁVALOS, MEXICO CITY, 1878, IN A SERMON ON THE SWEETNESS OF THE DIVINE NAME.

OVER THE COURSE OF his long term as archbishop of Mexico City (1863–1891), Pelagio Antonio de Labastida y Dávalos continued to promote the gendered vision of renewed piety and religious practice articulated in the pastoral letter he co-wrote with other bishops in 1875, in which values formerly associated with "the devout sex" were constructed as normative for all believers.[3] In an 1878 sermon, for example, he sounded themes similar to those found in other sermons from the mid-to-late nineteenth century, including a portrayal of Jesus in feminized terms. Instructively, the archbishop's sermon also touched on the crucial importance of the ongoing

1. Labastida y Dávalos, *Sermon* (1878), 3.
2. Ibid., 7.
3. See chapter 7 for analysis of this pastoral letter.

struggles in which the Church—led by the supreme authority of the Roman Pontiff—would need to engage against the errors and deceptions of the age. In this combination of feminized language with lively invocation of militant action, Labastida y Dávalos' sermon suggests that, by the last quarter of the nineteenth century, official Church discourses in Mexico City had, in a sense, come full circle.

In the Baroque period, as observed in chapters 1 and 2, sermons constituted a discursive space in which the transcendence of gendered social norms was encouraged. For example, Baroque sermons might celebrate female saints and remarkable contemporary women as virile warriors while praising the feminine qualities of extraordinary men. In the wake of trends and ideas associated with the Enlightenment, however, sermons and other discourses changed, as chapter 3 showed, featuring more rigid gendered language and narrower visions of proper gendered social roles. The exigencies of the Napoleonic and independence wars exaggerated these trends (chapters 4 and 5), resulting in sermons that both celebrated heroic, masculine deeds on the part of defenders of the Spanish *patria* and condemned vices associated with "the weak sex" as vaguely responsible for social and even political ills. However, the rise of competing public voices and sometimes oppositional political figures in the first decades following independence challenged the Church to defend its traditional place of prominence in Mexican society. As a result, official discourses changed once again, as chapter 6 and 7 argue, jettisoning condemnations of "pusillanimous" women in favor of praise for the piety and religiosity of "the devout sex" as the foundation for a new public offensive against anti-religious forces. By the second half of the century, official purveyors of Church discourses were enthusiastically expounding the virtues of feminized piety for all the faithful and positioning the institutional Church—often portrayed as a loving "mother"—as a tireless, unchanging admirer of women and their renowned devoutness precisely because women's pious dispositions and practices would inspire loyalty to the Church among their husbands and children and, through them, in the surrounding society.

In other words, by the latter part of the nineteenth century, Mexico City's high clergy were once again calling upon the faithful to transcend the limits of gender for a greater cause—in this case, the renewal and eventual resurgence of the Church following the losses of the Reform era. However, whereas eighteenth-century Baroque preachers proffered images of feminine-inspired devotion in men and virile militancy in women, the gender bending of the late nineteenth century followed a different course. First, it was less free-spirited and playful than earlier Baroque precedents; the gravity of contemporary threats to the Church's authority and social position precluded the kind of elaborate flights of imagination witnessed in earlier sermons. Second, its gender bending was more one-sided, advocating the cultivation of feminine virtues in both sexes and remaining largely silent on the assets of masculinity. With the strength of earlier tropes of masculine virtue compromised by mid-century turns of events—for example, men's increasingly secular opportunities and preoccupations within the nascent secular public sphere and the increasing openness with which anti-clerical ideas were expressed in speeches and the press, both associated with men—it would be the virtues of "the devout sex" that would now assure the Church's vindication and ultimate triumph. Though "soft" and "tender," women held the key to the Church's resurgence because it would be through their spiritual and moral influence that their husbands and children would remain loyal to religion and would support a type of renewal invigorated and emboldened from within. Similarly, by emulating the "sweet" and "loving" qualities of their wives, and even of Christ himself, men could join women in restoring the proper place of religious devotion in public and private life, thus giving witness to the triumph of religion over perfidious secularism.[4]

Nevertheless, militancy of the sort associated with sermons from earlier in the nineteenth century by no means had disappeared from official church discourses. As demonstrated in his sermon cited above, Archbishop Labastida y Dávalos and other official church representatives, for all their celebration of the tenderness of religion, were equally likely to call the faithful to do battle against the evils of anti-clerical forces. What was different now, however, was an important set of assumptions underlying the clerics' statements. In the opening decades of the nineteenth century Mexico City's archbishops and other preachers had fully expected and actively pursued the reunification of church and state as it had existed, at least in theory, during the colonial period. However, as the conflictive opening decades of Mexico's independence progressed and the state continued to chip away at its traditional rights and privileges, the Church gradually realized that it would need to move from a defensive position (seeking to restore what had

---

4. It is important to note, nevertheless, that not all women conformed fully to the Church's vision of idealized femininity. As recent scholarship has demonstrated, in pursuing this vision the Church would also be forced to enter into a process of negotiation and contestation with various women and other practitioners of local piety and devotions. See Wright-Ríos, *Revolutions*. As Wright-Ríos demonstrates in his study of the Church in Oaxaca, figures such as Bishop Eulogio Gillow exemplified tensions within the task of the late-nineteenth-century Church between promoting unassailable orthodoxy and recognizing and capitalizing on the dynamism of local devotions, many of which were associated with women's piety but whose female leaders and devotées did not always conform to ecclesiastical expectations and stipulations.

been lost) to an offensive one—a move that would require a radical reimagining of the nature of the institution's place at the core of Mexico's national consciousness.[5]

It is the argument of this book that it was precisely the newly feminized language developed by clergy in the mid-to-late nineteenth century that supplied this novel vision. The first step would be to replace the Church's now-defunct societal *raison d*'être (i.e., its status as effective coequal with the state) with a new source of authenticity—a goal accomplished in returning discursively to the Church's most fundamental, pristine essence as a peerless vehicle for and privileged arbiter of the divine. The second step would involve molding close and lasting associations between this fundamentally religious character of the Church and closely familiar and celebrated commonplaces of social life. Here the crucial importance of women emerged. As those members of society traditionally most closely associated with piety (i.e., as "the devout sex"), women supplied an ideal common referent which, when both enthusiastically celebrated by and purposefully associated with the Church, had the potential to underline precisely those values the institution was seeking to annex to itself. Finally, the third step was to convert this renewed, feminized emphasis on piety into the sort of religious energy that could stand up to and do battle with reigning ambient secularist and antireligious forces—a task that would take on increasing urgency once more in subsequent decades. Indeed, as the history of twentieth-century Mexico demonstrates, it appears that this conversion process of feminized piety into militarized religious zeal more than amply met its goals.

In a word, by the period of Archbishop Labastida y Dávalos' leadership official church discourses had circled back to earlier precedents but in an original way. After celebrating playfully the flexible and fluid possibilities of gender in the Baroque period and then asserting a studied rigidity under the influence of enlightened science and rationality, by the middle and latter decades of the nineteenth century the time had come to exploit the pliability of these discourses once more. Now that piety and religious sentiment were paramount for an institution in need of revitalization, it was logical that church leaders would turn to the portion of society they had traditionally associated with those feelings and emphasize the normative character of their habits and practices for all.[6] Buttressed by the power of the laity

---

5. For this transition from a defensive to an offensive position, see Lida, "La iglesia."

6. See Olimón Nolasco, "Proyecto," 291–92. As Olimón Nolasco puts it, efforts on the part of Church leaders to promote renewal from within by means of reinvigorated piety constituted a kind of refounding of the Mexican Church in a way that would prove even more significant than Porfirian conciliatory politics for the Church's survival and recovery in subsequent years.

Preaching Power

(a power that originated from intense, often feminized piety), the Church would be prepared to confront once more the secularizing, anti-religious forces which opposed it. Paradoxically, then, it would be the "tender" and "sweet" qualities of femininity that would embolden the new militancy of the Church in the late nineteenth-century and beyond, eliciting a return to fundamental religious values through renewed piety and thus supplying the strength and vitality needed for the institution to emerge victorious against ever-pressing foes. Perhaps it would have stirred the "militant" and "virile" souls of some of the remarkable female saints and laywomen celebrated in earlier Baroque sermons to know that it was precisely through a fresh refashioning of the virtues of femininity that the Catholic Church in Mexico would emerge from the bitter challenge of the anti-clerical Reform to continue to play a powerful role in Mexican history.

Bibliography

Abogado, Rafael. *Sermón de Nuestra Señora de Guadalupe*. Mexico City, 1850.
Achim, Miruna. "Mysteries of the Heart: The Gift of Bishop Fernández de Santa Cruz to the Nuns of Santa Mónica." *Colonial Latin American Review* 14/1 (2005) 83–102.
Adoración nocturna al Santísimo Sacramento. Mexico City, 1869.
Aguirre, Juan de. *Panegirico que en honor del glorioso San Ladislao Rey predicó en la Iglesia del convento de Religiosas Dominicas de Jesus Maria de esta ciudad el dia 28 de junio de 1829 el R P. Lector Fr. Juan de Aguirre. Religioso Mercedario de este Convento de Nuestra Señora de la Merced*. Mexico City: Rodríguez, 1829.
Alamán, Gil. *Sermón predicado por el Padre Don Gil Alaman presbítero de la Congregacion del Oratorio de San Felipe Neri de México, el dia 17 de junio de 1855, primero de los tres dias en que celebró solemnemente la misma congregacion en su iglesia la declaracion dogmática de la Inmaculada Concepcion de la Santísima Virgen María Madre de Dios*. Mexico City: Andrade & Escalante, 1856.
Alberro, Solange. "Barroquismo y criollismo en los recibimientos hechos a Don Diego López Pacheco Carer y Bobadilla, Virrey de Nueva España, 1640: Un estudio preliminar." *Colonial Latin American Historical Review* 8/4 (1999) 443–60.
Albers, Irene, and Uta Felten, editors. *Escenas de transgresión: María de Zayas en su contexto literario-cultural*. Madrid: Iberoamericana/Vervuert, 2009.
Alcalá, Alfonso, and Manuel Olimón. *Episcopado y gobierno en México, Cartas pastorales colectivas del Episcopado mexicano*. Mexico City: Paulinas, 1989.
Alcalá, Luisa Elena, et al., editors. *Fundaciones Jesuíticas en Iberoamérica*. Mexico City: Fundación Iberdrola, 2002.
Alcayde y Gil, Manuel. *Oracion que en la solemne accion de gracias que anualmente se celebra en la ultima noche de cada año en el sagrario de la Santa Iglesia Catedral de Mexico, dixo el 31 de diciembre de 1811 a presencia del Excmo. Señor Virey, el Dr. D. Manuel Alcayde y Gil, presbítero, capellan del número de la real Armada, Regente Theolgi-académico, Exâminador Sinodal de los obispados de Santander y Cadiz, y Comisionado en estos reynos, por el supremo consejo de Regencia*. Mexico City: Fernández de Jáuregui, 1812.
Alejos-Grau, Carmen José. "La contribución de los eclesiásticos novohispanos a la formación de la conciencia nacional mexicana (siglos XVII y XVIII)." *Hispania Sacra* 53/107 (2001) 285–309.
———. "Génesis de los ideales americanistas." In *Teología en América Latina*, edited by Josep-Ignasi Saranyana and Carmen-José Alejos Grau, 2/1:691–786. Madrid: Vervuert/Iberoamericana, 2005.

Bibliography

Allaín Bracamonte, Jorge. "Los nefandos placeres de la carne: la iglesia y el estado frente a la sodomía en la Nueva España, 1721–1820." *Debates en Sociología* 25 (2000) 73–90.

Alonso de Diego, Mercedes. "Retórica, predicación y vida cotidiana en la Ciudad de México (1735), según Francisco de la Concepción Barbosa, O.F.M." PhD diss., Universidad de Navarra, 2002. ProQuest (AAT C816100).

Alvarado, Juan de. *Parecer de el M. R. P. Fr. Juan de Alvarado, del Orden de Predicadores, Presentado en Sagrada Theologia, Qualificador del Santo Officio de la Inquisicion desta Nueva España, Doctor Theologo por la Real Universidad de esta Corte, y en ella Cathedratico proprietario del Angel Doctor Santo Thomas.* In Bartolomé Felipe de Ita y Parra, *La libertad en la esclavitud. Sermon panegyrico, de las benditas almas del Purgatorio. Predicado en el Anniversario, que celebra la Congregacion de los Esclavos de las Almas del Purgatorio, todos los años, en el mes de Noviembre, en la Santa Iglesia Cathedral Metropolitana de esta Ciudad de Mexico, en donde con Authoridad Apostolica está fundada.* Mexico City: Herederos de la Viuda de Miguel de Rivera Calderón, 1720.

Amphoso, Juan. *Parecer del M. R. P. M. Fr. Juan Amphoso, Vicario de la Casa de Doctrina de Gueguetlán.* In *Octava Maravilla del Nuevo Mundo en la Gran Capilla del Rosario dedicada y aplaudida en el Convento de N. P. S. Domingo de la Ciudad de los Angeles el dia 16 del Mes de Abril de 1690 al Illvsmo. y Revmo. Señor D. D. Manuel Fernández de Santa Cruz Obispo de la Puebla del Consejo de su Magestad.* Puebla: Junta de Mejoramiento Moral, Cívico y Material del Municipio de Puebla, 1985.

Ampudia, Ricardo. *La Iglesia de Roma: estructura y presencia en México.* Mexico City: Fondo de Cultura Económica, 1998.

Anderson, Margaret Lavinia. "The Divisions of the Pope: The Catholic Revival and Europe's Transition to Democracy." In *The Politics of Religion in an Age of Revival: Studies in Nineteenth-Century Europe and Latin America*, edited by Austen Ivereigh, 22–42. London: Institute of Latin American Studies, 2000.

Andrés-Gallego, José, editor. *Tres grandes cuestiones de la historia de Iberoamérica: ensayos y monografías: derecho y justicia en la historia de Iberoamérica; Afroamérica, la tercera raiz; impacto en América de la expulsion de los jesuitas.* Madrid: Fundación Mapfre Tavera/Fundación Ignacio Larramendi, 2005.

Anna, Timothy E. "Agustín de Iturbide and the Process of Consensus." In *The Birth of Modern Mexico, 1780–1824*, edited by Christon I. Archer, 187–204. Lanham, MD: Rowman & Littlefield, 2003.

———. "The Finances of Mexico City during the War of Independence." *Journal of Latin American Studies* 4/1 (1972) 55–75.

Año crisitano, ó ejercicios devotos para todos los días del año. Mexico City: Galván, 1835.

Aparición milagrosa del Apóstol Santiago por P. M. Mexico City: García Torres, 1861.

Apuntes biográficos de los trece religiosos dominicos que en estado de momias se hallaron en el osario de su Convento de Santo Domingo de esta Capital. Mexico City: Inclán, 1861.

Archer, Christon I. *The Army in Bourbon Mexico, 1760–1810.* Albuquerque: University of New Mexico Press, 1977.

Archer, Christon I., editor. *The Birth of Modern Mexico, 1780–1824.* Lanham, MD: Rowman & Littlefield, 2003.

Bibliography

Arenal, Electa, and Stacey Schlau. *Untold Sisters: Hispanic Nuns in Their Own Works*. Translated by Amanda Powell. Albuquerque: University of New Mexico Press, 1989.

Aroche, Miguel de. *Aprobacion del M. R. P. Fr. Miguel de Aroche, del Real Orden de Nuestra Señora de la Merced Redempcion de Captivos, Mrô del numbero de su Provincia de la Visitacion, Provincial, que fué de ella, y Definidor, Rector del Colegio de S. Pedro Pasqual, Comendador del Convento principal de esta Corte, y Calificador del Santo Oficio. In Juan José de Eguiara y Eguren, El primero de los martires de Christo por su magisterio, y primero entre los maestros christianos por su martyrio. Panegyrico de San Estevan protomartyr, que el dia 13 del mes de Octubre de 1729, por espacio de una hora, con termino de quarenta y ocho, y asignacion de puntos, en oposicion â la Canoniga Lectoral de la Santa Iglesia Metropolitana de Mexico, presente el Muy Ilustre Venerable Señor Dean, y Cabildo Sedevacante*. Mexico City: Berardo de Hogal, 1729.

Arrom, Silvia Marina. *The Women of Mexico City, 1790–1857*. Stanford: Stanford University Press, 1985.

Arrupe, Pedro. "Art and the Spirit of the Society of Jesus." *Studies in the Spirituality of Jesuits* 5/3 (1973) 83–92.

Artículos publicados en el Semanario Católico de México, con motivo de la festividad de la Inmaculada Concepción de la Madre de Dios, y de la apertura del concilio ecuménico vaticano. Mexico City: Lara, 1869.

Asociación para el culto perpétuo del castísimo patriarca Señor San José, contiene la obligación que se contrae y las indulgencias concedidas por esta prácticapiadosa. Mexico City: Lara, 1874.

Atienza López, Ángela. "De beaterios a conventos. Nuevas perspectivas sobre el mundo de las beatas en la España moderna." *Historia Social* 57 (2007) 145–68.

Atkin, Nicholas and Frank Tallett. *Priests, Prelates and People: A History of European Catholicism since 1750*. Oxford: Oxford University Press, 2003.

Ávila, Alfredo. "El cristiano constitucional. Libertad, derecho y naturaleza en la retórica de Manuel de la Bárcena." *Estudios de Historia Moderna y Contemporánea de México* 25 (2003) 5–41.

———. "La crisis del patriotismo criollo: Mariano Beristáin." In *Religión, poder y autoridad en la Nueva España*, edited by Alicia Mayer and Ernesto de la Torre Villar, 205–24. Mexico City: Universidad Nacional Autónoma de México, 2004.

———. "Interpretaciones recientes en la historia del pensamiento de la emancipación." In *La independencia de México: temas e interpretaciones recientes*, edited by Alfredo Ávila and Virginia Guedea, 17–39. Mexico City: Universidad Nacional Autónoma de México, 2007.

Ávila, Alfredo, and Pedro Pérez Herrero, editors. *Las experiencias de 1808 en Iberoamérica*. Mexico City: Universidad Nacional Autónoma de México, 2008.

Bailey, Gauvin A. *Art of Colonial Latin America*. London: Phaidon, 2005.

Baird, Joseph Armstrong, Jr. *The Churches of Mexico, 1530–1810*. Berkeley: University of California Press, 1962.

Baker, Keith Michael. *Inventing the French Revolution*. Cambridge: Cambridge University Press, 1990.

Barajas, Pedro. *Sermon panegírico, que en la festividad del angélico doctor Santo Tomás de Aquino, predicó el dia 7 de marzo de 1835 en el convento grande de N. P. Santo Domingo de México, el señor licenciado don Pedro Barajas, prebendado de la Santa*

Bibliography

Iglesia Catedral de Guadalajara, y Diputado al Congreso general. Mexico City: Testamentaria de Don Alejandro Valdés, 1835.

Barcelo Miller, María F. "De la Polilla a la virtud: visión sobre la mujer de la Iglesia jerárquica de Puero Rico." In *La Mujer en Puerto Rico: ensayos de investigación*, edited by Yamila Azize Vargas, 49–88. Rio Piedras, Puerto Rico: Ediciones Huracán, 1987.

Barnes-Karol, Gwendolyn. "Religious Oratory in a Culture of Control." In *Culture and Control in Counter-Reformation Spain*, edited by Anne J. Cruz and Mary Elizabeth Perry, 51–77. Minneapolis: University of Minnesota Press, 1992.

Barnes-Karol, Gwendolyn and Nicholas Spadaccini. "Sexuality, Marriage, and Power in Medieval and Early Modern Iberia." In *Marriage and Sexuality in Medieval and Early Modern Iberia*, edited by Eukene Lacarra Lanz, 235–45. New York: Routledge, 2002.

Batchelor, Jennie. "Fashion and Frugality: Eighteenth-Century Pocket Books for Women." *Studies in Eighteenth Century Culture* 32 (2003) 1–18.

Bautista, Cecilia. "Hacia la romanización de la Iglesia Mexicana." *Historia Mexicana* 55/1 (2005) 99–144.

Bazant, Jan. *Alienation of Church Wealth in Mexico: Social and Economic Aspects of the Liberal Revolution, 1856–1875*. Translated and edited by Michael P. Costeloe. Cambridge: Cambridge University Press, 1971.

———. "From Independence to the Liberal Republic." In *Mexico Since Independence*, edited by Leslie Bethell, 1–48. Cambridge: Cambridge University Press, 1991.

Belaunzarán, José María de Jesús. *Discurso panegirico que en la solemne accion de gracias celebrada en la iglesia del convento grande de N. S. P. S. Francisco de esta imperial corte, por el feliz excito de la gloriosa empresa de la emancipacion de esta septentrional america, dijo el dia 16 de Noviembre de 1821 el M. R. P. Fr. Jose Maria de Jesus Belaunzaran, religioso descalzo de la Santa Provincia de S. Diego de la misma Corte; y lo dedica al primer gefe de la nacion, generalisimo de mar y tierra, serenisimo señor D. Agustin Iturbide y Aramburu*. Mexico City: Abadiano y Valdés, 1837.

Benito Artigas, Juan. "Juegos de barroco desde México: la desmaterialización de la esctuctura en el barroco iberoamericano." Online: http://www.upo.es/depa/webdhuma/areas/arte/3cb/documentos/053f.pdf.

Bergosa y Jordán, Antonio. *Nos el Dr. D. Antonio Bergosa y Jordan, por la gracia de Dios, Obispo de Antequera de Oaxaca, Arzobispo electo de Méxcio, Caballero de la real y distinguida orde de Carlos III del consejo de S. M. etc.* Mexico City: Fernández de Jáuregui, 1814.

———. *Sermon que en la funcion que celebró la Santa Iglesia Metropolitana de Mexico en accion de gracias por el feliz regreso a su trono del señor Don Fernando VII rey catolico de ambas españas; y del sumo pontifice Pio VII a su sagrado solio y capital de Roma, predicó el dia 8 de diciembre de 1814 el Illmô. Sr. Dr. D. Antonio Bergosa y Jordan, Obispo de Oaxaca, y Arzobispo de México, Caballero de la Real y distinguida Orden Española de Cárlos III del Consejo de S. M. etc.* Mexico City: Fernández de Jáuregui, 1814.

Beristáin, José Mariano. *Elogio de los soldados difuntos en la presente guerra, que en las solemnes exequias de los militares celebradas en la metropolitana de Mexico el dia 22 de noviembre de 1794, y presididas del Exmô. Señor Marqués de Branciforte, Virrey de esta Nueva España, dixo el Sr. Dr. Don Joseph Mariano Beristain, canónigo de dicha Santa Iglesia*. Mexico City: Los Herederos de Don Felipe de Zúñiga y Ontiveros, 1795.

Beristáin de Sousa, José Mariano. *Oracion panegirico-eucaristica, pronunciada en esta festividad por el caballero eclesiastico Don Joseph Mariano Beristain de Sousa*, in *Solemne accion de gracias que tributaron al todo poderoso en la Metropolitana de Mexico los caballeros de la real y distinguida orden española de Carlos III en el dia de su inmaculada patrona, por la instalacion de la soberana junta de gobierno de España y de sus Indias*. Mexico City: Fernández de Jáuregui, 1809.

Borges Moran, Pedro. *Los métodos misionales en la cristianización de América, siglo XVI*. Madrid: CSIC, 1960.

Bosse, Monika, Barbara Potthast, and André Stoll, editors. *La creatividad femenina en el mundo barroco hispánico. María de Zayas, Isabel Rebeca Correa, Sor Juana Inés de la Cruz*. Vol. 2. Kassel: Reichenberger, 1999.

Bowers, Teresa. "The Golden Age of Choral Music in the Cathedrals of Colonial Mexico." *Choral Journal* 40/9 (2000) 9–13.

Boyer, Richard. *Lives of the Bigamists: Marriage, Family, and Community in Colonial Mexico*. Albuquerque: University of New Mexico Press, 1995.

Brading, D.A. "Bourbon Spain and its American Empire." In *Colonial Spanish America*, edited by Leslie Bethell, 112–62. Cambridge: Cambridge University Press, 1987.

———. *Church and State in Bourbon Mexico: The Diocese of Michoacán, 1749–1810*. Cambridge: Cambridge University Press, 1994.

———. "Tridentine Catholicism and Enlightened Despotism in Bourbon Mexico." *Journal of Latin American Studies* 15/1 (1983) 1–22.

Brading, David. *Miners and Merchants in Bourbon Mexico, 1763–1810*. New York: Cambridge University Press, 1971.

———. "La ideología de la Independencia mexicana y la crisis de la Iglesia Católica." In *México en tres momentos: 1810–1910–2010. Hacia la conmemoración del bicentenario de la Independencia y el centenario de la Revolución Mexicana. Retos y perspectivas*, edited by Alicia Mayer and Juan Ramón de la Fuente. 1:357–76. Mexico City: Universidad Nacional Autónoma de México/Instituto de Investigaciones Históricas, 2008.

———. "Ultramontane Intransigence and the Mexican Reform: Clemente de Jesús Munguía." In *The Politics of Religion in an Age of Revival: Studies in Nineteenth-Century Europe and Latin America*, edited by Austen Ivereigh, 115–42. London: Institute of Latin American Studies, 2000.

Brading, David A. *The First America: The Spanish Monarchy, Creole Patriots, and the Liberal State, 1492–1867*. Cambridge: Cambridge University Press, 1991.

———. *Mexican Phoenix: Our Lady of Guadalupe: Image and Tradition Across Five Centuries*. Cambridge: Cambridge University Press, 2001.

———. *Nueve sermones guadalupanos (1661–1758)*. Mexico City: Centro de Estudios de Historia de Méxcio Condumex, 2005.

Bravo Rubio, Berenise. "La gestión episcopal de Manuel Posada y Garduño. Cambios y permanencias en el gobierno del clero secular del arzobispado de México (1840–1846)." Master's thesis, Universidad Nacional Autónoma de México, 2006.

Bravo Ugarte, José. *Diócesis y obispos de la iglesia mexicana (1519–1965)*. Mexico City: Jus, 1965.

Bringas y Encinas, Diego. *Sermón politico-moral que para dar principio á la misión extraordinaria, formada de venerables sacerdotes de ambos cleros, dirigida a la*

Bibliography

 concordia y union de los habitantes de esta América, y el restablecimiento de la paz, predicó en la plaza de Santo Domingo de Mexico el 17 de enero de 1813, y repetió a peticion de muchos sugetos celosos del bien público en la iglesia de nuestra Señora de la Merced de la misma ciudad el 24 del propio mes, con asistencia del Excmô, sr. virrey, nobilisima ciudad, etc. Mexico City: Bautista de Arizpe, 1813.

Burke, Marcus B. *Treasures of Mexican Colonial Painting: The Davenport Museum of Art Collection.* Davenport, IA: Davenport Museum of Art, 1998.

Burkhart, Louise M. *The Slippery Earth: Nahua-Christian Moral Dialogue in Sixteenth-Century Mexico.* Tucson: University of Arizona Press, 1989.

Buxó, José Pascual. "Sor Juana and Luis de Góngora: The Poetics of *Imitatio*." In *Baroque New Worlds: Representation, Transculturation, Counterconquest,* edited by Lois Parkinson Zamora and Monika Kaup, 352–93. Durham, NC: Duke University Press, 2010.

Cabranes-Grant, Leo. "The Fold of Difference: Performing Baroque and Neobaroque Mexican Identities." In *Baroque New Worlds: Representation, Transculturation, Counterconquest,* edited by Lois Parkinson Zamora and Monika Kaup, 467–86. Durham, NC: Duke University Press, 2010.

Calendario de la Asociación Universal del Sr. S. José, para el año de 1878 dedicado á los devotos del Santísimo Patriarca. Mexico City: Tipografía Religiosa, 1878.

Calendario de las señoritas megicanas para el año 1838, dispuesto por Mariano Galván. Mexico City: Librería del Editor, 1838.

Calendario de la señoritas megicana, para el año 1839, dispuesto por Mariano Galván. Mexico City: Librería del Editor, 1839.

Calendario de la señoritas megicanas, para el año bisiesto de 1840 dispuesto por Mariano Galván. Mexico City: Librería del Editor, 1840.

Calendario de las señoritas para el año 1859. Mexico City, 1859.

Calendario de las señoritas para el año de 1866. Mexico City: Murguía, 1866.

Calendario de las señoritas, para el año bisiesto de 1864. Mexico City, 1864.

Calhoun, Craig, ed. *Habermas and the Public Sphere.* Cambridge, MA: MIT Press, 1992.

Callahan, William J. *Church, Politics, and Society in Spain, 1750–1874.* Cambridge, MA: Harvard University Press, 1984.

Calloway, Stephen. *Baroque Baroque: The Culture of Excess.* London: Phaidon, 1994.

La Camelia. Semanario de literatura, variedades, teatros, modas, etc. dedicado a las señoritas mejicanas. Mexico City: Navarro, 1853.

El camino verdadero. Coloquio entre el dulcísimo Jesús y la alma su esposa, deseosa de agradarle y servirle, y ansiosa por amarle y gozarle en su divina unión. Mexico City: Abadiano y Valdés, 1851.

Cañizares Esguerra, Jorge. "Racial, Religious, and Civic Creole Identity in Colonial Spanish America." *American Literary History* 17/3 (2005) 420–437.

———. *Puritan Conquistadors: Iberianizing the Atlantic, 1550–1700.* Stanford: Stanford University Press, 2006.

Canseco, José Juan. *Esplicación ulterior sobre los inconvenientes que obstan al establecimiento de la libertad de cultos en la República Mexicana por J. J. C.* Oaxaca: Rincón, 1849.

Capel, Rosa María, and Margarita Ortega. Introduction to *Textos para la historia de las mujeres en España.* Edited by A. María Aguado et al. Madrid: Cátedra, 1994.

Cárdenas, José. "La cruz y la espada." *El Universal* (Mexico City, Mexico), Jan. 12, 2010.

Cardaillac, Louis, ed. *Dos sermones panegíricos sobre Santiago* El Mayor *pronunciados en la Ciudad de México años de 1802 y 1809*. Zapopan: El Colegio de México, 2002.

Carner, Françoise. "Estereotipos femeninos en el siglo XIX." In *Presencia y transparencia. La mujer en la historia de México*, edited by Carmen Ramos Escandón, 93–109. Mexico City: El Colegio de México, 1987.

Carrasco y Enciso, Luis. *Oracion eucaristica por la libertad gloriosa y feliz restitucion del rey nuestro señor al trono augusto de sus mayores, que en la solemne funcion celebrada por el batallon tercero de patriotas distinguidos de Fernando septimo amado soberano de España, é Indias dixo en la Iglesia del Convento de N. P. S. Francisco en 16 de Diciembre de 1814 el R. P. Doctor Fr. Luis Carrasco y Enciso, ex-Prior del convento imperial de N. P. Santo Domingo, Calificador del Santo Oficio, Teologo Consultor de Cámara, y Exâminador Sinodal del Arzobispado*. Mexico City: Fernández de Jáuregui, 1815.

———. *Sermon moral del fuego vengador de la caridad y de la dureza de las palabras con que se han de redarguir las impiedades de Napoleon y sus sectarios. Para el triduo de las rogaciones que con el fin de impetrar los tirunfos de la religion y la patria celebraron ante la imagen portentosa de Maria Santisima de los Remedios las M. RR. Religiosas Dominicas del Convento de Santa Catalina de Sena de México en el dia 15 de Julio de 1810 y pronunció el R. P. ex-lector Fr. Luis Carrasco y Enciso, del Sagrado Orden de Predicadores, doctor teologo por la real y pontificia universidad, calificador y predicador el Santo Oficio de la Inquisicion*. Mexico City: Sánchez Espinosa, 1810.

———. *Sermon panegirico de Santiago el Mayor, que en la solemne funcion que le hace anualmente la real congregacion de los naturales y originarios del reino de Galicia en la iglesia del Convento Grande de N.P.S. Francisco de México*. Mexico City, 1809.

Carrera, Magali M. *Imagining Identity in New Spain: Race, Lineage, and the Colonial Body in Portraiture and Casta Painting*. Austin: University of Texas Press, 2003.

Carta de un amigo a otro, contra la introducción de sectas en México. Guadalajara: Rodríguez, 1848.

Carta pastoral que el ilustrisimo venerable señor presidente y cabildo de la Santa Iglesia Metropolitana de Mexico, gobernador sede vacante, dirige a los fieles de este arzobispado. Mexico City, 1811.

Carta pastoral que los Illmos. Sres. Arzobispos de México y Michoacan y obispos de Puebla, Oaxaca, Caradro, Querétaro, Tulancingo, Chiapas, Veracruz, Zamora y Chilapa, dirigen a sus diocesanos con motivo de la entrada de sus majestades el emperador Maximiliano Primero y la Emperatriz Carlota a la capital. Mexico City: Andrade y Escalante, 1864.

Casado, Dionicio. *Sermon que en la profesion religiosa, que en el Convento de la Encarnacion de Méxcio hizo el dia 6 de julio la R. M. Sor Maria Genara de Santa Teresa, hija del Señor Don Felix Quijada y Ovejero, Oidor que fué de esta Real Audiencia*. Mexico City: Zúñiga y Ontiveros, 1806.

———. *Sermon que en la solemne funcion de gracias que los naturales y originarios de las montañas de Santander, celebraron en su capilla sita en el atrio de San Francisco, por las brillantes victorias de las armas Españolas, sobres las Francesas: dixo el dia 6 de noviembre de 1808 el R. P. Fr. Dionisio Casado, Prior del convento grande de N. P. S. Agustin de Méxcio*. Mexico City: Arizpe, 1809.

Casaús Torres, Ramón. *Sermon panegírico del doctor angélico Santo Tomas de Aquino, que en la solemne festividad celebrada por la real y pontificia universidad, y*

Bibliography

    por el imperial convento de Sro. Domingo de México, el dia 7 de Marzo de 1799 predicó en la Iglesia del expresado convento el R. P. Fr. Ramon Casaus, Torres y Las Plazas, del Orden de Predicadores, Doctor en Sagrada Teologia de la dicha Universidad, Calificador del Sto. Oficio de la Inquisicion, Examinador Synodal de este Arzobispado, y Regente Primario de Estudios en el Pontificio Colegio de Santo Domingo de Porta-Coeli. Mexico City: Ber. D. José Fernández Jáuregui, 1799.

———. *Sermon panegírico de Santa Ines virgen y martir predicado en el Convento de Religiosas del mismo nombre de México en el dia 21 de enero de 1802 por el R. P. Fr. Ramon Casaus y Torres del Orden de Predicadores, Doctor Teólogo y Catedrático Propietario de Santo Tomas en la Real y Pontificia Universidad, Calificador del Santo Oficio, y Exâminador Sinodal de este Arzobispado de México, y de los Obsipados de la Puebla de los Angeles y de Antequera de Oaxaca*. Mexico City: Zúñiga y Ontiveros, 1802.

———. *Sermon tercero de San Pedro Martir de Verona, predicado en 29 de Abril de 1807 por el Illmô. y Rmô. Sôr. Dôr. Don Fr. Ramon Casaus, Torres y Lasplazas, del Orden de Predicadores, Maestro por su Religion, Calificador del Santo Oficio, Catedrático de Santo Tomás en la Universidad de México, Académico Honrario de la Real Academia de S. Carlos de N. E., Socio de mérito de la Real Sociedad de Jaca, del Consejo de S. M., Obispo de Rosen, y Auxiliar de Antequera de Oaxaca; en la fiesta que el Illmô. y Santo Tribunal de la Inquisicion con su Ilustre Cofradia celebró en la Iglesia del Imperial Convento de nuestro Padre Santo Domingo de México*. Mexico City: Bautista de Arizpe, 1807.

Casaús Torres y Las Plazas, Ramón. *Sermon de nuestra señora de Cobadonga, y de la Victoria que con su Patrocinio consiguió el Infante Don Pelayo en las Montañas de Asturias*. Mexico City: Fernández de Jáuregui, 1805.

———. *Sermon de S. Pedro Martyr de Verona, predicado el dia 29 de Abril de 1794 por el R. P. Fr. Ramon Casaus Torres y Las Plazas, del Orden de Predicadores, Doctor en Sagrada Teologia por la Real y Pontificia Universidad de México, y Maestro de Estudiantes en el Pontificio Colegio de Porta-Coeli en la fiesta que el Santo Tribunal de la Inquisicion con su ilustre cofradia celebrò en la Iglesia del Imperial Convento de N. P. Stô. Domingo de México*. Mexico City: Los Herederos del Lic. D. Joseph de Jáuregui, 1794.

———. *Sermon Segundo de San Pedro Martyr de Verona, predicado el dia 29 de Abril de 1796 por el R. P. Fr. Ramon Casaus Torres, y Las-Plazas del Orden de Predicadores, Doctor en Sagrada Teologia por la Real y Pontificia Universidad de Méxcio, su Consiliario y Catedrático Substituto del Doctor Angélicao Santo Tomás, y Lector de Prima de Teologia en el Pontificio Colegio de Porta Coeli.. En la fiesta que el Sto. Tribunal de la Inquisicion con su ilustre cofradia celebró en la Iglesia del Imperial Convento de Nrô. P. Stô. Domingo de Mexico*. Mexico City: Fernandez Jáuregui, 1796.

Casillas, Rodolfo. "La discusión sobre el patronato eclesiástico." In *Hacia una historia mínima de la Iglesia en México*. Edited by María Alicia Puente Lutteroth. Mexico City: Jus, 1993.

Castañiza González de Aguero, Juan Francisco de. *Relación del restablecimiento de la Sagrada Compañía de Jesús en el reyno de Nueva España, y de la enrega á sus religiosos del Real Seminario de San Ildefonso de México*. Mexico City: Ontiveros, 1816.

Bibliography

Cayetano Orozco, José M. *Sermon de honras de los venerables sacerdotes, predicado el dia 26 de enero de 1849 en la catedral metropolitana de Mexico por el Dr. D. José M. Cayetano Orozco, catedratico de elocuencia y de historia en el seminario de Gudalajara, examinador sinodal del arzobispado de México, y diputado al soberano congreso general*. Mexico City: Lara, 1849.

———. *Sermon predicado por el Sr. Dr. D. José Maria Cayetano Orozco, canónigo de la Santa Iglesia Catedral de Guadalajara, en la funcion que dedica a la Sma. Virgen de Guadalupe, hizo en la insigne y nacional colegiata el dia trece del corriente septiembre la asamblea de notables, para darle las gracias a la misma Purisima Virgen por el feliz exito de sus deliberaciones*. Mexico City: Literaria, 1863.

Ceballos Ramírez, Manuel. "Un siglo de la Iglesia en México: entre la Reforma liberal y la Revolución Mexicana (1850–1940)." In *México en tres momentos: 1810–1910–2010. Hacia la conmemoración del bicentenario de la Independencia y el centenario de la Revolución Mexicana. Retos y perspectivas*, edited by Alicia Mayer and Juan Ramón de la Fuente, 1:377–98. Mexico City: Universidad Nacional Autónoma de México/Instituto de Investigaciones Históricas, 2008.

Chartier, Roger. *The Cultural Origins of the French Revolution*. Translated by Lydia G. Cochrane. Durham, NC: Duke University Press, 1991.

Chiampi, Irlemar. *Barroco y modernidad*. Mexico City: Fondo de Cultura Económica, 2000.

Chincilla Pawling, Perla. *De la* Compositio Loci *a la república de las letras: predicación jesuita en el siglo XVII novohispano*. Mexico City: Universidad Iberoamericana, 2004.

Chowning, Margaret. "The Consolidación de vales reales in the Bishopric of Michoacán." *Hispanic American Historical Review* 69/3 (1989) 451–78.

———. "Convent Reform, Catholic Reform, and Bourbon Reform: The View from the Nunnery." *Hispanic American Historical Review* 85/1 (2005) 1–38.

———. "La feminización de la piedad en México: Género y piedad en las cofradías de españoles. Tendencias coloniales y poscoloniales en los arzobispados de Michoacán y Guadalajara." In *Religión, política e identidad en la Independencia de México*, edited by Brian Connaughton, 475–514. Mexico City: Universidad Autónoma Metropolitana/Benemérita Universidad Autónoma de Puebla, 2010.

———. "The Laywomen of the Vela Perpetua: Gender, Religion, and Political Culture in Mexico, 1750–1930." Paper presented at Annual Meeting of the American Historical Association, San Diego, CA, January 2010.

———. "The Management of Church Wealth in Michoacán, Mexico, 1810–1856: Economic Motivations and Political Implications." *Journal of Latin American Studies* 22/3 (1990) 459–96.

———. *Rebellious Nuns: The Troubled History of a Mexican Convent, 1752–1863*. Oxford: Oxford University Press, 2006.

Clark, Anna. *Desire: A History of European Sexuality*. New York: Routledge, 2008.

Clark de Lara, Belem, and Elisa Speckman Guerra, editor. *La república de letras: asomos a la cultura escrita del México decimonónico*. 3 vols. Mexico City: Universidad Nacional Autónoma de México, 2005.

Clenndinen, Inga. *Ambivalent Conquests: Maya and Spaniard in Yucatán*. Cambridge: Cambridge University Press, 1987.

Coakley, John W. *Women, Men, and Spiritual Power: Female Saints and Their Male Collaborators*. New York: Columbia University Press, 2006.

Bibliography

Cochrane, Eric W. "Counter-Reformation or Tridentine Reformation? Italy in the Age of Carlo Borromeo." In *San Carlo Borromeo: Catholic Reform and Ecclesiastical Politics in the Second Half of the Sixteenth Century*, edited by John M. Headley and John B. Tomato, 31–46. Washington, DC: Folger, 1988.

Comunicación que dirige Joaquín J. de Araoz, presidente general de la Sociedad Católica de la Nación Mexicana a los señores sus consocios. Mexico City: Díaz de León, 1875.

Conde y Oquendo, Francisco Xavier. *Oración fúnebre que en las exequias militares celebradas por la plaza de México en su Santa Iglesia Metropolitana el día 28 de noviembre de 1786, dixo el Dr. D. Francisco Xavier Conde y Oquendo, prevendade de la Catedral de Puebla*. Mexico City: Zúñiga y Ontiveros, 1787.

Connaughton, Brian F. "El ajedrez del sermón mexicano: entre la retórica redentora y la vida terrena (época colonial al imperio de Maximiliano)." In *Homenaje a Álvaro Matute*, edited by José Ortiz Monasterio, 197–248. Mexico City: Universidad Autónoma de México, 2009.

———. "El catolicismo y la doma del 'espíritu constitucional del siglo': la fragua del nacionalismo conservador mexicano en el universal tras la derrota bélica de 1846–1848." In *México: un siglo de historia constitucional (1808–1917)*, edited by Cecilia Noriega and Alicia Salmerón, 247–66. Mexico City: Suprema Corte de Justicia de la Nación/Instituto Mora, 2009.

———. *Clerical Ideology in a Revolutionary Age: The Guadalajara Church and the Idea of the Mexican Nation (1788–1853)*. Translated by Mark Alan Healey. Calgary, AB: University of Calgary Press, 2003.

———. "El clero y la fundamentación del Estado-nación mexicano." In *Las Fuentes eclesiásticas para la historia social de México*, edited by Brian F. Connaughton and Andrés Lira González, 353–68. Mexico City: Universidad Autónoma Metropolitana, 1996.

———. "Conjuring the Body Politic From the *Corpous Mysticum*: The Post-Independent Pursuit of Public Opinion in Mexico, 1821–1854." *The Americas* 55/3 (1999) 459–79.

———. "El cura párroco al arribo del siglo XIX: el interlocutor interpelado." In *El historiador frente a la historia: religión y vida cotidiana*, edited by Alicia Mayer, 189–214. Mexico City: Universidad Nacional Autónoma de México, 2008.

———. "Los curas y la feligresía ciudadana en México, siglo XIX." In *Las nuevas naciones: España y Méxcio 1800–1850*, edited by Jaime E. Rodríguez O., 241–72. Madrid: Fundación Mapfre, 2008.

———. *Dimensiones de la identidad patriótica. Religión, política y regiones en México. Siglo XIX*. Mexico City: Universidad Autónoma Metropolitana, 2001.

———. "The Enemy Within: Catholics and Liberalism in Independent Mexico, 1821–1860." In *The Divine Charter: Constitutionalism and Liberalism in Nineteenth-Century Mexico*, edited by Jaime E. Rodríguez O., 189–214. Lanham, MD: Rowan & Littlefield, 2005.

———. "Entre la palabra hablada y la palabra escrita: La cultura política nacional en el foro de la Alameda, 1827–1854." *Estudios del Hombre* 20 (2005) 117–52.

———. "Los lindes teóricos de una inquietud de época: Cádiz y las lecturas paradigmáticas de la década independentista." In *Independencia y revolución: pasado, presente y futuro*, edited by Gustavo Leyva, 108–42. Mexico City: Fondo de Cultura Económica/Universidad Autónoma Metropolitana, 2010.

———. "Modernización, religión e iglesia en México (1810–1910): vida de rasgaduras y reconstituciones." In *Nación, constitución y reforma (1821–1908)*, edited by Erika Pani, 238–75. Mexico City: Centro de Investigación y Docencia Económicas/ Fondo de Cultura Económica/Consejo Nacional para la Cultura y las Artes/ Instituto Nacional de Estudios Históricos de la Revolución Mexicana/Fundación Cultural de la Ciudad de México, 2010.

———. "Mudanzas en los umbrales éticos y político-sociales de la práctica religiosa." In *Mexico en tres momentos: 1810-1910-2010. Hacia la conmemoración del Bicentenario de la Independencia y del Centenario de la Revolución Mexicana. Retos y perspectivas*, edited by Alicia Mayer 2:241–67. Mexico City: Universidad Nacional Autónoma de México, 2007.

———. "Nación y religión en el México del siglo XIX." In *Los caminos de la ciudadanía. México y España en perspectiva comparada*, edited by Manuel Suárez Cortina and Tomás Pérez Vejo, 246–63. Madrid: Editorial Biblioteca Nueva/Publican-Ediciones de la Universidad de Cantabria, 2010.

———. "El ocaso del proyecto de 'Nación Católica', patronato virtual, préstamos, y presiones regionales, 1821–1856." In *Construcción de la legitimidad política en México en el siglo XIX*, edited by Brian Connaughton, Carlos Illades, and Sonia Pérez Toledo, 227–62. Zamora: El Colegio de Michoacán/Universidad Autónoma Metropolitana/Universidad Nacional Autónoma de México/El Colegio de México, 1999.

———. "¿Politización de la religión o nueva sacralización de la política? El sermón en las mutaciones públicas de 1808-1824." In *Religión, política e identidad en la Independencia de México*, edited by Brian Connaughton, 160–202. Mexico City: Universidad Autónoma Metropolitana/Benemérita Universidad Autónoma de Puebla, 2010.

———. "La religiosidad de los liberales: Francisco Zarco y el acicate de la economía política." In *Presencia internacional de Juárez, Asociación de Estudios sobre la Reforma, la Intervención Francesa y el Segundo Imperio*, edited by Patricia Galeana, 69–83. Mexico City: Carso, 2008.

———. "¿Una república católica dividida? La disputa eclesiológica heredada y el liberalismo ascendente en la independencia de México." *Historia Mexicana* 59/4 (2010) 1141–1204.

———. "República federal y patronato: el ascenso y descalabro de un proyecto." *Historia Moderna y Contemporánea de México* 39 (2010) 5–70.

———. "Una ruptura anunciada: los catolicismos encontrados del gobierno liberal y el arzobispo Garza y Ballesteros." In *Los obispados de México frente a la Reforma liberal*, edited by Jaime Olveda, 27–55. Zapopan: El Colegio de Jalisco, 2007.

———. "La sacralización de lo cívico: la imagen religiosa en el discurso cívico-patriótico del México independiente. Puebla (1827-1853)." In *Estado, iglesia y sociedad en México. Siglo XIX*, edited by Álvaro Matute, Evelia Trejo, and Brian Connaughton, 223–50. Mexico City: Universidad Nacional Autónoma de México, 1995.

———. "Soberanía y religiosidad: la disputa por la grey en el movimiento de la reforma." In *Clérigos, políticos y política. Las relaciones iglesia y estado en Puebla, siglos XIX-XX*, edited by Alicia Tecuanhuey, 101–21. Puebla: Benemérita Universidad Autónoma de Puebla, 2002.

Bibliography

———. "Voces europeas en la temprana labor editorial mexicana, 1820–1860." *Historia Mexicana* 55/3 (2006) 895–946.

Connaughton, Brian F., editor. *Poder y legitimidad en México en el siglo XIX: instituciones y cultura política*. Mexico City: Universidad Autónoma Metropolitana, 2003.

Connaughton, Brian F., and Carlos Rubén Ruiz Medrano, editors. *Dios, religión y patria. Intereses, luchas e ideales socioreligiosos en México, siglos XVIII y XIX*. Mexico City: El Colegio de San Luis, 2010.

Corder, Stephen J. "The Spiritual Senses in the Exercises of Ignatius of Loyola." PhD diss., Jesuit School of Theology at Berkeley, 2003.

Cordero, Vicente. *Sermon panegírico que en la solemne funcion de Nuestra Señora de Covadonga pronunció el Doctor D. Vicente Cordero canónigo magistral de la I.Y N. Colegiata de Santa María de Guadalupe el dia trece de noviembre de 1859*. Mexico City: Andrade y Escalante, 1859.

Correa Etchegaray, Leonor. "El rescate de una devoción jesuítica: el Sagrado Corazón de Jesús en la primera mitad del siglo XIX." In *Memoria del I Coloquio Historia de la Iglesia en el Siglo XIX*, edited by Manuel Ramos Medina, 91–122. Mexico City: Centro de Estudios de Historia de México/CONDUMEX, 1998.

Costeloe, Michael. "The Administration, Collection, and Distribution of Tithes in the Archbishopric of Mexico, 1810–1860." *The Americas* 23 (1966) 3–27.

———. *The Central Republic in Mexico, 1835–1846: Hombres de bien in the Age of Santa Anna*. Cambridge: Cambridge University Press, 1993

———. *Church and State in Independent Mexico: A Study of the Patronage Debate, 1821–1857*. London: Royal Historical Society, 1978.

———. *Church Wealth in Mexico: A Study of the 'Juzgado de Capellanías' in the Archbishopric of Mexico, 1800–1856*. London: Cambridge University Press, 1967.

Covarrubias, José María. *Sermon que en la parroquia del Sagrario Metropolitano de México, predicó el Sr. Dr. D. José María Covarrubias, prebendado de esta santa iglesia, provisor y vicrio general de este arzobispado, el dia 9 de abril de 1853. En la solemne accion de gracias por la conclusion de la proroga del Santo Jubileo concedido por Nuestro Santísimo Padre el Sr. Pio IX*. Mexico City: Lara, 1853.

Cuadriello, Jaime. "Ministry of Saint Joseph." In *Painting a New World: Mexican Art and Life, 1521–1821*, edited by Donna Pierce, Rogelio Ruiz Gomar, and Clara Bargellini, 260–265. Denver: Denver Art Museum, 2004.

Cubero Ramírez de Arellano, Joseph, fray. *Musica sagrada, que aplaude la coronacion augusta de Maria Santissima N. Sra. Sermon, que en la Santa Iglesia Metropolitana de Mexico en el dia de la Assuncion de Nuestra Señora, con asistencia de la Rl. Audiencia, Tribunales, Sagradas Religiones, y muy noble Ciudad predicó el Rmo. P. Mro. Fr. Joseph Cubero Remirez de Arellano, Maesto en Santa Theologia de los de el numero de su gravisima Provincia de Castilla, Secretario, que fue de ella, Comendador de los Conventos de Burgos, Logroño, y Toledo, Examinador synodal de el Arzobispado de Burgos, y Obispados de Calaborra, y Goatemala, Calificador del Santo Oficio, Juez Apostolico Conservador de las Santas Iglesias Catedrales de Burgos, y Toledo, y al presente Difnissimo Vicario General de todas las Provincias de Nueva España, Mexico, Goatemala, Isla Española de Santo Domingo, y sus adiacentes, de el Real, y Militar Orden de Nuestra Señora de la Merced, Redencion de cautivos, etc*. Mexico City: Bernardo de Hogal, 1728.

Dallo y Zavala, Manuel Romualdo, fray. *San Pedro Martyr. Sermon Panegirico en la Iglesia del Imperial Convento de N.P. Santo Domingo de la Cesarea, y Nobilisima*

Ciudad de Mexico el dia 29 de Abril de 1743. Mexico City: La viuda de J. B. de Hogal, 1743.

———. *El Trono del Supremo Juez Maria Santisima por su Concepcion en gracia. Sermon panegírico, que el día veinte de diciembre de mil setecientos quarenta y cinco, último de la Solemnísima Octava con que se celebra en la Pontificia Universidad de Mexico, y en que la aplaudió su Sapientisimo Claustro de Doctores, y Maestros*. Mexico City, 1745.

Danés Rojas, Edgar. *Noticias del edén: la Iglesia católica y la Constitución Mexicana*. Ciudad Victoria: Universidad Autónoma de Tamaulipas/Miguel Ángel Porrúa, 2008.

Dargan, Edwin Charles. *A History of Preaching*. Vol. 1, *From the Apostolic Fathers to the Great Reformers A.D. 70–1572*. Grand Rapids: Baker, 1954.

Davidoff, Lenore and Catherine Hall. *Family Fortunes: Men and Women of the English Middle Class, 1780–1850*. Chicago: University of Chicago Press, 1987.

Dávila, Ramón. *Panegirico que en honor de la augusta Madre de la Merced, pronunció en su Convento Grande de México el M. R. P. Provincial Maestro Fray Ramón Dávila, el día 24 de septiembre de 1850*. Mexico City: Lovis Morales, 1850.

Dávila, Salvador. *Aprobacion del Padre Salvador Dávila, de la Sagrada Compañia de Jesus*. In Joseph Julián Parreño, *El ilustre, y real colegio de abogados, patron de las causas y derechos de Nuestra Señora de Guadalupe*. Mexico City: Colegio de San Ildefonso, 1762.

Defensa de la Compañía de Jesús, Núm. 1, Introducción a la refutación de las cartas del Señor Palafox, y de las Provinciales. Mexico City: Abadiano, 1841.

Defensa de la petición al soberano congreso por varios individuos solicitando la restitución de la Compañía de Jesús en la República Mexicana, y satisfacción a los señores editores del Cosmopolita que la han impugnado. Mexico City: Lara, 1841.

de la Bárcena, Manuel. *Sermon exhortatorio que en la solemne funcion annual, que hace la imperial orden de Guadalupe a su celestial patrona, predico el Exmo. Sr. Dr. D. Manuel de la Bárcena: Arcediano, Dignidad de la Santa Iglesia Catedral de Valladolid de Michoacan, Caballero Gran-Cruz de la misma Orden, y Consejero de Estado, el dia 15 de diciembre del año de 1822, en la Iglesia de San José el Real de esta Córte, con asistencia de S. M. el Emperador, y de SS. AA. el Príncipe Imperial y el Príncipe D. Angel*. Mexico City: Supremo Gobierno, 1823.

de la Cruz, Sor Juana Inés. "Sor Juana Inés de la Cruz's Letter to Sor Filotea." In *Colonial Latin America: A Documentary History*, edited by Kenneth Mills, William B. Taylor, and Sandra Lauderdale Graham, 207–14. Wilmington, DE: Scholarly Resources, 2002.

de la Garza y Ballesteros, Lázaro. *Carta pastoral que el Illmo. Señor Arzobispo de México Dr. D. Lazaro de la Garza y Ballesteros dirige a sus diocesanos*. Mexico City: Andrade y Escalante, 1858.

———. *Cuarta carta pastoral del Illmo. Sr. Arzobispo de México Dr. D. Lazaro de la Garza y Ballesteros, dirigida al V. Clero y fieles de este Arzobispado con motivo de los proyectos contra la Iglesia, publicados en Veracruz por D. Benito Juarez antiguo presidente del supremo tribunal de la nacion*. Mexico City: Lara, 1859.

———. *Edicto de llustrisimo Sr. Arzobispo Dr. D. Lazaro de la Garza y Ballestreros, para publicacion del Santo Jubileo, concedido por N. S. P. el SR. Pio IX*. Mexico City: Lara, 1852.

Bibliography

———. *Opusculo sobre los enviados de la silla apostólica. Su autor el Doctor Don Lázaro de la Garza y Ballesteros, Arzobispo de México*. Mexico City: Lara, 1854.

———. *Pastoral que el Ilmo. Señor Arzobispo Doctor D. Lázaro de la Garza, dirige a los fieles de su diócesis comunicándoles haber condenado S. S. el Señor Pío IX la obra que se espresa*. Mexico City: Lara, 1852.

———. *Sermon que en la insigne y nacional colegiata de Ntra. Señora de Guadalupe predicó el Doctor D. Lázaro de la Garza y Ballesteros, arzobispo de México, el dia 12 de Agosto del presente año, en que se celebró en dicho templo la Declaracion dogmática de la Inmaculada Concepcion de la Virgen María*. Mexico City: Lara, 1855.

———. *Sermones predicados en la iglesia de Jesus María, por el Doctor D. Lázaro de la Garza y Ballesteros, arzobispo de México*. Mexico City: Voz de la Religión, 1852.

———. *Varias cartas sobre diversas materias que el Illmo. Sr. Doctor D. Lázaro de la Garza y Ballesteros, Arzobispo de Mexico: siendo obispo de Sonora, dirigió al clero de aquella diócesis y hoy dedica al de la iglesia mexicana*. Mexico City: Colegio N. de San Gregorio, 1851.

de la Hera, Alberto. "El regalismo español y su proyección en Indias en tiempos del Arzobispo Lorenzana." In *España y América entre el Barroco y la Ilustración (1722–1804): II Centenario de la muerte del Cardenal Lorenzana (1804–2004)*. Edited by Jesús Paniagua Pérez. León: Universidad de León, 2005.

de la Maza, Francisco. "La decoración simbólica de la capilla del Rosario de Puebla." *Anales del Instituto de Investigaciones Estéticas* 6/23 (1955) 5–29.

———. *Las piras funerarias en la historia y en el arte de México, grabados, litografías y documentos del siglo XVI al XIX*. Mexico City: Universitaria, 1946.

del Arenal Fenochio, Jaime. "El Plan de Iguala y la salvación de la religión y de la Iglesia novohispanas dentro de un orden constitucional." In *Memoria del I Coloquio Historia de la Iglesia en el Siglo XIX*. Edited by Manuel Ramos Medina. Mexico City: Centro de Estudios de Historia de México/CONDUMEX, 1998.

de la Rocha, Juan Ignacio. *Dictamen de el Dr. y Mrô. D. Juan Ignacio de la Rocha, Canonigo Lectoral de esta Santa Iglesia Metropolitana, etc.*, in Fray Joseph Manuel Rodríguez, *Oracion funebre, que en las exequias, que de orden del Excmo. Sr. D. Carlos Francisco de Croix, Virrey de esta Nueva España, etc. se celebraron por los militares españoles difuntos, en la Iglesia del Convento Grande de N. S. P. S. Francisco de Mexico, el dia 6 de Noviembre de 1767. Con asistencia de los tribunales*. Mexico City: Nuevo Rezado de los Herederos de Doña María de Ribera, 1767.

———. *Parecer del Señor Doctor, y Maestro Don Juan Ignacio de la Rocha, Colegial que fuè del Tridentino Seminario de esta Corte, y Cathedratico Jubilado de Philosophia en la de propriedad de la misma facultad de la Real, y Pontificia Universidad de esta Ciudad, Cura de la Parroquia de Santa Catharina Martyr, y mas antiguo del Sagrario de esta Santa Iglesia Cathedral, y Prebendado de la misma Stà. Iglesia*. In Joseph Julián Parreño, *El ilustre, y real colegio de abogados, patron de las causas y derechos de Nuestra Señora de Guadalupe*. Mexico City: Colegio de San Ildefonso, 1762.

de la Torre Villar, Ernesto. "Eguiara y Eguren, orador sagrado." *Estudios de Historia Novohispana* 10 (1991) 173–88.

de la Vega, Tranquilino. *Opúsculo que contiene una corta defensa de la religion de Jesucristo, y un sumario de los fundamentos que hay para probar, que en Mexico no puede establecerse la tolerancia de cultos*. Mexico City: Arévalo, 1849.

Bibliography

del Barrio y Rengel, José María. *Sermon predicado por el P. D. José M. del Barrio y Rengel, presbitero de la V. Congregacion del Oratorio, en la solemne funcion que el comercio de Méxcio dedicó á María Santísima de Guadalupe, su augusta patrona, el martes 6 de enero de 1857, en la Iglesia de N. S. P. S. Francisco*. Mexico City: Lara, 1857.

del Castillo, Joseph. *El Salomon de España. Oracion panegyrica, con que el dia 1 de s Mayo de 1761 años celebrò en la Iglesia del Hospital de la Concepcion, y Jesus Nazareno de la Ciudad de Mexico la feliz Coronacion de nuestro Rey, y Señor Don Carlos III (Que Dios Guarde) Catholico Monarcha de las Españas, y Augusto Emperador de las Indias, el Real Tribunal del Protho-Medicato: Que predicò el P. Joseph del Castillo, professo de la Compañia de Jesus, Maestro de Prima de Sagrada Theologia en el Colegio Maximo de S. Pedro, y S. Pablo de la Ciudad de Mexico*. Mexico City: Real y más Antiguo de San Ildefonso, 1762.

De Los Reyes-Heredia, José Guillermo. "Sodomy and Society: Sexuality, Gender, Race and Class in Colonial Mexico." PhD diss., University of Pennsylvania, 2004. ProQuest (AAT 3138002).

del Valle, José. *Sermón que dixo el día quarto el M. R. P. M. Fr. Ioseph del Valle, Prior que fuè de los Conventos de N. P. Santo Domingo de la Puebla, de Isucar, y actual Rector, y Regente de Nuestro Real Colegio de San Luis de la Ciudad de los Angeles. In Octava Maravilla del Nuevo Mundo en la Gran Capilla del Rosario dedicada y aplaudida en el Convento de N. P. S. Domingo de la Ciudad de los Angeles el dia 16 del Mes de Abril de 1690 al Illvsmo. y Revmo. Señor D. D. Manuel Fernández de Santa Cruz Obispo de la Puebla del Consejo de su Magestad*. Puebla: Junta de Mejoramiento Moral, Cívico y Material del Municipio de Puebla, 1985.

del Valle Pavón, Guillermina. "El apoyo financiero del clero al gobierno de Agustín de Iturbide." In *Memoria del I Coloquio Historia de la Iglesia en el Siglo XIX*, edited by Manuel Ramos Medina, 113–26. Mexico City: Centro de Estudios de Historia de México/CONDUMEX, 1998.

De Nicolas, Antonio T. *Powers of Imagining: Ignatius de Loyola*. Albany: State University of New York Press, 1986.

Desan, Suzanne. *Reclaiming the Sacred: Lay Religion and Popular Politics in Revolutionary France*. Ithaca, NY: Cornell University Press, 1990.

Diario de los niños. Mexico City: González, 1840.

Díaz Calvillo, Juan Bautista. *Noticias para la historia de Nuestra Señora de los Remedios desde el año de 1808, hasta el corriente de 1812*. Mexico City: Casa de Arizpe, 1812.

———. *Sermon predicado en la iglesia del convento de religiosas de Santa Inés Virgen y Martir de esta ciudad, el dia 18 de julio de 1810, y tercero de la rogacion circular que allí se hacía á la portentosa imagen de Maria Santisima de los Remedios por las presentes necesidades de la antigua España*. Mexico City, Casa de Valdés, 1810.

———. *Sermon que en el aniversario solemne de gracias a Maria Santisima de los Remedios, celebrado en esta santa iglesia catedral el día 30 de octubre de 1811 por la Victoria del Monte de las Cruces*. Mexico City: Arizpe, 1811.

Díaz y Díaz, Manuel C. "La pasión de S. Pelayo y su diffusion." *Anuario de estudios medievales* 6 (1969) 97–116.

Díaz Pérez y Calvillo, Juan Bautista. *Elogio de San Ignacio de Loyola, fundador de la Compañia de Jesus, predicado en su primera festividad despues del restablecimiento de dicha compañia en esta corte, el 31 de julio de 1816. En la capilla del real y mas antiguo Colegio de S. Ildefonso, por el P. Dr. D. Juan Bautista Diaz Perez y Calvillo, examinador sinodal de este arzobispado, presbítero secular y director de los*

Bibliography

    exercicios espirituales del mismo San Ignacio en las casas de hombres y mugeres del real oratorio de San Felipe Neri de esta capital. Mexico City, 1816.

Díaz Romero, Miguel, fray. *Ornamento sacro de la santidad mas elevada, y vestido acendrado de la virtud mas suprema. Capa de pureza virginal, y manto de castissimo amor*. Mexico City: Rivera Calderón, 1720.

Diez de Sollano, José María. *Sermon que en la celebridad de la declaracion dogmatica de la Inmaculada Concepcion de Maria Santisima, predicó el dia 8 de mayo de 1855 en la capilla del seminario conciliar, el Sr. Dr. y Mtro. D. José Maria Diez de Sollano, rector del mismo Colegio mas antiguo del Sagrario Metropolitano, Caballero de la Nacional y distinguida Orden de Guadalupe, etc. etc*. Mexico City: Lara, 1855.

Diccionario biográfico universal de mugeres célebres, o compendio de la vida de todas las mugeres que han adquirido celebridad en las naciones antiguas y modernas, desde los tiempos remotos hasta nuestros días. Vol. 1. Mexico City: Voz de la Religión, 1851.

Diéguez, Matías fray. *Espejo de luz, que deshace las tinieblas de la ignorancia, y hace ver con su luz los engaños de la vanidad, y soberbia, descubre, y enseña a las mugeres, y todo genero de personas entregadas loca, y ciegamente à trages, y vanidades profanas, el camino mas solido, y verdadero para seguridad de sus conciencias: compuesto de las doctrinas mas santas, claras, y verdaderas de la Sagrada Escritura, SS. PP. DD. y maestros sagrados, concilios, decretos, y constituciones apostolicas, declaraciones pontificias, sagrados canones, revelaciones y doctissimos tratados de varios, eruditos theologos. Dispuesto en estylo escriptuario, y theologico, moral y ascetico: provechoso para todo prelado eclesiastio, y seglar: utilissimo para padres de familia, y demas superiores, que tienen a su cargo almas de que cuidar: muy conveniente para los predicadores, y mucho mas necesario para confessores*. Mexico City: La viuda de D. Joseph Bernardo de Hogal, 1748.

Dickens, A.G. *The Counter Reformation*. London: Thames & Hudson, 1992.

di Stefano, Roberto. *El púlpito y la plaza: Clero, sociedad y política de la monarquía católica a la república rosista*. Buenos Aires: Siglo XXI, 2004.

Domingo, Manuel María. *Sermon panegirico de la Concepcion Inmaculada de la Virgen Maria. Predicado en el Convento Grande de N.S.P. San Francisco de Mexico, implorando su intercession para el acierto del capitulo provincial el dia 8 de mayo de 1829 por el P. Fr. Manuel Maria Domingo*. Mexico City: Testamentaría de Ontiveros, 1829.

Domínguez, Juan Francisco. *Discursos sobre el amor puro y bien ordenado con que se debe veer a las mugeres. Explicados en cinco sermones que predicó en el Sagrario de esta Santa Iglesia Metropolitana el Sr. Lic. D. Juan Francisco Dominguez, Colegial Real de Oposicion en el Real mas antiguo de S. Ildefonso, Cura mas antiguo de la misma Parroquia*. Mexico City: Fernández Jáuregui, 1807.

Dommanget, Maurice. *La déchristianisation à Beauvais et dans l'Oise (1790–1801)*. Paris: Millot, 1918.

La doncella cristiana santificada en el siglo XIX o manual de las hijas de Maria. Traducida del francés bajo la dirección del Illmo. Sr. Munguía. Mexico City: Escalante, 1875.

Doyle, William. *The French Revolution: A Very Short Introduction*. Oxford: Oxford University Press, 2001.

Early, James. *The Colonial Architecture of Mexico*. Dallas: Southern Methodist University, 1994.

Edwards, O. C., Jr. *A History of Preaching*. Nashville: Abingdon, 2004.

Bibliography

Eguiara y Eguren, Juan Joseph de. *La muger fuerte dichosamente hallada, y desgraciadamente perdìda en la muerte de la Serenissima Señora Da. Maria Barbara de Portugal, Catholica Reyna de las Españas y Emperatriz Augusta del Nuevo Mundo. Panegyrico que en sus reales exequias celebradas en la Metropolitana de Mexico predicò el dia 19 de Mayo de 1759 el Dr. D. Juan Joseph de Eguiara y Eguren, Obispo que fue electo de Yucatan, antes Canonigo Magistral, Thesorero electo, y actual Dignidad Maestrescuela de dicha Metropolitana, Cancelario de la Real Universidad de dicha Corte, y su Cathedratico Jubilado en Prima de Sagrada Theologia, Calificador del Santo Oficio, Inquisidor Ordinario por el Obispado de la Puebla, Examinador Synodal del Arzobispado de Mexico, Theologo de Camara de Su Ilmâ, Juez Conservador de la Provincia del Santissimo Nombre de JESUS del Orden de S. Agustin, Capellan de las Religiosas Capuchinas de esta Ciudad.* Mexico City: Bibliotheca Mexicana, 1760.

———. *La Purificacion Triplicada de la Purisima. Panegirico de la Purificacion de María Santisima Nuestra Señora, que el dia 25 de febrero de este año, Sabado después de la Dominica primera de Quaresma, por espacio de una hora, con asignacion de puntos, y termino de cuarenta y ocho. En oposicion a la canoniga magistral de esta Santa Iglesia Metropolitana de Mexico.* Mexico City, 1748.

Elliott, J. H. *The Count-Duke of Olivares: The Statesman in an Age of Decline.* New Haven: Yale University Press, 1986.

———. *Empires of the Atlantic World: Britain and Spain in America, 1492–1830.* New Haven: Yale University Press, 2006.

Enebro, Miguel Auerelio, fray. *Sermon que se predico al nacimiento de Nuestro Serenissimo Infante el Señor Don Carlos Clemente de Borbon (que Dios guarde) en el Sagrado Orden de la Caridad, titulo de S. Hippolyto Martyr, por el R. P. Fr. Miguel Aurelio Enebro, de el Orden de los Ermitaños de Nuestro Padre S. Augustin, Lector Jubilado, y Regente de Estudios en el Convento Principal de Mexico, en el dia 26 de Henero de 1772.* Mexico City: Antonio de Hogal, 1772.

Enríquez Perea, Alberto. "La república de Juárez: laica, plena de libertades, sumisa a la ley." In *Experiencias republicanas y monárquicas en México, América Latina y España. Siglos XIX y XX,* edited by Marco Antonio Landavazo and Agustín Sánchez Andrés, 133–56. Morelia: Universidad Michoacana de San Nicolás de Hidalgo/Instituto de Investigaciones Históricas, 2008.

Eriksen, Erik Oddvar, and Jarle Weigård. *Understanding Habermas: Communicative Action and Deliberative Democracy.* London: Continuum, 2003.

Escamilla González, Francisco Iván. *José Patricio Fernández de Uribe (1742–1796): el cabildo eclesiástico de México ante el Estado Borbónico.* Mexico City: Conaculta, 1999.

Escobar, Diego Antonio de, fray. *Ultimo quid de el mysterio de la Immaculada Concepcion de Maria Santissima Señora Nuestra, revelado (y piadosamente creydo) por la Santissima Trinidad. Sermon historio-panegyrico que el dia 12 de Diziembre de 1723 años predicó en el Convento de la Limpia Concepcion de la Ciudad de Mexico, estando patente el SS. Sacramento, el R. P. F. Diego Antonio de Escobar de los Menores Descalços de N. P. S. Francisco, Examinador Synodal del Obispado de Oaxaca, y Lector de Visperas de Sagrada Theologia en el Convento de San Diego de dicha Ciudad de Mexico.* Mexico City: Los Herederos de la Viuda de Miguel de Rivera, 1724.

Bibliography

Espinosa, José de. *Triumpho festivo, Dedicación Plausible, de la sumptuosa, preciosa, y rica Capilla de Nuestra Señora de el Rosario, en el Convento de Nuestro Padre Santo Domingo, de la Puebla de los Angeles Año de 1690.* In *Octava Maravilla del Nuevo Mundo en la Gran Capilla del Rosario dedicada y aplaudida en el Convento de N. P. S. Domingo de la Ciudad de los Angeles el dia 16 del Mes de Abril de 1690 al Illvsmo. y Revmo. Señor D. D. Manuel Fernández de Santa Cruz Obispo de la Puebla del Consejo de su Magestad.* Puebla: Junta de Mejoramiento Moral, Cívico y Material del Municipio de Puebla, 1985.

Esposición que hace al público la junta de señoras, encargada de la dirección de la casa de niños expósitos de esta capital, por disposicion del Illmo. y Venerable Cabildo Metropolitano, referente á los trabajos que ha impendido en obsequio de este piadoso establecimiento, y de todo cuanto concierne á dar una idea de su manejo, sobre la inversion de los caudales que han ingresado á su poder en los diez y siete meses que han transcurrido desde 10. de Agosto de 1838, en que se publicó la primera esposicion, hasta 31 de Diciembre de 1839. Mexico City: Cumplido, 1840.

Esposición que varias señoras mexicanas presentaron al Exmo. señor general D. Vicente Guerrero, electo Presidente de los Estados-Unidos Mexicanos, sobre la ley general de expulsion de españoles, la noche del 24 de marzo de 1829. Mexico City: Arévalo, 1829.

Estatutos para las señoras archicofrades de la muy ilustre archicofradia de ciudadanos de la Santa Veracruz: Mandados observar en Junta general de la misma, y aprobados por las potestades eclesiástica, política y civil, en el presente año de 1825. Mexico City: Ciudadano Alejandro Valdés, 1825.

Evenett, H. Outram. *The Spirit of the Counter Reformation.* Edited by John Bossy. Cambridge: Cambridge University Press, 1968.

Exaltacion y nobleza, a que aspira el elma haciendose esclava de la Divina Infantita Maria Santisima, pagandole tributo cada año, cada mes, cada semana, cada dia y cada hora. A devocion de dos amantes Esclavas é Hijas de la Inmaculada Concepcion de esta Divina Niña. Mexico City: Abadiano y Valdés, 1843.

Fabián y Fuero, Francisco. *Oracion que en alabanza del Angelico Doctor Santo Thomas de Aquino pronunció el Illmô. Sr. Dr. D. Francisco Fabian y Fuero, Obispo de la Puebla de los Angeles, del Consejo de Su Mag. etc. En la solemne Funcion que el Quarto Concilio Provincial Megicano, celebrado el año de MDCCLXXI hizo en culto del Glorioso Angel de las Escuelas el dia de su festividad en el Convento de Santo Domingo de la Ciudad de Megico.* Mexico City: Oficina de dichos Seminarios Palafoxianos, 1773.

Farriss, Nancy M. *Crown and Clergy in Colonial Mexico, 1759–1821.* London: Athlone, 1968.

Fernández Álvarez, Manuel. *La sociedad española del siglo de oro.* Madrid: Editoria Nacional, 1984.

Fernández de Lizardi, José Joaquín. *The Itching Parrot/El periquillo sarniento.* Translated by Katherine Anne Porter. Garden City, NY: Doubleday, 1942.

Fernández de Uribe, José Patricio. *Solemnes exêquias del Exmô. Señor D. Matías de Galvez, García, Madrid y Cabrera, Teniente General de los Reales Exércitos, Virey, Gobernador y Capitan General del Reyno de Nueva España, y Presidente de su Real Audiencia etc. Celebradas en la Santa Iglesia Catedral de la Imperial Corte Mexicana en los dias IV y V de Marzo de MDCCLXXXV. Dispuestas por sus albaceas testamentarios. Las describe a su nombre el Sr. Dr. y Mrô. Don Joseph Patricio*

Bibliography

Fernandez de Uribe, Catedrático de Retórica en la Real y Pontificia Universidad, y Canónigo Penitenciario de la misma Iglesia Catedral de México. Mexico City: Nueva Imprenta Mexicana de Don Felipe de Zúñiga y Ontiveros, 1785.

El fin del hombre y de la muger. Por un Sacerdote de la Congregacion de la Mision. Mexico City: Albadiano, 1867.

Flores, Francisco Fernando de. *Sermon panegyrico al celestial cingulo de la pureza del angelico doctor Santo Tomas, que en la solemne festividad, celebrarda por la Ilustre Congregacion de la Castidad, o Milicia Angélica, fundad en la advocacion del Santo en su Convento titular de esta Corte, el dia 9 de Junio de 1794, Lunes Pasqua de Espíritu Santo predicó el Doctor D. Francisco Fernando de Flores, Capellán de Honor de S. M. y de su Real Iglesia de las Salesas de Madrid, Teologo Consultor de Cámara del Emmo. Señor Cardenal de Lorenzana, Arzobispo de Toledo, Inquisidor General, etc.* Mexico City: Zúñiga y Ontiveros, 1795.

Flores Caballero, Romeo. "La Consolidación de vales reales en la economía, la sociedad y la política novohispanas." *Historia Mexicana* 18/3 (1969) 334–78.

Florescano, Enrique and Margarita Menegus. "La época de las reformas borbónicas y el crecimiento económico (1750–1808)." In *Historia general de México*. Mexico City: El Colegio de México, 2000.

Folgar, Antonio Manuel de. *Las circunstancias del divinisimo sacramento, maravillosamente excedidas en la portentosa Aparicion de Nuestra Señora de Guadalupe*, in *Semones Panegiricos en la Imperial Ciudad de Mexico*. Madrid: Marin, 1753.

———. *Competencias de Amor, entre el Eterno Padre, y San Jose. Panegirico que en glories de este Santisimo Patriarca, en su propio dia 19 de Marzo, ano de 1734, en la Iglesia del Convento de Senoras Religiosas del Dulcisimo Nombre de MARIA, y San Bernardo, de esta Imperial Ciudad de Mexico*. Mexico City: Real del superior govierno de doña María de Rivera, 1734.

———. *La mayor victoria de Santa Ines. Sermon Panegirico, que en su propio dia veinte y uno de enero del ano de 1752 y en su propia Iglesia de Religiosas de este Titulo, de la Imperial Ciudad de Mexico, patente el Augustisimo Sacramento, se predicó*, in *Semones Panegiricos en la Imperial Ciudad de Mexico*. Madrid: Marin, 1753.

Ford, Caroline. *Divided Houses: Religion and Gender in Modern France*. Ithaca, NY: Cornell University Press, 2005.

Foucault, Michel. *The History of Sexuality*. Translated by Robert Hurley. Vol. 1, *An Introduction*. New York: Vintage, 1990.

Fraguas, Lorenzo, fray. *Hermanada idea de sacerdotes y religiosas, mystico sol Christo Sacramentado; sermon, que el dia 28 de Agosto de este Año de 1720, predicó en el Religiosissimo Convento de Señoras Capuchinas de esta Corte, y Ciudad de Mexico: el R. P. Fr. Lorenzo Fraguas, Hijo de la Santa Provincia de Menores Descalzos de N. S. P. S. Francisco, de esta Nueva-España, y Lector de Prima de Sagrada Theologia, en el Convento de S. Diego*. Mexico City: Ortega y Bonilla, 1721.

Franco, Jean. *Plotting Women: Gender and Representation in Mexico*. New York: Columbia University Press, 1989.

Francois, Marie. "Cloth and Silver: Pawning and Material Life in Mexico City at the Turn of the Nineteenth Century." *The Americas* 60/3 (2004) 325–62.

French, William E., and Katherine Elaine Bliss. *Gender, Sexuality, and Power in Latin America Since Independence*. Lanham, MD: Rowman & Littlefield, 2007.

Friedrich, Carl J. *The Age of the Baroque: 1610–1660*. New York: Harper & Row, 1952.

Bibliography

Gacetas de México: Castorena y Ursua (1722)—Sahagún de Arévalo (1728 a 1742). 2 vols. Mexico City: Secretaría de Educación Pública, 1949.

Galeana de Valadéz, Patricia. *Las relaciones Iglesia-Estado durante el Segundo Imperio.* Mexico City: Universidad Nacional Autónoma de México, 1991.

Gallegos, Joseph. *Dechado de la castidad. Oracion panegyrica, que en la solemne fiesta de la milicia angelica del celestial cingulo del Doctor Angelico Santo Thomas, dixo en la Iglesia del Imperial Convento de N. P. Sto. Domingo, de Mexico, dia 28 de Enero del año de 1771 el R. P. Fr. Joseph Gallegos, Lector de Sagrada Escritura, y de el Illmo. Melchor Cano.* Mexico City: Imprenta del Lic. D. Joseph de Jáuregui, 1771.

———. *Glorias de España deducidas de su restauracion milagrosa. Oracion panegyrica, que en la solemne fiesta, que hasen [sic] los S. S. Asturianos a Maria Santisima de Cobadonga dixo en la Iglesia del Convento Imperial de N. P. Santo Domingo dia 14 de Noviembre del año de 1773 el R. P. Fr. Joseph Gallegos, Lector de Sagrada Theologia, quien insertando una breve Apología del Método de Estudios, impuesto por S. Rma. la dedica a N. Rmo. P. Fr. Juan Thomas de Boxadors, Maestro General del Orden de Predicadores. Por mano de N. M. R. P. Fr. Pedro Garrido, Mtro. En Sagr. Theologia, Exâminador Synodal, de este Arzopdo, y Ex-Provincial de esta Provincia de Santiago de México.* Mexico City: Biblioteca Mexicana, 1774.

García Ayluardo, Clara. "A World of Images: Cult, Ritual, and Society in Colonial Mexico City." In *Rituals of Rule, Rituals of Resistance*, edited by William H. Beezley, Cheryl English Martin, and William E. French, 77–94. Wilmington, DE: SR, 1994.

García de Torres, José Julio. *Sermon de accion de gracias a Maria Santisima de Guadalupe, por el venturoso suceso de la Independencia de la América Septentrional, predicado en su santuario insigne imperial colegiata, el 12 de octubre de 1821 por el Sr. Dr. y Mtrô. D. José Julio Garcia de Torres, Prebendado de la misma, presente el Supremo Consejo de Regencia, presidido por el Excmô. Sr. D. Agustin de Iturbide, Generalisimo de las armas del Imperio, Gefe y Promotor de la libertad americana.* Mexico City: Imprenta Imperial de D. Alejandro Valdés, 1821.

García Peña, Ana Lidia. "El encierro de las esposas y las prácticas policiacas en la época de la independencia." In *1750–1850: La independencia de México a la luz de cien años*, edited by Brian Connaughton, 103–31. Mexico City: Universidad Autónoma Metropolitana/Ediciones del Lirio, 2009.

García Ugarte, Marta Eugenia. *Poder político y religioso. México, siglo XIX.* 2 vols. Mexico City: Universidad Nacional Autónoma de México/Miguel Ángel Porrúa, 2010.

———. "Provisión de las sedes diocesanas vacantes en México (1825–1831)." In *La iglesia hispanoamericana de la colonia a la república*, edited by Rodolfo Aguirre and Lucrecia Enríquez, 45–98. Mexico City: Plaza y Valdés, 2008.

Garofoli, Joe. "Salvatore Cordileone's Key Prop. 8 Role." *San Francisco Chronicle*, July 27, 2012.

Garza Carvajal, Federico. *Butterflies Will Burn: Prosecuting Sodomites in Early Modern Spain and Mexico.* Austin: University of Texas Press, 2003.

Gibson, Charles. *The Aztecs Under Spanish Rule: A History of the Indians of the Valley of Mexico, 1519–1810.* Stanford: Stanford University Press, 1964.

Giraud, François. "Mujeres y familia en Nueva España." In *Presencia y transparencia: la mujer en la historia de México*, edited by Carmen Ramos Escandón, 61–78. Mexico City: El Colegio de México, 1987.

Gómez de Escontría, José. *Oracion funebre que en las Honras anniversarias de los Militares Difuntos de la Monarchia Española, celebradas en la Iglesia Cathedral de Mexico, dixo, en presencia del Excmo. Sr. Marques de Croix, Cavallero del Orden de Calatrava, Comendador de Molinos, y Laguna Rota en la misma Orden, Capitan General de los Reales Exercitos de S. M.. Virrey Governador, y Capitan General del Reynos de Nueva España, Presidente de su Real Audiencia, Superintendente General de Real Hacienda, y Ramo del Tabaco, Juez Conservador de este, Presidente de su Junta, y Subdelegado General de la Renta de Correos Maritimos en el mismo Reyno, el dia 23 de Noviembre de el año de 1770, el P. Dr. D. Joseph Gomez de Escontria Presbytero de la Congregacion de San Phelipe de Neri, de esta Corte*. Mexico City: Imprenta Real del Superior Govierno del Br. D. Joseph Antonio de Hogal, 1770.

———. *Sermon, que en la Santa Iglesia Catedral de Megico predicó el dia de la festividad de la Asuncion de la Madre de Dios, el Padre Dr. D. Josef Gomez de Escontría, Presbytero de la Real Congregacion de San Felipe Neri, y Calificador del Santo Oficio de la Inquisicion de esta Corte*. Mexico City: Imprenta del Br. D. Josef Antonio de Hogal, calle de Tiburcio, 1772.

Gómez de la Parra, José. *Aprobación del Señor Doctor Don Joseph Gómez de la Parra, Colegial, que fue en el Insigne, y Viejo de Nuestra Señora de Todos Santos, Canónigo Magistral que fue de la Santa Iglesia Cathedral de Mechoacán, Racionero de la de la Puebla de los Angeles, y Examinador Synodal en uno, y otro Obispado. In Convento de N. P. S. Domingo de la Ciudad de los Angeles el dia 16 del Mes de Abril de 1690 al Illvsmo. y Revmo. Señor D. D. Manuel Fernández de Santa Cruz Obispo de la Puebla del Consejo de su Magestad*. Puebla: Junta de Mejoramiento Moral, Cívico y Material del Municipio de Puebla, 1985.

Gómez Marín, Manuel. *Meditaciones para todos los días del año que por orden de la Congregación de S. Felipe Neri de Méjico dispuso el Reverendo Padre Doctor y Maestro D. Manuel Gómez Marín, presbítero de la misma*. Vol. 1. Mexico City: Abadiano y Valdés, 1835.

Gómez Marín, Manuel. *Oracion panegírica, que en la funcion, con que el oratorio de S. Felipe Neri de Mexcio solemnizó la beatificacion del venerable siervo de Dios Sebastián Valfré, presbítero y prepósito del Oratorio de Turín, pronunció, con asistencia del exmo. Ayuntamiento, el R. P. Dr. y Mtro. D. Manuel Gomez Marin, Presbítero y Director de egercicios del dicho Oratorio de Méxcio, Catedrático jubilado de Prima de Sagrada Teología, y Deacano de esta facultad en la Nacional y Pontificia Universidad*. Mexico City: Abadiano y Valdés, 1836.

Gómez Martínez, Javier. *Historicismos de la arquitectura barroca novohispana*. Mexico City: Universidad Iberoamericana, 1997.

Gonzalbo, Pilar. "Autoridad masculina y poder femenino: los recursos de dominio en la vida familiar." In *Religión, Poder y Autoridad en la Nueva España*, edited by Alicia Mayer and Ernesto de la Torre Villar, 367–79. Mexico City: Universidad Nacional Autónoma de México, 2004.

———. "Nuevo mundo, nuevas formas familiares." In *Género, familia y mentalidades en América Latina*, edited by Pilar Gonzalbo Aizpuru, 13–38. San Juan: Universidad de Puerto Rico, 1997.

———. "Tradición y ruptura en la educación femenina del siglo XVI." In *Presencia y Transparencia: la mujer en la historia de México*, edited by Carmen Ramos Escandón, 33–59. Mexico City: El Colegio de México, 1987.

Bibliography

Gonzalbo Aizpuru, Pilar. "Del decoro a la ostentación: los límites del lujo en la ciudad de México en el siglo XVIII," *Colonial Latin American Review* 16/1 (2007) 3–22.

———. *Las mujeres en la Nueva España: educación y vida cotidiana*. Mexico City: El Colegio de México, 1987.

———. "Las mujeres novohispanas y las contradicciones de una sociedad patriarcal." In *Las mujeres en la construcción de las sociedades iberoamericanas*, edited by Pilar Gonzalbo Aizpuru and Berta Ares Queija, 121–40. Seville: Consejo Superior de Investigaciones Científicas/El Colegio de México, 2004.

González, Juan. *Sermon historico eucaristico, que en la annual y solemne funcion, que la real congregacion de naturales y originarios del principado de Asturias y obispado de Oviedo hace a su singular patrona Maria Santisima de Covadonga en la Iglesia de N. P. Santo Domingo de Mexico, predicó el dia 12 de noviembre de 1815 el R. P. Dr. Fr. Juan Gonzalez del orden de Predicadores, examinador sinodal de este arzobispado y del obispado de Merida y Yucatan, regente primario de estudios de dicho convento y catedratico del Angelico Dr. Santo Tomas en esta real y pontificia Universidad*. Mexico City: Benavente, 1816.

———. *Sermon panegirico de Santa Ines virgen y martir, que en el convento de religiosas de su misma advocacion de esta corte, predicó el dia 21 de enero de 1816 el R. P. Fr. Juan Gonzalez, del Orden de Predicadores, Doctor Teólogo, y Catedrático de Santo Tomás en la Real y Pontificia Universidad, Calificador del Santo Oficio, Exâminador Synodal de este Arzobispado, y del Obispado de Mérida de Yucatan, y Regente primero de estudios en el Imperial Convento de N. P. Stô. Domingo de México*. Mexico City: Imprenta de la calle de Santo Domingo, y esquina de Tacuba, 1816.

González Casanova, Pablo. *La literatura perseguida en la crisis de la colonia*. Mexico City: Secretaría de Educación Pública, 1986.

González Díaz, Bernardo. *Sermon que en la solemne accion de gracias al Dios de los exercitos y Señor de las batallas por la feliz restitucion de nuestro catolico monarca el SR. D. Fernando VII al trono de las Españas, celebrada por el segundo batallon de Patriotas distinguidos de la imperial ciudad de México, en la capilla de su cuartel la real y pontificia Universidad, el dia de la Natividad de nuestro Señor Jesucristo del año de 1814, dixo Fr. Bernardo Gonzalez Diaz, religioso agustino calzado, rector del real colegio de San Pablo de esta capital, calificador del Santo Oficio y exâminador sinodal de este arzobispado*. Mexico City: Benavente, 1815.

Gonzlez Díaz, Bernardo Antonio. *Sermon que en la solemne fiesta de Nuestra Señora de Covadonga, celebradda por la Real Congregacion de Naturales y Originarios del Principado de Asturias y Obispado de Oviedo, en la Iglesia del Convento Imperial de Santo Domingo de México , el dia 15 de Noviembre de 1807, dixo el M. R. P. Fr. Bernardo Antonio Gonzalez Diaz, del Orden de San Agustin, Regente que fué de Sagrada Teología en el Colegio mayor de San Gabriel de Valladolid de España, y despues Lector de la misma Facultad en el Real de San Pablo de Méxcio, Calificador del Santo Oficio de esta Corte, y Definidor actual de la Provincia del Santísimo*. Mexico City: Arizpe, 1808.

———. *Sermon que en las publicas, solemnes y devotas rogativas hechas a Maria Santisima de los Remedios, por la muy noble y fidelísima Ciudad de México, por todo el venerable Clero secular y regular de esta Corte imperial, por las observantes Religiosas de todos sus Monasterios, y por todos los respetables Cuerpos de esta gran Capital, para la restauracion de nuestra católica Monarquía, para la restitucion de nuestro amado Soberano el Señor D. Fernando VIII á su Trono, y de nuestro*

Bibliography

Santísimo Padre el Señor Pio VII á su Silla, y para confusion de Napoleon Bonaparte, *usurpador del trono de los Borbones, protector de los impíos, y perseguidor de la Religion de Jesuchristo, dixo el dia 2 de agosto del año de 1810 en la iglesia de la monjas de Regina Coeli, el M. R. P. Fr. Bernardo Antonio Gonzalez Diaz, Religioso Agustino Calzado, Regente que fuue de Sagrada Teologia en el Colegio mayor de S. Gabriel de Valladolid de España, Calificador del Santo Oficio, y Definidor actual de la Provincia del Santísimo Nombre de Jesus de esta Nueva España.* Mexico City: Zúñiga y Ontiveros, 1810.

Goode, Luke. *Jürgen Habermas: Democracy and the Public Sphere.* London: Pluto, 2005.

Goodstein, Laurie. "Bishops Defend Fight Against Obama's Policy on Birth Control Coverage." *New York Times,* June 13, 2012.

Gorospe, Juan de. *Sermón que en el Segundo día dixo el M. R. P. M. Fr. Juan de Gorospe, Rector, y Regente que fue del Colegio Real de San Luis de la Ciudad de los Angeles, Prior del Convento de N. P. S. Domingo, y Vicario General de la Provincia de San Miguel, y Santos Angeles, y Actual Provincial Suyo.* In *Octava Maravilla del Nuevo Mundo en la Gran Capilla del Rosario dedicada y aplaudida en el Convento de N. P. S. Domingo de la Ciudad de los Angeles el dia 16 del Mes de Abril de 1690 al Illvsmo. y Revmo. Señor D. D. Manuel Fernández de Santa Cruz Obispo de la Puebla del Consejo de su Magestad.* Puebla: Junta de Mejoramiento Moral, Cívico y Material del Municipio de Puebla, 1985.

Green, Stanley C. *The Mexican Republic: The First Decade, 1823–1832.* Pittsburgh: Pittsburgh University Press, 1987.

Gruzinski, Serge. "The Ashes of Desire: Homosexuality in Mid-Seventeenth-Century New Spain." Translated by Ignacio López-Cavlo. In *Infamous Desire: Male Homosexuality in Colonial Latin America,* edited by Pete Sigal, 197–214. Chicago: University of Chicago Press, 2003.

Guardino, Peter. *The Time of Liberty: Popular Political Culture in Oaxaca, 1750–1850.* Durham, NC: Duke University Press, 2005.

Guerra, François-Xavier. "La desintegración de la monarquía hispánica: revolución de independencia." In *De los imperios a las naciones: Iberoamérica.* Edited by Antonio Annino, Luis Castro Leiva, and François-Xavier Guerra. Zaragoza: IberCaja, 1994.

———. "Revolución Francesa y revoluciones hispánicas: una relación compleja." In *Modernidad e independencias: ensayos sobre las revoluciones hispánicas,* edited by François-Xavier Guerra, 35–77. Madrid: Editorial Mapfre, 1992.

———. "La ruptura originaria: mutaciones, debates y mitos de la Independencia." In *Mitos políticos en las sociedades andinas,* edited by Germán Carrera Damas et al., 21–44. Caracas: Equinoccio, 2006.

Gunnarsdóttir, Ellen. *Mexican Karismata: The Baroque Vocation of Francisca de los Angeles, 1674–1744.* Lincoln: University of Nebraska Press, 2004.

Guridi y Alcocer, José Miguel. *Exortacion que para el juramento de la constitucion en la parroquia del sagrario el dia 11 de junio de 1820, hizo su cura mas antiguo el Dr. D. José Miguel Guridi y Alcocer.* Mexico City: Valdés, 1820.

———. *Sermon predicado en la solemne funcion que celebró el ilustre y real colegio de abogados de esta corte, en accion de gracias à su Patrona nuestra Señora de Guadalupe por la Jura de nuestro Católico Monarca el señor Don Fernando VII hecha en 13 de agosto de 1808.* Mexico City: Arizpe, 1808.

Gutiérrez Haces, Juana. "Sacred Heart of Jesus with Saint Ignatius of Loyola and Saint Louis Gonzaga." In *The Arts in Latin America, 1492–1820,* edited by Joseph J.

Bibliography

Rishel and Suzanne Stratton-Pruitt, 387. Philadelphia: Philadelphia Museum of Art, 2006.

Habermas, Jürgen. *The Structural Transformation of the Public Sphere: An Inquiry into a Category of Bourgeois Society*. Translated by Thomas Burger and Frederick Lawrence. Cambridge, MA: MIT Press, 1989.

Hahn, Lewis Edwin, editor. *Perspecitves on Habermas*. Chicago: Open Court, 2000.

Hale, Charles A. *Mexican Liberalism in the Age of Mora, 1821–1853*. New Haven: Yale University Press, 1968.

Halperin, David M. "Is There a History of Sexuality?" *History Theory* 28/3 (1989) 257–74.

Hamill, Hugh. *The Hidalgo Revolt: Prelude to Mexican Independence*. Gainesville: University of Florida Press, 1996.

Hamill, Hugh M. "¡Vencer o morir por la patria! La invasión de España y algunas consecuencias para México, 1808–1810." Translated by Helene Levesque Dion. In *Interpretaciones sobre la independencia de México*, edited by Josefina Zoraida Vázquez, 71–101. Mexico City: Nueva Imagen, 1997.

Hamnett, Brian R. "Antonio Bergosa y Jordán (1748–1819), Obispo de México: ¿Ilustrado? ¿Reaccionario? ¿Contemporizador y oportunista?" *Historia Mexicana* 233 (2009) 117–36.

Harbison, Robert. *Reflections on Baroque*. Chicago: University of Chicago Press, 2000.

Heredia y Sarmiento, Ignacio. *Oracion funebre que en las solemnes exequias celebradas en la parroquia de San Miguel Arcangel de Mexico por las benditas animas de los que murieron en la reconquista y defensa de Montevideo y Buenos-Ayres*. Mexico City: Arizpe, 1808.

———. *Sermon panegírico de Nuestra Señora de Covadonga, que en la solemne funcion que le hace anualmente la Real Congregacion de los naturales y originarios del principado de Asturias y obispado de Oviedo, en la Iglesia del Imperial Convento de Santo Domingo de México, pronunció el dia 9 de noviembre de 1806, el Dr. D. Joseph Ignacio Heredia y Sarmiento, Colegial de Oposicion, Catedratico que ha sido de Latinidad, de Filosofia, y lo es ho de Retórica en el Real y Pontificio Colegio Seminario de dicha Corte, y Cura Juez Eclesiástico interno que fué de Metepec, de S. Felipe el Grande, de Ozolotepec, de Ozumba, y de la Nueva Villa de Santa Maria de Peña de Franicia*. Mexico City: Zúñiga y Ontiveros, 1807.

Las Hermanas de la Caridad a los mexicanos. Opúsculo por un católico. Mexico City: Poliglota, 1874.

Herr, Richard. *Rural Change and Royal Finances in Spain at the End of the Old Regime*. Berkeley: University of California Press, 1989.

Herrejón Peredo, Carlos. "Catolicismo y violencia en el discurso retórico, 1794–1814." In *Memoria del I Coloquio La Iglesia en el siglo XIX*. Edited by Manuel Ramos Medina. Mexico City: El Colegio de México, 1998.

———. *Del sermón al discurso cívico: México, 1760–1834*. Zamora: El Colegio de Michoacán/El Colegio de México, 2003.

———. *Hidalgo: razones de la insurgencia y biografía documental*. Mexico City: Secretaría de Educación Pública, 1987.

———. "La oratoria en Nueva España." September 7, 1993. Online: http://acadmexhistoria.org.mx/PDF/SILLON_22_CARLOS_HERREJON.pdf.

———. "La potestad política en algunos sermones novohispanos del siglo XVIII." In *Religión, poder y autoridad en la Nueva España*, edited by Alicia Mayer and

Ernesto de la Torre Villar, 159-78. Mexico City: Universidad Nacional Autónoma de México, 2004.

———. "La Revolución Francesa en sermones y otros testimonios de México, 1791-1823." In *La Revolución Francesa en México*, edited by Solange Alberro, Alicia Hernández, and Elías Trabulse, 97-110. Mexico City: El Colegio de México, 1992.

———. "El sermón barroco en el mundo hispánico, estudio de dos latitudes." In *México en el mundo hispánico*, edited by Óscar Mazín Gómez, 343-51. Zamora: El Colegio de Michoacán, 2000.

———. "El sermón en Nueva España durante la segunda mitad del siglo XVIII." In *La Iglesia Católica en México*, edited by Nelly Sigaut, 251-64. Zamora: El Colegio de Michoacán /Secretaría de Gobernación, 1997.

———. "Sermones y discursos en el Primer Imperio." In *Construcción de la legitimidad política en México en el siglo XIX*, edited by Brian Connaughton, Carlos Illades, and Sonia Pérez, 153-68. Zamora: El Colegio de Michoacán, 1999.

———. "Los sermones novohispanos." In *Historia de la literatura mexicana, desde sus sorígenes hasta nuestros días*, edited by Raquel Chang-Rodríguez, 2:429-47. Morelia: Universidad Michoacana de San Nicolás de Hidalgo, 2002.

Herrera Peña, José. *Hidalgo a la luz de sus escritos*. Morelia: Universidad Michoacana de San Nicolás de Hidalgo, 2003.

Herrero Bervera, Carlos. *Revuelta, rebelión y revolución en 1810: historia social y estudios de caso*. Mexico City: Porrúa, 2001.

Herrero García, Miguel. *Sermonario clásico*. Madrid: Escelicer, 1942.

Herrero Salgado, Félix. *La oratoria sagrada española de los siglos XVI y XVII*. Madrid: Fundación Universitaria Española, 1996.

Higgins, Antony. "(Post-) Colonial Sublime: Order and Indeterminacy in Eighteenth-century Spanish American Poetics and Aesthetics." In *Colonialism Past and Present: Reading and Writing about Colonial Latin America Today*, edited by Alvaro Félix Bolaños and Gustavo Verdesio, 119-50. Albany: State University of New York Press, 2002.

Homenaje a la Inmaculada Concepción de la Santísima Virgen María. Breve noticia de las solemnidades con que en la capital del orbe católico ha sido celebrada la definición dogmática de este misterio, con una instrucción muy importante y oportuna sobre el mismo piadoso objeto. Mexico City: Gardida, 1855.

Hsia, R. Po-Chia. *The World of Catholic Renewal, 1540-1770*. Cambridge: Cambridge University Press, 1998.

Hufton, Olwen. "The Reconstruction of a Church, 1796-1801." In *Beyond the Terror: Essays in French Regional Social History, 1794-1815*, edited by Gwynne Lewis and Colin Lucas, 21-52. Cambridge: Cambridge University Press, 1983.

Hunt, Jocelyn. *The French Revolution*. New York: Routledge, 1998.

Ibarra, Ana Carolina. *El clero de la Nueva España durante el proceso de independencia, 1808-1821*. Mexico City: Universidad Nacional Autónoma de México, 2010.

———. "La crisis de 1808 en la iglesia novohispana." In *Las experiencias de 1808 en Iberoamérica*, edited by Alfredo Avila and Pedro Pérez Herrero, 323-41. Mexico City: Universidad Nacional Auntónoma de México, 2008.

———. "De tareas ingratas y épocas difíciles: Francisco Xavier de Lizana y Beaumont." In *Poder civil y catolicismo en México, siglos XVI al XIX*, edited by Francisco Javier Cervantes Bello, Alicia Tecuanhuey Sandoval, and María del Pilar Martínez López-Cano, 337-58. Mexico City: Universidad Autónoma de México, 2008.

Bibliography

El Ilustrador Católico Mexicano. Vol. 1. Mexico City: Tipografía de R. Rafael, 1847.

Instrucción pastoral que los Ilmos. Sres. Arzobispos de México, Michoacán y Guadalajara dirigen á su venerable clero y á sus fieles con ocasión de la ley orgánica expedida por el soberano congreso nacional en 10 de diciembre del año próximo pasado y sancionada por el supremo gobierno en 14 del mismo mes. Mexico City: Lara, 1875.

Irizarri y Peralta, Juan Manuel. *Pastoral del Illmo. Sr. arzobispo de Cesarea, sobre la guerra: Nos, Juan Manuel Irizarri y Peralta, por la gracia de Dios y de la santa sede apostólica arzobispo de Cesarea, dean de la metropolitana de Mèxico y vicario capitular de su diócesis etc., á mis muy amados hijos en Jesucristo Nuestro Señor, los diocesanos del arzobispado de Mèxico.* Mexico City: Imprenta de la calle de Medinas, 1847.

Ita y Parra, Bartolomé Felipe de. *Canonizacion en vida de San Juan de la Cruz, Sermon Panegyrico, que en la plausible solemnidad de sus nuevos Sagrados cultos, con que le celebró unido con su Religiosisima Descalzèz el Illmo. y Venerable Señor Dean, y Cabildo Sede-Vacante de esta Ciudad de Mexico en su Santa Iglesia Cathedral Metropolitana, patente el Santisimo Sacramento, con asistencia de la Real Audiencia, y demás Tribunales, el dia 6 de Enero de 1729.* Mexico City, 1729.

Itinerario para una peregrinación espiritual que se practicará por los fieles católicos del Arzobispado de México en el próximo mes de Octubre a algunos de los principales santuarios del país y del extranjero. Mexico City: Tipografía Escalerillas, 1874.

Itta y Parra, José Mariano Gregorio de Elizalde. *El desempeño de la omnipotencia. Oracion panegirica, que patente el Santisimo Sacramento predico en la dedicacion de la iglesia de Sra. Sta. Ana.* Mexico City: La viuda de J. B. de Hogal, 1754.

Ivereigh, Austen, editor. *The Politics of Religion in an Age of Revival: Studies in Nineteenth-Century Europe and Latin America.* London: Institute of Latin American Studies, 2000.

Jantzen, Grace M. *Power, Gender and Christian Mysticism.* Cambridge: Cambridge University Press, 1995.

Jesús, José Manuel de. *Sermon fúnebre en las honras, que el dia 26 de octubre de 1825 hizo en su iglesia de México la Provincia de Carmelitas Descalzos de S. Alberto al Illmo. y Rmo. Señor Don Fr. Bernardo del Espiritu Santo, hijo de la misma provincia, y obispo de Sonora y Sinaloa. Predicado por el R. P. Prior del Convento de México Fr. José Manuel de Jesus.* Mexico City: Oficina del ciudadano Alejandro Valdés, 1825.

Jesús María, Nicolás de. *El codicioso, y codiciado, santo a pedir de boca, codiciado por boca de los santos. Panegyrico, que el dia de San Bernardo predicó en su Convento de Señoras Religiosas de la Ciudad de Mexico el P. Fr. Nicolas de Jesus Maria, Religioso Carmelita Descalzo: Lector, que fue de Sagrada Theologia Escholastica de Visperas: Prior de su Convento de Oaxaca, Examinador Synodal de su Obispado, y Diffinidor actual de su Provincia: este Año de 1734.* Mexico City: Joseph Bernardo de Hogal, 1735.

Johnson, Lyman L. and Sonya Lipsett-Rivera, editor. *The Faces of Honor: Sex, Shame, and Violence in Colonial Latin America.* Albuquerque: University of New Mexico Press, 1998.

Jones, Jennifer M. "Repacking Rousseau: Femininity and Fashion in Old Regime France." *French Historical Studies* 18/4 (1994) 939–68.

———. *Sexing La Mode: Gender Fashion and Commercial Culture in Old Regime France.* Oxford: Berg, 2004.

Bibliography

Jordan, Mark D. *The Invention of Sodomy in Christian Theology*. Chicago: University of Chicago Press, 1997.

Jove y Aguiar, José Alejandro. *Oracion funebre pronunciada en las solemnes exequias por los españoles difuntos en la presente guerra con la Francia, que hizo el M. Ilustre y Real Colegio de Abogados en el Convento Grande de N. P. S. Francisco*. Mexico City: Imprenta de Arizpe, 1808.

Kahle, Günter. *El ejército y la formación del Estado en los comienzos de la independencia de México*. Translated by María Martínez Peñaloza. Mexico City: Fondo de Cultura Económica, 1997.

Kamen, Henry. *Golden Age Spain*. New York: Palgrave Macmillan, 2005.

Kates, Gary, editor. *The French Revolution: Recent Debates and New Controversies*. New York: Routledge, 2006.

Katz, Friedrich. "The Liberal Republic and the Porfiriato, 1867–1910." In *Mexico Since Independence*, edited by Leslie Bethell, 49–124. Cambridge: Cambridge University Press, 1991.

Katzew, Ilona. *Casta Painting: Images of Race in Eighteenth-Century Mexico*. New Haven: Yale University Press, 2004.

Kellner, Douglas. "Habermas, the Public Sphere, and Democracy: A Critical Intervention." In *Perspecitves on Habermas*, edited by Lewis Edwin Hahn, 259–88. Chicago: Open Court, 2000.

Kerber, Linda. "Separate Spheres, Female Worlds, Woman's Place: The Rhetoric of Women's History." In *No More Separate Spheres! A Next Wave American Studies Reader*, edited by Cathy N. Davidson and Jessamyn Hatcher, 29–66. Durham, NC: Duke University Press, 2002.

Kirk, Stephanie L. *Convent Life in Colonial Mexico: A Tale of Two Communities*. Gainesville: University Press of Florida, 2007.

Klaus, Susanne. *Uprooted Christianity: The Preaching of the Christian Doctrine in Mexico Based on Franciscan Sermons of the 16th Century Written in Nahuatl*. Schwaben: Saurwein, 1999.

Kubler, George, and Martín Soria. *Art and Architecture in Spain and Portugal and their American Dominions 1500–1800*. London: Penguin, 1959.

Kuznesof, Elizabeth Anne. "Gender Ideology, Race, and Female-Headed Households in Urban Mexico, 1750–1850." In *State and Society in Spanish America during the Age of Revolution*, edited by Victor M. Uribe-Uran, 149–72.Wilmington, DE: Scholarly Resources, 2001.

Labastida y Dávalos, Pelagio Antonio de. *Carta pastoral que el Illmo. Sr. Dr. D. Pelagio A. de Labastida y Davalos dirige al venerable clero y fieles del arzobispado de Mexico con motivo de su promocion à aquella Archidiòcesis*. Puebla: Tipografía de Pedro Alarcón y Ca., 1863.

———. *Edicto del Excelentísimo e Ilustrísimo señor Doctor don Pelagio Antonio de Labastida y Dávalos en que se anuncia a los fieles la continuación de la visita general y establece el orden que se ha de conservar en ella, seguida de una instrucción pastoral sobre el sacramento de la confirmación*. Mexico City: Imprenta de Andrade y Escalante, 1866.

———. *Sermon predicado por el Illmo. Sr. Arzobispo de México, Dr. D. Pelagio Antoino de Labastida y Dávalos en la Parroquia del Tenango del Valle, el 20 de Enero de 1878, festividad del Dulce Nombre de Jesús*. Mexico City, 1878.

Bibliography

Landavazo, Marco Antonio. *La máscara de Fernando VII: discurso e imaginario monárquicos en una época de crisis, Nueva España, 1808–1822*. Mexico City: El Colegio de México/Universidad Michoacana de San Nicolás de Hidalgo/El Colegio de Michoacán, 2001.

Landavazo, Marco Antonio and Agustín Sánchez Andrés. "La opción monárquica en los inicios del México independiente." In *Experiencias republicanas y monárquicas en México, América Latina y España. Siglos XIX y XX*, edited by Marco Antonio Landavazo and Agustín Sánchez Andrés, 253–74. Morelia: Universidad Michoacana de San Nicolás de Hidalgo and Instituto de Investigaciones Históricas, 2008.

Landes, Joan. *Women and the Public Sphere in the Age of the French Revolution*. Ithaca, NY: Cornell University Press, 1988.

Larkin, Brian. "Baroque and Reformed Catholicism: Religious and Cultural Change in Eighteenth-Century Mexico." PhD diss., University of Texas, Austin, 1999. ProQuest (AAT 9956871).

———. *The Very Nature of God: Baroque Catholicism and Religious Reform in Bourbon Mexico City*. Albuquerque: University of New Mexico Press, 2010.

Lavrin, Asunción. *Brides of Christ: Conventual Life in Colonial Mexico*. Stanford: Stanford University Press, 2008.

———. "The Execution of the Law of Consolidation in New Spain: Economic Aims and Results." *Hispanic American Historical Review* 53/1 (1973) 27–49.

———. "La religiosa real y la inventada: diálogo entre dos modelos discursivos." In *La creatividad femenina en el mundo barroco hispánico. María de Zayas, Isabel Rebeca Correa, Sor Juana Inés de la Cruz*, edited by Monika Bosse, Barbara Potthast, and André Stoll, 2:535–58. Kassel: Reichenberger, 1999.

Lavrin, Asunción, editor. *Sexuality and Marriage in Colonial Latin America*. Lincoln: University of Nebraska Press, 1989.

Lavrin, Asunción, and Edith Couturier. "Dowries and Wills: A View of Women's Socio- Economic Role in Colonial Guadalajara and Puebla, 1640–1790." *Hispanic American Historical Review* 59/2 (1979) 280–304.

Lemmon, A. E. "Los jesuitas y la música colonial en México." *Heterofonía* 10/53 (1977) 7–10.

Lemoine, Ernesto. *Insurgencia y República Federal, 1808–1824*. Mexico City: Miguel Ángel Porrúa, 1987.

León Zaragoza, Gabriel. "Inmorales y aberrantes, las reformas aprobadas: Norberto Rivera." *La Jornada* (Mexico City, Mexico), Dec. 22, 2009.

Lerdo, Ignacio María. *Sermon pronunciado en la solemne festividad con que el Colegio de San Gregorio de la Compañía de Jesus celebró la declaración dogmática de la Inmaculada Concepción de la Santísima Virgen María, el 22 de julio del presente año, por el R. P. Ignacio María Lerdo, de la misma Compañía*. Mexico City: Gardida, 1855.

Lerdo de Texada, Ignacio. *Discurso que en la profesion solemne de cuarto voto hecha por los RR. PP. de la Compañia de Jesus Jose Maria Castañiza y Pedro Canton en el dia quince de agosto de este año, y en la primera misa pontifical que celebraba el Illmo. Sr. Dr. D. Juan Francisco de Castañiza Gonzalez de Aguero, Marques de Castañiza y dignisimo obispo de la Santa Iglesia de Durango: pronunció el P. Dr. D. Ignacio Lerdo de Texada, presbítero secular de la Real Congregacion del Oratorio de San Felipe Neri de esta capital*. Mexico City, 1816.

Bibliography

Lida, Miranda. "La iglesia católica en las más recientes historiografías de México y Argentina. Religión, modernidad y secularización." *Historia Mexicana* 56/4 (2007) 1393–1426.

Lipsett-Rivera, Sonya. "Marriage and Family Relations in Mexico during the Transition from Colony to Nation." In *State and Society in Spanish America during the Age of Revolution*, edited by Victor M. Uribe-Uran, 121–48. Wilmington, DE: Scholarly Resources, 2001.

Lizana y Beaumont, Francisco Xavier de. *Carta pastoral que el Illmô. Señor doctor D. Francisco Xavier de Lizana y Beaumont Arzobispo de Mexico, del Consejo de Su Mag. etc. dirige á los fieles de su arzobispado sobre la grandeza de nuestra Santa Religion, en lo que enseña, manda creer y practicar.* Mexico City: Madrileña, 1803.

———. *Carta pastoral que el Illmô. señor don Francisco Xavier de Lizana y Beaumont Arzobispo de México, dirige á sus Diocesanos con el fin de exhortarlos, y prepararlos para unos exercicios espirituales públicos.* Mexico City: Zúñiga y Ontiveros, 1804.

———. *Carta pastoral que el Ilmô. Señor D. D. Francisco Xavier de Lizana y Beaumont, por la gracia de Dios, y de la Santa Sede Apostolica, Arzobispo de México, del consejo de S. M. etc. Dirige á sus Diocesanos sobre la santidad de nuestra sagrada Religion, y las obligaciones que nos impone.* Mexico City: Oficina de la Calle de Santo Domingo, 1807.

———. *Carta pastoral que el ilustrísimo señor Don Francisco Xavier de Lizana y Beaumont, del Consejo de S. M. arzobispo de México, dirige á sus Diocesanos sobre el modo de santificar el tiempo de Quaresma.* Mexico City: Fernández de Jáuregui, 1809.

———. *Exhortación del Exmô. Sr. Don Francisco Xavier de Lizana y Beaumont, Arzobispo de México, a sus fieles y demás habitants de este reyno.* Mexico City: Zúñiga y Ontiveros, 1810.

———. *Instrucccion del Illmô. Señor Don Francisco Xavier de Lizana y Beaumont, Arzobispo de México, del consejo de S. M. etc. Sobre la costumbre de llevar las Señoras el pecho y brazos desnudos.* Mexico City: Fernández de Jáuregui, 1808.

———. *Nos D. Francisco Xavier de Lizana y Beaumont, por la gracia de Dios y de la Santa Sede Apostólica Arzobispo de México, del Consejo de Su Magestad etc. A todos los Eclesiásticos de esta nuestra Diócesis salud en N. S. J. C. que es verdadera salud.* Mexico City, 1803.

———. *Nos Don Francisco Xavier de Lizana y Beaumont, por la gracia de Dios y de la Santa Sede Apostólica Arzobispo de México, Caballero Gran Cruz de la Real y Distinguida Orden Española de Cárlos III, del Consejo de S. M. etc.* Mexico City, 1810.

———. *Nos D. Francisco Xavier de Lizana y Beaumont, por la gracia de Dios y de la Santa Sede Apostólica Arzobispo de México, Caballero Gran Cruz de la Real Distinguida Orden Española de Cárlos III, del Consejo de S. M. etc. A nuestros amados Mexicanos, salud, paz, bendicion y toda clase de felicidades en nuestro Señor Jesucristo.* Mexico City, 1810.

———. *Sentimientos religiosos, con los que el Ilustrisimo Señor D. Francisco Xavier de Lizana y Beaumont, Arzobispo de Méxcio, desea instruir á sus amados Diocesanos. En la Semana Santa, Visitas y Estaciones que en ella se practican en las Iglesias.* Mexico City: Fernández de Jáuregui, 1808.

———. *Sermon moral que en la solemne accion de gracias, que se hace anualmente en el sagrario de esta Sta. Iglesia Metropolitana de Mexico por los beneficios recibidos de la divina piedad, predicó la noce del dia 31 de Diciembre de 1805 el Illô. Señor Don Francisco Xavier de Lizana y Beaumont, Arzobispo de dicha Santa Iglesia.* Mexico City: Fernández Jáuregui, 1806.

———. *Sermon que en las solmnes Rogativas que se hicieron en la Santa Iglesia Metropolitana de Mèxico implorando el auxîlio divino en las actuales ocurrencias de la Monarquía Española predicó en el dia 18 de Agosto de 1808 el Illmô. Sr. Don Francisco Xavier de Lizana y Beaumont Arzobispo de la misma Ciudad, del Consejo de S. M. etc.* Mexico City: Fernández de Jáuregui, 1808.

Lockhart, James. *The Nahuas After the Conquest: A Social and Cultural History of the Indians of Central Mexico.* Stanford: Stanford University Press, 1992.

Long, Pamela H. "Music and Theater in Colonial Mexico." *Ars Lyrica* 9 (1998) 67–78.

López, Rosalva Loreto. *Los conventos femeninos y el mundo urbano de la Puebla de los Ángeles del siglo XVIII.* Mexico City: El Colegio de México, 2000.

López-Cordón Cortezo, María Victoria. "Women in Society in Eighteenth-Century Spain: Models of Sociability." Translated by Eunice Anne Rojas. In *Eve's Enlightenment: Women's Experience in Spain and Spanish America, 1726–1839,* edited by Catherine M. Jaffe and Elizabeth Franklin Lewis, 103–14. Baton Rouge: Louisiana State University Press, 2009.

López-Portillo, Carmen Beatriz, ed. *Sor Juana y su mundo: una mirada actual.* Mexico City: Fondo de Cultura Económica, 1998.

López Rodríguez de Figueredo, Tomás Francisco. *Oración panegírica, que en la festividad que el escelentísimo ayuntamiento del Distrito Federal dedica anualmente a la patrona de los Estados-Unidos Mexicanos, Santa María de Guadalupe, dijo en su iglesia colegiata el día doce de diciembre de mil ochocientos treinta, el presbítero D. Tomás Francisco López, Rodríguez de Figueredo, cura encargado de San Lorenzo Tultitlán, con asistencia del Escmo. Sr. vice-presidente de la república D. Anastasio Bustamante, y Escmos. Sres. Secretarios del despacho general.* Mexico City: Águila, 1831.

———. *Sermon panegirico que en la festividad del Divino Redentor, en que se celebra a la imagen de Cristo Crucificado, conocida con el titulo del Buen Despacho, dijo en la Santa Iglesia Catedral de Méxcio, el dia 21 de Julio de 1839, el Br. D. Tomás Francisco Lopez Rodriguez de Figueredo, cura propio y juez eclesiástico de Santa Maria de la Asuncion de Xalatlaco.* Mexico City: Aguila, 1839.

Lorenzana, Francisco Antonio. *Cartas pastorales, y edictos del Illmo. Señor D. Francisco Antonio Lorenzana, y Buitron, Arzobispo de Méxcio.* Mexico City: Superior Gobierno, 1770.

Luque Alcaide, Elisa. "Los concilios provinciales hispanoamericanos." In *Teología en América Latina,* edited by Josep-Ignasi Saranyana and Carmen-José Alejos Grau, 2/1:423–523. Madrid: Vervuert/Iberoamericana, 2005.

Lynch, John. *Latin America between Colony and Nation: Selected Essays.* Houndmills, UK: Palgrave, 2001.

———. *The Spanish American Revolutions, 1808–1826.* New York: Norton, 1986.

MacHaffie, Barbara J. *Readings in her Story: Women in Christian Tradition.* Minneapolis: Fortress, 1992.

Mack Crew, Phyllis. *Calvinist Preaching and Iconoclasm in the Netherlands, 1544–69.* London: Cambridge University Press, 1978.

Macune, Charles W., Jr. "The Impact of Federalism on Mexican Church-State Relations, 1824–1835: The Case of the State of Mexico." *The Americas* 40/4 (1984) 505–29.

Bibliography

Manifestación que hacen al venerable clero y fieles de sus respectivas diocesis y á todo el mundo católico los illmos. señores arzobispo de Méxcio y obispos de Michoacán, Linares, Guadalajara y el Potosí, y el Sr. Dr. D. Francisco Serrano como representante de la mitra de Puebla, en defensa del clero y de la doctrina católica, con occasion del manifiesto y los decretos expedidos por el Sr. Lic. D. Benito Juárez en la ciudad de Veracruz en los días 7, 12, 13 y 23 de julio de 1859. Mexico City: Andrade y Escalante, 1859.

Manifiesto de los feligreses de la Veracruz en defensa de su párroco. Mexico City: Imprenta de la esquina de la calle de Tacuba, 1828.

Maravall, José Antonio. *Culture of the Baroque: Analysis of a Historical Structure.* Translated by Terry Cochran. Minneapolis: University of Minnesota Press, 1986.

Marichal, Carlos. *La bancarrota del virreinato. Nueva España y las finanzas del Imperio español, 1780–1810.* Mexico City: Fondo de Cultura Económica/El Colegio de México, 1999.

Martínez López-Cano, María del Pilar. *Iglesia, estado y economía, siglos XVI a XIX.* Mexico City: Universidad Nacional Autónoma de México/Instituto de Investigaciones Dr. José María Luis Mora, 1995.

Mayer, Alicia. *Flor de primavera mexicana. La Virgen de Guadalupe en los sermones novohispanos.* Mexico City: Universidad Nacional Autónoma de México/Universidad de Alcalá, 2010.

Mazín, Oscar. "El altar mayor y el de los reyes de la catedral de Valladolid, Morelia." *Anuario de estudios americanos* 48 (1991) 205–34.

———. *Entre dos majestades: el Obispo y la Iglesia del Gran Michoacán ante las reformas borbónicas, 1758–1772.* Zamora: El Colegio de Michoacán, 1987.

———. "El poder y las potestades del rey: los brazos espiritual y secular en la tradición hispánica." In *La iglesia en Nueva España: problemas y perspectivas de investigación.* Edited by María del Pilar Martínez López-Cano. Mexico City: Universidad Autónoma de México, 2010.

McManners, John. *The French Revolution and the Church.* New York: Harper & Row, 1970.

McMillan, James F. "Religion and Politics in Nineteenth-Century France: Further Reflections on Why Catholics and Republicans Couldn't Stand Each Other." In *The Politics of Religion in an Age of Revival: Studies in Nineteenth-Century Europe and Latin America.* Edited by Austen Ivereigh. London: Institute of Latin American Studies, 2000.

Megged, Amos. *Exporting the Catholic Reformation: Local Religion in Early Colonial Mexico.* Leiden: Brill, 1996.

Melvin, Karen. "Rearranging Spaces: Celebrations for an Old World Saint in the New." Paper presented at Annual Meeting of the Pacific Coast Branch of the American Historical Association, Santa Clara, CA, August 2010.

———. "Urban Religions: Mendicant Orders in New Spain's Cities, 1570–1800." PhD diss., University of California, Berkeley, 2005. ProQuest (AAT 3190842).

Memoria que el consejo superior de las asociaciones de Señoras de la Caridad del Imperio Mexicano, dirige al General de París, de las obras que ha practicado y cantidades é invertidas en el Socorro de los pobres enfermos, desde 10. de Julio de 1864 á 30 de Junio de 1865. Mexico City: Tipografía del Comercio, 1865.

El Mensajero Católico. Semanario de la Sociedad Católica de México, vol. 1. Mexico City: Escalante, 1875.

Bibliography

Meyer, Jean. *Historia de los cristianos en América Latina, siglos XIX y XX*. Mexico City: Vuelta, 1989.

Mijangos y González, Pablo. "The Lawyer of the Church: Bishop Clemente de Jesús Munguía and the Ecclesiastical Response to the Liberal Revolution in Mexico (1810–1868)." PhD dissertation, University of Texas, Austin, 2009. ProQuest (AAT 3407558).

Miranda, Francisco Javier. *Sermon panegirico que en aniversario de la gloriosa aparicion de Santa María de Guadalupe pronunció en su insigne colegiata el dia 12 de diciembre de 1852 el presbitero Don Francisco Javier Miranda*. Mexico City: Tipografía de R. Rafael, 1853.

Molina, Álvaro, and Jesusa Vega. *Vestir la identidad, construir la apariencia. La questión del traje en la España del siglo XVIII*. Madrid: Ayuntamiento de Madrid, 2004.

Montalvo, Felipe, fray. *Mistico vaso de santidad, y de honor. Sermon de la Serafica Madre, y Esclarecida Virgen Santa Clara, que en su anual, y Titular Fiesta de su Convento de Senoras Religiosas de esta Corte, celebrada el dia 12 de Agosto de 1748*. Mexico City: Nuevo Rezado de María de Ribera, 1748.

Mora Escalante, Sonia Marta. *De la sujeción colonial a la patria criolla. El periquillo sarniento y los orígenes de la novela en Hispanoamérica*. Heredia, Costa Rica: EUNA/Institut de Sociocritique, 1995.

Morales, Francisco, editor. *Franciscan Presence in the Americas: Essays on the Activities of the Franciscan Friars in the Americas, 1492–1900*. Potomac, MD: Academy of American Franciscan History, 1983.

Morales, María Dolores. "La distribución de la propiedad en la ciudad de México, 1813–1848." *Historias* 12 (1986) 80–89.

Morales Cruz, Joel. "The Origins of Mexican Protestantism: Catholic Pluralism, Enlightenment Religion and the *Iglesia de Jesús* Movement in Nineteenth-Century Mexico (1859–1872)." PhD diss., Lutheran School of Theology at Chicago, 2009. ProQuest (AAT 3353408).

Moreno, Agustín María. *Sermon predicado el dia 10 de junio de 1855 en la Iglesia de N. S. P. San Francisco por el R. P. Fr. Agustin Maria Moreno, lector de sagrada teología y regente de estudios en el colegio de S. Buenaventura (vulgo) Santiago Tlatelolco, con motivo del solemne triduo que para celebrar la declaracion dogmatica de la concepcion inmaculada de la Santisima Virgen Maria, hecha por N. S. P. el señor Pio IX, dispuso la provincia del Santo Evangelio de esta ciudad en los dias 1, 2 y 3 del mes citado*. Mexico City: Gardida, 1855.

Moreno, Francisco, fray. *Santa Gertrudis Haec mysterioso de la gracia, en lo que No Es, en los que Es, y No Es, y en lo que Es. Sermon, que en el primero dia que se celebra su plausible Octava, en el Religiosissimo Convento de Nuestra Señora de Monserrate de Religiosos del Patriarcha Señor San Benito, predicó el R. P. Fr. Francisco Moreno, Predicador General Jubilado, Qualificador del Santo Officio de la Inquisicion, Notario Apostolico, Padre de la Santa Provincia del Santisimo Nombre de Jesus de Goatemala, y Diffinidor actual de esta del Santo Evangelio de Mexico*. Mexico City: Los Herederos de la Viuda de Francisco Rodríguez Lupercio, 1723.

Moreno y Jove, Manuel. *Sermon panegírico del angélico joven San Luis Gonzaga, predicado en la iglesia del convento de señoras religiosas de la enseñanza de la nueva fundacion de esta ciudad, el dia 21 de julio del presente año, por Manuel Moreno y Jove, quien lo dedica al Exmo. Sr. Gobernador del Departamento de México D. Luis Gonzaga Vieyra*. Mexico City: Lara, 1839.

Morfi, Juan Agustín. *La nobleza, y piedad de los montañeses, demostrada por el Smo. Cristo de Burgos. Sermon, que en su primera fiesta, celebrada en el Convento grande de N. S. P. S. Francisco de México el dia 3 de Mayo de 1775 años predicó el P. Fr. Juan Augustin Morfi.* Mexico City: Imprenta del Lic. D. Joseph de Jáuregui, 1775.

Morgan, Ronald J. *Spanish American Saints and the Rhetoric of Identity: 1600–1810.* Tucson: The University of Arizona Press, 2002.

Mörner, Magnus. *The Expulsion of the Jesuits from Latin America.* New York: Knopf, 1965.

La mujer cristiana, ó biografia de Virginia Bruni, escrita por el M.R. P. Ventura de Raulica, antiguo general de los Teatinos, Consultor de la Sagrada Congregacion de los Ritos, Examinador de Obispos del clero romano. Mexico City: Tipografía de la Biblioteca de Jurisprudencia, 1875.

Mujica Pinilla, Ramón. *El barroco peruano.* Lima: Banco de Crédito, 2002.

Mullen, Robert J. *Architecture and Its Sculpture in Viceregal Mexico.* Austin: University of Texas Press, 1997.

Munguía, Clemente de Jesús. *Panegírico de San Vicente de Paul predicado en Mexico el dia 19 de julio de 1860 en la Iglesia del Espírituo Santo por el Illmo. Señor Doctor Don Clemente de Jesus Munguia, obispo de Michoacan.* Mexico City: Andrade y Escalante, 1860.

Murray, Paul V. "Fray José María de Jesús Belaunzarán y Ureña, Bishop of Linares, Mexico (1772–1857)." *The Americas* 11/3 (1955) 355–62.

Myers, Kathleen Ann. "A Glimpse of Family Life in Colonial Mexico: A Nun's Account." *Latin American Research Review* 28/2 (1993) 63–87.

———. *Neither Saints Nor Sinners: Writing the Lives of Women in Spanish America.* Oxford: Oxford University Press, 2003.

Negredo del Cerro, Fernando. "Levantar la doctrina hasta los cielos. El sermón como instrumento de adoctrinamiento social." In *Iglesia y sociedad en el antiguo regimen*, edited by Enrique Martínez Ruiz and Vicente Suárez Grimón, 1:55–64. Las Palmas de Gran Canaria: Filmarte, 1994.

Nesvig, Martin Austin, ed. *Religious Culture in Modern Mexico.* Lanham, MD: Rowman & Littlefield, 2007.

Niño Jesús, Pablo Antonio del. *Sermon predicado en la santa iglesia parroquial de la ciudad de cholula del imperio el dia 16 de agosto de 1863 en accion de gracias por la proclamacion y llamamiento al trono de México de su majestad imperial Fernando Maximiliano I por el R. P. Pablo Antonio del Niño Jesus, carmelita.* Mexico City: Andrade y Escalante, 1863.

———. *Sermon que en el dia 8 de septiembre de 1850, tercero del Novenario solemne dedicado por la junta guadalupana a Nuestra Madre y Señora la Vírgen Santísima de Guadalupe, en accion de gracias por la cesacion del cólera morbo, predicó en la Insigne y nacional Colegiata, á nombre de la Venerable Provincia de Carmelitas de S. Alberto de México, el R. P. Fr. Pablo Antonio del Niño Jesus.* Mexico City: Voz de la Religión, 1850.

———. *Sermon que en la solemne funcion del estreno de la iglesia del Colegio de los Carmelitas de San Angel, predicó el dia 18 de octubre de 1857 el R. P. Fr. Pablo Antonio del Niño Jesus, actual prior del Carmen de Puebla.* Mexico City: Cumplido, 1857.

Bibliography

Nos el Presidente y Cabildo de la Santa Iglesia Metropolitana de México, Gobernador Sede-Vacante. A los venerables Curas Parrocos de éste Arzobispado, salud en nuestro Señor Jesucristo, que es el Pastor eterno y pacifico de las almas. Mexico City, 1811.

Nos el Presidente y Cabildo, Gobernador Sede Vacante de este Arzobispado. Mexico City, 1811.

Nos el Presidente y Cabildo de la Santa Iglesia Metropolitana de México, Gobernador Sede-Vacante de este Arzobispado. Mexico City, 1813.

Noticia sobre las conferencias de la Sociedad de San Vicente de Paul, dependientes del Consejo Superior de México, durante el año de 1868. Mexico City: Lara, 1869.

Noticia sobre las conferencias de la Sociedad de San Vicente de Paul, dependientes del Consejo Superior de la República de México durante el año de 1870. Mexico City: Imprenta de la Viuda e Hijos de Murguía, 1871.

Noticias sobre las conferencias de la Sociedad de San Vicente de Paul, dependientes del consejo superior de México, durante el año de 1869. Mexico City: Tipografía de la V. de Murguía e hijos, 1870.

Novena que para el augusto misterio de la Purisima Concepcion de Maria Santisima dispuso J. M. C. indigno devoto de la misma Santísima Señora. Mexico City: Andrade y F. Escalante, 1856.

Noveno calendario curioso, dedicado á las señoritas para el año 1859. Mexico City, 1859.

Núñez Beltrán, Miguel Ángel. La oratoria sagrada de la época del barroco: doctrina, cultura y actitud ante la vida desde los sermones sevillanos del siglo XVII. Seville: Universidad de Sevilla/Fundación Focus-Abengoa, 2000.

Núñez de Haro y Peralta, Alonso. Nos el doctor don Alonso Núñez de Haro y peralta por la gracia de Dios y de la Santa Sede Apostólica arzobispo de México, caballero gran cruz prelado de la real y distinguida orden española de Carlos III, del consejo de su Majestad, etc. A nuestros muy amados venerables hermanos deán y cabildo de nuestra santa iglesia metropolitana, al abad y cabildo de la insigne y real colegiata de nuestra señora de Guadalupe, a nuestros provisores, vicarios generales de españoles e indios, a los vicarios foráneos, a los curas y demás clérigos de cualquiera orden que sean, a los reverendos prelados de las ordenes regulares, a los superiores y superioras de todos los conventos, colegios y hospitales, y atodos los fieles de ambos sexos de esta ciudad y arzobispado de cualquier grado, dignidad, calidad, estado y condición que sean, salud, paz y gracia en nuestro Señor Jesucristo, sobre la tradición de la portentosa imágen de María Santísima de Guadalupe frente a la fábula predicada por el doctor fray Servando Teresa de Mier. Mexico City, 1795.

Obra de la esposición y adoración nocturna del Santísimo Sacramento, establecida en la Ciudad de México. Mexico City: Lara, 1869.

Octava Maravilla del Nuevo Mundo en la Gran Capilla del Rosario dedicada y aplaudida en el Convento de N. P. S. Domingo de la Ciudad de los Angeles el dia 16 del Mes de Abril de 1690 al Illvsmo. y Revmo. Señor D. D. Manuel Fernández de Santa Cruz Obispo de la Puebla del Consejo de su Magestad. Puebla: Junta de Mejoramiento Moral, Cívico y Material del Municipio de Puebla, 1985.

O'Hara, Matthew D. A Flock Divided: Race, Religion, and Politics in Mexico, 1749-1857. Durham, NC: Duke University Press, 2010.

———. "Visions of the Future in Mexico's Independence Era." Paper presented at "1810–1910–2010, Mexico's Unfinished Revolutions," The Bancroft Library, University of California Berkeley, October 2010.

Bibliography

Old, Hughes Oliphant. *The Reading and Preaching of the Scriptures in the Worship of the Christian Church*. Grand Rapids: Eerdmans, 2002.
Olimón Nolasco, Manuel. "Proyecto de reforma de la Iglesia en México (1867 y 1875)." In *Estado, iglesia y sociedad en México. Siglo XIX*, edited by Álvaro Matute, Evelia Trejo, and Brian Connaughton, 267–91. Mexico City: Universidad Nacional Autónoma de México, 1995.
O'Malley, John W. *Praise and Blame in Renaissance Rome: Rhetoric, Doctrine, and Reform in the Sacred Orators of the Papal Court, c. 1450–1521*. Durham, NC: Duke University Press, 1979.
———. *Trent and All That: Renaming Catholicism in the Modern Era*. Cambridge, MA: Harvard University Press, 2000.
O'Malley, John and Gauvin Alexander Bailey. *The Jesuits and the Arts 1540–1773*. Philadelphia: Saint Joseph's University Press, 2005.
Omaña, Gregorio de. *Oracion funebre, que en las anniversarias Honras de los Militares Defuntos [sic] de España, celebradas en la Santa Iglesia de Mexico, dixo en presencia del Excmo. Sr. Marques de Croix, Cavallero del Orden de Calatrava, Comendador de Molinos, y Laguna Rota en la misma Orden, Theniente General de los Reales Exercicios de S. M. Virrey Governador y Capitan General del Reyno de Nueva España, Presidente de su Real Audiencia, Superintente General de Real Hacienda, y Juez Conservador de este Ramo, Subdelegado General del Establecimiento de Correos Maritimos en el mismo Reyno, el dia 19 de Noviembre de este año de 1768 el Dr. Don Gregorio de Omaña, Canonigo Magistral de dicha Santa Iglesia*. Mexico City: Imprenta Real del Superior Govierno del Br. D. Joseph Antonio de Hogal, 1768.
———. *Oracion funebre que en las anniversarias honra de los difuntos militares de España, celebradas de orden de S. M. en la Sta. Iglesia Cathedral de Mexico, dixo, el dia 22 de Noviembre de este año de 1769 en presencia del Excmô. Sr. Marques de Croix, Virrey de este Reyno; y con assitencia del Ilmô. Sr. Arzobispo, y los Estado Ecclesiastico, Politico, y Militar, el Dr. D. Gregorio de Omaña, y Soto-Mayor, Canonigo Magistral de dicha Santa Iglesia, Ordinario del Santo Oficio por el Ilmô. Sr. Obispo de Puebla, Examinador Synodal del Arzobispado, etc*. Mexico City: Imprenta de la Bibliotheca Mexicana del Lic. D. Joseph de Jáuregui, 1770.
———. *Parecer del Dr. y Mrô. D. Gregorio de Omaña, Canónigo Magistral de esta Santa Iglesia Metropolitana, etc*. In *Oracion funebre, que en las exequias, que de orden del Excmo. Sr. D. Carlos Francisco de Croix, Virrey de esta Nueva España, etc. se celebraron por los militares españoles difuntos, en la Iglesia del Convento Grande de N. S. P. S. Francisco de Mexico, el dia 6 de Noviembre de 1767. Con asistencia de los tribunales*. Mexico City: Imprenta del Nuevo Rezado de los Herederos de Doña María de Ribera, 1767.
Opúsculos católicos número 2. Pastoral de los Gobernadores de la Sagrada Mitra de México, publicando la constitución dogmática sobre la infalibilidad del Romano Pontífice. Mexico City: Fernández de Lara, 1870.
Oronsoro, Pedro Francisco de, fray. *Oracion panegyrica, Maria Santissima en su Concepcion Immaculada, electa Patrona Universal de todos los Dominios del Rey Catholico por la Santidad de Nuestro Santissimo Padre CLEMENTE XIII a peticion de Nuestro Catholico Monarcha D. Carlos III*. Mexico City: Bibliotheca Mexicana, 1762.

Bibliography

Osorio, Ignacio. *Conquistar el eco. La paradoja de la conciencia criolla.* Mexico City: Universidad Nacional Autónoma de México, 1989.

Ossorio, Diego, fray. *Exaltacion del Divino Esposo Jesus con el Sacrificio de un corazon amante, sermon que en la solemne profession que hizo de religiosa de coro y velo negro, Sor Josepha Maria de S. Antonio, en el Convento de Señoras Religiosas de la Purissima Concepcion de esta corte, el dia 20 de Julio de este año de 1760, hizo y dixo el M. R. P. Fr. Diego Ossorio, Predicador General Jubilado, Calificador del Santo Oficio, Ex Custodio de esta Santa Provincia del Santo Evangelio, Chronista general de ella, Cura Ministro de la Parroquia de Sr. S. Joseph de esta Ciudad.* Mexico City: Bibliotheca Mexicana, 1760.

Outhwaite, William, editor. *The Habermas Reader.* Cambridge: Polity, 1996.

Outram, Dorinda. *The Body and the French Revolution: Sex, Class, and Political Culture.* New Haven: Yale University Press, 1989.

Oviedo, Juan Antonio de. *La muger fuerte, sermon panegyrico, y funeral, que en las solemnes Honras, que la Casa Professa de la Compañia de JESUS de Mexico celebrò a su insigne bienhechora, y Patrona de su Iglesia, la mui ilustre Señora Marques de las Torres de Rada, la Señora Doña Gertrudis de la Peña, el dia 28 de Abril del año passado de 1738.* Mexico City, 1738.

Pani, Erika. "'Ciudadana y muy ciudadana'? Women and the State in Independent Mexico, 1810–30." *Gender & History* 18/1 (2006) 5–19.

———. "'Para difundir las doctrinas ortodoxas y vindicarlas de los errors dominantes': los periódicos católicos y conservadores en el siglo XIX." In *La república de las letras: asomos a la cultura escrita del México decimonónico,* edited by Belem Clark de Lara and Elisa Speckman Guerra, 2:119–30. Mexico City: Universidad Nacional Autónoma de México, 2005.

———. *Para mexicanizar el segundo imperio. El imaginario político de los imperialistas.* Mexico City: El Colegio de México/Instituto de Investigaciones Dr. José María Luis Mora, 2001.

———. "Una ventana sobe la sociedad decimonónica: los periódicos católicos (1845–1857)." *La Palabra y el Hombre*/99 (1996) 113–31.

Panorama de la señoritas. Periódico pintoresco, cientifico y literario. Contienen varias viñetas, algunas laminas sobre acero, estampas y musica litografiada. Mexico City: García Torres, 1842.

Paredes, Antonio de, fray. *La autentica del patronato, que en nombre de todo el reino voto la cesarean, nobilisima Ciudad de México, a la Santisima Virgen María Señora Nuestra en su Imagen Maravillosa de Guadalupe. Sermon, que en el dia octavo de las fiestas, que en concurrencia de la Real Casa de Moneda celebró la Religion de la Sagrada Compañia de Jesus, Patente el Augustisimo Sacramento. Martes 19 de Diciembre de 1747.* Mexico City, 1748.

Paz, Octavio. *Sor Juana, or the Traps of Faith.* Cambridge, MA: Harvard University Press, 1988.

Pedraza, José Francisco. *La oratoria en San Luis Potosí durante la época colonial.* San Luis Potosí: Cuadernos de Plata Letras Potosinas, 1967.

Peña, Margarita. "Manipulación masculina del discurso femenino en biografías de monjas. Ejemplos del <<Parayso Occidental>>, de Sigüenza y Góngora." In *La creatividad femenina en el mundo barroco hispánico. María de Zayas, Isabel Rebeca Correa, Sor Juana Inés de la Cruz,* edited by Monika Bosse, Barbara Potthast, and André Stoll, 2:597–610. Kassel: Reichenberger, 1999.

Bibliography

Pérez, Anastasio Antonio, fray. *El Vice-Dios de los Plateros, Mejor Platero de Dios, San Eloi. Sermon, que en la annual fiesta, que la Plateria de Mexico celebra, Dijo el ano proximo pasado de 1740 en la Santa Iglesia Catedral el P.F. Anastasio Antonio Perez, menor hijo de esta Santa Provincia del Santo Evangelio, Predicador en este Convento Grande, Notario Apostolico, y del Santo Oficio, Expurgador, y Revisor de dicho Santo Tribunal, y Cura-Teniente de los Naturales de esta Parrochia de Senor San Jose de Mexico*. Mexico City: La viuda de J.B. de Hogal, 1741.

Pérez Carballo, Jacinto. *Sermón octavo que dixo el R. P. Predicador General, y Presentado Fr. Jacinto Pérez Carballo, Vicario que fue de la Casa, y Doctrina de Thepapaecan, y actual Superior del Convento de Nuestro Padre Santo Domingo de la Ciudad de los Angeles. In Octava Maravilla del Nuevo Mundo en la Gran Capilla del Rosario dedicada y aplaudida en el Convento de N. P. S. Domingo de la Ciudad de los Angeles el dia 16 del Mes de Abril de 1690 al Illvsmo. y Revmo. Señor D. D. Manuel Fernández de Santa Cruz Obispo de la Puebla del Consejo de su Magestad*. Puebla: Junta de Mejoramiento Moral, Cívico y Material del Municipio de Puebla, 1985.

Pérez Martínez, Antonio Joaquín. *Sermon predicado en la Santa Iglesia Metropolitana de Megico el dia 21 de julio de 1822 por el Exmo. è Illmo. Sr. Dr. D. Antonio Joaquin Pérez Martínez, dignisimo obispo de la Puebla de los Angeles: con motivo de la solemne coronacion del señor D. Agustin de Iturbide, primer emperador constitucional de Megico*. Puebla: Valle, 1839.

Pérez Memén, Fernando. *El episcopado y la independencia de México (1810–1836)*. Mexico City: Jus, 1977.

Pérez Puente, Leticia. "El obispo: político de institución divina." In *La iglesia en Nueva España: problemas y perspectivas de investigación*. Edited by María del Pilar Martínez López-Cano. Mexico City: Universidad Autónoma de México, 2010.

Pérez Vejo, Tomás. "Las encrucijadas ideológicas del monarquismo mexicano en la primera mitad del XIX." In *Experiencias republicanas y monárquicas en México, América Latina y España. Siglos XIX y XX*, edited by Marco Antonio Landavazo and Agustín Sánchez Andrés, 327–48. Morelia: Universidad Michoacana de San Nicolás de Hidalgo/Instituto de Investigaciones Históricas, 2008.

Pescador, Juan Javier. *De bautizados a fieles difuntos: familia y mentalidades en una parroquia urbana: Santa Catarina de México, 1568–1820*. Mexico City: El Colegio de México, 1992.

———. "Vanishing Woman: Female Migration and Ethnic Identity in Late-Colonial Mexico City." *Ethnohistory* 42/4 (1995) 617–26.

Picazo, Miguel, fray. *Imagen humana, y divina de la Purisima Concepcion. Sermon panegirico, que en la annual fiesta de la Concepcion de Maria SS. Nuestra Señora, con el Título de Guadalupe, celebra a su ilustre archi-cofradia fundada con Autoridad Apostolica en el Convento de México del Real, y Militar Orden de Nuestra Señora de la Merced Redención de Cautivos*. Mexico City, 1738.

Pinzón, Manuel. *Sermon que en los cultos que la ilustre archicofradia de ciudadanos de la Santa Veracruz de esta capital tributa a la Santa Cruz, dijo el R. P. Fr. ManuePinzon, lector de sagrada teologia y prefecto de carceles, el 5 de Mayo de 1837*. Mexico City: Galván, 1837.

Pita Moreda, María Teresa. *Los predicadores novohispanos del siglo XVI*. Salamanca: San Esteban, 1992.

Ponce, Manuel. *La elocuencia sagrada en México*. Mexico City: Academia Mexicana, 1977.

Bibliography

Portes, Emilio. *La lucha entre el poder civil y el clero*. Mexico City: El Día, 1983.

Posada y Garduño, Manuel. *Pastoral del Ilustrísimo Señor Arzobispo de Mégico [sic], Dr. D. Manuel Posada y Garduño*. Mexico City: Oficina de Galván, 1841.

Powers, Karen Vieira. *Women in the Crucible of Conquest: The Gendered Genesis of Spanish American Society, 1500-1600*. Albuquerque: University of New Mexico Press, 2005.

Presente amistoso dedicado a las señoritas mexicanas por I. Cumplido. Mexico City, 1847.

Primer calendario curioso dedicaco a las señoritas, para el año 1851, arreglado al meridiano de México. Mexico City, 1851.

Primer calendario de S. Vicente de Paul para el año 1859. Mexico City: Navarro, 1858.

Primer calendario de la Sociedad Católica de México, para 1871. Mexico City: Tipografía de T. F. Neve, 1871.

Profecías de Matiana, sirvienta que fue en el Convento de S. Gerónimo de México, sobre los sucesos que han de acontecer en la espresada capital. Mexico City: Imprenta de la calle del Cuadrante de Santa Catarina, 1861.

Puente Lutteroth, María Alicia. *Hacia una historia minima de la Iglesia en México*. Mexico City: Jus, 1993.

———. "'No es justo obedecer a los hombres antes que a Dios'. Un acercamiento a algunas realidades socioeclesiales y político-religiosas de México en el tiempo del Concilio Vaticano I." In *Estado, iglesia y sociedad en México. Siglo XIX*, edited by Álvaro Matute, Evelia Trejo, and Brian Connaughton, 293-323. Mexico City: Universidad Nacional Autónoma de México, 1995.

Puga y Araujo, Rafael Antonio de. *La Judit de la ley de gracia. Elogio que en obsequio de la gloriosa viuda, Santa Monica, Madre del Gran Doctor San Agustin, dixo en la iglesia de la Real Congregacion del Oratorio de esta corte el R. P. D. Rafael Antonio de Puga y Araujo, Presbítero de la misma Congregacion, el dia 4 de mayo de 1804*. Mexico City: Zúñiga y Ontiveros, 1804.

Quinto calendario de la Sociedad Católica de México para el año de 1875. Mexico City: Barbedillo, 1875.

R. de la Flor, Fernando. *Emblemas: lecturas de la imagen simbólica*. Madrid: Alianza, 1995.

Raffi-Béroud, Catherine. *En torno al teatro de Fernández de Lizardi*. Amsterdam: Rodopi, 1998.

Ramírez, Edelmira. *Persuasión, violencia y deleite en un sermón barroco del siglo XVIII*. Vol. 1. Mexico City: Universidad Autónoma Metropolitana /Secretaría de Educación Pública, 1986.

Ramírez, J. Emilio. "Earthquake History of Colombia." *Bulletin of the Seismic Society of America* 23 (1933) 13-22.

Ramírez L., Edelmira. *María Rita Vargas, María Lucía Celis: Beatas embaucadoras de la colonia*. Mexico City: Universidad Nacional Autónoma de Méxcio, 1988.

Ramos, Luis. "Documentos para servir a la historia sobre las relaciones Iglesia-Estado en México durante el siglo XIX." In *Del archivo secreto vaticano: la iglesia y el estado mexicano en el siglo XIX*, edited by Luis Ramos, 17-66. Mexico City: Universidad Nacional Autónoma de México, 1997.

Ramos Domingo, José. *Retórica-Sermón-Imagen*. Salamanca: Publicaciones Universidad Pontificia, 1997.

Ramos Gómez-Pérez, Luis. "El emperador, el nuncio y el Vaticano." In *Estado, iglesia y sociedad en México. Siglo XIX*, edited by Álvaro Matute, Evelia Trejo and Brian

Bibliography

Connaughton, 251–65. Mexico City: Universidad Nacional Autónoma de México, 1995.
Ramos Medina, Manuel. *Místicas y descalzas: fundaciones femeninas carmelitas en la Nueva España*. Mexico City: Condumex, 1997.
Ramos Medina, Manuel, editor. *Memoria del I Coloquio Historia de la Iglesia en el Siglo XIX*. Mexico City: Centro de Estudios de Historia de México Condumex, 1998.
La Regeneración Social. Religión, política, literatura, ciencias, artes, industria, comercio, agricultura, mejoras materiales, medicina, minería, teatros, modas. Revista general de la prensa de ambos mundos—anuncios y comunicados. Mexico City, 1869.
Reglamento de la Asociación de las Señoras de la Caridad instituida por San Vicente de Paul en beneficio de los pobres enfermos, y establecida en varios lugares por los Padres de la Congregación de la Misión con licencia de los Ordinarios. Mexico City: Andrade y Escalante, 1863.
Reglamento de la Sociedad Católica de Señoras y deberes de estas. Mexico City: Fernández de Lara, 1870.
Reglamento de la Sociedad de la Purísima Concepción de la Sma. Virgen María. Mexico City: Segura, 1860.
Reglamento provisional de la Sociedad Católica de México. Mexico City: Lara, 1869.
Representación contra la tolerancia religiosa. Alcance al número 37 de "La Cruz." Mexico City: Andrade y Escalante, 1856.
Representación que algunas señoras morelianas eleven al soberano congreso constituyente, contra la tolerancia de cultos. Morelia: Arango, 1856.
Representación que la Congregación de San Pedro de esta capital dirige a las augustas cámaras de la unión contra el proyecto de establecer en la República la tolerancia de cultos. Mexico City: Rafael, 1849.
Representación que elevan al Soberano Congreso los vecinos de las municipalidades de Cuautitlán, Tepotzotlán, Huchuetoca, San Miguel, Tultepec, Tultitlán, y Teoloyucán pidiendo se repruebe el art. XV del proyecto de constitución, sobre tolerancia de cultos. Mexico City: Segura, 1856.
Representación que los habitantes de Zamora dirigen al Soberano Congreso Constituyente, pidiéndole que no se permita en la república la libertad de cultos que establece el artículo 15 del proyecto de constitución, presentado por la comisión respectiva el día 16 de Junio de 1856. Mexico City: Murguía, 1856.
Representación que han elevado a las augustas cámaras de la nación los vecinos de Orizava, contra el proyecto de introducir en la República la tolerancia de cultos. Mexico City: Rafael, 1849.
Representación que varias señoras de Páztcuaro dirigen al soberano congreso constituyente, contra la tolerancia de cultos. Mexico City: Imprenta de Ignacio Arango, 1856.
Revista universal de religión, política, variedades y anuncios. Mexico City, 1869.
Ricard, Robert. *The Spiritual Conquest of Mexico: An Essay on the Apostolate and the Evangelizing Methods of the Mendicant Orders in New Spain, 1523–1572*. Translated by Lesley Byrd Simpson. Berkeley: University of California Press, 1966.
Ringrose, David. *Madrid and the Spanish Economy, 1560–1850*. Berkeley: University of California Press, 1983.
Rodríguez, Joseph Manuel, fray. *Como deben haverse los vasallos con sus reyes. Platica doctrinal predicada por el R. P. Fr. Joseph Manuel Rodriguez ex-Lector de Sagrada Theología, Predicador General, Notario Apostolico, Chronista General de la Orden de N. S. P. S. Francisco en esta Nueva España, y Comissario Visitador de su Orden*

Bibliography

    Tercera de la Ciudad de Mexico a los terceros de la misma orden en la Dominica primera de Septiembre, en que en el año de 1768 terminaron las que desde la primera de Julio se predican annualmente en su Capilla de dicha Ciudad. Mexico City: Imprenta Real del Superior Govierno, 1768.

———. *Oracion funebre, que en las exequias, que de orden del Excmo. Sr. D. Carlos Francisco de Croix, Virrey de esta Nueva España, etc. se celebraron por los militares españoles difuntos, en la Iglesia del Convento Grande de N. S. P. S. Francisco de Mexico, el dia 6 de Noviembre de 1767. Con asistencia de los tribunales*. Mexico City: Imprenta del Nuevo Rezado de los Herederos de Doña María de Ribera, 1767.

Rodríguez, Ruth. "Rivera defiende derecho a criticar matrimonio gay." *El Universal* (Mexico City, Mexico), Jan. 11, 2010.

Rodríguez Arizpe, Pedro Josef. *Parecer del P. Dr. D. Pedro Josef Rodriguez Arizpe, de la Sagrada Congregacion del Oratorio de San Felipe Neri*. In Joseph Gallegos, *Dechado de la castidad. Oracion panegyrica, que en la solemne fiesta de la milicia angelica del celestial cingulo del Doctor Angelico Santo Thomas, dixo en la Iglesia del Imperial Convento de N. P. Sto. Domingo, de Mexico, dia 28 de Enero del año de 1771 el R. P. Fr. Joseph Gallegos, Lector de Sagrada Escritura, y de el Illmo. Melchor Cano*. Mexico City: Imprenta del Lic. D. Joseph de Jáuregui, 1771.

Rodríguez de Santo Thomás, Miguel, fray. *Memorial ajustado de la vida, y virtudes de la M. R. M. Sor Antonia del Señor S. Joaquin, Religiosa Professa de Choro, y Velo negro, en el Religiosissimo Convento de Santa Cathalina de Sena de esta Corte*. Mexico City: Imprenta de los Herederos de doña María de Ribera, 1760.

Rodríguez O., Jaime E. "New Spain and the 1808 Crisis of the Spanish Monarchy." *Mexican Studies/Estudios Mexicanos* 24/2 (2008) 245–87.

———. "The Struggle for Dominance: The Legislature versus the Executive in Early Mexico." In *The Birth of Modern Mexico, 1780–1824*, edited by Christon I. Archer, 205–28. Lanham, MD: Rowman & Littlefield, 2003.

Romano Moreno. Prologue to *Octava Maravilla del Nuevo Mundo en la Gran Capilla del Rosario dedicada y aplaudida en el Convento de N. P. S. Domingo de la Ciudad de los Angeles el dia 16 del Mes de Abril de 1690 al Illvsmo. y Revmo. Señor D. D. Manuel Fernández de Santa Cruz Obispo de la Puebla del Consejo de su Magestad*. Puebla: Junta de Mejoramiento Moral, Cívico y Material del Municipio de Puebla, 1985.

Romero Galván, José Rubén. "La manifestación de los obispos." *Estudios de Historia Moderna y Contemporánea de México* 7 (1979). Online: http://www.historicas.unam.mx/moderna/ehmc/ehmc07/088.html.

Roxas y Andrade, Francisco. *Sermon patriotico-moral predicado en el Convento de Religiosas de la Concepcion el dia 18 de diciembre de 1814 por el Doctor y Maestro Fray Francisco Roxas y Andrade, Exâminador Sinodal de este Arzobispado en la solemne accion de gracias a la divina magestad, por la restitucion al trono español de nuestro amado monarca el Señor Don Fernando VII*. Mexico City: Fernández de Jáuregui, 1815.

Rubial García, Antonio. *La santidad controvertida: hagiogrfía y conciencia criolla alrededor de los venerables no canonizados de Nueva España*. Mexico City: Fondo de Cultura Económica, 1999.

Rubio y Salinas, Manuel. *Carta pastoral que el Ilustrissimo Señor D. Manuel Rubio Salinas Arzobispo de Mexico dirige al clero y pueblo de su diocesi, con motivo de las noticias, que ultimamente se han recibido de España, del Temblor de Tierra, que en el dia 1 de Noviembre del año proximo passado de 1755 se sintió con lamentables estragos en todo aquel Reyno.* Mexico City: Imprenta de la Bibliotheca Mexicana, 1756.

Ruether, Rosemary, editor. *Religion and Sexism: Images of Women in the Jewish and Christian Traditions.* New York: Simon & Schuster, 1974.

Ruiz Barrionuevo, Carmen. "El barroco de Sor Juana Inés de la Cruz a la luz del neobarroco." *Colonial Latin American Review* 4/2 (1995) 227–37.

Ruiz de Alarcón, José Mariano. *Sermon de Nuestra Señora de Guadalupe. Elogio panegírico que dijo Don José Mariano Ruiz de Alarcon, canónigo de la Santa Iglesia Real Insigne Colegiata de Nuestra Señora de Guadalupe de México, el 19 de diciembre, octava de la aparicion, año de 1815 en la misma colegiata, manifiesto el divinísimo sacramentado y asistencia capitular.* Mexico City: Bautista Arizpe, 1819.

Ruiz Guerra, Rubén. "La aceptación de la diversidad religiosa. Una ruta ardua." In *México en tres momentos: 1810–1910–2010. Hacia la conmemoración del bicentenario de la Independencia y el centenario de la Revolución Mexicana. Retos y perspectivas*, edited by Alicia Mayer and Juan Ramón de la Fuente, 1:417–30. Mexico City: Universidad Nacional Autónoma de México/Instituto de Investigaciones Históricas, 2008.

———. "La libertad religiosa: pilar de la libertad política." In *Transición y cultura política. De la Colonia al México independiente*, 171–92. Mexico City: Universidad Nacional Autónoma de México, 2004.

Sainz de Alfaro y Beaumont, Isidoro. *Circular que el Señor Gobernador de la Sagrada Mitra dirige a los Parrocos y Eclesiasticos del Arzobispado de Mexico, recordando la obediencia y fidelidad a Dios y a nuestro cautivo Rey Fernando VII.* Mexico City, 1810.

Sainz Herosa, José María. *Sermon pronunciado en la I. Colegiata de Ntra. Señora de Guadalupe por el señor canónigo doctoral de la misma, Doctor Don José María Sainz Herosa, el día 12 de diciembre de 1861.* Mexico City: Literaria, 1862.

Salazar de Garza, Nuria. *La vida común en los conventos de monjas de la ciudad de Puebla.* Puebla: Bibliotheca Angelopolitana, 1990.

Sánchez Korrol, Virginia. "Women in Nineteenth- and Twentieth-Century Latin America and the Caribbean." In *Women in Latin America and the Caribbean*, edited by Marys Navarro and Virginia Sánchez Korrol, 59–106. Bloomington: Indiana University Press, 1999.

Sánchez Herrero, José. *Historia de la Iglesia en España e Hispanoamérica desde sus inicios hasta el siglo XXI.* Madrid: Sílex, 2008.

San Bartolomé, José de. *El liberalismo y la rebelion confundidas por una tierna y delicada doncella. Sermon predicado el dia 15 de mayo de 1816 en la profesion solemne de la R. M. Maria de la Encarnacion, religiosa de velo negro en el observantisimo convento de Santa Teresa la Antigua, hija de los señores D. Diego Garcia Fernandez, capitan retirado, y de su esposa Doña Maria Dolores Quintanar.* Mexico City: Oficina de la calle de Santo Domingo y esquina de Tacuba, 1817.

San Cirilo, Francisco de. *La mejor parte de la gloria de Maria. Sermon de la Asuncion de Nuestra Señora, que en el dia de su Festividad 15 de Agosto de 1788 dixo en la Santa Iglesia Catedral de México el M. R. P. Fr. Francisco de S. Cirilo, Provincial de los Carmelitas Descalzos, Consultor del Santo Oficio y Examinador Sinodal del*

Bibliography

    Arzobispado de Mexico. Mexico City: Imprenta de los Herederos del Lic. D. Joseph de Jáuregui, 1788.

———. *Obligacion de los Carmelitas como hijos de Maria. Sermon de Nuestra Señora del Carmen, que en el dia de su Festividad 16 de Julio de 1788 dixo en su Iglesia del Carmen el M. R. P. Fr. Francisco de S. Cirilo, Provincial de los Carmelitas Descalzos, Consultor del Santo Oficio y Examinador Sinodal del Arzobispado de Méxcio*. Mexico City: Imprenta de los Herederos del Lic. D. Joseph de Jáuregui, 1788.

———. *La señora de si misma. Sermon predicado en la iglesia del Observantisimo Convento Antigüo de Señoras Carmelitas Descalzas de Méxcio en las honras, que en ella se celebraron el dia 2 del mes de Junio de 1794 por el alma de la M. R. M. Sebastiana Mariana del Espiritu Santo, religiosa del mismo convento*. Mexico City: Oficina de los Herederos del Lic. D. Joseph de Jaúregui, 1794.

Sánchez, José. *Sermon que en la insigne colegiata de Maria Santísima de Guadalupe, pronunció el 6 de febrero de 1859 el R. P. Fr. José Sánchez, predicador y lector de sagrada teología en el Convento de Churubusco, en la solemen accion de gracias por las victorias obtenidas mandó celebrar el Exmo. Sr. General de Division y Presidente sustituto de la República Mexicana, D. Miguel Miramón*. Mexico City: Abadiano, 1859.

Sánchez Bella, Ismael. *Iglesia y estado en la América española*. Pamplona: Ediciones Universidad de Navarra, 1990.

Sánchez de Espinosa, José María. *Himno dedicado a la Divina Providencia, ó arrepentimiento de un pecador para alcanzar los auxilios divinos. Dispuesto por el Bachiller D. Jose Maria Sanchez de Espinosa*. Mexico City: Finado Valdes, 1836.

Sánchez Lora, José Luis. *Mujeres, conventos y formas de la religiosidad barroca*. Madrid: Fundación Universitaria Española, 1988.

Sánchez Ortega, María Helena. "La mujer, el amor y la religion en el antiguo regimen." In *La mujer en la historia de España (siglos XVI-XX)*. Edited by María Ángeles Durán. Madrid: Universidad Autónoma de Madrid, 1984.

San Juan Crisóstomo, Manuel de. *Sermon que en la festividad del patrocinio de Señor San José, en 24 de abril de 1831, predicó en la iglesia del Colegio de San Angel Fr. Manuel de S. Juan Crisóstomo, en accion de gracias por el capítulo de los carmelitas, celebrado por la provincia de San Alberto, en aquel año*. Mexico City: Galván, 1836.

Santillán, Gustavo. "La secularización de las creencias. Discusiones sobre tolerancia religiosa en México (1821–1827)." In *Estado, iglesia y sociedad en México. Siglo XIX*, edited by Álvaro Matute, Evelia Trejo, and Brian Connaughton, 175–98. Mexico City: Universidad Nacional Autónoma de México, 1995.

Saranyana, Josep-Ignasi, and Carmen-José Alejos Grau, editors. *Teología en América Latina*. Vol. 1, *Desde los orígenes a la Guerra de Sucesión (1493–1715)*. Madrid: Iberoamericana, 1999.

———. *Teología en América Latina*. Vol. 2/1, *Escolástica barroca, Ilustración y preparación de la Independencia (1665–1810)*. Madrid: Iberoamericana, 2005.

Sarria y Alderete, Juan de. *Oracion funebre que en las solemnes honras que se celebran todos los años en la Santa Iglesia Metropolitana de Mexico a la Gloriosa Memoria de los difuntos militares que han seguido las triunfantes vanderas españolas, dixo el dia 24 de Noviembre de 1791 el Sr. Dr. Don Juan de Sarria y Alderete Colegial que fue del Mayor de Osuna, y ahora Racionero de dicha Metropolitana Iglesia*. Mexico City: Zúñiga y Ontiveros, 1792.

Sartorio, José Manuel. *Gozo del Mexicano Imperio por su independencia y libertad. Oracion que en la fiesta de la instalacion de la junta suprema provisional gubernativa, celebrada en la Santa Iglesia Metropolitana de México, dijo el presbítero mexicano D. José Manuel Sartorio, vocal de la misma junta, el dia 28 de septiembre de 1821; y dedica al Exmô. Sr. D. Agustin Iturbide, primer gefe del Ejército Trigarante, D. Alejandro Valdés, Regidor de esta nobilísima ciudad, é impresor imperial.* Mexico City, 1821.

Schmidt, Peer. "Contra 'la falsa filosofía': la Contra-Ilustración y la crítica al reformismo borbónico en la Nueva España." In *La formación de la cultura virreinal*, edited by Karl Kohut and Sonia V. Rose, 3:231–54. Madrid: Iberoamericana/Vervuert, 2006.

Schüller, Karin. "¿Disputa teológica o autodefensa? Elementos para una reinterpretación de la 'Carta Atenagórica' de Sor Juana Inés de la Cruz." In *La creatividad femenina en el mundo barroco hispánico. María de Zayas, Isabel Rebeca Correa, Sor Juana Inés de la Cruz*, edited by Monika Bosse, Barbara Potthast, and André Stoll, 2:719–28. Kassel: Reichenberger, 1999.

Schwaller, John Frederick. *The Church and the Clergy in Sixteenth-Century Mexico*. Albuquerque: University of New Mexico Press, 1987.

Schwaller, Robert F. "The Episcopal Succession in Spanish America, 1800–1850." *The Americas* 24/3 (1968) 207–71.

Schwartz, Lía. "Discursos dominantes y discursos dominados en textos satíricos de María de Zayas." In *La creatividad femenina en el mundo barroco hispánico. María de Zayas, Isabel Rebeca Correa, Sor Juana Inés de la Cruz*, edited by Monika Bosse, Barbara Potthast, and André Stoll, 1:301–22. Kassel: Reichenberger, 1999.

Scott, Joan Wallach. "Gender as a Useful Category of Historical Analysis." *American Historical Review* 91/5 (1986) 1053–1075.

Seed, Patricia. *To Love, Honor, and Obey in Colonial Mexico: Conflicts over Marriage Choice, 1574–1821*. Stanford: Stanford University Press, 1988.

———. "Marriage Promises and the Value of a Woman's Testimony in Colonial Mexico," *Signs* 13/2 (1988) 253–76.

Segundo calendario de la Sociedad Católica de México para el año bisiesto de 1872. Mexico City: Ancona y Peniche, 1872.

Segura, Nicolás de. *Platica de la Milagrosa Imagen de Nuestra Señora de Guadalupe de Mexico. Sacada del tomo nono de los sermones del P. Nicolas de Segura de la Compañía de Jesús, Prefecto, que fue de la M. Illtre. Congregacion de la Purisima, Preposito acual de la Casa Profesa de Mexico, y Calificador del Santo Oficio*. Mexico City, 1742.

Selwyn, Jennifer D. *A Paradise Inhabited by Devils: The Jesuits' Civilizing Mission in Early Modern Naples*. Aldershot, UK: Ashgate, 2004.

La Semana de las señoritas mejicanas. Mexico City: Navarro, 1851.

Semanario Católico. Mexico City, 1869.

Semanario cristiano. Periódico religioso, científico y moral. Mexico City: Lovis Morales, 1843.

Semanario de las señoritas mejicanas: educacion cientifica, moral y literaria, del bello sexo, vol. 1. Mexico City: Torres, 1841.

Sermón de los hombres contra las mugeres. Mexico City: López, 1850.

Sermon pronunciado en la Santa Iglesia Catedral Metropolitana de México el dia 26 de noviembre del año de 1833 por el Br. D. J. M. M. Y B. quien lo dedica a su M. I. Y V. S. D. Y Cabildo Gobernador. Mexico City: González, 1833.

Bibliography

Serruto y Nava, Joseph. *Elogio funebre del muy excelso, muy poderoso, muy amable Señor Don Carlos III rey de España, y de las Americas, que en sus exequias magnificamente celebradas en la Santa Iglesia Metropolitana de México, pronunció el Señor Doctor, y Maestro Don Joseph Serruto y Nava canónigo magistral de élla el dia 27 de Mayo de 1789*, in *Reales exequias celebradas en la Santa Iglesia Catedral de México por el alma del señor Don Carlos III rey de España y de las Indias, en los dias 26 y 27 de mayo de 1789*. Mexico City: Zúñiga y Ontiveros, 1789.

Shiels, W. Eugene. "Church and State in the First Decade of Mexican Independence." *Catholic Historical Review* 28 (1942) 206–11.

Sierra Nava-Lasa, Luis. *El Cardenal Lorenzana y la Ilustración*. Madrid: Fundación Universitaria Española, 1975.

Sigal, Pete, editor. *Infamous Desire: Male Homosexuality in Colonial Latin America*. Chicago: University of Chicago Press, 2003.

Smith, Hilary Dansey. *Preaching in the Spanish Golden Age: A Study of Some Preachers of the Reign of Philip III*. Oxford: Oxford University Press, 1978.

Smith, Theresa Ann. *The Emerging Female Citizen: Gender and Enlightenment in Spain*. Berkeley: University of California Press, 2006.

La Sociedad Católica, cuaderno extraordinario dedicado a N. S. P. el Señor Pío IX. Mexico City: Escalante, 1869.

Sociedad de S. Vicente de Paul. Noticia para ayudar al establecimiento de las santas familias, redactada por el padre director y por el presidente de una de ellas. Mexico City: Lara, 1862.

Socolow, Susan Migden. *The Women of Colonial Latin America*. Cambridge and New York: Cambridge University Press, 2000.

Solemnes honras que a la buena memoria de los ciudadanos Br. José Manuel Sartorio, y teniente coronel Ignacio Paz de Tagle, dedicó la muy ilustre cofradía de ciudadanos de la parroquias de la Santa Veracruz de México. Mexico City: Ciudadano Alejandro Valdés, 1829.

Somellera, Félix María. *Panegírico de Nuestra Santísima Madre y Señora de la Merced, que en el Colegio de San Pedro Pascual de Belén de Mercedarios de México, dijo el M. R. P. Maestro Doctor y Ex-Provincial Fr. Felix Maria Somellera, el dia 2 de octubre de 1825*. Mexico City: Testamentaria de Ontiveros, 1826.

Sosa y Peña, José Domingo de, fray. *Complemento de la iglesia dado por N. Santisimo Padre Clemente XII. En la Solemne Beatificacion de la Beata Catarina de Riccijs, Monja Profesa del Sagrado Orden de Predicadores*. Mexico City, J.B. de Hogal, 1734.

Spadaccini, Nicholas and Luis Martín-Estudillo. *Libertad y límites. El Barroco hispánico*. Madrid: Orto, 2004.

Spurling, Geoffrey. "Honor, Sexuality, and the Colonial Church." In *The Faces of Honor: Sex, Shame, and Violence in Colonial Latin America*, edited by Lyman L. Johnson and Sonya Lipsett-Rivera, 45–67. Albuquerque: University of New Mexico Press, 1998.

Staples, Anne. *La iglesia en la primera república federal mexicana (1824–1835)*. Translated by Andrés Lira. Mexico City: Secretaría de Educación Pública, 1976.

———. "Mujeres y dinero heredado, ganado o prestado. Las primeras décadas del siglo XIX mexicano." In *Las mujeres en la construcción de las sociedades iberoamericanas*, edited by Pilar Gonzalbo Aizpuru and Berta Ares Queija, 271–94. Seville: Consejo Superior de Investigaciones Científicas/El Colegio de México, 2004.

——. "La participación política del clero: estado, iglesia y poder en el México independiente." In *Las Fuentes eclesiásticas para la historia social de México*, edited by Brian F. Connaughton and Andrés Lira González, 333–52. Mexico City: Universidad Autónoma Metropolitana, 1996.

——. "Sociabilidad femenina a principios del siglo XIX mexicano." In *Persistencia y cambio: acercamientos a la historia de las mujeres en México*, edited by Lucía Melgar, 99–120. Mexico City: El Colegio de México, 2008.

Stein, Stanley J., and Barbara H. *Apogee of Empire: Spain and New Spain in the Age of Charles III, 1759–1789*. Baltimore: Johns Hopkins University Press, 2003.

——. *The Colonial Heritage of Latin America: Essays on Economic Dependence in Perspective*. New York: Oxford University Press, 1970.

——. *Edge of Crisis: War and Trade in the Spanish Atlantic, 1789–1808*. Baltimore: Johns Hopkins University Press, 2009.

——. *Silver, Trade, and War: Spain and America in the Making of Early Modern Europe*. Baltimore: Johns Hopkins University Press, 2000.

Stern, Steve J. *The Secret History of Gender: Women, Men, and Power in Late Colonial Mexico*. Chapel Hill: University of North Carolina Press, 1995.

Stevens, Donald Fithian. *Origins of Instability in Early Republican Mexico*. Durham, NC: Duke University Press, 1991.

Stratton, Suzanne L. *The Immaculate Conception in Spanish Art*. Cambridge: Cambridge University Press, 1994.

Suárez y Navarro, Juan. *Juicio crítico sobre el restablecimiento de la Compañía de Jesús, o investigaciones filosófico-políticas, sobre si conviene en las presentes circunstancias reponerla en la República Mexicana*. Mexico City: García Torres, 1841.

Sugawara H., Masae. "Los antecedentes coloniales de la deuda pública de México." *Boletín del Archivo General de la Nación* 8/1–2 (1967) 131–402.

——, ed. *La deuda pública de España y la economía novohispana, 1804–1809*. Mexico City: Instituto Nacional de Antropología e Historia, 1976.

Sumaria seguida sobre el sermon predicado en la catedral de México el dia 30 de agosto, por el R. P. prior del convento de Santo Domingo, en el año de 1823. Mexico City: Oficina del ciudadno Alejandro Valdés, 1824.

Talamantes y Baeza, Melchor. *Panegírico de la gloriosa virgen y doctora Santa Teresa de Jesus, que en el dia 15 de Octubre de 1802 dixo en la Iglesia del Convento grande de los RR. PP. Carmelitas Descalzos de esta Corte de Méxcio el R. P. Presdo. Fr. Melchor Talamantes y Baeza, Doctor Teólogo, y Opositor á las Cátedras de Filosofia, Teólgia y Sagrada Escritura en la Real Universidad de San Marcos, Exâminador Synodal del Arzobispado de Lima, Difinidor general del Real y Militar Orden de nuestra Señora de las Mercedes, etc*. Mexico City: Imprenta de la Calle de Santo Domingo y esquina de la de Tacuba, 1803.

Tapié, Victor-L. *The Age of Grandeur: Baroque Art and Architecture*. Translated by A. Ross Williamson. New York: Praeger, 1961.

Taylor, Larissa, editor. *Preachers and People in the Reformations and Early Modern Period*. Leiden: Brill, 2001.

Taylor, William B. *Magistrates of the Sacred: Priests and Parishioners in Eighteenth-Century Mexico*. Stanford: Stanford University Press, 1996.

——. "Mexico's Virgin of Guadalupe in the Seventeenth Century: Hagiography and Beyond." In *Colonial Saints: Discovering the Holy in the Americas*, edited by Allan Greer and Jodi Bilinkoff, 277–98. New York: Routledge, 2003.

Bibliography

———. "Santuarios y milagros en la secuela de la Independencia mexicana." In *Religión, política e identidad en la Independencia de México*, edited by Brian Connaughton, 515–89. Mexico City: Universidad Autónoma Metropolitana/ Benemérita Universidad Autónoma de Puebla, 2010.

———. "La Virgen de Guadalupe, Nuestra Señora de los Remedios y la cultura política del período de Independencia." In *México en tres momentos: 1810-1910-2010. Hacia la conmemoración del bicentenario de la Independencia y el centenario de la Revolución Mexicana. Retos y perspectivas*, edited by Alicia Mayer and Juan Ramón de la Fuente, 2:211–38. Mexico City: Universidad Nacional Autónoma de México/Instituto de Investigaciones Históricas, 2008.

———. "The Virgin of Guadalupe in New Spain: An Inquiry into the Social History of Marian Devotion." *American Ethnologist* 14/1 (1987) 9–43.

Terán, Mariana. *El artificio de la fe. La vida pública de los hombres del poder en el Zacatecas del Siglo XVIII*. Zacatecas: Universidad Autónoma de Zacatecas/ Instituto Zacatecano de la Cultura, 2002.

Terán Fuentes, Mariana. "¿Recordar para qué? El discurso cívico-eclesiástico y la formación de la conciencia nacional. Zacatecas, 1821-1828." In *Revolución, independencia y las nuevas naciones de América*, edited by Jaime E. Rodríguez O., 259–78. Madrid: Fundación Mapfre, 2005.

Terán, Marta, and Norma Páez, editors. *Miguel Hidalgo: ensayos sobre el mito y el hombre (1953-2003)*. Mexico City: Instituto Nacional de Antropología e Historia/ Fundación Mapfre Tavera, 2004.

Tercer calendario de la Sociedad Católica de México para el año de 1873. Mexico City: Aguilar Ortiz, 1873.

Thompson, John B., and David Held, editors. *Habermas: Critical Debates*. Cambridge, MA: MIT Press, 1982.

Tiernos coloquios con que la alma devota de Maria Santisima da a la señora el pésame en su soledad, y la consuela en el doloroso triduo de la Pasion de su Hijo. Mexico City: Murguía y Compañía, 1853.

Torres, Luis de. *Sermon funebre, que en las honras, que hicieron en 29 de mayo de el año de 1767 las Señoras Religiosas de la Enseñanza de Mexico a su fundadora, y prelada la M. I. Sra. y R. M. Maria Ignacia de Azlor, y Echevers*. Mexico City: Imprenta Nueva Antuerpiana de D. Phelipe de Zúñiga, y Ontiveros, 1768.

Torres Puga, Gabriel. "Beristáin, Godoy y la Virgen de Guadalupe. Una confrontación por el espacio público en la ciudad de México a fines del siglo xviii." *Historia Mexicana* 52/1 (2002) 57–102.

Tortorici, Zeb. "Contra Natura: Sin, Crime, and 'Unnatural' Sexuality in Colonial Mexico, 1530-1821." PhD diss., University of California, Los Angeles, 2010. ProQuest (AAT 3441475).

Traslosheros Hernández, Jorge. "Santa María de Guadalupe: hispánica, novohispana y mexicana. Tres sermones y tres voces guadalupanas, 1770-1818." *Estudios de Historia Novohispana* 18 (1998) 83–103.

Tristes ayes de la aguila mexicana, reales exequias de la Serenissima Señora Da. Maria Magdalena Barbara de Portugal, Catholica Reyna de España, y Augusta Emperatriz de las Indias, celebradas en el Templo Metropolitano de la Imperial Ciudad de Mexico, los dias 18 y 19 de Mayo del año de 1759. Mexico City: Bibliotheca Mexicana, 1760.

Bibliography

"12 Priests Slain in Mexico Over Last 4 Years." *Latin American Herald Tribune* (Caracas, Venezuela), March 16, 2011.

Twinam, Ann. "The Negotiation of Honor: Elites, Sexuality, and Illegitimacy in Eighteenth-Century Spanish America." In *The Faces of Honor: Sex, Shame, and Violence in Colonial Latin America*, edited by Lyman L. Johnson and Sonya Lipsett-Rivera, 68–102. Albuquerque: University of New Mexico Press, 1998.

———. *Public Lives, Private Secrets: Gender, Honor, Sexuality, and Illegitimacy in Colonial Spanish America*. Stanford: Stanford University Press, 1999.

Uribe, Joseph. *Elogio funebre del Exmo. Señor Baylio Fr. Don Antonio Maria Bucareli y Ursua, Henestrosa, Laso de la Vega, Villacís y Córdova, Caballero Gran-Cruz y Comendador de la Tocina en el Orden de San Juan, Gentil Hombre de Cámara de S. M. con entrada, Teniente General de los Reales Exércitos, Virrey, Governador y Capitan General del Reyno de Nueva España y Presidente de su Real Audiencia etc. Que predicó en la Santa Iglesia Catedral de México el Dr. D. Joseph Uribe Cura de la misma Santa Iglesia, y Rector de la Real y Pontificia Universidad*. Mexico City, 1779.

Uribe-Uran, Victor M. "The Birth of a Public Sphere in Latin America During the Age of Revolution." *Comparative Studies in Society and History* 42/2 (2000) 425–57.

Valverde, José María. *El barroco: una visión de conjunto*. Barcelona: Montesinos, 1980.

Valverde, Mariana. "The Love of Finery: Fashion and the Fallen Woman in Nineteenth Century Social Discourse." *Victorian Studies* 32/2 (1989) 168–89.

Valverde Tellez, Emeterio. *Bio-Bibliografía Eclesiástica Mexicana (1821–1943)*. 3 vols. Mexico City: Jus, 1949.

Van Young, Eric. *The Other Rebellion: Popular Violence, Ideology, and the Mexican Struggle for Independence, 1810–1821*. Stanford: Stanford University Press, 2001.

Vargas Alquicira, Silvia. *La singularidad novohispana en los jesuitas del siglo XVIII*. Mexico City: Universidad Nacional Autónoma de México, 1989.

Vázquez, Josefina Zoraida. "De la crisis monárquica a la independencia (1808–1821)." In *Interpretaciones sobre la independencia de México*, edited by Josefina Zoraida Vázquez and Jaime Rodríguez O., 9–32. Mexico City: Nueva Imagen, 1997.

———. "El liberalismo gaditano y la independencia de Nueva España." In *La América hispana en los albores de la emancipación*, edited by Gonzalo Anes y Álvarez de Castrillón and Rafael del Pino y Moreno, 17–32. Madrid: Real Academia de la Historia/Fundación Rafael del Pino, 2005.

Vázquez Parada, Lourdes Celina. "Del barroco al neoclásico. El sermón mexicano en el siglo XIX." In *Cultura, religión y sociedad*, edited by Lourdes Celina Vázquez Parada and Laura María Muñoz Pini, 243–58. Guadalajara: Universidad de Guadalajara, 2007.

Vergara, Joseph, fray. *La virtud en la elevacion. Oracion panegyrico-moral, que en la capilla del real palacio de Mexico dixo el dia VII de marzo de este año de MDCCLXX el R. P. Fr. Joseph Vergara, del Sagrado Orden de Predicadores, Lector de Prima de Sagrada Theologìa en el Pontificio Colegio de Porta-Coelii*. Mexico City: Biblioteca Mexicana del Lic. D. Joseph Jáuregui, 1770.

Victoria Moreno, Dionisio. "La provincia de los Carmelitas Descalzos de México y la guerra de Independencia (Seis documentos para su historia)." *Historia Mexicana* 37/4 (1988) 657–67.

Victoria Salazar, Diego de. *Sermón que predicó el Doctor D. Diego de Victoria Salazar, Canónigo Magistral de esta Sancta Iglesia Cathedral de la Puebla de los Angeles,*

Bibliography

Vicario Superintendente, y Iuez hordinario de los Conventos de Religiosas de esta Ciudad, Examinador Sinodal de su Obispado, y Calificador de el Santo Oficio. In Octava Maravilla del Nuevo Mundo en la Gran Capilla del Rosario dedicada y aplaudida en el Convento de N. P. S. Domingo de la Ciudad de los Angeles el dia 16 del Mes de Abril de 1690 al Illvsmo. y Revmo. Señor D. D. Manuel Fernández de Santa Cruz Obispo de la Puebla del Consejo de su Magestad. Puebla: Junta de Mejoramiento Moral, Cívico y Material del Municipio de Puebla, 1985.

Vida de S. Vicente de Paul, fundador de la Congregacion de la Mision y de las Hermanas de la Caridad. Mexico City: Arévalo, 1845.

Villaneda, Alicia. "Periodismo confesional: prensa católica y prensa protestante, 1870–1900." In *Estado, iglesia y sociedad en México. Siglo XIX*, edited by Álvaro Matute, Evelia Trejo, and Brian Connaughton, 325–66. Mexico City: Universidad Nacional Autónoma de México, 1995.

Villarello, Felipe. *Sermon pronunciado en la solemne funcion que el comercio de esta capital dedicó a la declaración dogmática de la Inmaculada Concepción de María Santísima, en 23 de septiembre de 1855, en la iglesia del Oratorio de S. Felipe Neri, por el R. P. Don Felipe Villarello, de la congregacion del propio oratorio*. Mexico City: Andrade y F. Escalante, 1855.

Villaseñor Black, Charlene. *Creating the Cult of St. Joseph: Art and Gender in the Spanish Empire*. Princeton: Princeton University Press, 2006.

———. "Love and Marriage in the Spanish Empire: Depictions of Holy Matrimony and Gender Discourses in the Seventeenth Century." *Sixteenth Century Journal* 32/3 (2001) 637–67.

———. "St. Anne Imagery and Maternal Archetypes in Spain and Mexico." In *Colonial Saints: Discovering the Holy in the Americas, 1500–1800*, edited by Allan Greer and Jodi Blinkoff, 3–30. New York: Routledge, 2003.

Villegas Revueltas, Silvestre. *El liberalismo moderado en México, 1852–1864*. Mexico City: Universidad Nacional Autónoma de México, 1997.

Villoro, Luis. *El proceso ideológico de la revolución de independencia*. Mexico City: Universidad Nacional Autónoma de México, 1983.

———. "La revolución de Independencia." In *Historia general de México*, 489–524. Mexico City: El Colegio de México, 2000.

Viqueira Albán, Juan Pedro. *Propriety and Permisiveness in Bourbon Mexico*. Translated by Sonya Lipsett-Rivera and Sergio Rivera Ayala. Wilmington, DE: Scholarly Resources, 1999.

Virginia, la doncella cristiana. Historia siciliana, que se propone por modelo a las señoras que aspiran a la perfeccion. Escrita en frances por el B. Miguel Angel Marin, religioso minimo y traducido al castellano por Doña Cayetana Aguirre y Rosales, vol. 1. Mexico City: Voz de la Religión, 1853.

Voekel, Pamela. *Alone Before God: The Religious Origins of Modernity in Mexico*. Durham, NC: Duke University Press, 2002.

Vovelle, Michel. *Religion et Révolution: La déchristianisation de l'an II*. Paris: Hachette, 1976.

———. *La Révolution contre l'église: De la Raison à l'Etre Suprême*. Paris: Editions Complexe, 1988.

Wagstaff, Grayson. "Processions for the Dead, the Senses, and Ritual Identity in Colonial Mexico." In *Music, Sensation, and Sensuality*, edited by Linda Phyllis Austern, 167–80. New York: Routledge, 2002.

Bibliography

Walker, Charles. *Shaky Colonialism: The 1746 Earthquake-Tsunami in Lima, Peru and its Long Aftermath*. Durham, NC: Duke University Press, 2008.
Walker Bynum, Caroline. *Jesus as Mother: Studies in the Spirituality of the High Middle Ages*. Berkeley: University of California Press, 1982.
Weeks, Jeffrey. *Making Sexual History*. Cambridge, UK: Polity Press, 2000.
Weismann, Elizabeth Wilder. *Art and Time in Mexico: Architecture and Sculpture in Colonial Mexico*. New York: Icon Editions, 1995.
———. *Mexico in Sculpture, 1521–1821*. Cambridge: Harvard University Press, 1950.
White, James F. *Roman Catholic Worship: Trent to Today*. Collegeville, MN: Liturgical, 2003.
Wobeser, Gisela von. *Dominación colonial. La consolidación de vales reales, 1804–1812*. Mexico City: Universidad Nacional Autónoma de México, 2003.
Wölfflin, Heinrich. *Renaissance and Baroque*. London: Collins, 1964.
Worcester, Thomas. "Catholic Sermons." In *Preachers and People in the Reformations and Early Modern Period*, edited by Larissa Taylor, 3–34. Leiden: Brill, 2001.
Wright, A. D. *The Counter-Reformation: Catholic Europe and the Non-Christian World*. Aldershot, UK: Ashgate, 2005.
Wright-Ríos, Edward. *Revolutions in Mexican Catholicism: Reform and Revelation in Oaxaca, 1887–1934*. Durham, NC: Duke University Press, 2009.
Zaret, David. "Religion, Science, and Printing in the Public Spheres in Seventeenth-Century England." In *Habermas and the Public Sphere*, edited by Craig Calhoun, 212–35. Cambridge, MA: MIT Press, 1992.
Zayas de Lille, Gabriela. "Los sermones políticos de José Mariano Beristáin de Souza." *Nueva Revista de Filología Hispánica* 40/2 (1992) 719–59.

www.ingramcontent.com/pod-product-compliance
Lightning Source LLC
Chambersburg PA
CBHW071245230426
43668CB00011B/1601